Radical Innocent:
Upton Sinclair

RANDOM HOUSE

NEW YORK

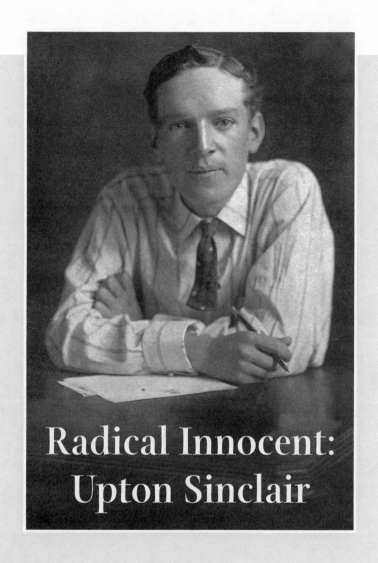

Radical Innocent:
Upton Sinclair

ANTHONY ARTHUR

Published in the United States by Random House, an imprint
of The Random House Publishing Group, a division of
Random House, Inc., New York.

RANDOM HOUSE and colophon are registered trademarks
of Random House, Inc.

Permissions acknowledgments can be found on page 379.

LIBRARY OF CONGRESS CATALOGING-IN-PUBLICATION DATA
Arthur, Anthony.
Radical innocent: Upton Sinclair / Anthony Arthur.—1st ed.
p.   cm.
Includes bibliographical references and index.
ISBN 1-4000-6151-2
1. Sinclair, Upton, 1878–1968. 2. Novelists, American—20th century—
Biography. 3. Social reformers—United States—Biography. I. Title.
PS3537.I85Z56 2006
813'.52—dc22   2005044931

Printed in the United States of America on acid-free paper

www.atrandom.com

2 4 6 8 9 7 5 3 1

First Edition

Book design by Victoria Wong

For John Ahouse

CONTENTS

PROLOGUE

Indiana University, Bloomington, Indiana
October 19, 1963

In 1895, when Upton Sinclair was sixteen years old, his English teacher in New York commended him for giving a speech that demonstrated "earnestness, feeling, spirit, and appreciation of his piece." Particularly appealing to his classmates, the perceptive teacher noted, was the young scholar's "freedom from affectation."

Upton Sinclair's audience on this autumn evening in 1963 was much larger than it had been in 1895—an overflow crowd of more than three thousand, mostly students. At eighty-five years old, his slender body was stooped. The bright stage lights highlighted his thinning white hair, his age spots, his prominent beak of a nose and the round wire-rimmed spectacles that perched on it. His voice, as he announced the subject of his talk— "Changing America and What Will Happen to You if You Try"—was thin and high, but it was strong enough to hold the hall's attention for the next ninety minutes. Not once during that time did Sinclair refer to notes. They were not necessary, because he was doing what he had done for most of his life—telling a story that was close to his heart with "earnestness, feeling, spirit, and appreciation of his piece."

Sinclair's story was an appealing one for a generation of college students whose idealism had recently been aroused by the election as president of the energetic young John F. Kennedy. Simply put, it was that one man, fired by the zeal to end injustice, could do it—or at least he could come close and, in America, as opposed to most other countries, live happily ever after. The old warrior's talk concerned his various battles with captains of industry. Of these, the best known and most important was his first, with Ogden Armour, the Chicago meatpacker whose plant Sinclair made the key setting for *The Jungle* in 1906. That book, which helped secure the subsequent passage of Pure Food and Drug legislation, would by itself have guaranteed Sinclair a niche in American history. Indeed, it was for *The Jungle,* published when he was just twenty-seven years old, that most of his audience in Bloomington knew him.

For a time it appeared as though *The Jungle* would mark the end as well as the beginning of Sinclair's career. He was dismissed by some critics as a mere "muckraker," one of those pesky investigative reporters bent on stirring up trouble. He also had trouble handling his subsequent renown. After all, he had been praised in a review of *The Jungle* by Winston Churchill as a man of "very great gifts" and even invited to chat with Teddy Roosevelt at the White House. He became entangled in several communes and was unfairly tarred as a debauched advocate of free love. His first wife ran off with his best friend, an affair that his new notoriety guaranteed was front-page tabloid news. His second wife saw to it that he was estranged for decades from his only child—now a distinguished physicist seated in the front row of the audience. For a long time he was regarded as a one-book wonder, producing a string of failed novels over the next fifteen years.

But Sinclair bounced back, as he would do throughout his life—first with a series of popular nonfiction attacks in the 1920s on religion, the press, and education in modern America, and then as a politician, nearly becoming the governor of California in 1934. His true fulfillment as a writer would come after he turned sixty. Having spent a lifetime as a self-described socialist propagandist, he turned to historical fiction in a series of eleven novels about the wars of the twentieth century. His appealing hero Lanny Budd, through whose eyes these stories are told, knew everyone from Hitler and Göring to FDR and Truman. In 1943 Sinclair won the Pulitzer Prize for *Dragon's Teeth,* which described the rise of Nazi Germany.

Even the intrepid Lanny was a relatively passive observer compared to his creator, who both witnessed and shaped the history of the twentieth century. As a young man, Upton Sinclair knew Mark Twain, Jack London, and Theodore Roosevelt. In his middle years, he formed a political alliance with Franklin Delano Roosevelt, and won the admiring friendship of men as various as Albert Einstein, Charlie Chaplin, Thomas Mann, and George Bernard Shaw. As an old man, he was corresponding with Carl Jung and Albert Camus, and in 1967 President Lyndon Johnson honored him at a special White House ceremony.

Sinclair was the most conservative of revolutionaries. The author of some ninety books and innumerable articles and essays, he had no patience with stream-of-consciousness narratives or even free verse. "He liked a writer to have something to say, and to say it with clarity and precision," Sinclair said of his alter ego Lanny Budd, just as "he disliked loud noises and confusion, and obscurity cultivated as a form of exclusiveness." He was also a straitlaced puritan concerning sex—this, despite at least one extramarital fling and an intemperate habit when young of linking marriage with prostitution and slavery. In a period when heavy drinking was widely seen to be a social necessity, if not a virtue, he despised alcohol, which had killed his father. Indeed, he disdained any form of indulgence: he even worried about his fondness for cakes and pies, fearing that he had it in him to become a "food drunkard."

These attributes, coupled with Sinclair's customary insistence that he knew best what was right for everyone else, encouraged extreme views among both his admirers and his detractors. To one disciple he was a "dearly beloved saint"; to another, "one who has been marked by the Gods as one who shall blaze the trail." And to a third, a woman suffering from multiple sclerosis, he was someone who "understands": "PLEASE PLEASE, Mr. Sinclair, write to me," she begged. "That is all I ask." His quick response, she replied gratefully, was "a purest ray serene. You have been sweet and kind to write to me."

But the saint could also be self-righteous and petulant, even absurd. His friend and onetime protégé Sinclair Lewis—the general public still confuses the author of *Babbitt* and *Main Street* with Upton Sinclair—howled when Sinclair chided him in print for making too much money: "My God, Upton, go and pray for forgiveness, honesty, and humility!" H. L. Mencken traded letters and barbs for many years with Sinclair and teased him for his "credulity complex," for not seeing that the "common people are damned to be diddled forever." Sinclair's own socialist publisher threw up his hands in dismay over his belief in ESP and ghosts, calling him an "egregious sucker," a "zanie," and "the Daniel Boone of Spookology." And these were his friends. His enemies compared him to Peter the Hermit and to Savonarola, the fanatical Florentine monk who got himself burned at the stake.

Sinclair himself used characters from history, religion, and literature as favored points of reference and departure. His typical plot sent a naive seeker in search of truth: Voltaire's Candide was one of his models, as was Christian in *The Pilgrim's Progress,* a traveler in what John Bunyan called the wilderness of the world. Another Sinclair favorite was Siddhartha, the Indian prince who gave up "his land and his treasures, and went out to wander with a beggar's bowl, in the hope of finding some truth about life that was not known at court."

Above all, there was Don Quixote, whose adventures prompted Sinclair to ask the question that guided him throughout his life: "What shall be the relation of the idealist, the dreamer of good and beautiful things, to the world of ugliness and greed in which he finds himself?" If he tries to apply his vision of the good, "the world will treat him so badly that before he gets through he may be really crazy."

As the breadth and depth of these allusions suggest, Sinclair was a far more sophisticated man of letters than most of his critics were willing to acknowledge. At the same time, it was his calculatedly naive manner that had let him find so many readers among workers, shopkeepers, and the poor; it was in this way that he became, as this biography suggests, a "radical innocent." The manner of the innocent seeker after knowledge had finally become the man—and yet, as his closing anecdote for the audience in Indiana revealed, the child had been father to the man all along.

When he was a very small child, Sinclair said, his family's fortunes fluctuated wildly. Sometimes he was sent to stay with his mother's wealthy relatives in Baltimore, though generally he lived with her and his pathetic father in New York tenements and boardinghouses. One day he asked his mother to explain the reasons for such obvious and unnecessary pain in a land of plenty, saying "Why, Mama?"

He had gone on to ask that same question for the next eighty years, he said. Even though he had done his best, he had to admit failure: "I haven't found the answer yet." But he was still looking, he told his rapt listeners, still asking "Why, Mama?" He hoped they would continue to ask that question, too.

Radical Innocent:
Upton Sinclair

CHAPTER ONE

THE PENNILESS RAT

(1878–1903)

In May 1903, when Upton Sinclair was twenty-four years old, he thought he was a failure at the end of his rope. He called himself a "penniless rat." His sole achievement of any merit was an autobiographical novel whose hero drowns himself. Less than three years later, in February 1906, the Doubleday, Page Company published Sinclair's novel *The Jungle*. Within weeks, he was the literary lion of two continents: "Not since Byron awoke one morning to find himself famous," marveled the *New York Evening World*, "has there been such an example of world-wide celebrity won in a day by a book as has come to Upton Sinclair."

Sinclair himself was startled by this miraculous transformation from abject failure to shattering success, and he tried in two autobiographies and several other commentaries to account for it. Certainly there was little in his early life pointing toward the slaughterhouses of Chicago, much less his many later accomplishments. He was born September 20, 1878, into relative prosperity, in Baltimore. His mother, Priscilla Harden, combined southern pretensions to aristocracy with a puritanism that discouraged the consumption of coffee or tea, and especially of liquor, because they fostered self-indulgence. Her father, John S. Harden, was a wealthy businessman, the secretary-treasurer of the Western Maryland Railroad. Priscilla's older sister, Maria, married a scion of the famous Randolph family of Virginia, John Randolph Bland, who became the richest man in Baltimore.

Priscilla's husband, Upton Beall Sinclair, was a Virginian with a worthy heritage; he came from a distinguished line of naval officers, one of whom had fought during the Revolution and helped to found the Naval Academy at Annapolis. His own father had adopted the lost cause of Virginia and the South over the Union at the outset of the Civil War, becoming an admiral in the Confederate Navy. But the admiral's son was himself a lost cause.

Morally weak and slothful, physically short and paunchy, Upton Sinclair's father was nonetheless vain: he thought his little hands and feet were aristocratic, his son and namesake later said, and he was a "natty" dresser who knew how to wear "the right kinds of shoes and vests and hats and gloves." Amiable and ingratiating, he made a decent living as a salesman of men's hats and clothing, and then, disastrously, of liquor, sampling his wares too freely. Upton Beall Sinclair became a periodically unemployable alcoholic not long after the birth of Upton junior.

The family drifted north to New York City in 1888 when Upton was ten years old, away from Baltimore and the reproachful presence of Priscilla's respectable family. The three of them—Upton would be the only child— lived a hand-to-mouth existence for the next several years, sliding steadily downward through a series of boardinghouses that catered to displaced southerners like themselves. They were remnants of an aristocracy who didn't know they were dead, Sinclair recalled of his fellow lodgers, in language that suggests one of his favorite books, John Bunyan's *Pilgrim's Progress:* "There was an incredible amount of drunkenness, and of debauchery scarcely hidden; there was pretense strutting like a peacock, and avarice skulking like a hound." It was a world of "jealousy, and base snobbery, and raging spite" that these failed aristocrats inhabited.

Equally repellent to the young Sinclair were the laborers and shopgirls who shared his lodgings: "The men who shoveled with their knives or plastered things on their forks as hod-carriers do mortar! The women who sucked in their soup, and the children who smeared their faces and licked their lips and slopped upon the table-cloth!" Clearly the author who would describe his subject as class warfare was not going to be operating on sentimental notions of essential human nobility in any segment of society.

Sinclair's pronounced and lifelong disdain for failures of will and for people who let themselves be defined by their indulgences was the chief legacy left him by his "little, fat, kind-hearted father." The son, hardly five feet seven inches tall when he was fully grown and undersized as a boy, hated having to search through saloons, at his mother's insistence, to retrieve his father and drag him home. In prose that suggests the lurid scenes of the famous temperance tract of the 1850s, *Ten Nights in a Bar-Room,* Sinclair recalled his late-night excursions along "the Highway of Lost Men," passing prostitutes who tried to lure him with their lascivious come-hither eyes and teasing cajolery. His search typically ended with a tearful encounter in a dingy bar, the guilty father sobbing out "all the terror and grief of a defeated life" on the slender shoulder of his son.

Priscilla Sinclair's stubborn strength stood out in contrast to Sinclair's father's weakness, and it endeared her to her son in his early years. The family was physically close, out of sheer necessity. They never had more than a single room; Sinclair slept either on a couch or with his parents. Sometimes unwelcome occupants shared their bed: fleetly scurrying bedbugs that stank when crushed beneath a shoe. More than once, when his saloon searches for his father had proved fruitless and he returned to their tiny rented room with its lone bed, he and his mother curled up together. The boy admired Priscilla's fortitude even as he lamented the need for it; he grew to hate alcohol as a destroyer of both the weak, like his father, and the strong, like his later friend Jack London, among many others.

During his father's long absences or periods of incapacitation, Sinclair and his mother often stayed at her wealthy sister's country estate or at her family's King Street home in Baltimore. He retained no memories of adventures with his cousins, of whom there were several near his age; there is only one scornful reference to a girl who married a millionaire and gave him some exposure to "dances and parties, terrapin suppers, punch, dresses, gossip—everything that is called 'society.' " This was a world, Sinclair would later understand, much like that of Thackeray's *Vanity Fair* a half-century earlier: one of ostentatious wealth, snobbery, and pretension.

Sinclair was getting a firsthand sense of what Thorstein Veblen would soon call "conspicuous consumption." His aunt and uncle's world was like the one that Edith Wharton would describe in *The House of Mirth,* published in 1905, the year before *The Jungle,* and like that in F. Scott Fitzgerald's *The Great Gatsby* (1925). Sinclair, born sixteen years after Wharton and eighteen before Fitzgerald, would see the moral and social flaws of this world as clearly as they did. Unlike them, he would conclude that societal flaws were economic in origin, and therefore curable, rather than rooted in unchanging human nature.

Like his social upbringing, the young Sinclair's education was erratic; his parents, concerned about his health, kept him out of school until he was ten. Luckily, they also encouraged his voracious reading; by the age of five he could read by himself, and from that time forward he was continually immersed in books. Partly out of sheer enjoyment, partly to shut out the distractions and dissensions of their cramped household, he escaped into *Gulliver's Travels,* the tales of the Brothers Grimm and Hans Christian Andersen, the dime-novel adventures of Horatio Alger. He also read *The Story of the Bible,* leading his mother to hope he would make a career in the Episcopal Church (as a bishop, of course). And he ranged widely in his Uncle Bland's encyclopedia, paying particular attention to the history of warfare.

When Sinclair's formal education did begin, he crammed the first eight grades into two years of study and was qualified to start high school as a ninth-grader when he was twelve. Forced to wait a year because regulations would not admit anyone so young, he repeated the eighth grade at a public school on East Twenty-third Street, where many of his classmates were tough Irish, German, and Italian immigrant kids from the East Side tenements. They teased Sinclair for his high, thin voice, his perfectly formed oral paragraphs when called upon in class to answer a question, and his soft southern accent. But he later recalled no bullying or persecution; he had already learned to camouflage his aggressively critical nature with the pleasing, open manner that later led his friend Charlie Chaplin to say Sinclair always spoke through a smile.

Sinclair was a few days shy of his fourteenth birthday when he embarked on his final year of high school, in 1892. He found the instruction tedious, requiring no more than rote learning of Latin, algebra, solid geometry, physics, and drawing. English instruction was a particular ordeal, he complained, because it consisted entirely of grammar drills.

Far more satisfying than formal study, Sinclair soon discovered, was the thrill of telling stories and getting paid for it. In his 1932 autobiography, *American Outpost,* Sinclair told how a classmate proudly announced one day that a magazine published by a Hebrew orphans' home would soon feature a short story he had written. Sinclair promptly wrote his own first story, based on his experience raising baby birds that he had plucked from their nests, and sold it to *Argosy,* a respected magazine with a wide circulation. His friend had not been paid for his story, so the $25 that Sinclair earned—when a prime rib dinner at Delmonico's cost about $2—was especially satisfactory.

Only fifteen years old, Sinclair became one of the youngest freshmen at the City College of New York in the fall of 1893. Goaded by the need for money to pay for his education and to help support his parents, and inspired by his early and easy success at making money through writing, Sinclair methodically studied the market for freelance writers. He soon found that the most profitable and least onerous writing was not stories or sketches, though he did many of both, but jokes. Filler material for newspapers and magazines, the jokes poked fun at drunken Irishmen, tightfisted Scots, lazy tramps, shrewish wives, henpecked husbands. Sinclair saw that they were all little stories, each put together according to a formula that started with a category and a desired response. His self-taught method was disciplined free association. Why were tramps supposed to be funny? Because they don't like bulldogs, they don't like to work, they don't like to bathe. Concentrate on "bathe," Sinclair said, and you will come up with "all the words and phrases having to do with water, soap, tubs, streams, rain, etc., and of puns or quirks by which these words can be applied to tramps." One result: a tramp who "calls attention to a sign, 'Cleaning and Dyeing,' and says he always knew those two things went together."

On a rather more elevated intellectual level, Sinclair also found the time to study the violin, with old friend and grammar school classmate, Martin Birnbaum, as his tutor. An even greater passion was the newly fashionable game of tennis. Sinclair loved tennis not because it offered social mobility but because it was one-on-one combat that a boy who was slight but well coordinated and fiercely competitive could win—as he would, in half a dozen amateur tournaments, for the next half-century.

Spread thin as he was, and indifferent to grades, Sinclair graduated in the middle of his City College class of 1897. He was still just eighteen years old. With money earned from his freelance writing, he began graduate studies at Columbia University in September of that year to prepare for a career as a lawyer, probably influenced by Martin Birnbaum, who had done the same. He quickly abandoned the law in favor of casual grazing among the offerings at Columbia, where he admired the practice of allowing unlimited dropping and adding of classes at no extra cost. Sinclair exploited the system accordingly, sampling some forty courses over two years. He attended most of these just long enough to get the book lists and to evaluate the professors' attitudes and methods of presentation. He discovered scores of authors; among his favorites were Shelley, Carlyle, Emerson, and Sir Walter Scott, all Romantics who seemed to embody or describe revolutionary idealism.

Sinclair wanted to be able to read European literature in its original tongues, particularly German and French. The study of foreign languages at this time was based almost entirely on grammar drills and recitation exercises, a dry and discouraging process that he rejected. He attended classes long enough to master pronunciation, but in lieu of the assigned texts, he read the Bible, parts of which he already knew by heart in the King James version, in whichever language he was studying, absorbing its vocabulary and grammar by virtue of his familiarity with the English equivalent text. His study of foreign languages was enhanced by his ability, as his son enviously confirmed years later, to look at a word once and fix it in his memory. By the time he left Columbia, Sinclair claimed later, he had "taught himself French and Italian, as well as German, and had read all the best literature in those languages."

As an only child, Sinclair was indulged by his parents, insofar as their circumstances permitted. They confirmed his growing sense of being set apart, as more than simply precocious. As he grew older and increasingly certain of his intellectual superiority, he came to think of himself as blessed with special gifts, capable of doing whatever he turned his hand to. He also was prone to exaggerate his considerable achievements: few well-read and mature Americans then or now could honestly claim to have read "all the best literature" in any foreign tongue, let alone three.

Sinclair's egotism was leavened by a degree of ingenuous charm, as when he called the chapter in *American Outpost* dealing with his education "Genius," but it often annoyed those whose authority he questioned—which would be, throughout his life, virtually everyone. At Columbia, he found only a few teachers to admire, including the composer Edward MacDowell, then head of the music department, and George Edward Woodberry, who earned his gratitude for two excellent comparative literature courses. But most of his professors, including those who taught writing and poetry, he despised as narrow pedants. Not even the renowned philosophy professor and Columbia University president Nicholas Murray Butler impressed Sinclair as a teacher; he thought "Nicholas Miraculous" was a pompous bore. Worst of all was his poetry instructor, a learned scholar who called attention one day to a grammatical error in Byron ("There let him lay") and was sure he could find even worse solecisms in Shelley if he tried.

===

Sinclair's disdain for his teachers was already that of the professional for the dilettante, for by his nineteenth year he was himself a self-supporting writer of published novels. To be sure, these were only juvenile entertainments similar to the Horatio Alger stories or the Rover Boys books, but they offer a valuable perspective on Sinclair's development. His chance came about as a consequence of his successful jokes and anecdotes, which favorably impressed Henry Harrison Lewis, a Street and Smith editor. Lewis commissioned Sinclair to write a continuing saga about life at the United States Military Academy. West Point, as the academy was more familiarly known, was just half a day's ferry ride up the Hudson River. Armed with an introduction to the appropriate authorities, Sinclair spent several days wandering around the academy, soaking up the atmosphere and pumping cadets for details of their lives there. A pompous plebe was transformed into the charming Mark Mallory, leader of a "rollicking" group of cadets at the outset of their military careers. A few days of research blossomed into a thirty-thousand-word novel, and Upton Sinclair became the pseudonymous author "Frederick Garrison, USA." So successful was this series that soon after it began Sinclair was sent by his grateful editor to Annapolis, where, "haunted by the ghosts of [his] grandfathers," he became "Ensign Clarke Fitch, USN," author of yet another series.

For months on end Sinclair turned out eight thousand words a day, including Sundays. Later, like most professional writers, he would regard one thousand words as a good day's work. But now he was famished for success, he said, "a young shark, ready to devour every thing in sight." He kept two full-time stenographers busy taking dictation one day and transcribing the next. "In the afternoon I would dictate for about three hours, as fast as I could talk; in the evening I would revise the copy that had been brought in from the previous day, and then take a long walk and think up the incidents of my next day's stunt." In the mornings, he attended lectures at Columbia and practiced his violin.

At his peak during this period, Sinclair earned $40 a week for his efforts—no small sum, about $850 in today's currency. He later adopted a pose of amused tolerance for his early hack work. His young heroes were graduating just in time to take part in the Spanish-American War of 1898, so he obligingly sent them off to Cuba to fight for country and glory. The war was a "romp" for Sinclair. When his mother asked what he was "going to do today," he said, "I have to kill Spaniards," as many and as bloodily as possible: "I thought nothing of sinking a whole fleet of Spanish torpedo boats to make a denouement, and the vessels I sank during that small war would have replaced all the navies of the world."

But he was less frivolous than he sounds. Proud of his military heritage, Sinclair was an enthusiastically patriotic young American who had seriously considered going to Annapolis for a career in the navy. By one account, he obtained a West Point cadet's uniform as a disguise; that is unlikely, though his erect posture and brisk but respectful manner would have let him impersonate a young cadet with ease. What is certain is that he did not tell the cadets he talked to that he was writing novels about them.

Working undercover, then, on assignment, the young Sinclair persuaded people he didn't know to talk to him at great length, often revealing more than they knew. An avid and intelligent listener, he flattered his confidants with his attention. He then quickly turned his material into gripping stories.

Especially important in his stories of youthful heroism is the absence of ironical subtext (despite his later sardonic reflections on killing Spaniards): his readers did not have to fear that their legs were being pulled. Sinclair's straightforward tone and the authority conferred by his method of gathering information about West Point and Annapolis anticipate his later success in Chicago while writing *The Jungle*.

Upton Sinclair's jaunty summation in *American Outpost* of his early professional and intellectual achievements masks an increasing desperation. He was tethered to a treadmill, a compulsive loner who participated in no youthful escapades other than once finding himself night-crawling with a crowd of students until their "barbaric screechings" drove him away in disgust. As for sex, or even innocent feminine companionship, these seem to have canceled each other out. He could not have been entirely innocent, after a childhood spent rescuing his father from bars and prostitutes. But Sinclair was a romantic idealist as a young man (and for the rest of his life); he was not, as he acerbically put it, a slum-dweller coupling in an alley or a barnyard animal. He was committed to swearing truthfully to the woman he finally married that he was a virgin.

Still, every passing female provoked in him volcanic fits of desire. He was so consumed by lust that he had to give up his self-directed study of Renaissance art and its overwhelming masses of glowing female flesh. Only textbook sublimation, as it would now be regarded, could distract him from his obsession with women and sex—complete immersion every waking moment in his studies, his violin, his tennis, the writing of his juvenile novels.

Helping him in his resolve to remain pure was a young clergyman, the Reverend William Wilmerding Moir, at the Church of the Holy Communion at Sixth Avenue and Twentieth Street. Sinclair was a devout believer when his mother joined Moir's church, which she did in large part because of Moir's attention to the spiritual and social welfare of his young charges. Moir placed special emphasis upon the virtue of chastity, and he was not shy about scaring Sinclair and his friends with threats of horrible venereal diseases if they strayed.

Moir was less successful in persuading Sinclair, as he grew older, to continue believing in Christianity as the revealed truth of God. Sinclair tortured the young clergyman with the questions that all bright young people think they are the first to pose. If "Jesus had been God, could he really have been tempted? To be God and man at the same time—did that not mean both to know and not to know?" Learned counterarguments by church scholars pressed on Sinclair by Will Moir merely confirmed his apostasy: "The only convincing parts of their books were where they gave a resumé of the arguments of their opponents."

What stood in for a revealed God was nature as perceived through the eyes of a sensitive artist, as Sinclair had come to think of himself. Sinclair rightly valued his rational powers of analysis and description, but he also believed he was capable of spiritual insights typically described by mystics, religious seers, and poets. One such moment in his sixteenth year is similar to that of Jonathan Edwards's ecstatic perception in his "Personal Narrative," though Sinclair does not seem to have known that essay. It occurred during a winter walk in a garden after midnight. The snow crunched under his feet as he gazed at the gleaming, quivering stars, and he felt a part of some "strange and portentous experience." He lost any sense of self, giving way instead "to the people of his dreams, the companions and lovers of his fancy." He felt a particular affinity with "Shelley and Milton, and the gentle and troubled Hamlet, and the sorrowful knight of la Mancha," and he understood that only in such creations and such creators would he ever find truth.

In the spring of 1900, his twenty-second year, Upton Sinclair made a conscious decision to become a literary artist of the first rank. He had undeniable gifts. When he later used the word "genius" to describe himself in his autobiography, he meant it in the sense of "special inclination" rather than extremely high intelligence; he knew well at least one true genius during his lifetime, Albert Einstein, and did not make that claim for himself. But there is no doubt that his powers of apprehension, understanding, and memory were extraordinary. Furthermore, not many American writers before or since have been as well educated as Upton Sinclair. Finally, he awed everyone he knew with his capacity for the hard work that writing involves.

At this point in his life, no one else understood Sinclair's burning sense of mission, of being specially selected to do great things, because he seldom spoke of this; he had not yet determined the purpose for his gifts. He knew only that he was destined to be a pure artist. He would give up writing merely for money and devote himself wholeheartedly to a career as a serious novelist—serious in the same intensely feeling way as his midnight epiphany in the frozen garden six years earlier suggests.

Not surprisingly, one of Sinclair's favorite writers was Henry David Thoreau, who made a religion of opinionated self-sufficiency. In April 1900, Sinclair moved into a log cabin in the forest near Lake Massawippi, a few miles north of the border between Quebec and Vermont. He had enough money saved from his writing to live on through the summer, as well as a plan for a novel called *Springtime and Harvest,* about "a woman's soul redeemed by high and noble love." Day after day, Sinclair walked for hours in the pine forests, working out whole scenes, including dialogue, before committing them to paper in his large, looping, neat script.

As a reader, Sinclair had a genuine capacity for delight; a friend would re-call seeing him nearly tumble from a hammock with laughter reading George Bernard Shaw's *Man and Superman.* But *writing* for him meant inspi-ration controlled by ascetic discipline. He could sit shivering in his cold and drafty shack for six hours without moving, afflicted by indigestion and headaches, yet consumed by the vision of truth and beauty that he saw him-self creating.

Something of his intensity, as well as a hint of the problems that he would soon face, comes through in Sinclair's lengthy preface to his first novel. Re-ferring to himself in the third person, he writes: "Last spring, because his heart was shaken with the beauty of it, he went away to wrestle with his vi-sion. Because he knew he had to give all his soul to the labor, he cut himself off absolutely from the world—found a little cabin in the wilds of Quebeck, where for five months he lived entirely alone, doing a work so fearful that now, as he looks back upon it, it makes him tremble. Each day, as he wrought at his story, the wonder of it took hold of him more and more, until it took the form of a very demon of beauty that was lashing him and would not let him rest."

The humorless aura of priestly self-importance marks a writer who lacks a capacity for self-criticism. Earlier, in his juvenile novels, the need to write according to a formula had given Sinclair direction and discipline. And later he would find subjects, as he did in *The Jungle,* that made those flaws he did not outgrow seem less important. But the heart of the problem with *Spring-time and Harvest* was its subject. Sinclair was writing about something he did not know well or understand: a woman in a moral quandary concerning her choice of a husband.

The potential solution to this problem, a real woman, arrived on the doorstep of Sinclair's cabin on a sunny afternoon in mid-June. Nineteen years old, lissome, sensuous, as lovely as a Pre-Raphaelite painting, and with artistic pretensions of her own, Meta Fuller seemed well prepared to serve both as Sinclair's muse and as his subject.

Meta and Sinclair had known each other casually since she was ten and he was thirteen. Her mother, Mary Eaton Fuller, belonged to one of the First Families of Virginia, and Mrs. Fuller had naturally found kindred spirits in Priscilla Sinclair and her husband. Like the Sinclairs, Mrs. Fuller had been reduced to boardinghouse living for a time until her husband, a former re-porter, secured a better-paying position as a court clerk. The women re-mained friends and occasional companions on summer trips to mountain and lake resorts, which were plentiful and inexpensive. Their children, however, had been less than close: Sinclair thought Meta was a pest and

once smacked her when she interrupted him while he was reading a newspaper. She kept her distance thereafter, awed by the way he could talk to
grown-ups and a little frightened at his intense self-absorption.

Now Meta and Mrs. Fuller had joined Priscilla, who had written her son
that she would come to stay for a month in a lodge on Lake Massawippi.
Sinclair met the three women at the train station in North Hatley, saw them
to their hotel, and invited them to dinner that evening in his cabin. In *Love's
Pilgrimage,* his 1911 autobiographical novel, Sinclair revised the facts of this
first dinner with Meta to eliminate the older women. Only Meta remains,
her dark eyes glowing as he, "picturesque in his old corduroy trousers and
his grey flannel shirt," prepares her supper of rice and raisins, bacon and
eggs, and freshly baked bread and butter. The lovely young woman strikes
the young author as the "perfect specimen" of the audience he knows his
story must reach. He tells her about his novel, and she eagerly agrees to
read it.

A summer romance followed, Meta arriving each afternoon having read
another chapter of *Springtime and Harvest.* The two strolled daily through
fields of wildflowers until dusk, returning to the cabin that Sinclair called
Fairy Glen, where he read Keats aloud and played his violin for the enchanted girl—who was often described as "elfin." He overwhelmed her with
his attention. He also lectured her about many things: about George Eliot's
Middlemarch, about Nietzsche and George Bernard Shaw, about the need to
develop "intellect, feeling, and will." He disparaged the folly of self-sacrifice,
that virtue so often praised in bourgeois novels. And he explained how romantic love is an "ignoble thing" unless the two lovers can lose themselves
together in some "great ideal, some purpose, some vision of perfection."

More alarmingly, he warned Meta later, after their romance had blossomed, that he was a bad prospect for her as a husband. She should know
this poem by Sir Walter Scott, Sinclair said; it was one of his favorites:

> Maiden! A nameless life I lead,
> A nameless death I'll die;
> The fiend whose lantern lights the mead
> Were better mate than I!

A true artist, Sinclair insisted, must be a ruthless monomaniac, loving no
one and nothing but his own vision of truth. When he looked deeply into
himself, he said, "I do not believe I am a kind man. I have no patience with
human hearts, their suffering and their weakness. There is only one thing
that I value and that is my fidelity to my ideal." Asked if he did not love

human beings, Sinclair said "Not as a rule": "God made me for an artist and not for a lover!" If they did marry, it would be not because he loved Meta as she was, but because "I love the woman you are to be . . . I give my life to you and I shall make of you a perfect woman—or else kill you."

Even allowing for literary exaggeration, Sinclair represents himself here as a borderline fanatic; he resembles Hawthorne's mad scientist in "The Birthmark," who kills his beloved in an operation to remove a tiny blemish that mars her perfection. He also anticipates Shaw's *Pygmalion* (which appeared in 1916). Indeed, there was something of Eliza Doolittle in Meta, who perceived life through her senses and her emotions rather than, like Sinclair, through her mind. Her father had refused to send her to college, and neither of her parents encouraged her vague longings for a stage career in the fashion of her heroine Eleonora Duse. She was a beautiful young woman, but without education or resources or prospects for a career. She was bright enough to be flattered by Sinclair's demands on her attention and his high expectations for her intellectual development, but not bright enough to meet those expectations. A forest sprite during those early days at Lake Massawippi, Meta's essence was physical, not intellectual. She was sensuous and flirtatious—"all female, and all feline," as another woman later described her. When Meta purred to Upton that he must have come to her "as an inspiration direct from God," that he was her "only means of breathing," the resistant carapace of the young object of her affection dissolved into jelly.

On October 17, 1900, Upton Sinclair and Meta Fuller were married. He had completed *Springtime and Harvest* and delivered it to Macmillan, a reputable publisher, which had agreed to consider it for publication. Sinclair felt sure that a generous contract would be forthcoming soon: he and Meta could therefore marry with some security. Having previously voiced their concern about the suitability of marriage without an income, neither set of parents was told about the occasion. The service was performed not by the proper Episcopalian Wilmerding Moir but by Minot Savage, a Unitarian who sympathized with the couple's impatience with formality, and perhaps with their need to consummate an increasingly passionate courtship.

Sinclair's upbringing and his attitudes concerning the family unit were in most ways conventionally Victorian, and would remain so throughout his life. He was never a bohemian. But like many young intellectuals at the beginning of the twentieth century, he regarded the *institution* of marriage as a bourgeois convention, a trap for men and slavery for women. So-called free thinkers, particularly artists and writers in Greenwich Village, married and divorced with impunity, indifferent to acceptance in the more rigid world depicted by Henry James and Edith Wharton. Many simply cohabited, justifying their behavior as "free love," and some, like Frank Harris and H. G. Wells, became notorious libertines. Sinclair felt caught between the forces of convention, which he disdained, and of indulgence, which he despised. He married Meta because, as a healthy young man, he needed to satisfy his sexual urges and didn't want to take advantage of her. But having married her, he became obsessed with the fear that sex would lead to childbirth— meaning not just one drag on his career as a writer but two. His apprehension only intensified when Macmillan, followed by half a dozen other publishers, rejected *Springtime and Harvest* because of its cluttered plot, its unconvincing characters, and its stilted language.

Unwilling to give up on his novel, Sinclair borrowed $200 from his Uncle Bland in January 1901 and printed a thousand copies of *Springtime and Harvest*. As he would do throughout his career, he sent free copies around to friends and to potential reviewers at newspapers and magazines. A brief burst of publicity resulted, in the form of two newspaper stories about Sinclair as a young artist, but he earned just enough from sales of his first book to repay the loan to his uncle.

Broke and disillusioned, living in a tiny room whose only window overlooked an airshaft, Sinclair grew increasingly fearful that Meta would become pregnant. They cast about in vain for reliable information on birth control, information readily available to the wealthy and to the poor ("Mrs. Frick's French Pills for Female Complaint") but less so to the respectable middle classes. Although one could openly condemn the institution of marriage, it was an offense punishable by a stiff fine and a possible jail sentence for anyone to publish or distribute guides to sexual behavior, including contraceptive techniques. Even the doctor whom Sinclair consulted about birth control before the marriage offered little advice beyond watching the calendar.

The doctor did not recommend abstinence, regarding it as unnatural, but Sinclair decided that for the time being he and Meta should live together as "brother and sister." He drilled her in German verb conjugations and exposed her to the poetry of Browning and Tennyson. They played Mozart duets, Meta's dutiful piano accompanying Sinclair's excited violin, wandered through the Central Park Ramble, attended lectures at the New School for Social Research. But living with Meta was like living with a Rossetti figure come to life. No amount of brotherly distance could prevail against such propinquity. By April 1901, Meta was pregnant.

Sinclair reacted with an inadvertently comical despair to the news that he was about to be a father. He remembered Maeterlinck's *Life of the Bee,* in which the pathetic male lives as "a mere accident in the scheme of Nature," his only reason for existence to impregnate the female. Now he, Upton Sinclair, the would-be creator and artist, had had his brief orgasmic fling and was tossed aside, "disemboweled and torn, an empty shell!" Meta offered to get an abortion, but as this was not only illegal but dangerous, she tried to induce miscarriage during the coming months through vigorous exercise, herbal teas, even deliberate falls out of bed.

A ray of hope for a rebirth of *Springtime and Harvest* appeared at about the same time as the dread news of Meta's pregnancy. Funk & Wagnalls agreed to reissue it with a new title, *King Midas.* The author was identified, for the first time, as Upton Sinclair, rather than Upton B. Sinclair, Jr. Though only about two thousand copies were finally sold, Sinclair's self-confidence was rekindled. In June 1901, he and Meta traveled north to camp for the summer in the Thousand Islands, at the mouth of the St. Lawrence River where it enters Lake Ontario. Here he would work on a new novel, to be called *Prince Hagen.*

Sinclair had come to maturity believing in the virtues of the strenuous life so vividly advocated by Theodore Roosevelt. He prided himself on his physical stamina, once bicycling a hundred miles in a day through the hills and forests of upstate New York, and on his survival skills, hunting squirrels for food with a slingshot and catching mackerel on a birch pole. Nothing pleased him more than setting up a wall tent, securing the mosquito netting, and settling in for the evening on his cot, reading Henry James's *The Ambassadors* or Nietzsche's *Will to Power* by the light of a kerosene lamp.

He also loved the violence of nature, as seen in the wild storms that rolled off Lake Ontario and across the tiny island where he and Meta stayed that summer. One storm in particular stayed in his memory. He stood in the doorway of his tent, holding on to the front pole to help it withstand the wind. A guy rope was tied to a nearby tree, not ten feet away. A flash of lightning struck the tree, in a terrifying brilliant white spectacle of light and sound. Afterward he found a nest of baby birds at the foot of the tree. Two peewees—sparrows with green wings—had survived the storm and the fall. He adopted them, feeding them mosquitoes and flies and worms, and they followed him everywhere, declining to leave after they learned to fly. They even sat on his hat or on the prow of his little boat when he rowed over to the mainland to get his mail. When he and Meta took them back to the city, a cat ate one of them. Sinclair thought about killing the cat, but didn't, because "a cat couldn't help being a cat."

Meta, saddled with cooking and cleaning and morning sickness, enjoyed this summer idyll less than her husband did. But he was contented, at least, and hard at work on *Prince Hagen,* the novel that he would come to regard as his first work of social criticism. Discarding the Victorian framework of *Springtime and Harvest,* Sinclair turned now toward allegory and myth. His narrator, a poet, happens into the underground world of the Nibelungen that Wagner had made famous in his operas. It is a world of fabulous wealth, ruled by an enlightened king who is concerned about the moral upbringing of his son, Prince Hagen. The poet is engaged to bring the youth into his own world, and to show him how to use his wealth and power wisely when that time arrives.

The young prince, it turns out, is a cunning predator who scorns his teacher's moral instruction and becomes an archetypal robber baron. Life for Prince Hagen means a struggle for survival of the fittest: "It is like a barrelful of rats—there is only a certain number that can keep on top, and the rest must sweat for it till they die. All that a man can do, that I see, is to take care that he comes out on top." Everything else—morality, ethics, culture, taste—is secondary if not trivial.

Jack London would develop the same idea as Sinclair's a few years later in *The Sea-Wolf,* his 1904 novel about the brutal superman Wolf Larsen and his instructor-slave, the idealist poet, Humphrey van Weyden. Wolf tells Humphrey that they are both, like everyone, merely bits of yeast in a fermenting vat, with no more purpose in life than to eat smaller pieces and avoid being eaten by larger. London's vivid characterization of Wolf Larsen and his driving plot gave *The Sea-Wolf* life. Sinclair's didactic fantasy, though it anticipated London's hard-boiled romance, had little appeal for publishers. Once again, they turned their backs on its irate author.

Sinclair's frustration with the world of publishing for turning down his novels was largely his own fault; he failed to capitalize on the recent breakthroughs in literary realism by his slightly older contemporaries. There were more outlets for writers when he was coming to maturity than ever before, and many people with a fraction of his talent were making a living with their pens—or typewriters. Jack London, two years older than Sinclair, had shown how a writer could be both popular and serious with his collection of stories about the Yukon, *The Son of the Wolf: Tales of the Far North,* in 1900. Frank Norris, born to a wealthy San Francisco family in 1870, was well connected to the world of publishing by virtue of his job as an editor at Doubleday, Page, but it was the strength of his writing, not his connections, that made *McTeague* (1899) the success that it was. Stephen Crane, who died in England at the age of twenty-nine when Sinclair was working on *Springtime and Harvest,* may have been the greatest writer of his generation; neither his bad health nor his stubborn independence had kept him from publishing his classic account of the Civil War, *The Red Badge of Courage* (1895). Theodore Dreiser was Sinclair's senior by eight years; his great novel *Sister Carrie* had almost vanished without a trace when it appeared in 1900, but he would eventually land on his feet as an editor for the Butterick chain of magazines and establish himself as a literary powerhouse nevertheless.

All of these writers had struggled successfully against the conservative critical temper of the time, which was admittedly formidable. The austere literary scholar Paul Elmer More informed Sinclair that he had "given up" on realism, and Bliss Perry, the *Atlantic Monthly* editor, turned down *Prince Hagen* because it would offend what he called his "very conservative, fastidious, and sophisticated constituency." Sinclair took rejection personally and held grudges. Harry Thurston Peck, a Columbia professor who moonlighted as a reader for Dodd, Mead and Company, read Sinclair's manuscript for *Prince Hagen,* praised it, and promised Sinclair he would recommend it for publication. Sinclair waited patiently for a time. Hearing nothing, he then pestered the editors at Dodd, Mead for weeks before learning that Peck had never said a word about *Prince Hagen* to them. Thirty years later not even the memory of "the suicide of poor Harry Peck" after being fired from Columbia for moral turpitude had appeased Sinclair's anger: he said that if Peck had been attending to business, i.e., Sinclair's manuscript, he might have stayed out of trouble with women and not had to kill himself.

Sinclair's desperation grew as the birth of Meta's child approached in December 1901. Her father, who had been giving the couple $25 a month, said it was time for his son-in-law to get a regular job and support his wife and baby. Sinclair resisted, as he had when his uncle offered him a job in his bank two years earlier, with the promise of soon heading up the Paris branch at an excellent salary. His whole purpose in life was to work, he wrote in a begging letter to the poet Edwin Markham, but not for money: "I *want* to give every second of my time and of my thought, every ounce of my energy to the worship of my God and to the uttering of the unspeakable message that I know he has given me. I have no other joy or care in the world but this; and I tell you my dear Mr. Markham before heaven I can not stand what I have stood much longer."

Meta gave birth to a baby boy they named David on December 1, 1901, after fourteen hours of painful labor. Just a few days later her husband was telling Markham that he had "no other joy or care" than his writing. To be sure, Sinclair did give the event lavish attention later in *Love's Pilgrimage*—though it appears in a chapter he titled "The Capture Is Completed."

Sinclair was so ruthlessly honest about his self-absorption that we can believe his subsequent delight in the initial joys of fatherhood, described with considerable tenderness in *Love's Pilgrimage*. But it is also clear that just as some females are not natural "mother-women," as Kate Chopin scandalously wrote in *The Awakening* (1899), some males are not by nature "father-men." At any rate, Sinclair seems not to have objected too much when the Fullers took Meta and the baby home with them soon after David's birth, or even when Mr. Fuller told him not to come back to see them until he had a job.

On June 9, 1902, the following brief obituary appeared in *The New York Times*: "Stirling. —By suicide in the Hudson River, poet and man of genius, in the 22nd year of his age, only son of Richard T. and Grace Stirling, deceased, of Chicago." The sad event prompted a number of handwringing letters from readers about the precarious nature of art in a commercial society, and when the dead genius's monument to himself appeared in print the following February as *The Journal of Arthur Stirling,* it received some favorable comment from reviewers. They agreed that a man who kills himself is always allowed a certain amount of latitude for sarcastic and bitter humor. Since Stirling had been writing only for himself, he had been under no obligation to be polite, or to pretend to be a lover of all humanity. In a typical outburst, disgusted with his landlady and her two friends who waste their time "jabbering about dresses," Stirling fulminates about these "vile, ignorant serving-women" as "poisoned thorns in my flesh. The infinite degradation of it all, the shame, the outrage!"

Stirling sounded repellent, crazy, maybe dangerous: "Who knows what I suffer—who has any idea of it? To have a soul like a burning fire, to be hungry and swift as the autumn wind, to have a heart as hot as the wild bird's, and wings as eager—and to be chained here in this seething hell of selfishness, this orgy of folly." Still, he did have his inspired moments: "I saw my soul to-day. It was a bubble, blown large, palpitating, whirling over a stormy sea; glorious with the rainbow hues it was, but perilous, abandoned." He could even be funny, as when he tries eating raw eggs: "I record it for future generations of poets, that the experiment is not a success. You taste raw egg all day." Stirling was a doomed genius, agreed the few reviewers. His death was a great pity.

Arthur Stirling was soon forgotten, but its author was hardly dead. Upton Sinclair, in the first of many efforts over the course of his career to generate publicity for his work, had planted the *Times* obituary notice through a reporter friend. This was the final stage in a plot he concocted with Ripley Hitchcock, his editor at D. Appleton and Company. The hoax was exposed after the reviews appeared, generating even more publicity for the delighted Sinclair. Everything he had wanted to say about art and society, his paranoia, his resentment, his ambition, had been set forth in Stirling's journal. He would not be ignored, even if he had to resort to trickery.

The Journal of Arthur Stirling marked an advance over Sinclair's earlier work in that it was about a recognizable human being, and an occasionally fascinating one at that. Within the next year, it would affect one reader strongly enough to turn the author's life around radically. But *Arthur Stirling* did poorly in the literary marketplace. Stories about lonely poets cut off in the bud spoke more to other frustrated artists than to the general book-buying public, and Stirling was too frantic for even his more sympathetic readers. His voice was "strained," a wise editor had told Stirling, "hysterical and overwrought," and giving an "effect of crudeness." These were his own faults, Sinclair would come to realize; he reluctantly conceded that he was an author still in search of a voice, a form, and a subject.

In the autumn of 1902, Sinclair was living alone in a Harlem boardinghouse, unable to support himself, let alone his wife and baby. He was so broke that he resorted, like Hurstwood in *Sister Carrie,* to playing poker for money. Dreiser made Hurstwood lose and kill himself. Sinclair, in his typical all-or-nothing fashion, became fascinated with the possibility of winning money, but quit entirely when he saw himself falling into a trap—gambling as a vice was as familiar to southern gentlemen as the drinking that had ruined his father.

Paternal guidance having failed him, Sinclair had several times chosen older men as models for conduct and achievement—Will Moir, Minot Savage, and his two most admired professors at Columbia, George Woodberry and Edward MacDowell, among them. In October, as he was dropping off an article for consideration at *The Literary Digest,* he fell into conversation with a young English writer named Leonard Abbott. An active socialist, Abbott pressed Sinclair to read some recent pamphlets on social issues, including one by George Herron, a former minister and college professor. Sinclair liked what Herron had said and wrote him an admiring letter. Herron replied a week later, in early November 1902, inviting Sinclair to join him for dinner at his hotel.

The address Sinclair had been given was that of a dignified residential hotel on West Forty-fourth Street. George Herron greeted him warmly and introduced him to a tall, slender woman who wore an Empire gown of green velvet, and to Gaylord Wilshire, a thin little man with a Vandyke beard and mustache and an amused smile that struck Sinclair as Mephisophelean. Like Wilshire, Herron was a small man in his early forties of considerable presence, also in formal attire; his black beard, immaculately trimmed, set off his pale complexion. Sinclair's hair was shaggy over his frayed collar and his cracked shoes were rounded at the heel. He gazed wonderingly at his socialist hosts and the sumptuously appointed apartment, with its marble statuary, its thick Persian rugs, and its original oil paintings.

Over dinner in the hotel dining room, the two older men complimented Sinclair on the interest in social matters that his writing had demonstrated. They quizzed him closely about his background and asked what he knew, if anything, about socialism: had he read Kropotkin's *Mutual Aid: A Factor of Evolution*? Marx's *Capital*? Veblen's *The Theory of the Leisure Class*? Bellamy's *Looking Backward*? What was his position on the Fabians' quarrel with the anarchists and the nihilists? Was reform possible without violent revolution, or must the modern world be cured by destroying it?

The questions stumped Sinclair, and his ignorance infuriated him. Why, he wondered, had he come across none of these writers or books in his years of college and graduate school? His new instructors, who assured Sinclair that he could quickly remedy his deficient education, were on the face of it an unlikely pair. Wilshire was a Harvard graduate who had worked for two years in his father's Cincinnati steel mill before moving to Los Angeles in the mid-1880s and ultimately making his fortune in land speculation along the corridor that would become one of the city's most famous thoroughfares, Wilshire Boulevard. He lost his only political campaign, running for Congress in 1890 as "the Socialist millionaire," but won a reputation for showmanship, once offering to bet William Jennings Bryan $1,000 that the audience would side with him in their scheduled debate. In 1901, he invited the New York police to arrest him "at, say, 4:30 o'clock, Thursday afternoon, if convenient for you"—he said he intended to speak without a permit at that time in Central Park. He needed the publicity for his new magazine, he told the police, "which does considerable blowing about the menace of plutocracy." Would they please send their most brutal officers with a patrol wagon in "apple-pie order"?

George Herron shunned publicity as avidly as Wilshire sought it. A scholarly Congregational Church minister, he had been fired from his post as a professor at Iowa's Grinnell College in 1899 for adultery. He was not yet married to the elegant lady in the Empire dress, Carrie Rand, for whom he had deserted his harridan wife. The New York press had "tortured him hideously" for living in sin, as Sinclair wrote later. One story even claimed that Herron's farm in New Jersey was the site of an attempt to found a "free-love colony," prompting an editorial attack on Herron and Carrie Rand as having "the morality of the higher apes." But it was clear to Sinclair that Herron was no more a libertine than he was; he was a moral philosopher, a man of reason, and a proper model of conduct. To express his appreciation for their interest in him, Sinclair sent both Wilshire and Herron copies of *The Journal of Arthur Stirling.*

═══

The immediate consequence of Sinclair's momentous meeting with two prominent socialists was his second effort, after *Prince Hagen,* at social criticism. Although he still lacked the coherent philosophy that he would come to find in socialism, he created a properly vicious capitalist villain in his third novel, *The Captain of Industry.* Robbie van Rensselaer, the ruthless financier, is crudely drawn, but Sinclair's insights into the language of class and the complexities of commerce sometimes anticipate his later work. For example, he creates a brilliant aphorism to explain the significance of a cliché like "being born with a silver spoon in your mouth." Such a phrase is a "petrified inspiration. Once upon a time it was a living thing, a lightning flash in some man's soul; and now it glides off our tongue without our ever thinking of its meaning." Sinclair also deftly shows how a Wall Street bear can manipulate the market, swindle the public, and—to switch metaphors—clamber over the other rats in the barrel.

But Sinclair's tone darkens as Robbie's story continues; he loses control of both it and his structure, perhaps because his own life was so discordant while he was writing the novel. In a crashing operatic sequence, Robbie seduces a girl, not realizing that she is his long-lost illegitimate daughter. The lightning flash into his own soul does the captain of industry little good: he ends up drowned and devoured by crabs in a scene more gruesome than anything in *The Jungle.*

Sinclair's new novel read like a revenge fantasy by the ghost of Arthur Stirling, a melodrama gone haywire. Considered purely as social commentary, it was so profoundly negative about the chances for ameliorating social and economic conditions in America that it left no room for hope. With incest, best left to the ancient Greeks, thrown into the mix, the many publishers whom Sinclair pressed to buy his manuscript through the spring of 1903 had no trouble rejecting it. *The Captain of Industry* was an even more resounding failure than *Springtime and Harvest* and *The Journal of Arthur Stirling*. It would not be seen by readers until after the publication of *The Jungle*.

"Sir, I exist!" proclaims the indignant speaker to "the universe" in one of Stephen Crane's droll philosophical poems. In May 1903, Sinclair shouted his own angry challenge to the universe in an article headlined "My Cause." "I, Upton Sinclair, would-be singer and penniless rat," he began, "being in body very weak and in heart very weary, but in will yet infinitely determined, have sat myself down to compose this letter to the world." Henceforth, he planned to concentrate his energies on writing a trilogy of novels about the Civil War; on the establishment of his own Sinclair Press, which would circulate his work and circumvent his ostracism by the New York publishers; and on starting a foundation, to be called the American University of Literature, that would support young writers, liberating them from the slavery of writing for money. Too angry to realize that he was insulting the readers of the radical newspaper in which his screed appeared, he said they might "sneer" at such defiance and such grandiose schemes, but they would "live to blush for that sneer."

In Crane's poem, "the universe" dryly advises the excited speaker that his existence "has not created in me a sense of obligation." Sinclair was luckier, perhaps because he was louder and more persistent, or because some agreed his cause was just. He sent a copy of "My Cause" to George Herron and appealed to him for financial support; he knew that Herron's wife-to-be was from a wealthy family and of a generous disposition—she would later persuade her mother to fund the Rand School of Social Science at the New School for Social Research.

Herron had read and admired the copy Sinclair sent him of *Arthur Stirling;* he was especially sympathetic to its attacks on public taste and values, having suffered so much himself from both. As a writer himself—his later books on diplomatic history would be highly praised—he saw what Sinclair might accomplish with a subject worthy of his talents, such as the Civil War, which Sinclair hoped to treat. Like a wise and tolerant father, Herron excused the blustering rant of "My Cause." He invited Sinclair to visit him again in New York, where he offered to lend him enough money to help him write his first Civil War novel. The total amount of the loan would come to $800, or about $16,000 in today's currency.

Sinclair's alter ego Arthur Stirling drowned himself because nobody cared enough to offer him a helping hand. Now George Herron had tossed a line to a sinking Sinclair. It meant nothing less, Sinclair said later, than his "survival as a writer." He was "entirely unable to imagine" how he would have carried on without Herron's aid. It was a remarkable gesture, testimony both to Herron's perceptiveness concerning Sinclair's abilities and to Sinclair's capacity for inspiring confidence.

CHAPTER TWO

THE AMERICAN HOMER

(April 1903–October 1904)

Upton Sinclair began life anew when he, Meta, and David moved to a farm near Princeton in May 1903. His formal education, as well as his self-directed and often erratic apprenticeship as a novelist, was over. His early novels had failed because his true gifts were as a teacher and a preacher, and because the stories lacked both practical lessons and moral coherence. Sinclair had not yet found the subject that he wanted to teach or the religion that he wanted to preach. In Princeton, he would find both his lasting subject—the conflict between idealism and materialism in America—and the wellspring of his belief in socialism. He would also begin to develop his extraordinary talent for mastering difficult subjects and making them accessible to a wide audience of readers.

Carrie Stout, the seven-year-old granddaughter of the old couple on whose farm the Sinclairs lived for a year and a half, wrote a brief but touching account late in her life of her close association with Meta, David, and Sinclair. She first saw them on a Sunday late in April. Sinclair had rented a horse and buggy in Princeton, three miles southeast of their farm in Cedar Grove. He left Meta and David in the buggy by the porch and climbed the steps to introduce himself to the Stouts, saying that he was a writer and would be using the Civil War collection at the Princeton University library for at least a year. He and his family needed a place to stay. Would the Stouts consider renting him a piece of their property, perhaps in the stand of maple trees by the creek at the end of their long drive? He would want to put up a wall tent for the summer and to build a small cabin in the fall, Sinclair said. He was living on a grant from a friend of only a few hundred dollars a year, and could not offer much for the rental, but he promised to buy whatever he needed in the way of provisions such as bread, milk, butter, and eggs from the Stouts.

George Stout owned two farms but neither brought in much money, so even the pittance the young couple could pay would be a help. But Mrs. Stout, a kindhearted woman, said she was afraid that a young mother so far from town and from friends her own age would feel isolated and helpless. Sinclair assured her that his wife could easily travel the ninety minutes by train to New York to visit with her parents if she felt lonely; but they would both be so busy with establishing their new home that he did not think boredom would be a problem. Besides, the location in the grove was so lovely, after several years of dingy New York flats, that it was impossible to conceive of being less than contented living there.

Carrie Stout recalled that Sinclair seemed to like to saw and hammer and knock things together—first the platform for the big tent where the family lived during the summer, then the cabin and some homely pine furniture for it, and even three little bridges across the stream that curled through their acre.

Carrie often saw Sinclair walking when she delivered buttermilk, cottage cheese, vegetables, and fruits in her homemade wagon. He always walked with his head down and his hands clasped behind him, and didn't respond to her cheery hello. Meta explained that her husband didn't mean to be rude or unfriendly; his concentration was so deep that he simply didn't see Carrie or hear her. Sinclair was, in fact, often kind, bringing Carrie candy, along with boxes of nuts for her grandparents, when he came back from his frequent visits to New York. Meta was also nice to Carrie, and obviously grateful for her company. It seemed to Carrie that her grandmother might have been right in worrying that young Mrs. Sinclair would get lonely, because she and David spent a lot of time in the Stouts' parlor. It was there that David took his first steps, wobbling over to Carrie—quite late, when he was almost three. The little boy had suffered from rickets, which Meta's doctor had feared might prevent him from walking at all.

For weeks after their arrival at the Stout farm the young pioneers were caught up in the joy of their fresh beginning—together again for almost the first time since David's birth. The weather when they first set up camp by the spring that May had been glorious, one blue and golden day after another. Sinclair passed the mornings playing hide-and-seek with David among the flowering dogwood trees, while Meta puzzled over how to arrange the tent. It was the same one they had bought used in the Thousand Islands, musty and mildewed in places, which would lead to problems when the rains began. Though the tent looked big, at twelve by eighteen feet, the side walls were so low, at less than five feet, that movement was restricted. It was also crowded, with a small stove, a washstand, a crib purchased from the

Stouts for a dollar, a folding table, a packing box fitted with shelves for dishes, a steamer trunk for their clothing, and a small bookcase at the head of the double bed. Sinclair drew a chalk line across the middle of the tent floor, marking out his study area, and explained to David that he was not allowed to cross it. When Meta protested that he was going over the line himself, Sinclair threw up a smaller tent for himself as a study, where he kept a cot and a desk and a canvas folding chair.

By midsummer, Meta's enthusiasm for rural life was wearing thin, largely because of the demands of looking after David. The special diet that her doctor had prescribed for the baby's illness shortly before they left New York was expensive and arduous to prepare. She followed the doctor's regimen to the letter, fixing six meals a day of hot cereal, poached eggs, oranges, chicken broth, stewed prunes, chopped beef, mashed potato, and canned beets. Sinclair too was pressed into service, trimming fat and gristle from the meat and pounding it to a pulp, even peeling the skin off the prunes and peaches and apples as the doctor had demanded. While the diet cured the rickets, it led to bouts of diarrhea, requiring Meta to make frequent trips to the laundry—an exposed flat rock downstream from the spring where they drew their water. The diapers were hung out to dry on the tent's guy ropes.

David's health remained precarious. A bout with boils was followed by measles during the hottest weeks of the summer, in mid-August, and he was stung twice by bees. Trips to the doctor in New York meant mounting medical bills, which alarmed Sinclair. He was fast running through the first half of the loan from Herron, which had to last until December, when the second installment of the loan would arrive.

Sinclair considered money a necessary evil. He had no taste for luxuries and no expensive vices like gambling or liquor, or even coffee. Left to his own devices, he could have lived in a tent for much of the year. But he was now a man with hostages to fortune, a wife and baby who depended on him. Because of them—and because of the materialistic world in which he had to live—Sinclair thought that his career as a writer was in jeopardy. Generous himself when he had money, especially in later years, he assumed others should be generous too, especially fellow writers and intellectuals.

Accordingly, it was to a prosperous writer that Sinclair now turned, even though they had never met. This was Owen Wister, whose 1902 bestseller, *The Virginian,* had made him an international celebrity. Born in 1860, Wister came from a wealthy Philadelphia family and was a Harvard College friend and contemporary of Theodore Roosevelt. Like Roosevelt, he had gone west for his health as a sickly young man. Even before *The Virginian,* Wister had achieved renown as "the American Kipling" for his stories, including the famous "Balaam and Pedro" and *Lin McLean*—the novel that tickled Roosevelt for its account of the hero's strolling off after being "lightly stabbed."

In April 1901, Sinclair had sent Wister a copy of *Springtime and Harvest* and received in return a detailed analysis of its faults. Sinclair gratefully replied that though Wister's comments were "by no means the most favorable" analysis his novel had received, they were the "very best." Wister had been "beautifully kind." Sinclair suggested that he go to visit Wister in Philadelphia, where the master might explain his faults in more detail: "I write to you as a kind of oracle, for I have passed a deadly dull winter of despair," lightened only by Wister's writing, which was all "cymbals and trumpets, . . . so brilliant and so dazzling that I'd have been quite in despair about my own work if I'd thought of it."

Wister did not respond to this rather fulsome implied request for literary sponsorship. Undeterred, Sinclair sent him a copy of *Prince Hagen* in the early spring of 1903 with a note describing how he had sat out in a meadow reading *The Virginian* in a transport of joy. The correspondence resumed, as Darwin Payne explains in his biography of Wister, with the older man offering advice on everything from writing to "the kind of nursery Sinclair should construct for his son" on the Princeton farm. Soon Sinclair began to plead with Wister to send him some money. Wister's wife, Molly, visited him and Meta in August for an afternoon, making a trip down from the Wisters' summer house in Saunderstown, Rhode Island, and followed up with a gift of some groceries and other supplies.

Sinclair thanked Wister but said what he really needed was some cash. Wister said no. Sinclair tried once more, in what Payne calls a "lengthy, self-pitying plea for just one hundred dollars. His shanty-tent home was muddy inside, his wife was miserable and exhausted, his son was cutting teeth and constantly howling, and in trying to improve their primitive dwelling Sinclair had severely mashed his finger with a hammer. Finally, he wrote, while they ate the meal that Sinclair himself had prepared under these conditions the baby vomited, whereupon Mrs. Sinclair threw herself into the middle of the muddy floor and exclaimed, 'Oh how I *wish* Mrs. Wister in this hole tonight!' "

Sinclair told Wister that he and Meta had then laughed about pretending that Mrs. Wister was sharing their squalor. But he was serious about needing the money. Couldn't Wister spare a hundred dollars (about $2,000 today)? It would be so "helpful to a woman who has to wait endlessly for the book to be born," to buy "a rug, a blanket, a foot scraper (oh the mud in the tent!)." All he needed was a "fair chance" to write a book that would "shake men to the depths of their souls." Wister answered briskly that Sinclair had already had a hearing for his three books, without much response. Perhaps he ought to think about working at some menial job, even as a clerk, and get his family back on his feet instead of feeling sorry for himself. Sinclair hotly defended himself in his reply.

═══

Owen Wister had achieved fame because of his accurate sense of the American West as an epic subject. Sinclair must have thought his own excitement with the epic subject of the Civil War, and his need for more thoughtful reflection on it than would have been possible working as a clerk, should have inspired Wister to be openhanded. He shrugged off his disappointment, warned Meta to keep a closer eye on their budget, and continued his research—refusing, as always, to write anything but notes until he had read and absorbed everything he needed to know.

Sinclair's alter ego Arthur Stirling had eloquently argued that the war was a fit subject for an American epic: "Is there anything more fearful in history, any more tremendous effort of the human spirit? And so far it has not made one great poem, one great drama, one great novel." Nearly a decade later, in *Love's Pilgrimage,* Sinclair said again that there was "not one" novel about the war "above the grade of juvenile fiction" (presumably other than his own). His pointed omission of Stephen Crane is puzzling until we recall the bitter irony and cynicism at the heart of *The Red Badge of Courage*—whose hero, Henry Fleming, receives his wound, his red badge, while fleeing in a panic from the battlefield. Sinclair disliked cynicism generally, and thought it was inconsistent with his own effort to write a national epic. He was an unembarrassed patriot who believed—as Crane, though a minister's son, never could—in the special, God-given provenance of America. Arthur Stirling's words reflect Sinclair's own feelings: "Passionately, more than words can utter, I love this land of mine. If I tear my heart till it bleeds . . . it is for this consecration and this hope—it is for this land of Washington and Lincoln. There never was any land like it—there may never be any like it again; and Freedom watches from her mountains, trembling." If this was the greatest country, Sinclair reasoned, then it deserved the highest tribute, an epic after the fashion of Homer's *Iliad,* free of demeaning irony. His self-appointed task was nothing less than to write a novel about the Civil War that would be "worthy of comparison with that greatest of all epics!"

Unlike Crane, who drew much of his material for *Red Badge* from interviews with veterans, Sinclair relied on printed sources; he was an assiduous if self-trained researcher and there were vast resources of personal narratives on hand in the Princeton library. He was allowed to take some of these that had been published back to the farm with him, as well as campaign histories and biographies of Lincoln and Lee and Grant and dozens of others. But the valuable primary sources—the division and regimental histories, the Northern abolition tracts and the Southern denunciations they provoked, the recruiting literature and speeches, the unpublished diaries and letters in the collection—could not leave the building. Sinclair was frequently absent from home for hours, and when he was back at the farm he hid himself in his tent-study.

In late September, Sinclair took time off from his research to help a team of carpenters build a small cabin, his family's first real home. Meta's mood, depressed from tending a sick baby in a cramped tent, soon brightened. The cabin's added space and the protection it afforded against the rain and chilly evenings of early fall were pleasant, and she enjoyed using, instead of their tiny camp stove, the secondhand kitchen range and potbellied stove they bought from a neighbor. Sinclair constructed a concrete cistern in the spring and installed a pump in the kitchen so that Meta had running water. Best of all, the baby now had his own room.

So too did his father; using leftover lumber from the cabin project, Sinclair knocked together an eight-by-ten hut, a stone's throw from the cabin, with his own little stove, desk, shelving, and bed. To mollify Meta, who complained about the cheap and ugly black paint he used for the exterior, he trimmed the single window, the edges of the roof, and the door frame in bright red.

Now that they were settled into their new home, the baby's health improved. Meta finally had time to settle down to the reading program that Sinclair devised for her. She had frequently complained that she was uncomfortable when they spent an evening with the Herrons or Sinclair's other intellectual friends. She knew nothing about art or literature or politics, and felt that she was being dismissed as shallow, just a pretty face. Sinclair sympathized. He told Meta that she needed to become intellectually independent both of him and of the orthodox opinions of the day concerning women, who at that time still could not vote or hold property, in most states, apart from their husbands. He encouraged his wife to read widely in philosophy, economics, and political science; he also introduced her to two books by a woman he greatly admired, Charlotte Perkins Gilman, that have since become staples of feminist literature.

The first of these two books, *The Yellow Wall-Paper,* grew out of the treatment prescribed for Charlotte Perkins during her first marriage, when she suffered a nervous breakdown. The noted physician (and novelist) S. Weir Mitchell believed that in some highly sensitive and intelligent people the circuits of the brain become overloaded and break down, causing extreme depression. He advocated complete rest and, above all, the absence of any kind of mental, intellectual, or artistic stimulation. This treatment did work with some of his patients, but, as Gilman compellingly showed in her novella, which appeared in 1892, it nearly killed her. In *Women and Economics* (1898), Gilman argued that women were prone to the kind of depression from which she had suffered because they allowed their definition as mothers to enslave them. A newly enlightened society should allow women to realize their true potential by freeing them from caring for children and the home through cooperative or collective associations.

Meta responded enthusiastically to Gilman's books, especially *The Yellow Wall-Paper,* but she resisted Sinclair's efforts to instruct her in philosophy. Kant's categorical imperative left her cold, and she could not comprehend the substance or the appeal of Emerson's Transcendentalism. Veblen's *The Theory of the Leisure Class* (1899), which Sinclair said he consumed in "a continuous ebullition of glee," she found amusing; but she resented Sinclair's teasing insinuation that she bore some similarities to the useless dependent woman satirized by Veblen. She read and loved without reservation, however, the plays of Henrik Ibsen. The pathetic Nora in *A Doll's House,* who dedicates her existence to an ungrateful husband, and the suicidal Hedda Gabler, also unhappy in her marriage, spoke to Meta in ways that she barely comprehended—between caring for David and trying, however ineptly, to run their small household, she had little time for reflection.

Efficiency in small matters was not Meta's strong suit, and she frequently spent more money on her trips to town for food and staples than Sinclair thought she should. One day late in the fall, when the brilliantly colored leaves had vanished and her little house seemed particularly dark, Meta splurged on a bright red tablecloth. Proudly showing it off to her husband, she said it had cost only 30 cents. Sinclair exploded in anger. Thirty cents was their food budget for a whole day, he said. She was impoverishing them with her foolish indulgences, such as drinking coffee and diluting its poison with expensive cream and sugar. Now she wanted a "fool piece of rag for which they had no earthly need!" Meta dissolved in tears and returned the tablecloth the following day.

Very little color brightened Meta's life that first long winter in the country, marked as it was by frozen black tree trunks starkly silhouetted against white snow and crusted ice. It was the coldest winter anyone could remember, with temperatures dropping well below zero at night and barely climbing above the teens during the day for weeks on end. It was too cold for Meta to take the baby to town or to visit her parents in New York, or even to move more than a few feet from the cabin stove. By the middle of February she had grown tired of reading. Even the book that she liked the best after *The Yellow Wall-Paper,* Frederick Douglass's story of his life as a slave, only reminded her of her own imprisonment in what Gaylord Wilshire called "the soapbox on the marsh."

Meta knew that her husband was disappointed in her lack of mental growth. German verbs, Ricardo's iron law of wages, Bellamy's *Looking Backward,* all bored her. Upton was a thinking machine, she told herself. She was a creature of the heart, and of the soul. She determined to appeal to him as a creative spirit, a fellow artist, "a poetess." One evening, as he sat reading by the stove after David had gone to bed, she asked Sinclair to listen to a poem she had written about the rain.

> I am the rain that comes at night,
> When all in slumber is folded light—
> Save one by weary vigils worn
> Who counteth the drops unto the morn.

Sinclair's encouraging response was a heartbeat too late. Crushed, Meta cried, "You don't like it! You don't think it's good at all!" He hadn't said that, Sinclair protested weakly. It was just that of all the arts, poetry was the most difficult, and "there are so many standards . . . a thing can be good, and yet not good! The heights are so far away. . . ."

Sinclair regretted hurting Meta's feelings, especially as he was feeling increasingly optimistic about reaching new creative heights of his own. By Christmas he had finished his research, worked out the story line, and determined on a title: *Manassas,* after the location of the first significant battle of the Civil War, better known in the North as Bull Run for the creek that runs through the area. Sinclair's protagonist, Allan Montague, was a southerner from a slaveholding family. Educated in the North, and imbued with its abolitionist fervor, he embodies the split personality of the nation as he works against members of his own family to save the Union. Most of Allan's story takes place in the critical years before the war; it opens in 1846 with his grandfather receiving the news of Andrew Jackson's death and recalling his experiences with Jackson, fighting the British during the Revolution and in the War of 1812. Only the final pages are devoted to the Battle of First Manassas itself, a section of eight thousand words that merits comparison with the best combat narratives to come out of the Civil War, including Crane's *The Red Badge of Courage.*

By the end of February 1904, Sinclair was satisfied that he had his story well in hand. His theme would be the triumph of idealism over the threat of destruction from immoral forces, chiefly those relating to slavery. He was confident that *Manassas* would be his best work so far, and he was right. But even as he was beginning to realize his ambitions as a writer, his marriage was beginning its long, painful, and inexorable deterioration.

Later, when he described their marriage in *Love's Pilgrimage,* Sinclair gave himself and Meta the names of two shepherd boys from a Greek pastoral eclogue. Sinclair was Thyrsis, and Meta became Corydon. The device strikes the modern reader as arch, but it freed Sinclair to be objective about himself, his behavior, and his attitudes concerning sex, which were so different from those of most of his progressive friends.

Sinclair not only condemned sex outside of marriage (although he would not always live up to his code in this regard); he went further, arguing that not even marriage justified sexual intercourse purely for the pleasure it afforded. Only the desire to create a child, Sinclair told Meta, could give married sex the "dignity and meaning" it required. Since they both agreed that one child had been more than enough, logic dictated that they should again try to eschew sex. For the time being, they would return to living as "brother and sister." Like the lads in the pastoral legend, they would simply be good friends. The same idea had failed earlier, resulting in the birth of David, but they were wiser and stronger now.

Sinclair said he understood Meta's problem. Hers was "a love-nature" that sought to be loved in return. His own nature was "Hebraic," dedicated to the stern call of duty. In *Arthur Stirling,* Sinclair had cited the great European critic Georg Brandes, who in turn referred to Nietzsche, who was echoing Carlyle: Only a fool ever sought to be happy. To be *useful*—"to shine in use," like Tennyson's Ulysses—was the most one could ask of life. The highest use was to live the "heroic life," striving against great difficulties for "the good of all." The work he was now doing, Sinclair told Meta, was of this nature. It required sacrifices beyond the usual of him, and of her, including sexual relations.

But theory and practice often conflicted. The little cabin got so cold that they had to heap their extra blankets on David to keep him alive. Then they snuggled close in their own bed under overcoats, throw rugs, even the muslin curtains—"like two animals which crawl into the same hole to keep each other from freezing," in Sinclair's chilling simile. It was Meta's sensuality that had drawn him to her in the first place, and her own need for more than verbal assurances that Sinclair loved her was great. But as before, they had no secure sense of methods of birth control or contraception; they lived in constant terror of another pregnancy, "like people drawing lots for a death sentence." When he did surrender to impulse, Sinclair, according to Meta in her unpublished novel, "Thyrsis and Corydon," got the whole production over with as quickly as possible: "he needed the barest of stage settings," she wistfully recalled, while she "always wanted scenery and music."

In March, the freezing weather finally gave way to ceaseless, driving rain. The creek flooded and the cabin was surrounded by a sea of mud that reached above Meta's ankles. She was afraid to allow David onto the porch; if he fell from it into the mud he might drown. She began to let herself go, neglecting to brush the lustrous hair that was her pride, seldom changing clothes, leaving greasy dishes stacked in the sink for days on end. Sinclair now spent all but one or two days a week writing in his hut, frequently well past midnight. When he interrupted his work early in the evening for dinner, "faint and exhausted," he often found that Meta had neglected to prepare it. By the time she did, they sat down at the bare table and wordlessly wolfed their food "like savages."

They had less and less to talk about, beyond Meta's complaint that Upton had forgotten again to take out the garbage, or his that the diaper pail was overflowing again, and why wasn't that boy toilet-trained anyway. Sinclair read the newspapers at the library, and tried to interest his wife in world affairs: Madame Curie's recent talk about radium and the transmutation of metals, the opening of the Panama Canal, the hopeful signs of revolution coming in Russia. Meta failed to show any interest in such far-off events, preferring to talk about her feelings. If Upton loved her, could he not tell her so occasionally? Sinclair protested that talking about love was useless, then reproached himself for his "blundering insensitivity": he was "a hippopotamus to Meta's butterfly," a "spiny monster" who had imprisoned a beautiful maiden. Meta sighed and assured him that his work took precedence over her complaining. They would make do.

Caught up in his writing, Sinclair often slept only a few hours a night. He preferred to nap in his hut rather than disturb Meta, but she begged him not to leave her alone all night, so he always returned. Early one morning in mid-March, shortly after two o'clock, he approached the cabin and was surprised to see that the front window was glowing faintly. Inside, Meta sat by the dying fire, a shawl over her shoulders. She was quietly sobbing. This was not the first time Sinclair had found his wife crying. He comforted her and fell asleep.

When he awoke some time later, the full moon was shining brightly through the window, beside which Meta was sitting. He heard a clicking sound, then saw a flash of metal in the moonlight. He leaped out of bed and grabbed the revolver that Meta had cocked and placed against her temple. She shrieked and collapsed into his arms, crying "Save me!"

By dawn Sinclair had what he thought of as the full story. Meta had been thinking for several days of killing herself, using the revolver that Sinclair had given her for protection during his absences. She was too cowardly to go through with it, she said, having already tried and failed several times. Sinclair was shaken as he had never been before, and tearfully vowed to do whatever he could to make her happy. But as he described this event in *Love's Pilgrimage* it is clear that he believed Meta was in the power of forces beyond his reach. He did not refer to Gilman's *Yellow Wall-Paper,* behind which the distraught heroine sees her trapped reflection, but the echoes seem obvious to the reader today: there was a "subliminal woman" within Meta, Sinclair said, whose "deep chambers" he could not probe. He would never forget the picture of her "sitting in the cold moonlight with a blanket flung about her, her wild hair tossing, and in her hand the revolver with which she had meant to destroy herself."

Images of combat litter the landscape of Sinclair's work, no doubt because he saw his own life as a series of battles. He fought two of these simultaneously during that difficult first year in Princeton. Professionally, he was struggling to write a great novel about the greatest story he knew, and to define himself as an artist as he did so. He was also trying to save Meta from "the wolves" of her "black anguish and despair." This was a personal battle, but enlarged by Sinclair in terms that suggest both his paranoia and his egotism: "The world was trying to crush" his genius, using his wife's misery as its weapon. He would fight back, just as Samson and Roland and "the Greeks at Thermopylae" had fought back, even though they were destroyed.

Happily, no such dramatic martyrdom was necessary, for in early May Sinclair received an offer from George P. Brett, the noted Macmillan editor, to publish *Manassas* the following August. Brett was a shrewd man with an eye for new writers and for blockbuster books: within the past two years he had overseen the publication of London's *The Call of the Wild* (1903) and Wister's *The Virginian.* It was a coup for Sinclair to enlist Brett as his editor, a confirmation that he had finally been discovered. (Neither Wister nor

London apparently had anything to do with Brett's signing of Sinclair. Wister was less than friendly to Sinclair by this time, and London would not actually meet him for the first time until 1905, despite their continuing correspondence. But it couldn't have hurt Sinclair with Brett that his name was so closely linked to his most famous authors.)

Despite some strong reviews, *Manassas* was not the masterpiece that Sinclair had hoped for, nor a commercial success; it sold fewer than two thousand copies after its publication in the summer of 1904. But it did mark a considerable advance over his earlier work, anticipating Sinclair's later achievements in the Lanny Budd novels. Through young Allan Montague's eyes the reader meets Harriet Beecher Stowe and Frederick Douglass, and runs with a slave for freedom on the Underground Railroad. Among the novel's key events are John Brown's execution, the Lincoln-Douglas debates, the frustration of the plot to kill Lincoln in Baltimore en route to his first inauguration, and the attack on Fort Sumter. The narrative gets cluttered and the plot relies on improbable coincidence in order for its hero to be in on so many important events. But for readers interested in American history, *Manassas* is seldom dull. One highlight, in addition to the concluding section already noted, is a long passage describing the hunting down and murder of an escaped slave; clearly indebted to *Uncle Tom's Cabin,* it is superior to Stowe in the quality of its prose.

Brett's advance of $500 against royalties for *Manassas* was enough to lift the sword of financial doom a few more inches from Sinclair's neck. Meta could have her red tablecloth now, and even pay Mrs. Stout to look after David while she traveled to Princeton to wander around campus during the occasional days when Sinclair needed to work in the library. Politeness compelled him to introduce to her some of the undergraduates he had met. She thought the young men were charming in their blue and red blazers and straw boaters, though Sinclair was less pleased by the air they adopted of privileged indifference to the world outside their beautiful cloister. The few who cared enough to talk with him about literature were narrow and conventional in their tastes. The theology students were even worse, caught up in trivial debates about how "transubstantiation" differed from "consubstantiation." In his grumpier moods, the complacent stupidity of the Princeton undergraduates could send "a black shadow stealing" across Sinclair's soul.

Sinclair resented the Princeton men more than he might have a year earlier because of the "strange and sinister fact" he believed he had uncovered in the course of his Civil War research. During his formative years he had been exposed to attacks on civic and corporate corruption in the Hearst newspapers and in magazines like *McClure's, Everybody's,* and *Collier's.* These accounts had appalled him. But except for a few weeks in 1898, when he worked as a volunteer for the New York City reform candidate for mayor, he had been only a sympathetic observer of the growing progressive movement. Now, though, he thought he understood the causes and the significance of the rampaging profiteering that occurred during and after the Civil War, in the forty-year period that Mark Twain called "the great barbecue" and "the Gilded Age."

Sinclair's research led him to conclude that there were two groups of men who had worked to save the Union, one noble and the other ignoble. The noblest were the soldiers, who had suffered unspeakably, returning home, if they did, impoverished and crushed by their sacrifice. The ignoble were those who made illicit fortunes from the war, providing shoddy goods and rotten food to the troops. The heroic sacrifices of a few good men had enabled the many bad men who followed in their wake to exploit and degrade the republic. The money-grubbers had left their ill-gotten fortunes to their children, among whom were these spoiled Princeton undergraduates.

And who now opposed the exploiters and their heirs? Certainly not the existing political parties, the Republicans or the Democrats. Granted, there were honorable men in both parties, some in positions of authority and influence—including both President Theodore Roosevelt and the current president of Princeton, Woodrow Wilson. But even the best were too often stymied by the system itself—what Sinclair would often call "interlocking directorates"—and too many others had been corrupted by the ready availability of money. Based as it was on capitalism, the system was broken beyond repair or reform.

Convinced of these truths, and in search of a remedy, Sinclair now turned in earnest to the books that Wilshire and Herron had pressed on him the previous year. Other than proofreading the galleys for *Manassas,* he was free to read voraciously through the late spring and well into the summer of 1904. He grounded himself in economic theory, as explained in the works of Karl Marx, Karl Kautsky, and Veblen, and found confirmation of those theories in the continuing exposés by his fellow writers in *McClure's* and other publications.

Sinclair's self-study plan left him with a simple formula that he would devote his life to explaining, and with a program that he would advocate with the zealous devotion of a priest. The formula was implied by what Karl Marx called "surplus value"—meaning that workers created more value through their labor than it cost to feed, clothe, and house them. The "surplus" was accumulated by those who employed or staked the workers, men who did nothing else than accumulate capital—and the power to exploit those who gave them the surplus. The program was designed to correct this problem. It centered on public ownership of the means of production, the key plank in the socialist platform both in Europe and in the United States.

The abstract formula underlying socialism and its concrete recommendations for reshaping society would give Sinclair's life and writing the focus they had lacked until this point. He was about to become a proud and determined propagandist—his word—for the cause of socialism. From the beginning, though, he would approach socialism as a moralist, not as a political theorist. Both his strengths and his weaknesses derived from his simplistic belief that all injustice stemmed from greed, whether for money or power. He rejected the Christian doctrine that original sin and "natural depravity" were the key components in shaping human character. He also disputed the contention of secular philosophers like Thomas Hobbes, who said life was "nasty, brutish, and short," because people were at heart selfish and cruel when it served their interests—which was most of the time. On the contrary, said Sinclair: people were naturally good, not evil; social, not antisocial. When they had what they needed they were generous and kind. It was "the system"—religious in the past, economic now—that exploited them and made them prone to bad conduct and foolish ideas. Change the system, and you will change the people. Human nature was not fixed, it was malleable, capable of being improved—even, as Shaw would argue in *Back to Methuselah* (1921), of evolving finally toward an essence of pure thought.

But people could also regress into the purest savagery if the system failed to change, or so H. G. Wells speculated in his 1895 novel *The Time Machine*. In the distant future, the descendants of today's upper classes appear to Wells's Time Traveler to continue their lives of pampered uselessness. Yet they also lived in fear of dark forces beneath the earth, and every so often a few of them vanished. Soon Wells's hero learns the awful truth: the descendants of the lower classes, victimized in the past, were now strong and ruthless cannibals who kept their former rulers as cattle and slaughtered them when they were hungry.

——

Sinclair grew up in a time when many Americans worried, like Wells, that a literal war between the classes was imminent. In 1888, the year he published *Looking Backward,* Edward Bellamy flashed forward to 1988, imagining that in a century all the problems of his day—poverty, discrimination, and most of all labor violence—would somehow have been solved. Practical and energetic leaders arose to suggest how Bellamy's vision might be realized, among them Eugene Debs, who ran for president of the United States in 1900 as the candidate of the tiny Social Democratic Party. The Socialist Party of America (SPA) was not formed until 1901, but it grew rapidly during the next fifteen years—Debs won only 95,000 votes in 1900, but in 1912, running as the SPA candidate, he got nearly one million votes, a respectable 6 percent of the total number cast.

Popular support for the SPA came primarily from labor, inspired by Debs, and from the farm states of the Midwest—the party's founding convention took place in Indianapolis, and the SPA was profoundly influenced by the prairie populism that made William Jennings Bryan so powerful a leader. On the left, the SPA included the Industrial Workers of the World, or Wobblies, whose sometimes violent methods caused the major parties to link the SPA with communists and anarchists. At the other end of the spectrum, consistently opposed to violence, were the Christian Socialists; their leader and spokesman for many years would be kindly, idealistic Norman Thomas. Upton Sinclair, who joined the SPA in 1904, was a Christian Socialist in fact if not in name.

At its peak, in 1912, the SPA had a hundred thousand dues-paying members. They tended to be much more active than most Republicans or Democrats, and they swung many local elections—hundreds of towns and cities, ranging from Berkeley to Toledo, had socialist mayors and city councils. The SPA's influence was greatly magnified by the qualified support of liberal members of the major parties who identified with mainstream politicians, like Theodore Roosevelt and Woodrow Wilson, and who hoped to mend the system, rather than change it entirely. Though the "Progressives" would form their own party in 1912 and drain away much of the SPA's support, some socialist ideas continued to appeal to many Americans. The word "socialism" never could shed its aura of foreign radicalism, and most people continued to believe in the capitalist system, for all its flaws; even so, many socialist ideas such as Social Security—supported by Theodore Roosevelt in 1912—would later become part of Franklin D. Roosevelt's New Deal.

All those who wanted the bloodless overthrow of capitalism agreed that it would have to come about through educating and persuading American citizens to demand it. Change had to come from the bottom up, not from the top down. The only way to reach enough people to effect change in this period was through print: newspapers, magazines, and books. Rising rates of literacy in a public increasingly outraged by what they read turned a number of talented and committed writers into household names. Thanks to Theodore Roosevelt, they would be lumped together as "muckrakers," including among their members Upton Sinclair.

The constant references to Sinclair's youthful appearance during this time are more than coincidence. Born in 1878, he was in fact the youngest, and the last, of the muckrakers. Ida Tarbell, who denounced John D. Rockefeller in her 1904 book *The History of the Standard Oil Company,* was born in 1857. Charles Edward Russell, whose series in *McClure's* magazine on the meat-packing industry became *The Greatest Trust in the World,* was eighteen years older than Sinclair. Arthur Brisbane, the Hearst editor who sometimes cam-paigned for reform and who later befriended Sinclair, was fourteen years his senior. Ray Stannard Baker was born in 1870, though his groundbreaking study of race, *Following the Color Line,* did not appear until after *The Jungle,* in 1908. David Graham Phillips, who wrote about malfeasance in Washington in *The Treason of the Senate* (1905), was eleven years older than Sinclair.

The dean of this group was Lincoln Steffens, whose influence on its youngest member was deep and whose later friendship Sinclair cherished. Born in 1860, Steffens published his greatest work, *The Shame of the Cities,* in March 1904, just as Sinclair was finishing *Manassas.* A collection of articles on municipal corruption in Pittsburgh, Chicago, and other cities that had previously appeared in *McClure's, The Shame of the Cities* spurred Sinclair to write a long letter in April to Steffens—in effect, an essay-review of his book. He reminded the older man that they had met briefly in 1902 through Leonard Abbott at the *Literary Digest.* He said he was thrilled by what Stef-fens had written, but regretted Steffens's failure to advocate socialism as the cure for the corruption he so vividly described. Impressed by Sinclair's ar-gument, Steffens tried without success to get the letter published as an arti-cle in *McClure's.*

Robbie Collier, described by Sinclair as the impetuous son of the "vul-gar" but "jovial" magazine publisher, said he would get the letter into *Col-lier's* and invited him to dinner with his father. "It was like a scene in a comedy," Sinclair later wrote, when Peter Collier realized what his son had done: "What's this? You are going to publish an article like that in my mag-azine? *No, no!* I won't have it! It's preposterous!" Calming down, Collier put his arm around Sinclair's shoulders and told him he was a nice boy, and he could see that he had "brains." But he should put his ideas in a book and not try to "scare away my half-million subscribers." (Sinclair was being less than fair to Peter Collier, whose magazine under the editorship of Norman Hap-good would soon become a major outlet for the muckrakers.)

His letter to Steffens was Sinclair's first effort at pure social criticism, as opposed to tract fiction; it would appear substantially unchanged, after *The*

Jungle had made him famous, in *The Industrial Republic* (1907). His first *successful* effort to arouse public opinion, the one that would lead directly to the writing of *The Jungle,* appeared on September 17, 1904, in a midwestern socialist weekly newspaper called *Appeal to Reason.* Its founder and publisher, J. A. Wayland, was another of those eccentric businessmen like Gaylord Wilshire who abandoned real estate speculation in favor of socialist agitation. But whereas Wilshire's magazine appealed primarily to a relative handful of intellectuals and theorists, Wayland's reached out to the broadest audience possible. By 1904 the *Appeal* had a subscription list of 250,000, growing every year. The *Appeal*'s readers were generally farmers, mechanics, carpenters, teachers, and small-businessmen, many living in villages and small towns like Girard, Kansas, where the *Appeal* was based.

The *Appeal* was indignant but folksy; "it was full of ginger and spice, of Western slang and hustle," Sinclair wrote, always griping about the "plutes" (the plutocrats) and praising the "American working mule." Cheap enough at a nickel a copy for even its poorest admirers, the paper made just enough to scrape by. It plowed its slender profits into broadsides during political campaigns, like those promoting Eugene Debs for president. In the early summer of 1904, it supported the Chicago stockyards workers in their losing strike against the meatpackers.

In early September, Sinclair sent Wayland a passionate article that implored the recently defeated strikers not to give up their longer-term struggle. Wayland and his editor, Fred Warren, accepted the article, which their readers reacted to with enthusiasm. (In *The Jungle,* Sinclair lauds his own effort and character by having his hero, Jurgis Rudkus, vigorously approve his article's opening challenge: "You have lost the strike! And now what are you going to do about it?" Jurgis sees that this "incendiary appeal" was written "by a man into whose soul the iron had entered," and ultimately achieves his redemption because of it.)

As proof of his credentials, Sinclair also sent Wayland a copy of *Manassas.* He explained that he thought the "chattel slavery" of blacks before the Civil War was analogous to the "wage slavery" of workers in the early 1900s, as in Chicago. Wayland authorized Fred Warren to ask Sinclair if he would be interested in writing a book about "wage slavery" for serial publication in the *Appeal.* Sinclair said yes. He saw no point in continuing with his Civil War trilogy if there was no market for it, and was open to a new project. He asked for a stake of $500, enough to live on for a year. Warren agreed, and Sinclair chose the Chicago stockyards as his setting—an almost inevitable choice, given the history of labor unrest in Chicago, as well as Sinclair's earlier article on the strike there.

As was his habit, he buried himself for several weeks in reading every-thing he could find on the meatpacking industry. In mid-October he ap-proached George Brett at Macmillan with a proposition. He explained that he was working out the plan for a new novel, to be published serially the next year, 1905, in a radical newspaper. The midwestern audience for *Appeal to Reason,* he said, did not overlap with the readers of Macmillan's books. Would Brett consider publishing his new novel separately, after its run in the *Appeal*? He had no plot or characters yet, but Sinclair described his goal with passion: he "intended to set forth the breaking of human hearts by a system which exploits the labor of men and women for profits." For the first time, he was going to make "a definite attempt to write something popular." Brett had been favorably impressed with the quality of *Manassas,* if not by its sales; he agreed to advance Sinclair $500 against royalties on the promised novel.

A jubilant Sinclair now had $1,000 in the bank and two publishers in his pocket. On November 2, 1904, he kissed his wife and child goodbye and set out for Chicago, where he would see for himself what life was like for the wage slaves in the slaughterhouses.

CHAPTER THREE

THE MUCKRAKER

(November–December 1904)

Ernest Poole, writing in 1940, vividly recalled Sinclair's appearance in the lobby of the Transit House upon his arrival in Chicago. A huge, rambling hotel next to the Union Stockyards, the Transit House was surrounded by porches and—in 1904—hitching posts. It was always jammed with cowboys, ranchers, and cattle dealers. It had also been the central meeting place for the stockyard workers' strike committee, to which Poole had offered his services. A favorite hangout for newspapermen and for writers looking for local color, the Transit House was the first place an inquisitive reporter new to town would visit. Poole was thus amused but not surprised when "in breezed a lad in a wide-brimmed hat, with loose-flowing tie and a wonderful warm expansive smile. 'Hello! I'm Upton Sinclair!' he said. 'And I've come here to write the *Uncle Tom's Cabin* of the Labor Movement!' "

Poole's memory of Sinclair's comment about Harriet Beecher Stowe's stirring novel sounds slightly apocryphal, echoing as it does what would come to be Jack London's later plug for *The Jungle.* But there is no doubt that Sinclair, fresh from an arduous year of work on *Manassas,* had *Uncle Tom's Cabin* in mind when he arrived in Chicago. In *Manassas* he had linked Stowe's novel with two of his other favorites, *Pilgrim's Progress* and *Robinson Crusoe,* as great books "which make their way into the world of literature from below, and are classics before the *literati* have discovered them." It was still "the fashion" to denigrate *Uncle Tom's Cabin,* Sinclair wrote, "as having historical rather than literary interest." He admitted that as a work of literary art it was less than perfect—"its skeleton sticks through its every joint"— "but he who can read a hundred pages of it, for the first or the twentieth time, with dry eyes, is not an enviable person." *Uncle Tom's Cabin* remained, despite its imperfections, "the most unquestionable piece of inspiration in American fiction."

It certainly inspired Sinclair. He also envied what he considered Stowe's easier task, for she had the murderous Simon Legree to lash slaves and hound them across ice floes. The plight Sinclair wanted to describe seemed dull by comparison, and he was uncertain how to deal with it: "Who can thrill the reader with the tale of a man-hunt in which the hunted is a lousy and ignorant foreigner, and the hunters are the germs of consumption, diphtheria and typhoid? Who can make a romance out of the story of a man whose one life adventure is the scratching of a finger by an infected butcher knife, with a pine box and a pauper's grave as the denouement?"

Another problem for Sinclair was that slavery in pre–Civil War America had been a tangible reality, inflicted on black people who had often been dragged from their native villages, and who were routinely beaten, sometimes even killed when they protested or tried to escape. "Wage slavery" in the twentieth century was not a literal fact but a metaphor; no workers were chained to their jobs or shot for trying to quit. Moreover, as Sinclair noted, most of the workers in Chicago were foreigners who, rather than being kidnapped, had chosen to come here. The plight of workers in general might stir sympathy, even indignation, but their protests often came in the form of strikes that inconvenienced and antagonized the public—unlike the pre–Civil War uprisings by black slaves, which were far away and quickly crushed. The hard fact was that the largely middle-class Americans, mostly women, who bought and read books in the early 1900s were not likely to demand the end of "wage slavery." Workers' problems for these readers were mostly distant and theoretical concerns, no matter how vividly described.

Food, however, was an immediate and practical matter. Everyone had to eat; most people ate meat; and the meatpacking industry had been the subject of intense scrutiny for a decade. Sinclair made a calculated decision to use Chicago's slaughterhouses as the *setting* for his book because doing so would broaden his base of readers and appeal to their self-interest. His true *subject*, however, was to be the working conditions that he thought approximated slavery. His argument would be that the capitalistic system behind such conditions should give way to socialism. He had virtually no interest in persuading readers that their meat was rotten except as a means of dramatizing the sad conditions of the workers who prepared it for them. People could always choose not to eat meat. Workers couldn't choose not to work if they wanted to live.

The dramatic setting of the stockyards and the universal appeal of food as a subject still did not guarantee that Sinclair would be able to write the best-seller he had in mind. Most of the public believed that the meatpacking industry was a tribute to American technology and a boon to consumers, not a threat to its health. Following the Civil War and the completion of the nation's railroad network, a few aggressive innovators—P. D. Armour and Augustus Swift among them—built slaughterhouses near railroad terminals in major cities like Chicago. They also bought controlling interests in the stockyards where the animals were penned until they were killed. Local, small-scale slaughterhouses scattered around the country could not compete with the big companies and their modern methods of manufacture, which depended on speed, size, and efficiency. By the end of the century, the livestock industry had become the nation's largest—even larger than mining or steel—and by the early 1900s it was becoming a force in the world market. Its greatest figure, Philip Danforth Armour, was lauded as "a sandy-haired, red-whiskered demigod of stock-yards mythology" by one contemporary, and generously profiled in a long interview with Theodore Dreiser as a "plain merchant," modest and courteous, who recoiled at the notion that he was "the Hercules of American industry."

Armour's challenge, and that of the other packers, was to turn living creatures into products. The work involved was unpleasant at best and often dangerous for workers; it entailed not only the risks of injury but of infection and disease at almost every turn both for them and for the meat they turned out. Added to these inevitable hazards were others imposed by innovations in modern science and technology. Most cities were within a day or two by train of a packing company distribution point; with insulated and, later, refrigerated cars, meat could reach consumers before it had a chance to spoil—usually. Chemical preservatives inhibited the process of decay in fresh meat, and were essential in the development of new products like "tinned" or canned meat. Beginning in 1899, the Hearst newspapers ran a series of articles on the hazards of what they called "embalmed" beef: canned meat preserved with formaldehyde and other chemicals, said to be responsible for killing more American soldiers in Cuba than had died fighting the Spaniards.

On the scientific front, substantial work had been done for decades by Dr. Harvey Wiley, chief of the bureau of chemistry at the U.S. Department of Agriculture from 1883 to 1912. Wiley's original interest in controlling patent medicines led him to form a "poison squad" that looked into adulterated foodstuffs, including meat. Political and legislative interest in the subject was heightened when Theodore Roosevelt became president in 1901. On a personal level, the famous "Rough Rider" hated the packers for, he said, poisoning his soldiers in Cuba. As a progressive Republican, he regarded their companies as among the worst of the great "trusts" he had vowed to tame—companies that set aside their differences to present a unified front when faced with dangers to their common well-being, such as governmental regulation. His Justice Department would later win felony convictions against half a dozen packing company executives for illegal competition, assisted by the evidence provided in Charles Russell's *The Greatest Trust in the World.*

Russell and Hearst had produced exposés that prompted outrage, but Sinclair understood that only a novel equivalent to *Uncle Tom's Cabin* would move readers on the emotional level needed for action. As James D. Hart explains in his study of American reading habits, *The Popular Book,* "The socially conscious Americans who planned to improve the cities were far fewer than those" who read simply for pleasure or to escape "the standardized anonymity of New York [and] Chicago." Muckraking exposés like Tarbell's book on Standard Oil or Steffens's *The Shame of the Cities* were no competition for bestselling novels like *The Little Shepherd of Kingdom Come* and *Rebecca of Sunnybrook Farm* (both published in 1903). Only through fiction could writers concerned about social problems and ideas hope to reach the widest audience—novels like Frank Norris's *The Pit,* about the Chicago commodities market, published posthumously in 1903, and Jack London's philosophical adventure *The Sea-Wolf,* in 1904.

=====

Sinclair agreed with Frank Norris that a novel could be as effective as a sermon in changing people's attitudes, and with Shelley's claim that writers should lead the way to social change as the "legislators of mankind." But his own choice of imagery as he approached his task in Chicago was distinctly martial. He had to get inside the "fortress of oppression" without the enemy watching him: "How to breach those walls, or to scale them, was a military problem." He admitted later that he probably did not overwhelm his new comrades as a warrior. He had just turned twenty-six, still so dewy-cheeked that he could go for several days without shaving. He was "young and ascetic-looking," suffering so often from nervous tension, headaches, and indigestion that "my cheeks are hollow and my skin is white and my eyes have a hectic shine." He knew that to the experienced social workers and tough labor organizers he met in Chicago he seemed to be "a sort of 'guy,' " easily "pigeon-holed with long-haired violinists from abroad, and painters with fancy-colored vests, and women suffragists with short hair, and religious prophets in purple robes." He was a bumptious "young poet" who "believed that he had 'genius,' and kept making a noise about it."

But Sinclair was warmly received by capable men and women who were willing to take their new recruit in hand. Several were writers who had already done much of his legwork for him. Ernest Poole, his welcomer at the Transit House, graduated from Princeton in 1902, just a year before Sinclair moved there. An unusual Princetonian, at least from Sinclair's point of view, Poole had worked for a year at a New York settlement house, then moved to Chicago and become an unpaid publicity agent for the meatpackers union. He wrote an article about the stockyards strike for *The Independent* in July 1904, which Sinclair had read while preparing his own piece for the *Appeal.*

Poole's follow-up piece in August also caught Sinclair's eye. It was supposedly an autobiography, as told to Poole, of a Lithuanian immigrant stockyard worker named Antanas Kaztauskis. Disappointed in the failure of the American dream, Kaztauskis complained most bitterly about his experiences working in the stockyards. He also described being cheated by real estate agents (themselves immigrants) who persuaded him to buy a worthless house on a usurious installment plan. Theodore Roosevelt, always an avid reader, saw Poole's story and told an aide in Chicago to find out more about Kaztauskis. Poole explained that no such individual existed. He had written the story of thousands of men and given them one name, "Kaztauskis," as a representative symbol.

Elements of Poole's short narrative turn up in Sinclair's plot, including the cheating real estate agents. Another writer, Algie Simons, acted as Sinclair's "inside man," providing him with contacts that would help him pose as a worker. Simons was a socialist and sometime labor organizer who worked for the Bureau of Charities as its agent in the stockyards. He also served as a volunteer inspector for the Chicago Health Department. In 1899 Simons had written a pamphlet called "Packingtown," which contained many of the details and anecdotes that would make *The Jungle* so controversial. One described the death of a worker's child in a roadside pool of "slime," which Sinclair would use himself to strong effect in his novel.

At least as important for Sinclair as these two energetic young men were two middle-aged women, Mary McDowell and Jane Addams. McDowell, then fifty years old, had directed the University of Chicago Settlement House since 1894, when it opened next to the Union Stockyards. She was called "the Angel of the Stockyards" for her sympathetic devotion to the workers, which extended to vigorous support of their strike in 1904. Sinclair stayed in the settlement house while he was in Chicago. Much less expensive than the Transit House, it also provided him with ready access to McDowell's expertise and to her influential friends.

Of these, Jane Addams was certainly the most important and the best remembered today. Born in Cedarville, Illinois, in 1860, she graduated from Rockford Female Seminary in 1881. Her interest in social work was stimulated during a trip to England in the mid-1880s, and in 1888 she converted the old Hull mansion, in what was then the outskirts of Chicago, into an experimental settlement house. By the time Sinclair met her, Addams and Hull House had become bywords in the growing community of social reformers in Europe and in the United States. Her emphasis was on practical measures: housing, sanitation, factory inspections, the eight-hour workday. She had little patience with wild-eyed theorists, which is how Sinclair struck her on their first meeting, shortly after he moved into his small room at McDowell's settlement house. As Sinclair later admitted, the "saintly" Jane Addams and her "consecrated band" quickly put him in his place.

Like many radicals then—especially new converts to the cause, as he was—Sinclair regarded charity and welfare work as well-meaning but futile. Such activities merely eased hardships, making people more comfortable and happier. They did not solve social problems. He told Addams that the only useful purpose of settlements like Hull House was "the making of settlement workers into Socialists." She let Sinclair know that she had been working hard for many years in Chicago and that his brief presence there did not allow him to lecture her; he was "a young man with a good deal to learn." Then, softening, she introduced him to a man she said was eminently qualified to be one of his teachers, an English medical writer named Adolph Smith. Of Sinclair's many valuable helpers in Chicago, Smith would be the most important.

Smith was researching a series of articles on the meatpacking industry to be published the following year in *The Lancet,* the respected British medical journal. Like Addams and McDowell, he was a generation older than Sinclair. A man of vast experience in both politics and medicine, he did not share Sinclair's aversion to capitalism; having witnessed the street fighting in Paris in 1876, he also feared the excesses of revolution. Smith's opposition to the meatpacking industry was not that of a socialist but of a man with unusual expertise in slaughterhouse practices in England and on the Continent, where the efficient means of mass production used in Chicago were considered inhumane.

Smith took Sinclair with him on at least one authorized tour of the P. D. Armour plant, explaining the differences between the European and American methods of processing meat and sharing with him the evidence that would crowd the pages of his forthcoming articles. The detailed titles of Smith's five articles—the first was "Chicago: The Dark and Insanitary [*sic*] Premises Used for the Slaughtering of Cattle and Hogs—The Government Inspection"—suggest something of his thoroughness. He concluded that the European method of slaughter was not only more humane but more hy-

gienic than the American method. It was also less likely to lead to worker injury and dissatisfaction. (A correspondent later sent Sinclair the reminder to
slaughterhouse workers he had seen in Braunschweig, Germany, which
began, "Bloody indeed is your task, O butcher / Therefore practice it hu-
manely!")

Sinclair's range of contacts and his body of information expanded geo-
metrically: everyone he met led him to three or four more people, who in
their turn did the same. He interviewed plant foremen and laborers, priests
and bartenders, policemen and politicians and undertakers. Carrying a
lunch bucket and wearing the same shabby clothes he had come to town
in—minus the dashing hat and flowing tie—he wandered unimpeded
through the vast Armour facilities, memorizing details of what he saw, then
rushing back to his room to write everything down. Gifted with an amoeba-
like quality of absorbing sights and sounds and information, and driven by a
messianic sense of purpose, he had nearly enough material within a few
short weeks to write his novel.

But by mid-November Sinclair was deeply worried. He had set out to
write a novel, and now, nearly midway through his self-allotted time in
Chicago, he had collected only data. What was his *story* to be? His experience
with writing boys' adventures, idealistic romances, poetic complaints, satirical allegories, and historical epics had not prepared him adequately for the
demands of the realistic novel. He needed characters. He needed a plot. And
he needed a new style, a form that he could adapt to what for him was a
unique situation. His was not the familiar dilemma of the novelist who feels
blocked but knows what he wants to say: it was a simple but terrifying anxiety that he was not up to what he had vowed to do.

═══

Sinclair's own account of how a Lithuanian wedding party in a saloon solved
most of his writing problems is charmingly self-effacing, considering that
his career properly began at that moment. He had been "wandering" aim-
lessly "back of the yards" on a Sunday afternoon when he came upon the
celebrants, who generously invited him to join them. "I slipped into the
room and stood against the wall. There the opening chapter of *The Jungle*
began to take form. There were my characters—the bride, the groom, the
old mother and father, the boisterous cousin, the children, the three musicians, everybody. I watched them one after another, fitted them into my
story, and began to write the scene in my mind." He stayed most of the
night, "sitting in a chair against the wall, not talking to anyone, just watching, imagining, and engraving the details on my mind. It was two months

before I got settled at home and first put pen to paper; but the story stayed, and I wrote down whole paragraphs, whole pages, exactly as I had memorized them."

Sinclair's modest memory of this critical moment, like Coleridge's claim that he simply recorded what he remembered of his dream of "Kubla Khan's" Xanadu, minimizes the achievement of his first chapter, surely one of the best not just in his own work but in American literature. It turns around music, allowing Sinclair to draw upon his own experience in playing the violin and on his concept of the role of the artist. The key figure of the wedding party is not Ona, the bride, or Jurgis, the bridegroom, but the violinist—a scrawny but inspired player who through his art holds the party together, providing the bridge between the old world and the new. Sinclair functions in *The Jungle* in the same way as the violinist at the wedding: he builds the interpretive bridge between the world he observes and his readers, for whom this is a strange new world indeed.

This particular violinist is not a great musician, Sinclair says: "His notes are never true, and his fiddle buzzes on the low ones and squeaks and scratches on the high; but these things they heed no more than they heed the dirt and noise and squalor about them—it is out of this material that they have to build their lives, with it that they have to utter their souls. And this is their utterance; merry and boisterous, or mournful and wailing, or passionate and rebellious, this music is their music, music of home."

At the outset of the party, the music is consistent with what the immigrants have brought from the old country: the wedding feast, the *veselija,* is carried out properly, in the traditional manner. Folk dancing and congratulatory speeches follow. But by the end of the evening it is clear that the old ways have been corrupted; freeloaders flout the tradition that everyone contributes toward the cost of the wedding so that the young couple will not start their marriage owing money. Jurgis shrugs off his unanticipated burden of debt, vowing, as he will so often, "I will work harder" to repay it. The harmonies of the old country are now replaced by the revelers' drunken renditions of a popular American tune, of which they know only the first line: "In the good old summer time—in the good old summer time! In the good old summer time—in the good old summer time!"

The Norwegian scholar Orm Øverland has praised Sinclair's opening chapter as "one of the most poignant sketches in American literature of a common experience of immigration: the loss of a culture in all its complexities—including language—and the acquisition of poorly understood fragments of a new one." Sinclair's cultural sensitivity let him lift his story beyond the level of simple exposé or mere sensationalism. It also aided him in devising a narrative that combined documentary realism with the traditional novelistic elements of character and plot. He could now attack "wage slavery" through the eyes of its victims, interpreting what they saw in his own words—words that he hoped would move his middle-class readers to sympathy and to action.

Everything Sinclair had seen before the wedding, and would see after it, soon took its place in a relatively simple plot. Though it would take him many months to put it down on paper, he now had the structure and many of the details in his head. After the opening chapter, he flashed back about thirteen months to describe the events preceding the wedding: the arrival of a dozen or so Lithuanian immigrants, all relatives or friends, in Chicago; their first jobs in the Durham yards (the Armour company); the courtship of Jurgis and Ona; and the purchase of a house in which they can live as a kind of extended family with their relatives and friends. During this period of time, covering about 50 of the novel's 325 pages, the characters live on a plateau of relative contentment. But the Chicago winter that follows the wedding is cruel and jobs are scarce. Neither Ona nor Jurgis can find work until spring. In August, after their baby boy, Antanas, is born, Jurgis loses his job after a panic-stricken steer breaks free on the killing floor and seriously injures him. While Jurgis recovers, Ona leaves him with the baby and returns to her job in a canning factory.

By the time Jurgis is able to work again, someone else has taken his job. He finds a job in a fertilizer plant, an even lower circle, as Sinclair notes, in his Dantean hell. Jurgis turns to drink. Ona is raped by her foreman, Connor, who warns her she will lose her job if she complains. Jurgis finds out anyway, beats Connor, and is thrown into jail as well as blackballed from future employment in the meatpacking industry. While Jurgis is in jail, Ona dies giving birth to her second baby, probably Connor's; the baby also dies. Jurgis briefly finds work in the steel mills as a laborer, though in his grief he squanders his money on drink. In what appears to be the final blow, his two-year-old son falls into a deep mud puddle in the unpaved street and drowns (as Meta had feared David might in New Jersey).

Following a brief pastoral interlude, working in the countryside at a harvester plant, Jurgis returns to the city. He works for crooked politicians until another confrontation with Connor lands him in jail again; then he becomes a petty thief, and finally a scab, taking the place of striking stockyard workers. Approaching bottom, he stumbles into a rally for the strikers. The charismatic Socialist Party speaker is the unnamed Eugene Debs, whose revivalist cadences stimulate a quasi-religious awakening in Jurgis. The speaker persuades him that salvation is possible, not for individuals alone but for the many, working together for the common good. The coming strike will trigger the overturning of the system that made possible such terrible things as those that have happened to Jurgis and his family. The novel concludes with the famous call to revolution—"Chicago will be ours!" Jurgis's sad but instructive journey will continue, with a meaning and a power that it never had before.

═══

Like *Uncle Tom's Cabin, The Jungle* is hardly flawless. Some readers find their compassion for Jurgis and his family and friends giving way to incredulity at such an implausible accumulation of disasters. They grow numb, and avert their eyes from such horrors as the child who goes into convulsions and dies from eating smoked sausage, or the young boy who falls into a stupor after drinking beer and is eaten by rats. The "message" part of the novel also presents problems; Sinclair himself thought the second half of his book was too episodic and preachy, and he disliked the happy ending for Jurgis that he had felt compelled to provide: he had wanted to send him to jail for two years. But these weaknesses pale in comparison to Sinclair's great strengths in *The Jungle:* powerfully descriptive prose, a sense of truthful authority, and an inspiring moral fervor.

Sinclair referred to Ernest Poole's "autobiography" of Kaztauskis while constructing his novel, but he wisely chose to write in the third person and not to limit himself to the vocabulary and perceptions of an unschooled immigrant. He stands behind Jurgis, as it were, and explains that the river is called "Bubbly Creek" because "the grease and chemicals that are poured into it undergo all sorts of strange transformations . . . it is constantly in motion, as if huge fish were feeding in it. . . . Bubbles of carbonic acid gas will rise to the surface and burst, and make rings two or three feet wide. Here and there the grease and filth have caked solid, and the creek looks like a bed of lava; chickens walk about on it, feeding, and many times an unwary stranger has started to stroll across, and vanished temporarily."

The drama and color of Sinclair's artfully chosen details give his passage a kinetic force, a dynamic intensity paradoxically drawn from filth and decay. Similarly, what in Poole is just a "big smell" becomes for Sinclair's immigrants a "strange, pungent odor. . . . You could literally taste it, as well as smell it." Most writers would have stopped here, but Sinclair continues, endowing the disgusting odors with a strangely aesthetic appeal and his immigrants with qualities of sophisticated insight and curiosity that go beyond simple realism into symbolism: "you could take hold of it, almost, and examine it at your leisure. They were divided in their opinions about it. It was an elemental odor, raw and crude; it was rich, almost rancid, sensual, and strong. There were some who drank it in as if it were an intoxicant; there were others who put their handkerchiefs to their faces."

Sinclair also brings the slaughterhouse chimneys to malevolent life: "tall as the tallest of buildings, touching the very sky—and leaping from them half a dozen columns of smoke, thick, oily, and black as night. It might have come from the center of the world, this smoke, where the fires of the ages still smolder. . . . One stared, waiting to see it stop, but still the great streams rolled out. They spread in vast clouds overhead, writhing, curling; then, uniting in one giant river, they streamed away down the sky, stretching a black pall as far as the eye could reach."

Finally, Poole's vague reference to "the dumps" becomes, in *The Jungle,* an explanation of how the workers' houses occupy old dump sites where the city's garbage still festers a few feet underground, resulting in "swarms of flies . . . blackening the air" and "a ghastly odor, of all the dead things of the universe."

Sinclair's descriptions often achieve a surreal intensity: Jurgis carefully watches the doomed hogs, who must approach "a great iron wheel, about twenty feet in circumference," studded with large iron rings. A "great burly Negro, bare-armed and bare-chested," tends the wheel, turning it as two men seize a pig, attach a loop of chain to its rear, and secure the other end of the chain to a ring of the wheel. The wheel revolves, and the hog is "suddenly jerked off his feet and borne aloft," shrieking in pain and fear until its throat is slit and it vanishes "with a splash into a huge vat of boiling water." This is "pork-making by machinery, pork-making by applied mathematics." Sinclair's description here is worthy of his admirer Franz Kafka, and is partly echoed, consciously or not, in Kafka's treatment of the ingenious killing machine in his story "In the Penal Colony."

In one of his more purple passages—which he later insisted, not very convincingly, he intended as satire—Sinclair allows Jurgis to speculate on the harmless victims of the machine: "they were so innocent, they came so very trustingly; and they were so very human in their protests. . . . And now was one to believe that there was nowhere a god of hogs, to whom this hog personality was precious, to whom these hog squeals and agonies had a meaning? Who would take this hog into his arms and comfort him, reward him for his work well done, and show him the meaning of his sacrifice? Perhaps some glimpse of all this was in the thoughts of our humble-minded Jurgis as he turned to go on with the rest of the party and muttered: '*Dieve*—but I'm glad I'm not a hog!' "

Sinclair's descriptions of the workers' lives and the conditions of their employment—his true subject in *The Jungle*—generally eschew symbolism in favor of graphic realism: "Of the butchers and floorsmen, the beef-boners and trimmers, and all those who used knives, you could scarcely find a person who had the use of his thumb; time and time again the base of it had been slashed, till it was a mere lump of flesh against which the man pressed the knife to hold it." In another passage Sinclair describes how the men working on the unheated "killing-beds" in subzero winter weather would bury their frozen hands and feet within the steaming carcass of the steer they had just killed. Much of *The Jungle* is devoted to similar depictions of such uncomfortable and dangerous working conditions. Hardly less important, though less sensational, is the persistent exploitation of the workers by everyone they encounter: saloonkeepers, aldermen, the police, and their own countrymen.

By comparison, relatively few pages, perhaps thirty in all, describe the details of unhealthy procedures relating to meat products. Lurid and revolting, these were the passages that would make *The Jungle* so controversial and so successful—and that completely overshadowed the plight of the workers so earnestly depicted by Sinclair.

Ironically, most of the abuses that led to public concern for the safety of their meat products stemmed from the excess of two great virtues prized by American business enterprises: the avoidance of waste and the maximizing of efficiency. Meatpacking was a labor-intensive enterprise, highly competitive, with a slender margin of profit. Then as now, Americans paid far less for their food than Europeans, which accounts in part for their tolerance of peculiarities, and even of abuses, in its manufacture. In their efforts to avoid waste, and to increase profits, the packers used everything they could from slaughtered animals, including snouts, tails, horns, hooves, eyeballs, entrails, and skins: "everything but the squeal." In order to increase production and hold down costs, they developed, as an admiring biography of P. D. Armour noted in 1938, "the basic device of modern straight line production. . . . The 'assembly line' and 'belt' of the modern motor car, chemical, or electrical equipment plant are merely an adaptation of the 'chain' which came into packing-plants in 1865 or thereabouts."

Although he deplored the dehumanizing effects of working at repetitive, boring tasks, Sinclair had no quarrel with the ideal of efficiency, and he revered the idea of work itself. Unlike the followers of William Morris and others who wanted to retreat to some kind of imaginary preindustrial utopia, he was, he said, "a Socialist who believes in machinery." There was "no reason why machines should not make beautiful and substantial things," instead of ugly ones, other than the system that allows people to make profits from them. Sinclair's memorable phrase, "pork-making by applied mathematics," does not signal ironic disdain but admiration, just as Jurgis's pride at being "a sharer in all this activity, a cog in all this marvelous machine" is sincere.

Equally sincere, and admirable for Sinclair, is Jurgis's evident belief that hard work has its own inherent satisfaction, even shoveling steaming heaps of guts. He wants to work, to belong. It was not the system of industrial production or the killing of animals for food that Sinclair was attacking, or the fact that some people had to do unpleasant but necessary work. He was attacking what he regarded as the *distortion* of the industrial system, the warping of the machine, caused by the uncontrolled drive for profit.

For Sinclair, this distortion showed itself in four ways. First, the packers' use of diseased or condemned animal parts; second, their use of chemical additives; third, their indifference to workers' health and welfare, resulting in dangerous contamination of food products; and fourth, their resistance to state and federal regulations that would control these practices and attitudes. Sinclair wove his objections into a series of passages that would frequently be excerpted in newspaper stories about *The Jungle*. Each read like a short horror story. Combined, they amounted to an indictment.

Worst of all was the making of sausage: "There was never the least attention paid to what was cut up for sausage; there would come all the way back from Europe old sausage that had been rejected, and that was mouldy and white—it would be dosed with borax and glycerine, and dumped into the hoppers, and made over again for home consumption. There would be meat that had tumbled out on the floor, in the dirt and sawdust, where the workers had tramped and spit uncounted billions of consumption germs. There would be meat stored in great piles in rooms; and the water from leaky roofs would drip over it, and thousands of rats would race about on it. It was too dark in these storage places to see well, but a man could run his hand over these piles of meat and sweep off handfuls of the dried dung of rats. These rats were nuisances, and the packers would put poisoned bread out for them; they would die, and then rats, bread, and meat would go into the hoppers together. This is no fairy story and no joke; the meat would be shovelled into carts, and the man who did the shovelling would not trouble to lift out a rat even when he saw one—there were things that went into the sausage in comparison with which a poisoned rat was a tidbit."

This was the passage that the Chicago satirist Peter Finlay Dunne had in mind when he imagined President Roosevelt sitting down to a plate of sausage and eggs and reading *The Jungle*. Dunne, who employed an exaggerated Irish dialect, explained how "Tiddy was toying with a light breakfast an' idly turn'n over the pages iv th' new book with both hands. Suddenly he rose fr'm th' table, and cryin': 'I'm pizened,' began throwin' sausages out iv th' window."

Federal and city inspectors tried to control illegal practices, but they were often frustrated and harassed. One doctor who was employed by the city (and who became one of Sinclair's major sources) "made the discovery that the carcasses of steers which had been condemned as tubercular by government inspectors, and which therefore contained ptomaines, which are deadly poisons, were left upon an open platform and carted away to be sold in the city, and so he insisted that these carcasses be treated with an injection of kerosene—and was ordered to resign the same week! So indignant were the packers that they went farther, and compelled the mayor to abolish the whole bureau of inspection; so that since then there has not been even a pretense of any interference with the graft" and "hush money" that oiled the system.

Some of Sinclair's more shocking details, relating both to food and to the workers' lives, never made it into the final published version of *The Jungle:* the unmarried woman who gave birth in a plant and dropped her baby into a cart full of beef on its way to the cooking vats; the prostitute who had to "sell herself to ten or a dozen men in a day"; the woman forced to become a prostitute to pay for her false teeth; the man "mashed in half" by an elevator. Others were modified: the story of the little boy whose frozen ears fell off when his boss rubbed them too hard remained, but without the final line, "and then the little fellow lay down and rolled on the floor in his agony."

But the most famous passage of all stayed, through all the many revisions that the novel would undergo in the months to come: for some men, "who worked in tank-rooms full of steam, and in some of which there were open vats near the level of the floor, their peculiar trouble was that they fell into the vats; and when they were fished out, there was never enough of them left to be worth exhibiting—sometimes they would be overlooked for days, till all but the bones of them had gone out to the world as Durham's Pure Leaf Lard!"

———

Exhausted after seven weeks of gathering such harrowing material, but certain that he had in his hands the greatest story of his life, Sinclair returned to Meta and David a few days before Christmas. One domestic task demanded attention before he could sit down to record the novel he had already written in his mind: the purchase of a house.

Before he had left for Chicago, Meta let Sinclair know that she would not even consider spending another winter in the soapbox on the marsh. With his new novel on the way, they should be able to borrow the money they needed to move into something better. What Meta had in mind, according to Sinclair, was a country home "with great open fire-places, and exposed beams, and a broad staircase, and a deep piazza, and, above all, a view of the sunset." All he wanted was a comfortable place with enough land to grow a few crops to defray their costs, as well as a barn for a horse, a cow, and a few chickens.

Indifferent to creature comforts, Sinclair could easily have continued living in their soapbox. He had no romantic illusions about the nobility of farm life—indeed, he showed far less sympathy for the poorer of his neighbors than he did for the Lithuanian immigrants he had come to know in Chicago. Most of the locals, he said, were inbred degenerates and imbeciles, degraded by poverty, disease, and drunkenness: one in particular, an Irish immigrant and the worst of the lot, "would work as a laborer in town for a day or two, and buy vinegar and make himself half insane," and then come home and beat his wife and their eleven children. His oldest sons were already thieves, and the youngest of the children "might be seen in midwinter, playing half-naked before the house."

George Stout, Sinclair's landlord, owned a small farm not half a mile away. He had despaired of finding a reliable tenant for it and was eager to sell. The Stouts took Meta and Sinclair through the house, which was unoccupied and unfurnished but clean, on a beautiful October day. It was located near the intersection of Province Line Road and Drake's Corner Road, a handsome old place surrounded by oaks and maples exploding in autumn colors. It was an easy walk through pleasant meadows from there to the Stouts' residence, which appealed greatly to Meta. The property could be theirs for $2,000, Stout said. Sinclair replied that he didn't have the money yet, but would try to get it together after he returned from Chicago.

Meta left David with Mrs. Stout and walked to the empty house several times while Sinclair was away, its charms growing on her with each visit. When Sinclair returned from Chicago he found on his desk a warm letter from Dr. Minot Savage, the clergyman who had married him and Meta four years earlier. Savage thanked Sinclair for sending him a gift copy of *Manassas* and invited him to call upon him whenever he was in the city. Meta suggested that they ask Savage for a loan to buy the Stout property. They still had more than half of the money from the two advances Sinclair had received, and could surely anticipate more coming in soon to repay Savage.

"Whereupon," Sinclair says, amused at his own ruthlessness, he headed for New York to launch "an assault upon this ill-fated clergyman." Savage said no at first, believing with Herbert Spencer and other Social Darwinists that such contributions undermined self-reliance and encouraged sloth and indolence. Sinclair protested in vain that he was asking for a loan, not for charity. Even his plea that he was on the verge of becoming a "murdered artist" failed to move the benign but stubborn minister to open his checkbook.

Sinclair then played his ace in the hole, his poor wife, as he had earlier tried to do with Owen Wister. He could perhaps survive himself, he bravely said. But "oh, the horror of having to kill his wife for the sake of his books!" Meta would never last another winter in their miserable shack; she had already tried once to kill herself, and "unless something were done, the spring-time would not find her alive."

"The suicide story" did the trick with Savage, Sinclair noted smugly. He deposited the minister's check in an escrow account the following day. Though the formal closing date was to be December 31, Stout helped the Sinclair family move into their new home on the morning of December 24. The soapbox on the marsh was left behind, but Sinclair's study shed was loaded onto a wagon and deposited on a slight rise a few yards from their new home.

Sinclair was satisfied with their situation, but Meta was ecstatic. The house itself was luxurious by their standards: eight rooms on two floors, a full basement, plastered walls, oak flooring, closets with shelves, a parlor, a dining room, a pantry. Outside, stretching for sixty acres, were fields and pastures and woodlots, one of which contained a twelve-foot pine just the right size for a proper Christmas tree. To celebrate their good fortune, as well as David's recent third birthday, they roasted a fat goose in the new kitchen oven. Snug and warm against the snowstorm raging outside, "an aroma of molasses taffy pervading the house," the young family enjoyed the most satisfying Christmas Eve dinner imaginable.

On Christmas morning 1904, Upton Sinclair sat down in his tiny study and began to write *The Jungle*.

CHAPTER FOUR

THE WARRIOR

(January 1905–June 1906)

For the first three months of 1905 Sinclair wrote "incessantly," every day, with "tears and anguish, pouring into the pages all that pain which life had meant to me. Externally, the story had to do with a family of stockyard workers, but internally it was the story of my own family," which had suffered so much in the past year from hunger, cold, and illness. "Ona" was Meta, "speaking Lithuanian, but otherwise unchanged." David, "our little boy," was so ill with pneumonia in February that he nearly died, "and the grief of that went into the book."

Sinclair's emotional investment in *The Jungle* was intense. So too was his gratification when, on February 25, 1905, the first chapter appeared in *Appeal to Reason,* introduced with an editor's note from Fred Warren praising his novel as the *Appeal's* "crowning achievement." Some 290,000 subscribers had the opportunity to read that soon-to-be-famous first chapter of *The Jungle;* assuming that each biweekly issue was passed around in a household, many thousands more saw the subsequent chapters during the novel's serialization over the next eight months.

The *Appeal to Reason* version of *The Jungle* is essentially a rough first draft of the version that readers know today, thirty thousand words longer and showing the haste with which it was written. But even in that form, for a midwestern audience that did not consider itself literary, it is not hard to see why it was successful. Beyond its eloquent descriptive passages and its gripping plot, it fulfilled the obligation that Frank Norris described of educating its readers: simply as an explanation of the way the commercial world of the meatpacking industry worked, *The Jungle* was often fascinating.

But there was another, deeper reason for readers' favorable responses to *The Jungle.* Even in comparison with the extraordinary men who would be his friends, associates, and rivals over the years—Steffens, London, Herron,

Markham, Wister, H. G. Wells, H. L. Mencken, George Bernard Shaw, Thomas Mann, and dozens more—Sinclair was an unusually "literary" writer. His many books abound in literary allusions and references, though they were seldom noticed by his less sophisticated readers. In the case of *The Jungle,* widely regarded as a landmark of twentieth-century American literary realism, the key to its deeper meaning—and to its surprisingly broad appeal—is provided by John Bunyan's seventeenth-century allegory, *Pilgrim's Progress.*

Nowhere does Sinclair make the associations between *Pilgrim's Progress* and *The Jungle* explicit, but they have struck many readers as self-evident. Indeed, the editor of a 1988 reissue of the *Appeal's* version of *The Jungle,* Gene DeGruson, argued that Wayland himself, a great admirer of *Pilgrim's Progress,* sent Sinclair to Chicago with a summary and an outline drawn from Bunyan's allegory. DeGruson's assumption of Wayland's influence rested entirely on circumstantial evidence, and Sinclair's own account significantly contradicts it, but it does indicate how clearly *Pilgrim's Progress* and *The Jungle* resemble each other. To some degree this may have been because *Pilgrim's Progress* was so deeply embedded in the popular as well as the literary culture of Sinclair's world. Countless editions of the adventures of Christian on the road to salvation had appeared since the book was written, many of them illustrated and revised for children; Sinclair would read the original to David when his son was only six years old.

Conscious or unconscious, the many similarities between the two works are unmistakable. They derive from the notion of being lost in a spiritual wilderness—the jungle that the world is—but progressing ultimately to a happy salvation in God. Sinclair's Jurgis is Bunyan's Christian (though he is far less well educated and doctrinaire than Bunyan's character). The City of Destruction is Chicago. Christian's Wicket Gate, the entrance to salvation, is Durham's deceptively open gate for the eager worker, Jurgis. The Delectable Mountains parallel Jurgis's job at the harvester works, a period of respite. The Meadow by the River of Life is like the stream beside which Jurgis rests while wandering through the countryside. Christian is thrown into the dungeon of Despair, as Jurgis is tossed into prison, and remains there until the Key of Promise unlocks the door. Finally, Christian at the Cross receives salvation and becomes one of the elect. Jurgis, "a man whose soul had been murdered, who had ceased to hope and to struggle," a man "for whom the world is a prison, a dungeon of torture, a tomb," is similarly saved. He converts to socialism, "the new religion of humanity" in Sinclair's key phrase—and "the fulfillment of the old religion, since it implied but the literal application of all the teachings of Christ."

Later commentators, including Christopher Hitchens, have found more sinister allegorical associations with *The Jungle:* it anticipates both the mechanization of death at Auschwitz and the totalitarian world depicted by George Orwell in *Animal Farm,* where the heroic but doomed horse, Boxer, echoes Jurgis's credo: "I will work harder." Clearly, Sinclair's novel provides a kind of template for human experience that transcends the limitations of his own time, and which accounts for the persistent appeal of such an admittedly unpleasant book—a book that almost never came into being in the form that we know it today.

Despite the vast readership provided by *Appeal to Reason,* Sinclair's contract with Wayland had been for a flat $500; there were no royalties beyond that amount, and no provision for publishing *The Jungle* as a book. It was on Macmillan that Sinclair had staked his hopes for a breakthrough that would win him renown as well as financial reward—for a book within respectable hard covers, not on flimsy newsprint that disintegrated almost at the touch. But by April 1905, George Brett, having read the first half of *The Jungle* and seen the plan for the rest, was more impressed by its deficiencies than by its virtues, evident or not. His Columbia University "readers" complained about the aesthetic deficiencies of the novel and warned him that suits by the Armour company, so clearly the model for Sinclair's Durham, were inevitable. They also worried that Macmillan's reading audience would be put off by Sinclair's sermonizing on socialism.

Brett pressed Sinclair to cut down on the gore and violence. Sinclair not only resisted making any changes but, in late April, requested a further advance because Meta had required hospitalization for a serious illness, and David's bout with pneumonia had left them broke. Brett ignored the request. In a subsequent plea, on June 10, Sinclair said that after paying for a second operation for Meta, he had just 27 cents in his pocket. Brett was unmoved to part with any more of Macmillan's money: he had come to agree with one of his Columbia readers, G. R. Carpenter, who said Macmillan might make a profit on Sinclair's book, but only if the author could be persuaded to tone down some of the more gruesome scenes and details. Carpenter did concede, however, that the book's indictment of the meatpackers was so vivid that it might even prompt corrective legislation by the Congress.

Correspondence and meetings between Brett and Sinclair continued well into the summer of 1905. A frustrated Sinclair complained to Lincoln Steffens that Brett wanted him to cut out all the "blood and guts," but Steffens gave Sinclair no satisfaction: he thought it was futile to harp on matters that were true but hard to believe. Fiction had to be truer than life, making sense of it no matter how irrational and grotesque it might in fact be.

Brett's negative turnabout on *The Jungle* coincided with a period of increasing strain between Sinclair and Meta. Sinclair had leaped at the chance to go to Chicago for two months in part because his relations with Meta had become so difficult. Similarly, his willingness to go into debt to buy the Stout farm had been prompted by the hope that somehow it would help revive their marriage. For a few hours, as on that magical Christmas Eve when they moved into the house, they had been happy. But winter in New Jersey, even though it was not on the marsh, was still winter, and Meta's initial euphoria soon gave way to her familiar lassitude and melancholy.

Her mood was further darkened by Sinclair's continuing dread that, just as he seemed poised to succeed as a writer, Meta might get pregnant again. A second child would destroy his career and their marriage. His fear expressed itself in different ways. In *The Jungle,* as he said, the moving depiction of family disintegration owes much to his own mood at the time of its composition: the reader is supposed to be stunned with sorrow for Jurgis's loss of wife and child. But a closer reading reveals that those deaths are the key to Jurgis's salvation: only when Ona and Antanas are gone is he free to follow his own destiny.

His combined worries during that spring caused Sinclair to suffer from insomnia, headaches, and indigestion. Meta frequently said her husband regarded the mind as a machine; so also was the body to him a machine, to be tinkered with and experimented upon. Good health, he said, was not an accidental gift but a goal to be achieved "by will and intelligence." He compelled Meta to join him in a new diet fad. This one was based on the quackish Horace Fletcher's conviction that all digestive ailments, as well as stomach and colon cancer, were caused by failure to chew food properly. Each mouthful had to be "Fletcherized": chewed at least twenty times, or as often as it took to turn solids into liquid, before it was swallowed. Within weeks, both Meta and Sinclair had lost so much weight that they had to abandon the diet.

Sinclair also fretted about controlling his sexual appetite, and Meta's, perhaps because nothing else so endangers "will and intelligence." In an astounding passage from *Love's Pilgrimage* he describes sex as a "marriage duty" requiring him to "squander" the "vital forces of his being"; the "body and soul of him were wrung and squeezed dry like a sponge." Their bedroom is a "chamber of terror," sex a "licensed preying of one personality upon another"; he fears that this "animal intimacy" must lead to both his own and his wife's constantly "discovering new weaknesses and developing new vices in themselves."

Sinclair later joked, attempting to disarm the armchair Freudians who were already becoming prominent in the field of literary criticism, that he was clearly a mass of neuroses at this time. But as his comments elsewhere reveal, he thought Meta was more at fault than he for their mutual failures. Not surprisingly, Meta herself would spend a good deal of time several years later under the care of Havelock Ellis and A. A. Brill, pioneers in the fields of sexual research and psychoanalysis.

The illness from which Meta suffered that spring, and for which she required two operations, was never specified. It might have been psychosomatic, which would have been consistent with her later behavior, or connected with an aborted pregnancy. Whatever the cause, both of them thought a trip to Florida in midsummer, paid for by Sinclair's wealthy Baltimore relatives, was a good idea—though Sinclair would later complain that Meta had become infatuated during their vacation with a handsome, wavy-haired young photographer who wouldn't leave her alone.

═══

One source of Sinclair's success throughout his life was his ability to escape frustration by channeling his energies in a new direction. Unwilling to meet Brett's demands for revising *The Jungle,* troubled by his relationship with Meta, he turned his attention in early August to launching a nationwide organization to encourage socialism on college campuses. It was to be called the Intercollegiate Socialist Society, the ISS. In typical Sinclair fashion, frenzied but efficient, he gathered a few dozen enthusiasts for a dinner meeting at a New York restaurant; with little discussion (and in his absence) Jack London was elected as the organization's first president. By September 12, when London was scheduled to speak to the ISS at Grand Central Palace, Sinclair had persuaded hundreds of idealistic students and immigrant workers from the East Side to attend. London's train was late and Sinclair was nervously preparing, he later wrote, to address the boisterous crowd himself—but then "came a roar of cheers, and Jack was there," swaggering down the aisle, handsome, broad-shouldered, waving his cap and grinning, ready to read his famous discourse, "Revolution."

Though they had corresponded for several years, this was the first time the two writers had met, and Sinclair was prepared to be impressed—as he said, to give his "hero the admiration of a slave." They spent the next day together, London drinking and chain-smoking cigarettes and regaling Sinclair with stories of sexual debauches, opium smoking, and week-long whiskey benders. Oyster pirate and roustabout, brawler and sailor, London was the archetype of the red-blooded, two-fisted intellectual, and he teased Sinclair mercilessly as a "mollycoddled" intellectual and puritan.

London may also have given the less experienced author some practical advice about the virtue of compromising with demanding editors. For on the same day that the two men talked, September 13, Sinclair wrote to Brett saying he was ready to cooperate. He offered not only to tone down some of the more repulsive details but also to solve the problem of the novel's unwieldy second half. He would end *The Jungle* with the death of Ona, the current *Appeal* version's Chapter 15, then do a sequel, a second novel following Jurgis through the corrupt world of Chicago municipal politics. Naturally, Sinclair added, a new novel would require a new advance.

But he was too late. On September 18 another Columbia reader advised Brett strongly against publishing *The Jungle* in any form: it was simply a doom-ridden tract of unrelieved misery, written not out of love for the poor but out of hatred for the rich. Brett by this time had lost patience with his temperamental author. He had already spoken several times with Fred Warren about coordinating Macmillan's publicity efforts for *The Jungle* with those of the *Appeal*, but Warren himself now indicated some reservations about the last part of the novel. When Brett added up the reasons for Macmillan not to publish *The Jungle*—lawsuits, minimal profits, a problematical manuscript, a difficult author—he decided to cancel the deal. On September 23 he wrote Fred Warren to say that Macmillan was pulling out. Sinclair presumably heard the bad news on or before that day.

Brett did not ask Sinclair to return his advance—a good thing, as that money was long gone, along with the $500 that the *Appeal* had paid him. Sinclair pleaded with Warren to publish his novel in hard covers, but Warren said he had neither the facilities to print the book nor the marketing connections to get it reviewed.

Fred Warren had in fact wearied of trekking through *The Jungle*. Brett, who may have had an excessively delicate literary sensibility in this instance, thought *The Jungle* was too violent. Warren, who lacked any semblance of literary sensibility, thought it was too dull—despite his early praise. Six years older than Sinclair, Warren was less amiable than Sinclair's account of the *Appeal* in *The Jungle* might suggest. He was a wiry, combative small-town editor who liked big headlines in red ink, juicy exposés about murders and sexual misconduct, and energetic attacks on public figures. Since he had taken over the active management of the paper a few years earlier from J. A. Wayland, the *Appeal*'s circulation had surged. Its older, less demonstrative readers had been Sinclair's fans; its newer readers, aggressive and opinionated, expected shock and scandal along with their political uplift, and they let Warren know that after Ona's death, Jurgis's adventures had ceased to enthrall them.

Warren came out to Sinclair's farm in early October to talk about the problems he saw with the novel. After dinner, Meta took David to bed and the two men sat together by the fire, Sinclair reading the final chapters aloud with his customary intense concentration. These passages contained the heart of Sinclair's message: Jurgis's religious conversion to socialism. Warren delivered the cruelest of verdicts for any author, Sinclair wryly recalled. He fell sound asleep.

Two weeks later, on November 4, Warren told his readers to say goodbye to *The Jungle*. Though there were several chapters to go, reader response didn't justify continuing the serial beyond the current Chapter 28, in which Jurgis is released from jail. Any readers who cared enough about what happened to Jurgis after that could mail the *Appeal* a postcard and Warren would print and send the last chapters along when they were ready.

Abandoned now by both his editors, Sinclair struggled to resolve the problems they had noted. Warren may have lacked subtlety as a literary critic, but, as Sinclair admitted later, *The Jungle* did lag in its later sections: "I went crazy at the end of that book and tried to put in everything I knew about the Socialist movement." He now pruned some of the excesses and circulated the manuscript among other publishers. Most of these, he was disappointed to learn, had never heard of the novel's success with the *Appeal*'s readers. Nor had the big-city newspapers picked up on Sinclair's charges of worker exploitation or bad meat. While he was waiting for the several publishers to make up their minds about *The Jungle*, he resolved to publish and promote the book himself.

Sinclair's first effort at self-publishing, with *Springtime and Harvest*, had fizzled, but that was with a lesser product. Now he revealed a growing talent for marketing, sales, and public relations—he often boasted that he was as much a businessman as any of his targets were, and saw nothing shameful in that. On November 18, in a note that Warren agreed to print in the *Appeal*, he suggested to his readers that they purchase an amended hardcover version of *The Jungle*. Printed from the *Appeal*'s plates, and including several new illustrations, this version of the novel was to be called a "sustainer's edition." A rousing plug by Jack London—solicited by Sinclair—appeared with this announcement; it proclaimed that all good socialists should be heartened by *The Jungle*, which did for the "wage slaves of today" what *Uncle Tom's Cabin* had done earlier for black slaves.

Sinclair set the price for this edition, of which about a thousand were printed, at $1.20. He would have liked to offer the book at cost, he said, but he had been working for years for sixteen hours a day, living with his wife and baby in "tents and shanties and garrets," and he had to make a modest profit: that was why he called it a "sustainer's edition." (There is no record of Meta's reaction to Sinclair's claim that "there have been months when I have done all the housework, the cooking and washing of dishes, and taken care of a baby and sick wife besides.")

A month later, on December 16, Sinclair told his *Appeal* readers that he would print no more copies of his sustainer's edition because he had just received an excellent offer from a reputable New York publisher to publish *The Jungle.* Many thousands of copies of the novel, rather than just the relative handful he could issue, would soon be in the hands of readers throughout the nation.

The publishing house to which Sinclair referred was Doubleday, Page, equivalent to Macmillan in prestige. Frank Doubleday, the senior partner, had published Dreiser's *Sister Carrie* in 1900, a daring move; then, according to Dreiser's famous but now discredited account, he allowed it to languish and die, with sales of only a few hundred copies, because his wife so disliked it. More positively, Doubleday, Page had also been the home of Frank Norris, whose shining example in *The Pit* of using fiction to expose shabby commercial practices had so inspired Sinclair. It was Norris who had persuaded Doubleday to take a chance on *Sister Carrie,* and to whom Sinclair might have appealed for help but for his untimely death from peritonitis in 1902.

Though he did not know it, Sinclair did have a contact of sorts at Doubleday, Page: a former reporter named Isaac Marcosson, who had earlier written a favorable review of *The Journal of Arthur Stirling* for the *Louisville Times.* When Sinclair had arrived at the company's office on East Sixteenth Street one afternoon in late November, he was sent into Marcosson's office. Indicating the bulky envelope he was carrying, he said "I have the manuscript here of what I consider is a sensational book," Marcosson later recalled. Sinclair politely suggested that Doubleday, Page consider it for publication.

Marcosson was a self-assured young man, only two years older than Sinclair, who looked to him like a boy still in his teens. He had admired Sinclair's clever ploy to manipulate the public with the phony obituary of "Arthur Stirling." If the manuscript he had been handed lived up to its author's claims, he reasoned, both he and Sinclair might be well served. Marcosson took the typescript home with him at five o'clock and finished it at four the next morning, held "spellbound" by its power and originality. A few hours later he burst into Walter Page's office, saying that if they failed to publish this book they should "have guardians appointed" for them. It was destined to become "either a sensational success or a magnificent failure," though he was certain of the former if it were properly merchandised.

Page was inclined to listen to Marcosson, whose sound judgment he had come to value since hiring him two years earlier as a writer for *The World's Work*. This was Page's special love, a monthly magazine that ran earnest articles on hookworm, education, and voting registration. Marcosson wrote for *The World's Work* and solicited articles and interviews for it, but the money-losing magazine and its tedious subjects soon bored him. Instead, he turned his attention to the relatively new field of publicity and public relations.

Book publishing at that time, according to Marcosson, was hobbled by its habit of simply announcing new books with "amiable and sterilized 'Literary Notes,' " and by its reluctance to spend money on advertising. Recognizing that newspapers needed daily copy, Marcosson cultivated his contacts with reporters and editors, persuading them to think of books as news, especially when they carried a "message" about some current issue. If the message happened to be "commercialized race hatred," which Thomas Dixon admitted was the heart of his novel *The Clansman,* so be it: the more controversy it stirred up in the form of newspaper and magazine stories, the more free advertising and profits it generated. Marcosson worked out a publicity campaign that turned Dixon's novel into a bestseller in 1905—the book that, a few years later, became the landmark and perpetually controversial film *The Birth of a Nation.*

Marcosson now persuaded Page that Macmillan and George Brett had made a huge mistake in rejecting Sinclair's novel: *The Jungle* had far more news value than *The Clansman,* which had been such a moneymaker for the company. Page conferred with Doubleday, and they agreed that Marcosson should take over "the responsibility of launching and exploiting The Jungle," if and when a contract with the author was signed.

Walter Page then invited Sinclair to join him for a luncheon chat about his book. Twenty-five years Sinclair's senior, Page was a courtly southerner who had written widely about the South and its culture. As a young man, he declined a fellowship in classical studies at Johns Hopkins in favor of a more active life as a newspaper reporter. More recently, he had been the editor of *The Atlantic Monthly* before teaming up with Frank Doubleday in 1899. A thoughtful, accomplished man with a whimsical sense of humor, he was every writer's dream: a publisher and editor who actually wrote himself.

Page's obvious interest in his book encouraged Sinclair to assume that an offer to publish it was forthcoming. Much to his alarm, he was summoned a few days after Thanksgiving to a less pleasant meeting with Herbert S. Houston, the company's treasurer and most senior member after the two partners. Page had sent a copy of Sinclair's manuscript to James Keeley, the respected managing editor of the *Chicago Tribune,* for an appraisal of its accuracy. The report had just come back, and it was a damning indictment of the book. Houston showed it to Sinclair, who said it was a masterpiece of misdirection, evading the substantive charges to note trivial—and debatable— inaccuracies. Among these was a dismissal of Sinclair's statement that tuberculosis germs from infected workers might live for up to two years on the greasy, steamy walls of the packing plant's rendering rooms. This was simply an "unproven theory," the report complained—forcing Sinclair, as he joked later, to refer Houston to a bacteriology textbook confirming that "unicellular parasitic organisms are sometimes endowed with immortality."

Keeley vouched that a "competent and disinterested reporter" had written the report, but Sinclair was suspicious. The *Tribune,* published by the crusty Colonel Robert McCormick, had long advocated some form of pure food legislation, but McCormick despised outsiders who presumed to criticize local industry; he would soon attack *The Jungle* as "a cloak for calumny," the product of the "distempered imagination and credulous mind of a pseudo social reformer." Already knowing McCormick's likely position, Sinclair argued that the report was part of a conspiracy to silence him; they should send somebody to find out the truth. Houston summarized Sinclair's argument for Page, who agreed to send Isaac Marcosson and Thomas McKee, the company's attorney, to Chicago immediately.

Luckily, as McKee later told Sinclair, the first person he met in Chicago was "a publicity agent of the packers." Ignorant of McKee's mission, the agent said he knew all about *The Jungle*—he had read it closely and "prepared a thirty-two page report" for Mr. Keeley at the *Tribune.* Keeley never acknowledged any deception, but Sinclair's charge that the report was a fraud was obviously correct.

Marcosson earned his keep by searching out Dr. W. K. Jacques, the Chicago city bacteriologist who Sinclair said—without naming him in *The Jungle*—had been fired for doing his job too effectively, and soliciting an article by him for a forthcoming issue of *The World's Work.* Another Sinclair source, Dr. Caroline Hedger, agreed to write an article for the same issue that would further "bulwark" Sinclair's position. Marcosson also arranged for Tom McKee to contribute a third article, detailing his exposure of the McCormick-Keeley-Armour plot—for such it appeared to be—to discredit Sinclair.

When McKee returned from Chicago early in December, Sinclair agreed to sit down with him and take out anything in *The Jungle* that seemed libelous or likely to offend readers needlessly—a wrenching task. Doubleday, Page wanted to market a book that exposed the meatpacking industry and by so doing prompted reform; Sinclair had hoped to arouse enough outrage about wage slavery to provoke a socialist revolution. He never fully admitted the degree to which he was forced to compromise his original intentions. The title itself was challenged by Doubleday, Page as too provocative; Sinclair was supposedly encouraged to change it. He refused, but dropped almost all references other than the title itself to the world as a jungle: gone was the warning that it was "full of creatures which preyed upon each other," tracking you not for "your life-blood, but your money." Also omitted was the line "Thus again were the strong devouring the weak, according to the law which prevails in the jungle," as well as a sarcastic reference to "this glorious land of freedom."

Encouraged by Sinclair's newfound pliability, along with the boxes of documentation that supported his remaining assertions, Marcosson and McKee between them persuaded Doubleday and Page that their cannons were in place, their bulwarks firm. If Ogden Armour wanted to go to war over *The Jungle,* they were ready.

Sinclair signed his contract with Doubleday, Page on January 8, 1906. Only six weeks later, the first printing of twenty thousand copies was nearing completion; production time had been compressed in order to exploit the growing likelihood of governmental action to regulate the meatpacking industry. In line with Marcosson's notion of linking books and their authors with breaking news, he sent page proofs of the novel to the Associated Press and the United Press for distribution to their member newspapers. He made a point of advising editors that they were free to quote whatever they liked from the novel. When review copies became available, two weeks before the official release date of February 26, Marcosson sent *The Jungle* to President Roosevelt—the book's most important potential reader, and its strongest "bulwark" in case of attack. Sinclair also sent the president a copy, initiating a lively and prolonged correspondence.

Marcosson worked hard to sell Upton Sinclair as a commodity, rather grandly claiming that they stood "shoulder to shoulder in the front-line trenches of publicity," battlefield generals directing the campaign that "now interested the whole world." As Christopher P. Wilson has explained in *The Labor of Words,* Marcosson was not the first publicist to try to exploit the news value of new books: he was simply one of the best to do it, largely because he knew better than most that it was the author's celebrity as much as his book that caught and kept the public's attention. He had read and absorbed the argument by Frank Norris (who deplored what he described) that publishers now saw writers as potentially valuable commodities, seeking out those who could be turned into "money-making propositions."

As Marcosson saw the situation, he had a netted a rare bird in Sinclair: a retiring artist-scholar, he had gone to Chicago with a slender reputation as both a cranky *poète maudit* (*The Journal of Arthur Stirling*) and a thoughtful interpreter of American history (*Manassas*). Now he had proved himself to be a star investigative reporter, as probing as Tarbell and Steffens, yet creative enough to put his findings into a novel comparable to those of London and Norris. Even better: he was a déclassé southern aristocrat with a boyish charm, but brave enough to take on those fearsome industrial predators, the meatpackers.

There had been nothing like this scenario, or like Sinclair himself, in American literary history. Marcosson put all the elements together— Sinclair's reputation, his manner, his explosive manuscript, and the topicality of his subject, now clearly bad meat and not wage slavery—and turned *The Jungle* into more than just a book. It was an event, an extravaganza, unique and unparalleled, Marcosson said; writing about it many years later, he doubted whether "publishing history has ever developed such a strenuous and continuously dramatic situation as was brought about by *The Jungle*." The star of the drama was Sinclair himself.

No frightened ingénue, Sinclair hardly had to be dragged to the stage. Marcosson kept a photographer available for the nonstop interviews he set up for his author, feeling, he said, like a managing editor trying to keep track of a dozen breaking stories at once. Not surprisingly, he found Sinclair to be a handful "whose impulsiveness seriously embarrassed me at times." One such moment came when Sinclair offered "without consulting me" to let Arthur Brisbane, Hearst's managing editor at the *New York Evening Journal,* serialize *The Jungle* free of charge. Marcosson rescinded the offer, instead selling the rights to Hearst "for a considerable sum."

Perhaps the publicity had gone to Sinclair's head: just six months earlier he had been virtually unknown, broke, and abandoned by the two editors who had promised to support him. Now the *New York Evening World* was comparing him to Byron for the "world-wide celebrity won in a day" by his sensational book. Marcosson, observing the results of his handiwork, as he saw it, said, "Few men could have stood up under what was literally an almost overwhelming inundation of fame." Not very steady to begin with, Marcosson said, Sinclair grew ever more erratic with the "whirl of events."

Two men who wielded more power than Marcosson—one a great deal more power—agreed with him about Sinclair as an eccentric and difficult man, but each in his own way did much to guarantee his lasting fame. The first of these was Frank Doubleday, the second Theodore Roosevelt.

Unlike his partner, Frank Doubleday had shown little interest in *The Jungle,* whose author he considered a "wild man" and his book both repellent and doctrinaire. In early March, he was at his desk, reading a cable from the English publisher and newspaper magnate Alfred Harmsworth, Lord Northcliffe, requesting permission to reprint *The Jungle* in England and elsewhere in Europe. Doubleday was on the point of refusing permission, having decided that he and Doubleday, Page "had had about all the Jungle–bad meat business that we could stand, and we did not care to wash our dirty linen in all the capitals of Europe."

Then a distinguished-looking gentleman identified as an attorney for Ogden Armour was ushered into his office. Mr. Armour wished to invite Mr. Doubleday to join him for lunch in his private Pullman car at Grand Central Station, the lawyer said. Doubleday's reward for dining with Armour would be a lucrative advertising contract. In return, Doubleday, Page would curtail further publicity and distribution of *The Jungle,* particularly in Europe, where ruthless competitors of the American packing companies would use the novel as a weapon against them. As a sign of his good faith, Armour's man offered the publisher a large can of preserved meat.

Doubleday recoiled in disgust at such "unbounded cheek." "This chap made me so angry," Doubleday said, that "I showed him this telegram and told him we would give permission to have the book reprinted in Europe. He did not seem to understand why I was so angry. Of all the moral degenerates that I ever saw, he was the worst."

Thanks in large part to Frank Doubleday's high dudgeon, Upton Sinclair's international fame was assured. *The Jungle* appeared not only in England, where it would go through sixty-seven reprintings in twenty-six years, but around the world, with seventeen translations appearing within months of its American publication. Some idea of the respectful attention *The Jungle* elicited is suggested by an early review in England. Its author was the rising young journalist, soldier, and politician Winston Churchill. Not surprisingly, Churchill picked up on Sinclair's martial metaphors, extending them in a long two-part essay-review. Sinclair had marshaled his forces like the general of an army on the attack, wrote Churchill. His weapons were all "the conditions of life" that he found in Chicago, social, economic, moral, even "bacteriological." The "mind of the commander" was intently focused on inspiring his army of facts and opinions, "down to the humblest item which marches in the ranks," to make the Beef Trust "stink in the nostrils of the world, and so to contaminate the system upon which it has grown to strength." Churchill quarreled with Sinclair's conclusion that socialism was the answer to the problems he so convincingly described, but lauded him as one of those men "of very great gifts" bent on changing the political and social structure of the United States.

———

Theodore Roosevelt, to whom not only Marcosson but Sinclair had sent copies of *The Jungle*, also read the novel with care. On March 9 he wrote to Sinclair, suggesting that he get in touch with his commissioner of corporations to discuss the charges he had made against the meatpackers. Sinclair replied to Roosevelt directly, immodestly mentioning that a friend had praised him for joining the ranks of Zola, Tolstoy, and Gorky. On March 15, Roosevelt sent the young author an extraordinary three-page letter of literary criticism.

Of all American presidents before or after him, Theodore Roosevelt was the closest to being a professional writer, best known for his four-volume history of the American West. He was also, like Sinclair, something of a puritan himself, and he now advised Sinclair that his friend had done him no favors by linking him with the European novelists. Although some thought Emile Zola had single-handedly reformed the mining industry in France and exposed the evils of prostitution, "for every man who reads Zola and shudders at the wrong, a hundred are lured into depravity by his lasciviousness. The net result of Zola's writings is evil." Maxim Gorky might seem a hero who had exposed the evils of czarist Russia; but he was also a man who would "lead all the Russians into a Serbian bog," and one who flouted the common moral codes of behavior. And the great Count Leo Tolstoy? The president conceded that some of "his novels are good." But "only a man of diseased moral nature, both devotee and debauchee, could have written *The Kreutzer Sonata!*"

As for Sinclair's own novel, Roosevelt agreed entirely that action was needed to soften the pernicious effects of the arrogant and greedy meatpackers. But Sinclair was wrong about socialism. The idea that weaklings when they join other weaklings somehow become strong was a pathetic delusion. It's not in the group that men find their strength, Roosevelt insisted: it is in the development of what makes them individual.

In its length and its thoughtfulness, Roosevelt's March 15 letter was flattering evidence, even if it consisted largely of reproof, that the president considered Sinclair worthy of his attention. ("I have had three letters from his majesty so far; the latest one a three-page discourse upon the futility of Socialism," Sinclair wrote to Jack London.) Even more pleasant was his invitation to visit him at the White House, perhaps stimulated by the hundred letters he was getting every day demanding that he do something about what Sinclair had described in *The Jungle:* "If you can come down here during the first week in April I shall be particularly glad to see you."

Sinclair met Roosevelt in his White House study on Wednesday, April 4. Fresh from his own experience with Marcosson in marketing personality, Sinclair appreciated the legendary components of the president. Born frail and sickly, Roosevelt had, by sheer discipline, transformed his scrawny adolescent body into a physical fitness magazine image of muscularity, into the hunter who once kicked aside a pack of dogs that had treed a cougar and killed it himself with a knife thrust to the heart, and, most enduringly in the public mind, into the Rough Rider who led his men up San Juan Hill (in fact, up the more prosaic Kettle Hill). Roosevelt was now a portly forty-eight years old, weighing nearly two hundred pounds though he was only an inch or two taller than Sinclair. But he was still active, sometimes playing tennis for hours at a stretch with younger men on the new clay court he had had installed next to the White House.

Two members of his "Tennis Cabinet" had joined him to talk to Sinclair. The first was Francis Leupp, a laconic westerner who was familiar with ranching interests that were being adversely affected by the meat scandals. The other man, handsome, athletic, and elegantly tailored, was the commissioner of corporations Roosevelt had wanted Sinclair to meet, James Garfield; when Garfield's father, President James Garfield, was assassinated in 1881, Roosevelt had taken the dead president's son under his wing, and Garfield was one of his most intimate advisers. At Roosevelt's direction, Garfield had initiated a study in 1903 of the Beef Trust that laid the groundwork for its later investigation.

On the coffee table between Sinclair and the president were neatly piled staff reports, pending legislation, popular magazines like *McClure's* and *Century,* and the morning's major newspapers. Next to the president's chair on an end table lay a copy of *The Jungle,* bristling with index cards, and a similarly marked copy of David Graham Phillips's *The Treason of the Senate,* the second most sensational book of the current season, after Sinclair's own. Roosevelt asked Sinclair for his opinion of Phillips. Sinclair said he admired Phillips but considered him "longer on adjectives than on facts." Roosevelt said that Phillips had done a great deal of harm by naming names as he did;

anybody could do that, he said, tallying for Sinclair and the other guests his own examples of misbehavior in the Senate. (Roosevelt was on record as having at various times vilified one political leader as a "blue-rumped ape," another as a "circumcised skunk" and a "copper-riveted idiot," and a third, a famous publisher who aspired to become a senator, as an "unhung traitor.")

As he listened to Roosevelt describe the sins of the senators, Sinclair reflected that "Phillips in his wildest moment" never came close to Roosevelt for sheer vituperation. He asked himself, "What, after all, does Theodore Roosevelt know about me?" Was this meeting entirely off the record? It had to be, given what Roosevelt was saying. Perhaps the president assumed that because Sinclair and he were of the same class, blue bloods and gentlemen, the young reporter hardly needed to be reminded not to betray a confidence. (The truer explanation, Sinclair said later, was that Roosevelt often denied saying things he was known to have said, on the grounds that he had been speaking simply as Theodore Roosevelt the man, and not as the president of the United States.)

Returning to business, Roosevelt praised Sinclair for pointing out problems that needed to be investigated. He was sending a new team of investigators to Chicago, two men in whom he felt sure Sinclair would have confidence. He invited Sinclair to join them.

Sinclair pondered his response. The Agriculture Department had two inherently opposed missions. One was to support the meatpackers as an essential American industry, and the second was to reprimand and discipline the companies when they erred. Roosevelt's first investigative commission from the Agriculture Department, in March, had claimed not only that *The Jungle* was distorted and exaggerated, but that Sinclair had lied outright, making "willful and deliberate misrepresentations" in connection with charges against corrupt government inspectors. Sinclair had already told Roosevelt in a letter that sending these so-called investigators to Chicago had been like letting a burglar deliver the verdict on his own guilt. He suggested now that he was being invited to take part in a second investigation into his own culpability. He declined politely, saying he was too busy with his affairs in New York to go to Chicago. Roosevelt responded that he had already dismissed the earlier report as untrustworthy and inadequate and that he had reprimanded his agriculture secretary, James Wilson. He had told Wilson, Roosevelt said, that he "wanted his ideas on two good men who would meet with you [Sinclair] and do everything you suggest in terms of interviewing witnesses and gathering information."

That new team, so flatteringly assembled to please Sinclair, at least in part, consisted of the president's own commissioner of labor, Charles P. Neill, and a younger man, James B. Reynolds. Reynolds in particular was a welcome addition for Sinclair, he had done settlement work in New York with Ernest Poole, whose "Kaztauskis" story had so fascinated Roosevelt, and was close to an old friend of Sinclair's, Graham Phelps Stokes. Neill and Reynolds were leaving soon for Chicago, Roosevelt said, concluding the interview with a suggestion that Sinclair see them immediately.

Sinclair left the White House and met with the commissioners in Neill's office briefly, having only a few minutes to catch his train. He promised them he would keep silent about their mission, as Roosevelt had requested, and returned to Princeton that evening. There he found a letter waiting for him from a contact in Chicago who said the packers already knew the commissioners were coming, and had assigned hundreds of men to work around the clock, cleaning up the factories ahead of their arrival.

The next morning, Sinclair later wrote, he was visited by "a business gentleman with dollar signs written all over him." He wanted to offer Sinclair a large quantity of shares in a new "independent packing company," in return for which Sinclair would let his "name and reputation" be used to promote the company. The "business gentleman"—perhaps the same who had approached Frank Doubleday—came back several times after Sinclair's dismissal of his offer, eventually raising it to $300,000 worth of stock in a new packing company, an amount equivalent to about $6 million today.

The theme of temptation denied runs throughout Sinclair's work, usually as a version of Satan tempting Christ in the wilderness. Like Christ—with whom he was often accused of comparing himself—Sinclair represents himself as neither tempted by the bribe nor surprised by its size. He was apparently not even indignant at the presumption of its instigator. He may have welcomed the effort as a reason to break his promise to Roosevelt and the two commissioners that he would keep their visit a secret. Whatever the cause, he obviously felt justified in launching a secret strike of his own. He sent a telegram the same morning he first turned down the bribe—Thursday, April 5—to an old and colorful ally. She was Ella Reeve, who as a reporter for Hearst in 1901 had written some of the first exposés of the Chicago meatpacking industry.

Born in 1862 to a family that had its roots in pre-Revolutionary New Jersey, Ella Reeve had sat as a child at Walt Whitman's feet when the old poet was living in virtual retirement in Camden. She earned a living for a time writing fashion stories for newspapers, then married a gentle socialist named Louis Cohen. Inspired by Eugene Debs, as Sinclair was, she had worked against the exploitation of children as workers in mining and textiles. Sprightly and cheerful, Ella was well educated and deeply rooted in the

American traditions of self-help as well as philanthropy. She was now living quietly as a divorcee near Trenton, with her three younger children.

When Sinclair's telegram arrived, she was busy trying to install a new stove, with the aid of a young neighbor, a Welsh laborer and fellow radical named Richard Bloor. "Come to Princeton at once," Sinclair ordered. Ella replied, with maternal directness, "If you want to see me, come to Trenton" (less than an hour by train from Princeton). He couldn't do that, he said; his mother was coming to visit him. Ella gave in, entrusting her children to Bloor, and Sinclair met her at the Princeton station at ten o'clock that Thursday evening. He always called Ella "Lady," and now he said, "Lady, you have to go to Chicago tomorrow." Reynolds and Neill were due to arrive there on Monday. If she left in the morning, she could be there on Saturday. "Find these people and make sure they talk to Roosevelt's men," he told Ella, handing her a small notebook; they were his major contacts for his research for *The Jungle* and would back him up. He promised to pay all her expenses out of his own pocket. (They would come to a substantial amount: almost a thousand dollars.)

"All right, Upton," Ella said, "I'll go. But do you really think Roosevelt is interested in whether or not you're telling the truth? All this is just for show. He's playing to the cheap seats in the galleries."

Because a single woman traveling alone would be too conspicuous, Ella called her sister in Philadelphia to look after her children and asked young Richard Bloor to accompany her to Chicago, posing as her husband. On Sunday she wired Sinclair that she had lined up a number of appointments with workers and other witnesses from Sinclair's list for the Neill team, including Algie Simons.

On Tuesday Ella wired Sinclair again. She said that Neill and Reynolds had arrived late Monday, on schedule, but they seemed intent on avoiding "unpleasant facts," including one account that Dick Bloor had heard about a man disappearing into a lard vat—a new version of the notorious story that Sinclair had originally heard from Simons, one which, if provable, would have meant much to Sinclair's credibility. She also said that she thought someone from Roosevelt's office had sent a telegram to Colonel McCormick at the *Tribune* that had resulted in the meatpackers learning about the imminent arrival of the commissioners.

Greatly distressed at these reports, Sinclair rushed in to Princeton, where he spent the rest of Tuesday trying in vain to telephone Roosevelt. Finally, he wired instead to complain about the unaggressive posture of the commissioners and the supposed message from the White House. He also said he had heard that Roosevelt was going to attack *The Jungle* in a forthcoming speech.

Roosevelt wrote back at some length the next day. He knew nothing about a telegram from his office. No efforts had been made to undermine the commissioners by advertising their presence; he had told them to be discreet, but they were public figures and could hardly conduct their inquiries incognito. He gently mocked Sinclair for being upset at the recurring slurs on his integrity in the press, including charges that he had spent more time in whorehouses than in packinghouses during his weeks of research for his novel. "Really, Mr. Sinclair, you must keep your head," he admonished; he, the president, had to put up with "hundreds" of similar lies about him appearing "all the time, with quite as little foundation."

Roosevelt also stated firmly that he had no intention of "attacking *The Jungle* in my speech next Saturday," April 14. Here Roosevelt was being disingenuous, in a way that disguised an enormous blow aimed at Sinclair; for it was on that very date, April 14, that Roosevelt gave to the Senate one of the most famous speeches of his career—the one in which he coined the word "muckrakers" in its modern sense and attacked them as meddlers who caused more trouble than they cured. Like Sinclair a devoted reader of *Pilgrim's Progress,* Roosevelt used the image from Bunyan of a man so obsessed with raking up filth that he never looked up to see the stars. "There is filth on the floor" that must be attended to, Roosevelt said; but the man "who in this life consistently refuses to see aught that is lofty, and fixes his eyes with solemn intentness only on that which is vile and debasing," is not merely misguided; he "speedily becomes, not a help to society, not an incitement to good, but one of the most potent forces of evil."

Historians have assumed that because Roosevelt was addressing the Senate, which had been the object of David Graham Phillips's attack, his chief target was Phillips—who certainly thought this was the case and suffered greatly as a result. It is also true that Roosevelt mentioned neither *The Jungle* nor Sinclair by name. But given Roosevelt's obvious familiarity with *Pilgrim's Progress,* his recent close reading of *The Jungle,* and his growing irritation with its author—"Tell Sinclair to go home and let me run the country for awhile," he finally appealed to Frank Doubleday—it is obvious that Sinclair was high on his list of targets. It may even have been Jurgis's first job, and Sinclair's obvious identification with his hero, that triggered Roosevelt's recollection of Bunyan's muckraker: Jurgis is handed a stiff broom "such as is used by street sweepers, and it was his place to follow down the line the man who drew out the smoking entrails from the carcass of the steer; this mass was to be swept into a trap, which was then closed, so that no one might slip into it."

"Muckraker" before Roosevelt's speech was a seventeenth-century archaism, never employed by Sinclair, Steffens, Tarbell, Phillips, Baker, Russell, or a dozen other investigative reporters to describe their activities. Almost overnight, it became their common and dismissive sobriquet, an easy tag for detractors to hang on them, as "goo-goo" had become for the "good government" progressives—progressives like Theodore Roosevelt. The president no doubt intended merely to rescue his reform movement from those he considered extremists, a recurring problem in American politics, but he smoothed the path for Sinclair's real enemies—the meatpackers and their minions—who were now redoubling their attacks.

Sinclair's opponents used the same weapon that had made him so successful: the written word. Beginning in March, a series of articles under Ogden Armour's name in the widely read and influential *Saturday Evening Post* had sought to discredit Sinclair's book and to burnish the image of the meatpackers. George Horace Lorimer, the *Post*'s admired literary editor, had published writers as radical as Jack London and David Graham Phillips. But he had also once worked as the personal secretary to old P. D. Armour, Ogden's father, who had died in 1901. That alone was enough to suggest collusion to Sinclair. But there was more: Sinclair had assumed that Armour used one of his publicity staff to write the articles. Now he learned that the author was Forrest Crissey, on Lorimer's staff at the *Post*.

Another line of attack on Sinclair was that by Elbert Hubbard. Famous in his day as the author of the uplifting homily "A Message to Garcia" and as the founder of a crafts movement in East Aurora, New York, called Roycroft, Hubbard was a mild socialist, at least in his early years, with a wide following that overlapped Sinclair's. As a young man, Hubbard had made a fortune selling soap; his second fortune came from publishing eulogistic essays called "Little Journeys to the Homes of Good Men and Great." Clearly riding on the negative associations with muckraking kindled by Roosevelt's speech, he ridiculed *The Jungle* in a broadside that Sinclair said was reprinted by the packers "and mailed out to the extent of a million copies; every clergyman and every physician in the country received one." Citing from his own copy, Sinclair noted that the headline, stretching across four columns, read "Elbert Hubbard Lashes the Muck-Raker Crowd: Says The Jungle Book Is a Libel and an Insult to Intelligence, and That This Country Is Making Headway as Fast as Stupidity of Reformers Will Admit." "Can it be possible," Hubbard wondered, "that anyone is deceived by this insane rant and drivel?" Responding in kind, Sinclair called Hubbard "a worm."

Seeing all of these forces arrayed against him, Sinclair counterattacked: in mid-April he "moved into New York and opened an amateur publicity office in a couple of hotel rooms, with two secretaries working overtime. I gave interviews and wrote statements for the press until I was dizzy." It seemed at the time, he said, as though "the walls of the mighty fortress were on the point of cracking." All that was needed was "one push, and then another, and then another." His most vigorous pushes took the form of a series of articles throughout the spring and into the summer of 1906. They were published in *Collier's, Everybody's, The Arena,* and *The Independent,* provocatively titled "Stockyard Secrets," "Campaign Against the Wholesale Poisoners of the Nation's Food," and "The Condemned Meat Industry." In the most important of these articles, "Is *The Jungle* True?," Sinclair said that he had provided "an exact and faithful picture of conditions as they exist in Packingtown, Chicago," true "in the smallest detail," as true "as it should be if it were not of work of fiction at all, but a study by a sociologist." However, he added that he had reserved the right to "dramatize" and "interpret" what he reported. What this meant, his critics said, was that what he provided was Upton Sinclair's selected vision of the truth.

But it apparently was true enough. By mid-May the packers' walls began to crack. Despite Ella Reeve's misgivings, Neill and Reynolds had more than confirmed Sinclair's charges in *The Jungle;* they told him they thought he had actually understated the disgusting conditions that they had witnessed. However, their report was still not in writing and thus could not be made public; Roosevelt regarded it as so harmful to the meatpackers that he preferred not to use it unless absolutely necessary. A bill introduced on May 22 by Senator Albert Beveridge sailed through in three days. Its quick passage was due partly to the intense spotlight focused on its uneasy members by *The Treason of the Senate,* and partly to indifference to the packers' fortunes on the part of senators from other than midwestern states. The commissioners' report had not been necessary after all.

Sinclair feared the Beveridge bill would be killed in the House by the packers' chief ally, Congressman William "Blond Billy" Lorimer (he was not related to the *Saturday Evening Post* editor). A key member of the House Agriculture Committee, Lorimer swore that the measure would never come before the House if he, "Little Willy," could help it. At the very least, he could stall consideration until after the long summer recess. By that time, the short attention span of the public would have been exhausted.

By late May, Sinclair's access to the White House had vanished, the Neill report had still not been released, and the Beveridge bill seemed destined to die in committee. Sinclair went to Washington on Sunday, May 27, and spoke again with Neill and Reynolds, who were "amazingly frank" with him and anxious that their report come to light. He could see, Sinclair claimed later, that he was dealing with people who "desired publicity."

And thus it happened that Upton Sinclair broke the trail for those modern social activists who make their case by leaking documents to *The New York Times.* At ten o'clock that Sunday night, after stopping in Princeton to pick up a suitcase stuffed with letters, affidavits, and official reports, he found himself in a private office at the *Times* with its editor, Carr Van Anda, an aggressive man after his own heart. Sinclair explained his intent: by publicizing the essence of the Neill-Reynolds report as it had been conveyed to him orally (along with his own even more gruesome supporting materials), he hoped to force Roosevelt to release the entire report in writing. That would pry the bill from Billy Lorimer's clutches in the Agriculture Committee—and, hardly less important to Sinclair, vindicate his own honesty. Two stenographers took down his story in shifts for three hours, and by 1:00 A.M. it was ready to go to press.

Sinclair's story appeared on the front page of the *Times* on Monday, May 28, without his byline; it was ostensibly written by a *Times* reporter in Washington. Interviews with Ella Reeve, who was now being called Mrs. Bloor (soon to become famous as the communist "Mother Bloor") because of her association with the young Welshman who had accompanied her to Chicago, were also conducted by *Times* reporters. Sinclair's own interviews with reporters were full of devastating details more shocking than most of those in his novel. Some of them could not be proven, like "the little finger of a child" reportedly found in a can of meat by a Brooklyn woman, but most had the ring of truth, and were confirmed by sworn affidavits by stockyard workers. The relatively restrained Adolph Smith, who had shown Sinclair through Armour's plant, lent his support once again. The conditions in the Chicago yards were "worthy of medieval barbarism," Smith said, and "a disgrace to American civilization. The packers seem never to have heard of modern bacteriology, treating meat products as though they were dry goods."

Personalizing the dispute, as he always tried to do, Sinclair circulated his earlier blistering letter to the *Times* in which he had dared Armour to sue him. He summarized in that letter the charges that he said he had gathered from a variety of sources in Chicago: "The selling for human food of the carcasses of cattle and swine which have been condemned for tuberculosis, actinomyosis, and gangrene; the converting of such carcasses into sausage and lard; the preserving of spoiled hams with boric and salicylic acid; the coloring of canned and potted meats with saline dyes; the embalming and adulterating of sausages—all of these things mean the dealing out to hundreds and thousands of men, women, and children of a sudden, horrible, and agonizing death." Did that sound exaggerated? If one percent of what he charged was true, Sinclair said, those guilty should go "to the gallows." If one percent of what he charged could be proven false, then he ought to go to prison. He welcomed the chance to prove his statements in court.

On Tuesday, May 29, Sinclair wired the Democratic minority leader of the House, Representative John Sharp Williams of Mississippi, asking him to apply added pressure on Roosevelt. Williams obligingly introduced a resolution calling for the president to release the report. Roosevelt, partly as a result of Sinclair's leaks and maneuvers, ordered Neill and Reynolds to have their written report on his desk within forty-eight hours. On the evening of that same busy day, Roosevelt took the time to write Sinclair a letter that was remarkably equable, at least in part; he assured Sinclair that he had not been obligated or "bound to me" to sit on anything Sinclair saw fit to release to the public. But his own role as president was to see that nothing but the truth should emerge, and he reprimanded Sinclair for repeating "utterly reckless" and unproven statements.

When the written version of the Neill-Reynolds report was finally released to the public, on June 4, Sinclair was disappointed; it was only eight pages long and made no specific reference to his claims as they appeared in *The Jungle*. It was limited to what Reynolds and Neill had seen with their own eyes on guided tours through packing plants whose owners had advance notice of their visits. Even so, the plants revealed an indifference to sanitation and a sense of "universal" uncleanliness. "Dirt, splinters, floor filth, and the expectoration of tuberculous" workers were everywhere. It was obvious that meat products coming out of such conditions were a menace to the health of their consumers. Dry and factual in its presentation, the report nevertheless caught the public's attention; especially memorable was the commissioners' account of a freshly killed hog sliding into a men's privy, from which it was retrieved and hung up by the other carcasses with no effort to clean it.

The report caused less public stir than it might have because Sinclair had already provided much more graphic material, but at least it deflected attacks on him toward Reynolds and Neill. Their competence and integrity were roundly (and unfairly) condemned during congressional hearings by the allies of the Beef Trust. More positively, the release of the report foiled the packers' scheme of delaying a vote on the Beveridge bill until after the summer.

Victory came quickly—at long last. A compromise Pure Food and Drug bill was passed June 23 and signed by President Roosevelt on June 30, 1906, along with its important companion piece, the Meat Inspection Amendment. Neither Roosevelt nor Beveridge was pleased with the compromises they had been forced to make. The head fee Beveridge wanted to charge the packers to pay for tougher inspections was replaced by a flat yearly appropriation; the provision for dating canned meats had been dropped; and the courts, rather than the Agriculture Department, would have the final say in deciding disputes between the industry and the regulators. In hindsight, of course, the legislation turned out to be worth all the effort, establishing useful standards as well as precedents for greater control and supervision of the food industry.

President Roosevelt did not acknowledge Sinclair during the signing ceremony, concentrating his praise on Senator Beveridge. He also omitted any reference to Sinclair or to *The Jungle* in his 1913 autobiography. In a letter to the journalist William Allen White a few weeks after signing the bills, Roosevelt signaled the true degree of his exasperation with Sinclair: one had to work with the materials at hand on any venture, Roosevelt said, and Sinclair had been useful in revealing some "ugly things." But he "did not like the man." Sinclair had put him in the position time and again of having to apologize for the author's intemperate behavior. In fact, Roosevelt said, he had "an utter contempt for him. He is hysterical, unbalanced, and untruthful." He was also, Roosevelt said in another context, a "crackpot."

A harsh conclusion to what had begun so promisingly at their White House meeting a few months earlier—but it was foreshadowed by Roosevelt's warning remarks about Tolstoy, Zola, and Gorky: progressives like Roosevelt always loathed radicals like Sinclair, natural allies though they might seem, for their absolutism. "I want to let in light and air, but I do not want to let in sewer gas," Roosevelt wrote to Ray Baker. "If a room is fetid, and the windows are bolted[,] I am perfectly contented to knock out the window, but I would not knock a hole into the drain pipe."

Sinclair, for his part, acknowledged with amusement that he owed much of the success of *The Jungle* to Roosevelt as "the greatest publicity man of that time." He also parodied the president's emphatic manner of speech, recalling from his visit to the White House Roosevelt's attack on a senator from Maine. Beginning in a moderate baritone, Roosevelt's voice followed a rocketlike trajectory, ending in a virtual comet's trail of exploding falsetto exclamation points. He clenched his fist, bared his big teeth, and thumped the desk to emphasize every accented syllable: "The most in-*nate*-ly and es-*sen*-tial-ly mal-*e*-vo-lent *scoun*-drel that *God Almight*-y ev-er *put* on *earth!*"

Sinclair never quite forgave Roosevelt for his "muckraker" speech, which scholars now agree was wrongheaded. As Robert M. Crunden notes in his book *Ministers of Reform,* Sinclair and his allies "had forced both Roosevelt and America to face hard problems, and their tone was hardly more passionate than that of Roosevelt himself on many issues. They were clergymen, as it were, of different faiths, but all were preachers within an evangelical Christian moral environment."

Crunden's analogy is slightly misleading, for Roosevelt's importance in passing the necessary legislation was much greater than Sinclair's, significant though that was. The chief contribution of *The Jungle* had been in dramatically setting forth issues and fears of long standing; it did not set in motion the drive to pass the Pure Food and Drug Act, though it persuaded many people of the need for such legislation. Revising Crunden's analogy from evangelical Protestantism to Catholicism, Roosevelt and Sinclair were not contending cardinals, they were the pope and the obstreperous village priest. Roosevelt's impatience with Sinclair may well have come from his feeling that the young writer had won more renown than he deserved credit for.

Tempers cooled later, as they often do in political disputes. In 1915 Sinclair learned that Roosevelt would be visiting a resort near where he was staying. He sent the former president a note, hoping that they might finally be able to play some tennis. Roosevelt replied cordially that he looked forward to meeting Mrs. Sinclair but that his tennis days, sadly, were over. Two years later he wrote again, to thank Sinclair for sending him a copy of his latest book: "Mighty nice of you," Roosevelt said, offering his "hearty thanks."

But now, in the summer of 1906, Sinclair was "bitterly disappointed" with the final outcome of the battle he had fought for the past two years. Hoping to rouse sympathy for workers, he said, he had "aimed at the public's heart and by accident I hit it in the stomach." He didn't even think he had so much as dented the fortress walls he had hoped to topple—they had just been whitewashed. The wage slaves he had sought to save were left alone and helpless in their cells. His conviction that the system was fixed against the possibility of real reform was confirmed. His entry onto the great stage of national affairs had only convinced him of the impossibility of real change within the existing system.

On the other hand, his titanic effort had at least made him a fair sum of money. That was not the most important thing to Sinclair, as his prompt dismissal of the bribery attempt indicates. But after years of scrimping and scrounging, he had realized by midyear more than $30,000 from sales of *The*

Jungle at home and abroad—equivalent to $600,000 today—which was a great deal more than enough to pay back his debts to Herron, Savage, and others.

He was also famous, which he did indeed want to be. About a hundred thousand copies of the Doubleday, Page edition would be in print by the end of 1906, and untold millions of Americans soon knew his name almost as well as they knew their own. With his wealth and his fame, he was now a man of influence, able to count on drawing supporters to his newest crusade: an ambitious experiment in communal living that he had conceived even as he was fighting Armour, dueling with Roosevelt, and trying to keep peace with his wife. His next adventure would be called Helicon Hall.

CHAPTER FIVE

THE CZAR OF HELICON HALL

(June 1906–March 1907)

For someone who often characterized himself as "shy," Upton Sinclair had a remarkable facility for keeping himself in the public eye. Even as President Roosevelt prepared to sign the new law for safer meat that so disappointed the eager reformer, Sinclair was telling readers of *The Independent,* on June 14, that he had "a problem to solve," one which required him to "discuss what the world would call my 'private affairs.' "

He was, Sinclair said, a man "possessed of a small family and a small income" who wanted "to be free to turn his situation to intellectual pursuits." He knew there were many others like him, "authors, artists, musicians, editors and teachers and professional men, who abhor boarding houses and apartment hotels and yet shrink from managing servants, who have lonely and peevish children like my own and are no fonder of eating poisons or of wasting their time and strength than I am." He suggested that he and others of a similar disposition combine their efforts to solve their mutual problem. Together, they would launch a grand experiment, a "Home Colony."

Thus did Sinclair shift his attention from the national stage to the homely domestic affairs of everyday life. But as would often be the case, his personal life and his public activities were intricately connected. His true problem with Meta concerned more than housekeeping: as he admitted to Gaylord Wilshire a few years later, she was nearly insane because of him and because of David, who had cause to be "peevish." For his part, Sinclair had feared for several years that Meta was experimenting with lovers, most recently the "wavy-haired" photographer she had beguiled in Florida. He had hoped to salvage their marriage by buying the farm in Princeton. Now he would try a more ambitious scheme, one that would address Meta's loneliness as well as their difficulties in raising David. By bringing together others like themselves, idealistic innovators looking for a practical alternative to living in crowded cities, in stultifying villages, or on lonely farms, Sinclair hoped to create a model for harmonious living. He and his small family were to be the heart of that model.

Most of those who responded to Sinclair's appeal were well aware of its many precedents in American history. Some of these experiments were religious, like the various Shaker and Quaker communities in half a dozen eastern states and Robert Owen's New Harmony in Indiana; some were cultural, like Brook Farm, near Boston, and the dozens of villages around the country prompted by Bellamy's *Looking Backward* in the 1890s. Several more recent efforts in the New York area where Sinclair was directing his efforts had been tagged as offbeat or eccentric. Elbert Hubbard, Sinclair's enemy, had made Roycroft profitable, but only by selling medieval gimcrackery. Bernarr Macfadden, the food fanatic and popular magazine magnate, had planned a community of thirty thousand people, called Physical Culture City, about thirteen miles northeast of Princeton. Sinclair visited it before it folded, about 29,800 people short of its goal. George Herron's less ambitious effort a few years earlier on his farm near Metuchen, New Jersey, had been tarred with the "free love" label by the press and was doomed from the start.

The pool of people willing to gamble on a similar venture led by Upton Sinclair could not have been huge to start with, and surely had shrunk as a result of these failed or tarnished ventures. On the other hand, the country was prosperous in 1906 and reform was in the air, which was electric with new ideas on education, child-rearing, marriage, and the very concept of community itself. When a famous young reformer invited you to join him in a thrilling adventure, and promised to bankroll it with his own hard-earned money, why not give it a try?

About three hundred curious people came to an informational meeting in New York on July 17. The debonair Gaylord Wilshire introduced Sinclair, who took questions from the floor about funding, servants, food preparation, and schooling. The most pressing questions concerned location; everyone agreed it should be within easy commuting distance of New York, where they all worked.

"Smiling almost ecstatically," according to a reporter from *The New York Times,* Sinclair answered the questions in a general way; the specifics would have to come later, when a planning group of the truly committed would work them out. The critical points now centered around his vision for a Home Colony and its source, which was Charlotte Perkins Gilman's important book *Women and Economics.* Sinclair said he agreed entirely with Gilman's central argument that women had become slaves to their homes, just as wage slaves were indentured to their jobs. Instead of a hundred harried wives cooking, often badly, for a hundred households, Gilman argued, let them band together and hire twenty professionals to cook well for all of them. The way to get women out of the kitchen was to get rid of the kitchen. The same principle could apply to child care and instruction, housekeeping, laundry, routine gardening, and all the sundry chores that kept both women and men from living the life of the mind and soul that was their proper calling. Sinclair told the crowd he was going to put Gilman's theories to the test. He was sure he would succeed so well that his new Home Colony, wherever it might be, would quickly become a major tourist attraction, like the Brooklyn Bridge and the Statue of Liberty.

By mid-July Sinclair had assembled thirty core colonists as his organizational committee. They were pioneers, he later said, good-humored, thoughtful people with a common cause. They gathered several times at his farm, and once at Barnegat Bay where they chartered a sailboat for the day. Trying to anticipate all possible difficulties, the committee considered and rejected several possible locations for the home as well as rules for admission and standards of behavior for those who were admitted. They reached what for them was a routine decision—no Negroes—that was consistent with the surprising blind spot of many progressives at the time. Their feeling, rarely voiced, seems to have been that when black people had been brought up to the necessary level of culture, they would be welcome. The committee members were more concerned with establishing procedures for cooking, housekeeping, and education for the children, and with prohibiting annoying behavior by their middle-class peers, such as appearing for dinner in bare feet. (*The New York Sun,* keeping an eye on the deliberations, wondered if frying onions or playing "Waiting at the Church" at midnight on a Gramophone would qualify as nuisances to be proscribed.)

At the center of this furious activity was a pretty, nearsighted young woman named Edith Summers, blessed with a good mind, a lively sense of humor, and an ability to deal with a variety of difficult egos. A Canadian by birth, Edie, as she was known, was just twenty-two years old. Upon graduating in 1903 from the University of Toronto with honors in German and equivalent command of French and Italian, she had been hired by Funk & Wagnalls in New York to prepare indexes for the *Standard Encyclopedia* and other works. An aspiring and talented writer herself—her 1923 novel *Weeds* would be a critical success—Edie was soon bored by her job. In October 1905, she responded to Sinclair's advertisement for a secretary and took the train out to Princeton to be interviewed by him. He impressed her, upon their first meeting, as a "slight, pale young man carelessly dressed and with country mud still on his shoes. He had a high, thoughtful brow and looked at me candidly with a pair of large, earnest eyes of great beauty." She impressed Sinclair as a "golden-haired and shrewdly observant" young woman with a "gentle voice and unassuming ways." The two would work together closely over the next two years, first seeing *The Jungle* through to publication, then in connection with the Home Colony.

It pleased Edie Summers that Sinclair had decided to make his colonists physically comfortable. It may well be that he, like Meta, had finally had enough of living in hovels, tents, shacks, and roomy but isolated farmhouses. As his association with Wilshire and Herron had proved, socialism did not require one to live miserably while awaiting the revolution. The Home Colony would not be housed in tents on the Princeton farm.

Instead, Sinclair's committee agreed with him that they should purchase, for $36,000, an elegant former boys' school in Englewood, New Jersey, called Helicon Hall. Sinclair would put up the lion's share of the money, using his proceeds from *The Jungle*. Less than half a mile from the Hudson River, in a secluded neighborhood of large estates, Helicon Hall took its name from the mountain in Greece that was said by the ancients to be the home of the Muses—a fortuitous coincidence for a band of modern writers and intellectuals. Situated on nine and a half acres of grounds adjoining miles of forest preserve, the property afforded not only seclusion but a degree of self-sufficiency; with a barn and silo, apple and peach orchards, vegetable gardens and a corn patch, a dairy, and a poultry yard, the colony should soon be able to provide most of its own food. Winding paths connected the fields and orchards, leading contemplative strollers through groves of beech and oak and maple trees, past fish ponds and over streams spanned by stone bridges. From the nearby Hudson River scenic viewpoints, one could look across the river to the northern tip of Manhattan Island.

Built in 1894, the hall was a three-story white stucco building, meant to suggest the classical lines of Greek architecture, with a glass-roofed atrium at its core. Thirty-five bedrooms in addition to dormitories on the second and third floors opened on to wrought iron balconies that overlooked the central courtyard below. The first floor had a total usable area of eight thousand square feet; it contained a billiard room, a parlor, a reading room and library, and a dining room—plus an indoor swimming pool, a bowling alley, and a theater with a pipe organ. The courtyard at the center of Helicon Hall was fifty by twenty feet. Nicknamed "the jungle," in homage to Sinclair, it was filled with tropical ferns, palms, and a gigantic rubber tree, according to *The New York Times* "the largest to be found north of Mexico." The physical and social heart of Helicon Hall was its gigantic four-sided stone fireplace, dominating the north end of the courtyard; it was big enough for fifty people to gather around.

This was more room than the first contingent of settlers needed when it moved into Helicon Hall on November 1, 1906—twenty-four people, including seven children—though there would be nearly eighty by the following March. Sinclair and Meta each took a room on the second floor, and installed David in the nursery on the third. Having rented the Princeton farmhouse with the intention of selling it as soon as possible, they brought everything they owned with them, including all of Sinclair's papers and books. Convinced from his early years that he was destined for greatness, he had kept drafts of his manuscripts as far back as the cadet novels. Given the continuing controversy over *The Jungle,* he had been particularly careful to file and store in sturdy corrugated boxes everything related to his research, his writing, his publicity campaign, and, in case of need, his legal defense: depositions, transcripts, interview notes, and handwritten and typed drafts of his manuscript. He also saved all his correspondence with his informants, his editors and publishers, and scores of other interested parties, including President Roosevelt. Sinclair stored these and other papers and most of his books on pallets in a locked basement storeroom, keeping out one manuscript copy of *The Jungle;* this he wrapped in oilskin and secured in his study, a fourth-story tower retreat accessible only by means of a ladder he could pull up after him.

Edie Summers, who had been living in a tiny cold-water flat in lower Manhattan, had very little in the way of papers or material possessions to worry about. She moved into her room at Helicon Hall a few days before its formal opening. From her first day there to the last, she found Helicon Hall enchanting; it was a "vision of exotic beauty, a Persian garden out of some Arabian Nights tale," full of a "subtle perfume, a whiff of incense faint and elusive."

Another pioneering committee member and early resident was Michael Williams, a tall, swaggering Canadian, the son of a Welsh sailor who had been lost at sea. Mike Williams himself had been lucky to survive the San Francisco earthquake and fire earlier that year. Searching for firmer ground, he made his way east with his wife, Peggy, and their two toddlers. One of the few writers, of the many who lived at Helicon Hall, to leave a record of his stay there, Williams mocked the local citizens' uneasiness with their new neighbors. Englewood's rich businessmen and their ladies were "safe, sane, conservative, average, normal, suave, smooth, conventional" people whose most extreme intellectual experience, Williams said snidely, might have been a Methodist camp meeting. Now a gypsy caravan had rolled into their enclave, "throbbing with a perpetual brain-storm of radicalitis!" Or, as the local newspaper's editor put it, according to Williams, "complaining of the isness of the is and mentally reorganizing the universe."

Considering that many of the Heliconers eventually moved to what a later time would call countercultural enclaves—Woodstock, Carmel, and the lesser known Arden, near Philadelphia—the apprehension of their conservative neighbors was understandable. But in fact almost all the new residents were hardworking writers and academics. Their major excesses were endless talk and keeping each other awake at night by banging too hard on their typewriters. Most were in their thirties or younger. They included William Montague, an English instructor at Columbia who later became an eminent professor of philosophy, his wife, Helen, a medical student, and their two young sons; Freeman Tilden, a Boston newspaper reporter whom Edie liked for his quiet smile, his "quaint humor and gentle, wise philosophy"; and two plump and jolly sisters, both writers for popular magazines—Grace MacGowan Cooke and her two young daughters, and Grace's younger sister, Alice.

Among the few senior members was the formidable Edwin Bjorkman. Twenty-two years older than Sinclair, half a foot taller, as lean as Ichabod Crane, Bjorkman had arrived in the United States from Sweden in 1891 knowing not a word of English. He retained a strong accent but had mastered the language well enough to work as a newspaper reporter for the *New York Evening Post,* spending his spare time agitating for socialist causes. Early in 1906 he married a magazine writer, Frances Maule, a suffragist from Denver who had sworn she had two ironclad rules. The first was never to marry, the second never to keep house. Having broken her first rule, she leaped at the chance Helicon Hall offered her to keep the second. An enthusiastic supporter, she participated for a time in running the affairs of the colony.

Bjorkman would later become the translator of the arch-misogynist Swedish playwright August Strindberg and the co-founder, with Emma Goldman and Sadakichi Hartmann, of the radical magazine *Mother Earth.* Fiercely intelligent, acid-tongued, and a hypochondriac prone to fits of depression, Bjorkman had a stormy relationship with Frances and an intimidating one with everyone else—excepting Sinclair, to whom he deferred.

The only man approaching Bjorkman in age at Helicon Hall was another type entirely, the kindly, marginally pathetic William Noyes. Born in 1862 in India, where his father was a Congregationalist missionary, Noyes spent five years himself as a missionary in Japan with his first wife and their two children. He deserted them in 1897, in a period of spiritual and marital crisis reminiscent of George Herron's, to study with John Dewey at the Ethical Culture Settlement in Chicago. Following Dewey's advice to take up working with his hands instead of his head in order to overcome his personal problems, Noyes taught high school shop classes, wrote manuals on woodworking and the use of power tools, and built his own furniture. Sinclair at first dismissed him as "the very incarnation of insignificance," but soon came to appreciate Noyes; he brought invaluable practical experience to the operation of Helicon Hall's complicated physical plant, and he chaired the colony's later planning meetings.

Also essential to the experiment's success was Noyes's much younger wife, Anna, who was paid to run the household. Just four years older than Sinclair, Anna had earned two degrees from the Teachers College in New York, the most recent a BS, in 1906. Practical and self-sufficient, she believed in making whatever she could herself and in teaching others to do likewise; she wrote magazine articles on furnishing homes inexpensively with homemade furniture and on avoiding frivolous luxuries such as fashionable clothes. After spending endless hours in organizational meetings with Anna, Sinclair came to admire her as his good "right hand." He was also delighted by her vivacious indifference to convention: scorning the shocked colonist who protested that their weekly masquerade parties were unseemly, she showed up once as a cowboy. Helicon Hall was no place for a Baptist minister or prim old ladies, Anna said, but it was fine for her. Meta agreed with her husband's later assessment of both William Noyes, whom she found "pleasant and gentle," and Anna, who was "capable and charming."

Given Sinclair's admitted lack of interest in administering just his tiny household of three people over the past few years, one has to wonder why he took on the task of running such a large and complicated operation as Helicon Hall. The likely answer is that he anticipated its becoming self-operating once it was up and running. And indeed, thanks to the care with which he had drawn up the original prospectus and subsequent plans, and to practical assistants like Edie Summers and Mr. and Mrs. Noyes, the colony was functioning fairly smoothly by Christmas 1906.

It helped that there were no significant problems with money or financial control: when he set up the corporate structure for Helicon Hall, Sinclair offered a thousand shares for sale at $100 each. Of the 230 shares that were finally sold, he owned 160, or $16,000 worth—about half of his return from *The Jungle*, or $320,000 in today's currency. Operational control was limited to stockholders who owned ten shares or more, of whom there were only a few besides Sinclair—wielding the equivalent of 70 percent of the available votes, Sinclair was the "czar" of Helicon Hall, joked Grace Seymour, one of his subjects.

Sinclair and his directors determined that Helicon Hall could operate in the black if they charged for room and board and child care at rates slightly lower than equivalent costs in New York. Individual board was $25 per month; room rent was $12 for a twelve-by-fourteen-foot room, plus $25 for board and care of each child. Comparable rentals without board in New York were $40 to $75 per month. It was possible to rent more than one room, as William Montague and his wife did for themselves, placing their children in the third-floor dormitory.

John Dewey, then forty-seven years old and near the peak of his fame as the nation's most influential philosopher of education, had recently completed his move from the University of Chicago to Columbia University when Helicon Hall opened. He considered taking six rooms for himself and his wife. Mrs. Dewey, however, wanted no part of Helicon Hall. A month before it opened, she complained about her husband's fascination with an experiment that she considered ridiculous and doomed to failure. Dewey accepted Sinclair's invitation to join the board of directors, and visited several times for board meetings. Mrs. Dewey did not accompany him.

Dewey's money would have been welcome, as the costs of running such a large establishment were considerable. Sinclair tried in various ways to economize, including bringing in college students to do odd jobs, along the lines of what today would be unpaid internships. In mid-November two Yale undergraduates moved in and were set to work painting, hauling mattresses, and mopping floors. Edie Summers thought both of the young men were great fun, especially the "lean, lanky, red-headed youth in a brand new pair of blue overalls, stiff from the factory and as yet unsullied by spot or stain. The young man had everybody listening to his quips and cracks. The red hair and the bright blue overalls made a bold splash of color." The young man soon popped his head into Edie's office: "Hey there! Say, I don't know your name, but I think I'll call you Cherub, if you don't mind. What do you say we go for a walk?" His name was Harry Lewis, he said, or sometimes Hal. But she could call him Red. It would be some time yet before he began to use his middle name, Sinclair, as his first.

Sinclair Lewis, whose name is still understandably confused with Upton Sinclair's, was then just twenty-one years old, seven years younger than his new employer. Irreverent and irresponsible, he often let the furnace go cold while conjuring up practical jokes with his Yale friend Allen Updegraff (nicknamed "Upde"—also confusingly close to "Uppie," as Sinclair was sometimes dubbed). The boys soon aroused the ire, Edie said, of a "large, dark woman of commanding appearance" named Bertha Wilkins. Wilkins had already persuaded Sinclair, whom she had known when he was in Chicago, to banish the evening sing-alongs from the courtyard to the barn. A vegetarian and a philosophical anarchist, Wilkins had written a book in 1900 called *Moral Culture as a Science,* but was working as a chambermaid at Helicon Hall. In the course of her cleaning chores one day, she discovered several plaster copies of naked Greek statues in the Yale students' rooms: Lewis and Updegraff had rescued them from the attic. Wilkins spirited the offensive art back to the attic, proving to her own satisfaction, as Edie Summers sardonically noted, that loose morals were not necessarily part of the anarchist's character.

Beneath Red Lewis's boisterous surface whimsy, Edie thought, lay a "will-o'-the-wisp" quality and, in his awkward homeliness, an endearing vulnerability. The two young would-be writers took long walks through the woods to the Palisades, and they sat together during meals, with Allen Updegraff, at a special "literary table." By the time Lewis left Helicon Hall in December, he and Edie were engaged to be married. Sinclair, who spent hours every day with Edie, never even noticed what was happening. "I am not by nature personal," he said later, rather stiffly, "and it never occurred to me that something other than literature was being discussed at that table in Helicon Hall; that Edie and Hal were falling in love and getting engaged."

Lewis and Updegraff lasted only a month at Helicon Hall, despite their mutual interest in Edie Summers (who would marry not Lewis but "Upde," two years later). That was just enough time to give them amusing information for a satirical gibe at Helicon Hall, "Two Yale Men in Utopia," published in *The New York Sun* on December 16, 1906. Among their targets were the rules to which the colonists, including the philosophical anarchists, had agreed: No smoking in the parlor, reading room, or dining room. No suspenders. Bloomers acceptable, except when going into town. Items left behind in the bathrooms will cost a nickel to retrieve from lost and found. Shower before using the pool. Mark laundry with initials. No whistling in the halls. Rent due on time; no credit.

Then there was the food, which the Yale interns were not alone in finding amusing. Vegetarians, Fletcherites, meat eaters, and nuts-and-berries types all had to eat at the same tables at the same time. The result, Sinclair complained later, was that "three fourths of the energy of those who were running Helicon Hall was given to ordering food, and cooking and serving it, and cleaning up the wreckage three times a day. We used to have long and anxious debates as to whether people could exist without soft-boiled eggs on

Sunday morning." The colonists' fare included the familiar and the strange. The familiar were prunes, sweet potatoes, codfish, and onions. The strange meant "samp," a kind of hominy, and saltless crackers known as "educators." A typical dinner, one resident complained, was "beans, potatoes, turnips, peanuts, prunes, 'educators,' and cocoa," not exactly "what the average man returning from a hard day's work in the city (unsustained by zeal for reform), would denominate a square meal." Special orders to the kitchen meant that one virtuous diner could be served lentil loaf and unsalted vegetables while the reprobate beside him feasted on fried chicken and candied sweet potatoes. The cooks were driven to distraction: a Boston newspaper story claimed the food in general was so bad that Sinclair's dog refused to eat the scraps and ran away.

The true sustenance at Helicon Hall mealtimes was supposed to be intellectual. The colonists sat along two facing rows of tables, linked at one end by a single table with room for three chairs. In the center of that single table sat Upton Sinclair, the philosopher-king of his small world, benignly stimulating the conversational flow when he had to, which was seldom. At his right hand was Edwin Bjorkman, whose witticisms often inspired vigorous rebuttals from the women they targeted. On Sinclair's left sat Anna Noyes—not Meta, who found these dinner debating sessions tedious.

Edie Summers, accustomed to a "grumpy boardinghouse table surrounded by the usual boardinghouse types," loved the mealtime conversation. So did Grace Seymour, who looked forward to dinner as the "culmination" of her day: "Here would start discussions on socialism, atheism, agnosticism," on through the alphabet to theosophy and utopianism, touching on "everything under the sun from pessimism and optimism to Upton Sinclairism." Seymour's only complaint was that she was frozen out by the intellectual aristocracy: when Bjorkman discovered she knew nothing about Schopenhauer or Nietzsche, he had her moved from the "highbrow" section near Sinclair to the far end of the table. Stuck between a Russian anarchist dressmaker and the chief engineer and boiler tender, she could barely hear the banter among the few who had earned Bjorkman's esteem.

The dinner conversations often spilled over into evening gatherings around the great fireplace in the courtyard. Its four sides were whimsically dedicated to those with special interests in philosophy, philology, philanthropy—and philandery. Mike Williams caught the tone and mood effectively in his memoir, *Book of the High Romance:* everyone who met by the fireplace at Helicon Hall was well advanced in "soul development." All were endlessly "effervescing in monologue, sizzling in conversation, detonating in debate," and finally "exploding in many theories." Lyrical as well as ironic, Williams recalled how the glowing coals died away to a flicker under the moon beaming palely through the glass roof; then the talk would grow calmer, the mood "sweet and pensive, friendly and melting." All egoism, all ambition seemed to blend into "the swaying shadows by the fountain, and all the ideals and dreams and fantasies . . . seemed to materialize, and the world of fact evaporated quite out of existence."

The good fellowship at Helicon Hall reached its highest point on Christmas Eve 1906. Bobsledding in the afternoon was followed by the singing of carols in the great hall as the giant spruce tree was decorated and presents spread beneath its boughs. Fourteen stockings for the children were hung from the four fireplace mantels. After the children were put to bed, Edwin Bjorkman, the least likely of Santa Clauses, supervised the distribution of small teasing gifts to the colonists. The best, Edie thought, was the stuffed puppy for the lady who hated dogs. Bjorkman presented the puppy and read a parody, in his strong Swedish accent, of a famous line from "The Rime of the Ancient Mariner," "He prayeth best who loveth best / All things both great and small." The parody went, "He prayeth best who loveth best / All dogs, both great and small; / For the dear Lord who loveth us / He loves them, fleas and all."

═══

The snake in this Garden of Eden naturally resided in the Philandery corner of the fireplace. Edie Summers's romance with Sinclair Lewis was an innocent flirtation, as she remembered it, but everyone knew the press was obsessed with the notion that Helicon Hall was a hotbed of sexual intrigue where "free love" reigned. Sinclair bitterly resented the apparent assumption of the New York newspapers that he had started the colony in order "to have plenty of mistresses handy." He recalled later that William Montague had been accused of misbehaving with an Irish serving girl at a dance in the courtyard: "Since none of the colony workers were treated as social inferiors Minnie danced with everybody else, and had a good time; but it didn't look so harmless in the New York gutter press." Montague had to pay the price in terms of suspicious glares from the "lady dean" when he went to lecture young ladies at Barnard College. The newspapers had it all wrong, Sinclair said piously. He did not know "of any assemblage of forty adult persons where a higher standard of sexual morals prevailed than at Helicon Hall."

These remarks appeared in Sinclair's first autobiography, *American Outpost,* in 1932. He had cause to be grateful then, and again, two years later, when he ran for governor of California, that Meta remained silent about an uncomfortable session she had with her husband some time early in December. According to her unpublished autobiographical novel, Sinclair asked her to meet him in his office. When she did, she was not surprised to see Anna Noyes seated by his desk, since the two had to work together so closely. Sinclair asked Meta then if she remembered reading the copy he had given her of Edward Carpenter's *Love's Coming of Age* (1896). She remembered it well. Carpenter argued, as Sinclair often had, that marriage was slavery for women and demeaning to men, a mere social convention that prevented couples from reaching fulfillment and happiness either as marriage partners or as individuals. Sinclair told Meta, according to her recollection, that he and Anna were in love. Anna comforted Meta, telling her not to worry; regardless of their love for each other, it was impossible for her to go off with Upton. She planned to tell William about what had happened, and was certain that he would understand.

Sinclair described his affair with Anna in an unpublished sequel to *Love's Pilgrimage* that he called "Love's Progress." In the preface to this work, written some time after 1912, he writes that its purpose was "to illustrate the new attitude toward love and marriage, in which the equal rights of both parties to experiment and self-discovery are recognized." He describes a sexual encounter with "Hildegarde Vance" (whom Meta identified as Anna Noyes) in a cabin in the woods where they have stolen off together. As he did in a similar scene in *Springtime and Harvest,* Sinclair links music and sexual arousal: "song after song she sang, while he kissed her upon her heaving bosom, and felt the quiver of the music through all his flesh."

Despite the apparent intensity of the affair with Anna, it seems to have ended soon after Sinclair's revelation to Meta, perhaps because, as he told his wife, "It wouldn't do to have the papers get hold of it." This was not Sinclair's first extramarital adventure. Only two months earlier, Margaret Mayo, the attractive blond actress who was to play Ona in an unsuccessful, short-lived stage adaptation of *The Jungle,* had come to see him at the Princeton farm while Meta and David were visiting her parents in New York. As Meta recounted the story later, Sinclair told her that Mayo had tried to seduce him. Wearing only a flimsy shift and sitting on the bed beside him, she begged him to give her "a little happiness." When he resisted, she consented to leave him "inviolate."

It is not hard to see why the handsome and celebrated young author would be attractive to women, but Sinclair's conduct with both Anna and Margaret Mayo—who would hardly have been sitting on his bed in her shift without some encouragement—raises the issue of hypocrisy. Sinclair's speculations about Meta's affairs and his earlier insistence that sexual intercourse even in marriage needed to have procreation as its object both seem hollow, as does his indignation with the press for speculating about "free love" at Helicon Hall. Sinclair never indicated that he considered himself a hypocrite. The press deserved to be lied to, in his mind. Moreover, he openly scorned middle-class opinion and was certain that he was not a sexual debauchee. The best explanation for his attitude is that he subscribed to the socialist dogma that women were exploited and deserved to be free. He also agreed with his icon Shelley, who, as Leon Harris aptly says in his biography of Sinclair, felt "one should go, man or woman, married or single, wherever love led; that not love but only jealousy was an obscenity; that to the right-minded, love gave all rights and marriage took away none."

The fact is that Sinclair simply didn't think such passing infatuations were very important when compared to his real work—which he was continuing to carry on even while running Helicon Hall and consorting with Anna in their forest retreat. For one thing, he entered his first race for public office, as the Socialist Party's candidate for Congress from New Jersey's Fourth District. He didn't campaign, and won only a handful of votes, but he devoted some time to writing appeals to the voters on behalf of socialist positions.

He gave more serious attention during his months at Helicon Hall to enlarging the letter he had written earlier to Lincoln Steffens as a new book: *The Industrial Republic.* Not a novel, which might have been anticipated as natural following his huge success with *The Jungle,* but an extended essay on political and economic history, *The Industrial Republic* argued that a second social revolution equivalent to the Civil War was in the offing; this time the wage slaves would be freed, just as the black chattel slaves had been earlier. The book suffers from implausible generalizations ("the work of war is *done.* . . . There is no more need of conquest, and no possibility of it. . . . We have moved on to another kind of struggle"); hackneyed associations of the United States with the late decadence of the Roman Empire; and, notoriously, the prediction that William Randolph Hearst would lead the way to a peaceful socialist revolution as president in 1912. But some of his suggested links between past and present spokesmen for opposition to bondage are intriguing. He pairs Frederick Douglass with Jack London, for example, and William Lloyd Garrison with Eugene Debs. Sinclair was especially proud, not many years later, of explaining in this early book how Germany was fast becoming a threat to world peace.

The Industrial Republic disappointed most readers when it was published, in May 1907, and Sinclair later declined to reissue it himself, as he did many of his books. But it did find one reluctant admirer: Allen Updegraff wrote to

Edie in 1912 that he had sat up most of the previous night reading Sinclair's book, which he found "the best and clearest exposition of the sane Socialist's standpoint I've seen anywhere. . . . He is the stuff—I dislike him personally, I admit; but by Jove he can write, and he's got an excellent head!"

One of Sinclair's goals in *The Industrial Republic* was to challenge the idea that human nature cannot change, which meant that social change would not affect it. If anything could destroy Helicon Hall it was this "dreadful bugaboo." But certainly Meta's behavior after Sinclair's revelation of his infidelity suggests a constancy and a predictability in affairs of the heart, if not of human nature—as well as willful obtuseness on his part.

=====

Meta's chance for philandery arrived some time after her encounter with Sinclair and Anna, in the form of a brilliant but periodically insane theology student from Memphis named John Armistead Collier. Born in 1874, Collier had attended the University of Virginia, Stanford, Union Theological Seminary, and, most recently, Columbia, dropping out now and then to support himself as a newspaper reporter. In 1897 he had lived briefly with the Unitarian minister and author Edward Everett Hale, whose most famous work was "The Man Without a Country." When the elderly Hale reproached him for stealing food from his kitchen, Collier flew into a rage and beat him in a frenzy of "poetic and religious ecstasy," according to *The New York Times,* screaming that he was the second Messiah. Collier's father had him committed to an asylum for nine months, and had tried to have him recommitted earlier in 1906. The president of Union Theological Seminary argued against restraining Collier on the ground that his extraordinary intelligence and sensitivity placed him on a plane so superior to that of ordinary mortals that they could not hope to comprehend his motivation or his actions.

If Sinclair thought of himself as a Shelley, then here for Meta was a Byron, "mad, bad, and dangerous to know"—though Edie Summers thought Collier was gentle and charming, with his slow southern drawl, perhaps even a touch effeminate, yet also a "rather wild visionary" who was a bit far out even in this crowd. Dangerous or gentle, or both, he fascinated Meta, and she him. They spent hours together discussing what Meta called their "soul states." Meta said they only "petted." Collier grandly claimed that he extended nothing more than reverence toward Meta, but the woman he later married, who did not know Meta and was not bound by concepts of southern chivalry, was sure that there had been an affair. In any case, Sinclair was in no position to complain. He reluctantly accepted Collier, he wrote him testily some years later, "as a sort of inevitable family accessory."

Small wonder, then, that Edie Summers thought Sinclair began to "take on a harassed look" as Helicon Hall entered the new year of 1907. The "easy camaraderie, the pleasant casualness, void of strain or pretense" that she so enjoyed were challenged frequently by squabbles among the residents that Sinclair had to moderate. He took to hiding in his tiny tower study, emerging only when needed to attend to problems—and, as was frequently the case, when guests arrived.

Some of these guests were warmly welcomed. John Dewey came often. William James, then in his final year of teaching at Harvard, came at least once. Lincoln Steffens came, as did Edwin Markham and Bernarr Macfadden's staff writer, the novelist John Coryell, who created the Nick Carter detective stories and the Bertha M. Clay stories. Emma Goldman visited her niece Stella Cominsky, one of the residents. Will Durant, then a senior at St. Peter's College in Jersey City, stayed for a day and left favorably impressed by Sinclair as "an honest and dedicated man," remarkable for his "handsome, almost girlish face, his modest manners, his quiet voice."

Helicon Hall also attracted more than its share of people who thought Sinclair, in his words, kept an open house for them and who tended to be "a little dusty in their upper story." "Being freaks ourselves," Edie Summers joked, "we naturally attracted other freaks" from Greenwich Village—"besmocked young women and men with long hair and flowing ties, the artists and actors and dilettanti of all sorts." One of these—their leader, if taken at his own word—was the self-anointed "King of Bohemia," Sadakichi Hartmann. On February 16 Hartmann sent a card announcing his arrival that day "in the tone of a monarch notifying a subject," Sinclair said, "that he is about to be honored by a royal visitor."

Sinclair claimed never to have heard of Hartmann at the time, which is possible but surprising given Hartmann's long notoriety and his peculiar background. Born in Tokyo in 1867 to a German businessman and a Japanese mother who died in childbirth, he had grown up in Germany and America and gained fame as an art critic and connoisseur. He was one of the early champions of Ezra Pound, Winslow Homer, and Alfred Stieglitz. Self-consciously eccentric, he would appear later in Gene Fowler's Hollywood memoir, *Minutes of the Last Meeting,* for his involvement with John Barrymore and other heavy drinkers and riotous partiers in the 1920s. The gentle Edie Summers described Hartmann as a mismatched assemblage, "a great German body with a small Japanese head on top of it." Mike Williams thought he looked "seven or eight feet tall," and that his face was "like a grotesque mask."

With Hartmann were the sculptor Jo Davidson, then just twenty-three, and a woman named Bessie Lhevinne, who described herself mysteriously as "a teacher in elementary things." Williams, only slightly less mysteriously, called her a "tramp Madonna." Though nobody acknowledged having invited Hartmann and his friends to visit, as he said was the case, they were included for dinner: a sad affair, Davidson complained later, of hash, baked beans, something that passed for pudding, and bitter tea. After dinner, Hartmann, Davidson, and the Tramp Madonna settled in comfortably on the deep sofas by the fireplace. The conversation appears to have been strained. Davidson said the colonists were all dying of ennui, but more probably they were bored by Hartmann, waving what Williams called his "big black bottle of whiskey" and endlessly "theorizing on Art and Life and Love—Free art, Free life, and Free love, of course—until long after midnight." Finally the enraged Edwin Bjorkman, "in a fluttering bathrobe, with flashing eyes and a head looking like the head of a refined and elegant Ibsen, rushed forth from his bedroom and drove Sadakichi and the sculptor and the lady and the bottle out into the bitter night, and into the newspapers the next day" with bitter recriminations against Sinclair and his lack of hospitality.

Twenty-six years later, when Sinclair repeated in *American Outpost* his claim that Hartmann had been drunk and out of control, Hartmann responded indignantly: "Why don't you get things right?" He swore he hadn't touched the bottle he had with him until he was tossed out into the snow.

═══

The comic Hartmann episode was forgotten as winter waned into spring. Edie Summers on her days off occasionally visited the city with Armistead Collier, whose company she enjoyed. One fine morning in mid-March they decided to visit the Metropolitan Museum of Art, treat themselves to a proper dinner, and take in a play. They left just before noon, Edie recalled. It was a sublime day of "melting snow, sunlight dripping from the bare trees, bits of green life showing here and there, and a sky of that tender blue, at once soft and bright, that comes only with a northern springtime." The fig tree by the north stairway was about to burst into leaf. Alice MacGowan, the heavier of the two MacGowan sisters, was skipping rope on the south porch, trying to exercise her way to slimness; she cheerily called out to Edie and Army, as Meta and Edie called Collier, to enjoy themselves.

They did, but by late evening, when they caught the Fort Lee ferry, Edie was tired and cold. She shivered in the night wind as she watched the black water, spotted with gray ice, rush past the bow of the ferry, but smiled when Collier said, "Cheer up, Cherub. You might be worse off. Suppose you were running around barefoot in the snow and had no home to go to." When they did get home, around 2:00 A.M., the dying embers in the great fireplace warmed the tired pair for a few minutes before they said good night. Exhausted, Edie fell into a deep sleep.

She awoke abruptly about an hour later to the acrid smell of smoke and the sounds of banging doors and shouting voices. Throwing on her bathrobe and slippers and stepping onto her balcony, she saw that the north end of the hall by the fireplace, including the staircase, was a mass of roaring flames. The glass roof over the atrium had already shattered from the heat as she rushed down the stairway into the courtyard, across broken glass and through smoke and flying embers, toward the east door, still untouched by the flames. Outside stood clusters of people, most wrapped in blankets and bedsheets, some crying, others numbly watching the flames engulf the building. Edie ran to the south side of the house where she heard panicked voices that she thought she recognized as those of the MacGowan sisters. Sinclair, his bare feet bleeding on the snow, and an elderly poet, Bernard Nadal, were holding a blanket between them, below the second-story window where Grace was standing with her two little girls and her sister. Edie grabbed a third corner of the blanket and Sinclair yelled to Grace to drop the children into it. Grace and her sister "threw out little Katherine, and then Helen," and the children landed safely in the blanket. The sisters then jumped, first Grace and then Alice. The two slightly built men and the even smaller woman holding the blanket, lacking a fourth person for the remaining corner, could only partially break the fall of the sisters. Both hit the frozen ground with a thud, badly injuring their backs.

Other survivors—only one person, as it turned out, would die, a carpenter who was probably drunk—were more fortunate than the sisters. One jumped into the fish pond and was unhurt, though it was only eight inches deep. Another escaped by climbing down a rope he had bought the day before for 90 cents. Several climbed down drainpipes and the fig tree.

They all gathered, Sinclair and his colonists, before the blazing house. Someone shouted, "Where is the fire department?" Anna Noyes pulled frantically on the alarm bell rope; it was tangled and useless, so she shinnied up the pole and banged the bell clapper by hand. There was nothing more anyone could do, as the flames engulfed the second staircase. The fire trucks arrived, but too late. Within an hour after the fire started, apparently from a defective boiler in the furnace room, all four walls had collapsed onto the central courtyard. The tropical patio, the billiard room and the library, the bowling alley and the pipe organ, the three-story atrium and the iron balconies, were all smoldering ruins.

The only things that remained upright were part of the rear foundation and the four-sided stone fireplace, the building's broken heart and soul. Standing there in the cold early morning of March 16, Edie Summers remembered the "brave little fig tree" that only a few hours earlier had been so full of springtime hope and promise. Now the tree was dead, as were Helicon Hall "and all the plans and dreams that were woven into it."

CHAPTER SIX

THE WAYFARER

(March 1907–September 1909)

The stuffy Republican neighbors of Helicon Hall who so amused Mike Williams opened their homes to the cold and frightened colonists on the night of the fire, plying them with hot soup and coffee, clothing and shoes; they even followed up with cash donations raised by local churches to send the MacGowan sisters and others who had been injured to the hospital. The colonists expressed "heartfelt thanks" for such "notable friendliness and generosity" in a card published two days later by the local newspaper.

Soon, though, the mood turned sour on both sides. Because a man had died—the carpenter, Lester Briggs—there had to be a coroner's inquest, which was an ordeal for Sinclair. The inquest was held on March 21, five days after the fire. Hobbling into the hearing on crutches, his feet still heavily bandaged, Sinclair found himself under attack for inadequate safety provisions and preparations. How could the famous author who had worried so about the welfare of Lithuanian immigrants in Chicago have neglected the safety of those under his direct care, including his own wife and child? Why were there no fire escapes?

Indignant, Sinclair responded that an explosion and fire had leveled Helicon Hall within an hour, and all but one of nearly eighty people had survived. This was either a miracle, he said, or proof of effective and prompt response to an unforeseen emergency on the part of the inhabitants. As for fire escapes, the original school had not been required to install them, and he had recently placed an order for rope ladders to rectify that oversight. He granted that, due to ongoing construction, some materials that were previously stored in the barn, including kerosene and explosive powders, had been moved to the basement. (Earlier, two sticks of dynamite had been found in the basement and removed; it was never determined where they had come from.)

Sinclair bridled at questions intimating the possibility of arson for the insurance money—an anonymous letter to the coroner's jury signed "One who knows" had demanded that they put Sinclair "on the rack," suggesting that he stood to gain by the fire. His accountant, the letter alleged, had said that "because of dissentions [*sic*] among the colonists," the colony's financial affairs were "in a bad state." Not true, Sinclair retorted. The community had been filled to capacity, and was about to embark on its next phase of building kitchenless cabins. As for arson, he was the major investor for Helicon Hall. Why would he destroy it? In any event, what he had lost in the fire was beyond price: the first twenty-seven years of his life, both personal and professional, as recorded in dozens of boxes of correspondence, legal documents, photographs, notes, and manuscripts. The only thing left to him was the single manuscript copy of *The Jungle* that he kept in his tower study; it had fallen to the courtyard and been found later beneath the debris, unscathed.

The board in the end dismissed the possibility of arson. It also found no culpable liability in the death of Lester Briggs, but "severely censured" Sinclair for safety shortcomings.

Sinclair was furious, both with Briggs for being too drunk to save himself, as he repeatedly charged, and with the jury, which he contemptuously dismissed as "the village horse-doctor and the village barber and the village grocer." As he noted later, once the claims were paid, all who invested in Helicon Hall were made whole. Only he ended up losing money, an amount vaguely specified but more than was covered by insurance. Sought out, as always, by the press, and as usual unable to avoid headline-provoking assertions, Sinclair defended Helicon Hall against charges of being too standoffish to interact with the town (they were just too busy) and against morals charges (like every hotel manager, he'd had to put up with occasional indiscreet guests).

Sinclair stoked a new controversy in the press when he deflected the recurring arson rumor in the direction of the great industrial baron Andrew Carnegie. He had recently obtained documents, Sinclair said, showing that American battleships were flimsily constructed of "rotten steel" made by Carnegie. If anyone had cause to burn down Helicon Hall, it was Carnegie and the Steel Trust. Sinclair denied making the charge almost immediately, but it would surface again later.

Virtually ignored by Sinclair during the busy aftermath of the fire was the death of Upton Beall Sinclair, Sr., on April 5. He was only fifty-four years old. A failure, a weakling, and a drunk, the father had long since ceased to exist for his son. Although a moderately sympathetic portrayal of a sodden alcoholic in his temperance novel *The Wet Parade* (1931) is clearly based on Sinclair's father, no direct reference to his death or his funeral is to be found anywhere in the vast quantity of letters and memorabilia that Sinclair left when he died sixty-one years later.

By early summer the Helicon Hall furor had died away. Many of the colonists shared Edie Summers's sense of loss—including William Noyes, that patient and forgiving man, who wondered if his and Anna's time in Sinclair's colony had "spoiled us for any other way of life." Sinclair's reaction was more complicated. His public position was that he had created a "beautiful Utopia," no mean achievement. He had "lived in the future." When he moved with Meta and David into a New Jersey summer beach cottage, back into the "single-family mode of life," he thought it was "like leaving modern civilization" and retreating to the dark ages.

Helicon Hall's untimely end made objective judgment as to its success or failure difficult. It was not a socialist enterprise but an experiment in cooperative living, designed to make life more comfortable for its talented and creative participants. As such, it might have lasted indefinitely, given good management. On the other hand, its lack of an ideological basis might have driven away some of the idealists Sinclair had hoped to attract. Surprisingly, Charlotte Perkins Gilman argued that Sinclair had not "the least justification" for claiming Helicon Hall was modeled after her teachings. Gilman's husband was then Sinclair's lawyer—he arranged, among other things, for the sale of the Princeton farm in late 1907—and Sinclair had told her of the influence her books had had on both him and Meta. But Gilman believed Sinclair had erred in having mothers working together to look after all the children; her plan required the use of professional nurses in order to free their mothers for more creative activities.

Privately, Sinclair was torn by the Helicon Hall experience—and not just by its traumatic ending, as an unguarded remark made a few years afterward to Meta suggests: "God, what a fool I made of myself—shutting myself in a dungeon with that swarm of human insects!" Isaac Marcosson, his former publicity man, agreed. Although he should not be taken as the final word on the merits of Sinclair's effort at communal living, Marcosson did have his finger firmly on the public pulse: Helicon Hall, he said, was generally regarded as "a weird experiment in sociology" that made Sinclair "the butt of countless jokes and the target of much ridicule. No man, however gifted, can stand up against this kind of attack."

Sinclair's move to the isolated beach cottage had been triggered by another emergency in his life that spring, after the fire: an abortion that Meta underwent had been followed by a second operation, for appendicitis, that nearly killed her. This meant that she had undergone as many as five operations within two years, perhaps involving two abortions. In August 1907, Sinclair sent Meta and her mother to Battle Creek, Michigan, for an extended and expensive rest cure at Dr. William Kellogg's sanatorium. He then called Edie Summers down from New York to stay with David in the beach cottage, and repaired by himself to a lake deep in the Adirondacks. Repeating the pattern of hermitlike isolation he had established before meeting Meta, he lived in a tent for a month and worked on his new novel. He called it *The Metropolis.*

═══

The Metropolis grew out of Arthur Brisbane's suggestion the previous December that Sinclair might like to visit his Long Island home. After almost persuading the young author to let him publish parts of *The Jungle* for nothing the previous year, William Randolph Hearst's right-hand man had continued to show an interest in Sinclair. He teased him for thinking a slaughterhouse should be an opera house, persuaded him, for the only time in his life, to try a glass of champagne, and even offered to send him back to Chicago to write a series of columns for Hearst's newspapers—about boxing. Cynical, jaded, and generous, and perhaps maliciously anticipating what Sinclair might do with a novel about the haut monde, Brisbane promised to provide him with an introduction to some important people from the highest reaches of New York society. Sinclair, eager for a vacation from Helicon Hall, accepted Brisbane's offer. He whimsically decided to travel by pony. Man and beast caught the Fort Lee ferry to Riverside Drive, passed through Central Park, down Broadway, and across the Brooklyn Bridge onto Long Island, arriving shortly before dark at Brisbane's estate in Hempstead.

One of Brisbane's guests on this winter day was a heavy lady, encrusted in diamonds and smoking black cigars, who told Sinclair scandalous and frequently ribald stories about society life in New York. She was Mrs. Oliver Hazard Perry Belmont, the doyenne of New York society. Apparently for her own amusement, Mrs. Belmont provided Sinclair then and in later meetings with the materials for a damning portrait of contemporary American life among the wealthy, and with useful contacts for additional information. As he had done in Chicago, Sinclair used each new contact as a means of entry to several more, including a Wall Street lawyer and a sitting New York Supreme Court judge.

Earlier, Sinclair had hoped to write a trilogy of novels about the Civil War, delving deeply into the American past. Now he planned a new trilogy, not about the past but the present, set in New York City. In the first, *The Metrop-*

olis, he took the son of his hero in *Manassas,* also named Allan Montague, through the new jungle that Mrs. Belmont opened up to him: the morally bankrupt social world of the rich and foolish. In the second, *The Money-changers,* he argued that J. P. Morgan deliberately provoked the great bank crisis of 1907. Both would be published in 1908. The third novel, never written, was to describe politics and slum life in the city.

As often happens with a writer who has produced a blockbuster, Sinclair's first novel after *The Jungle* was a disappointment. Although *The Metropolis* sold a respectable eighteen thousand copies, readers who expected to find engaging characters were disappointed. As the Sinclair scholar John Ahouse has noted, it is "more a travelogue than a novel, striking one reviewer at the time as 'picturesque.' Montague, the newcomer to the city, is the author's eyes and ears, consciously noting the habits, conceits, appetites, possessions, and even the language of the wealthy as if they were a race apart."

=====

Among the objects of satire in *The Metropolis* were the ways in which the wealthy indulged in " 'rest cures' and 'water cures,' 'new thought' and 'metaphysical healing' and 'Christian Science.' " Underlying Sinclair's satire, though, was his own susceptibility to such nostrums, caused by his increasingly bad health. He was now nearly twenty-nine years old and a self-described physical wreck, a "regular experiment station in health." For ten years he had been working almost nonstop, afflicted with insomnia and routinely staying up until 2:00 A.M. Hardly a day passed without a headache. He suffered from indigestion, constipation, diarrhea, bad teeth, bronchitis, and even hair loss, which he began to combat by refusing to wear a hat. Now "nature" had applied the brakes. He was on the verge of a complete collapse: "I could feel my body going to pieces." He decided in late September to join Meta for a few weeks at the Battle Creek sanatorium.

Sinclair would be one of nearly three thousand patients who came every year to "the San," eager to be flushed and irrigated, pounded and massaged, exercised and exhorted, admonished and entertained. It was no place for the truly ill; only the reasonably healthy, suffering from such curable conditions as being too fat or too skinny, too tired or too nervous, were accepted. Dr. Kellogg's credentials were in order, and much of his regimen—plenty of exercise, simple food in modest quantities—made sense. He did no harm. But his success derived mostly from his marketing genius, which capitalized on the celebrities he drew to him and who in turn drew wealthy non-celebrities. During its heyday, as T. C. Boyle writes in his satiric novel *The Road to Wellville* (1993), Kellogg's "enema machine irrigated the most celebrated bowels in the country, yea, the world"—including those of Johnny Weissmuller, Amelia Earhart, Thomas Edison, Henry Ford, and William Howard Taft.

Meta and Upton Sinclair have walk-on roles in Boyle's novel. She passes through the halls like a Gypsy Ophelia, variously described as "Arabian," "exotic," and scandalous for her association with "sun worship, nudity, [and] free love" at Helicon Hall (the first two of which at least, given the dates of the colony, from November to March, are unlikely.) A character represented as a former colonist defends both the Sinclairs from charges of improper behavior; they simply "happen to feel that one should go wherever love leads and that it is not love but jealousy which is the obscenity. Love gives all rights, and a true marriage, a forward-thinking marriage, takes none away."

By the time Sinclair arrived at the San, Meta had already recovered her health sufficiently to flirt with a young Harvard man named Alfred Kuttner—later rechristened by her as "my sun-god," with the evocative and masterful name of Erik Steinhart, or "stone heart," when the flirtation grew more serious. Then just twenty-three years old, Kuttner was a brilliant young man. His closest friend at Harvard, and for many years afterward, was Walter Lippmann; the two would camp together in Maine during the summer of 1912, Lippmann writing the book that launched his career, *A Preface to Politics* (1913), while Kuttner worked on his translation of Freud's *Analysis of Dreams*. Austerely handsome but slightly misshapen, carrying one shoulder higher than the other, Kuttner was enthralled by Meta, and capable of spending twelve hours straight talking with her, as Armistead Collier had done, about her soul. In the draft of her unpublished novel, Meta represents Erik, the character modeled on Kuttner, as praising her "curious, Pre-Raphaelite way," and writing rhapsodic poems: "How glad we were that day beside the sea / Under the windy sky, when first we met / Untrammelled! Our souls as two bright diamonds set / Twin-like upon the brow of purity."

Fortunately for Sinclair, he could not foresee the three-year "endless vista of horrors and despair" that Kuttner and Meta, as he said later, had in store for him. Dr. Kellogg was so straitlaced that he encouraged "sterilized dancing—the men with the men and the women with the women," so Meta's dalliance with Kuttner seemed harmless. It took her off his hands, in fact, while he threw himself with his usual gusto into Kellogg's regimen. He "subjected his abdomen" to alternating heat and ice treatments, admitting to feeling better so long as he could be "boiled and frozen." He "listened solemnly while Doctor Kellogg read off the numbers of billions of bacteria per gram in the contents of the colon of a carnivorous person." He concluded that "meat-eating was killing me"; moreover, it "certainly seemed proper that the author of *The Jungle* should be a vegetarian, so I became one."

Like his satirized plutocrats in *The Metropolis,* Sinclair tried every new cure, both at the San and later: the "nature cure," the "raw food route," the "monkey and squirrel diet" of berries and grains. He ate no cooked food but shredded wheat for months, with occasional detours for "nuts and salads and fresh and dried fruits." He frequently found himself "bubbling with health," but realized at last that he simply felt better when he wasn't writing. His strange diets were no help when he was doing his "brain work," and indeed could have disastrous effects: "I assure you that until you try, you have no idea the amount of trouble that can be made in your stomach by a load of bananas and soaked prunes which has gone wrong!"

Then as now, there was a ready market for magazine articles and books about health, and Kellogg warmly welcomed writers who planned to do stories about his program. One of these was Sinclair's former colonist Michael Williams, who arrived in Battle Creek in October with more than just an article on the San in mind. Like Sinclair, he had lost everything in the Helicon Hall fire, including several uncompleted article manuscripts. He and Sinclair, Williams suggested, should take to the open road with their wives and children. He drafted a prospectus for them to pitch to the magazines for a "Helicon Hall on the hoof; a migratory home, warranted fireproof," just a couple of covered wagons and sturdy teams of horses wandering through the golden hills and along the shining shores of distant California.

Williams was familiar with California's attractions, having lived in San Francisco, and his pitch for prospective editors excited Sinclair. Williams proposed to visit "the Point Loma Colony; the Carmel group of literary people, the Anarchist 'Freeland' " located in "San Francisco, Berkeley, and the Yosemite Valley." He promised more than a mere travelogue; this was to be a "health pilgrimage, a paean to the outdoor life," with "brown-legged babies, and camp adventures galore." They would "use no alcohol nor tobacco, tea nor coffee, nor the corpses of our fellow-creatures." All involved would be suffused with the feeling of good-fellowship and camaraderie, "full of enthusiasm and the spirit of adventure."

Peggy Williams and Meta killed the western trip—housekeeping and child-tending in covered wagons while their new frontiersmen gathered huckleberries and scribbled poetry did not appeal to either woman. But the idea of packing up the families together, and of the men collaborating on a book of some sort, remained attractive. Bermuda was an acceptable substitute, Sinclair agreed. *The Metropolis* had earned him a sizable $5,000 advance from his new publisher, Moffat, Yard, which would carry them through for a year. Williams promised to reimburse Sinclair later for his share of the expenses. They would call their book *Good Health, and How We Won It.*

In mid-December 1907, the two families moved into a ruined mansion on the beach in Hamilton. It had the added benefit of a tennis court which Sinclair and Williams used every day that it was not raining. Williams worked on drafting the first version of the health book, while Sinclair wrote a play, later a short novel, called *The Millennium.* Set in the year 2000, his story eerily anticipates the now familiar genre of post-apocalypse literature and film. Ten people, a wealthy industrialist and his family and one servant, are the only survivors of a chemical-nuclear catastrophe that destroys all human life but leaves everything else untouched. Faced with the task of reorganizing society in miniature, the useless aristocrats give way to the powerful and ruthless former butler, Tuttle, who turns them into wage slaves.

This was the first of many efforts by Sinclair to write a salable play. None was ever commercially successful, though *The Millennium* briefly intrigued the celebrated producer David Belasco before he decided its heavy-handed message killed its dramatic appeal. *The Millennium* is of interest now mainly for its ingenious premise and for the insight it provides into Sinclair's unacknowledged ambivalence about human nature. Although the survivors have everything they need in terms of food and shelter, they immediately revert to the old bad habits of the race. As Tuttle says to another survivor, " 'It's really exactly the same as it used to be in the old world. You're the politician, the man that governs—and I'm the businessman, the one that owns things. The rest of 'em, they're the ones that do the work.' "

═══

Hamilton in 1907 was still a small town, so it was inevitable that Sinclair should meet Samuel Clemens, better known as Mark Twain, who was also wintering there. "The uncrowned king of America," as Sinclair thought of Twain, had sent him a note the previous year, saying that he had tried to read *The Jungle* but was forced to quit halfway through because, in Sinclair's words, of the "anguish it caused him." Sinclair resented Twain's refusal to "endure the anguish of knowing." He also recalled with distaste Twain's failure to rally behind Maxim Gorky in 1906 when the visiting Russian writer was thrown out of his New York hotel for immoral behavior—traveling openly with his mistress of many years and incurring the disfavor of both President Roosevelt and the New York press.

But Sinclair soon became fond of the elderly Twain, tidy but shrunken in his famous white suit, only three years from his death. He was "kind, warm-hearted, and also full of rebellion against capitalist greed and knavery." Not until many years later, after reading Van Wyck Brooks's revealing biography *The Ordeal of Mark Twain* (1920), would Sinclair learn that Twain had lived a double life, that he "was the most repressed personality, the most completely cowed, shamed, and tormented great man in the history of letters." It was his wife, Livy, that "frail woman, a semi-invalid," who tamed Mark Twain and stole his fire. Publicly escorting his wife to church every Sunday, privately "loathing Christianity," he died convinced that modern civilization was, as he wrote in the posthumous "What Is Man?," "a shabby poor thing and full of cruelties, vanities, arrogances, meannesses and hypocrisies. As for the word [civilization], I hate the sound of it, for it conveys a lie; and as for the thing itself, I wish it was in hell, where it belongs." Though Sinclair remembered his lazy afternoons on the hotel veranda with Mark Twain warmly, he thought the famous writer had had a duty to be outspoken and brave, and that he had evaded his responsibility in order to maintain his high style of living and to keep peace with his wife.

＝＝＝

The Sinclair family came home to New York in May 1908. Sinclair was physically refreshed but angry with Mike Williams, who he thought had cheated him in their collaboration on *Good Health*. The book was in fact almost entirely Williams's, Sinclair having written only the introduction, though both their names were on the title page because of Sinclair's fame. Williams had returned early to New York with the manuscript and pocketed all the advance offered by a publisher instead of sending Sinclair half, as agreed. Like Huckleberry Finn, he then "lit out for the territory": the West that he had described so vividly the previous year in his proposal to take Helicon Hall on the road.

Sinclair, Meta, and David spent the summer in the Adirondacks, in a cottage on Lake Placid, where he worked on the second novel of his planned New York trilogy, *The Moneychangers*. He had been thinking about his plot for that book since early December, when he had spent an evening with Edmond Kelley, a respected attorney whom he had met while writing *The Metropolis*. Kelley was distraught, having just returned from a visit with his old friend Charles T. Barney, who was on the verge of ruin caused, Barney claimed, by J. P. Morgan. The great financier had recently won the nation's gratitude for single-handedly rescuing the American banking system from failure and the nation from a great depression during the bank panic of 1907. But Barney assured Kelley that Morgan was the instigator and chief cause of the very panic he had vanquished. The morning after Kelley told Sinclair this story, Barney killed himself. Sinclair was convinced of Morgan's guilt in causing the panic and determined to expose it.

By summer's end Sinclair had finished the novel, but Moffatt, Yard turned it down, having lost money on *The Metropolis*. Only a third-rate publisher, B. W. Dodge, could be persuaded to issue it, for a mere $600 advance. *The Moneychangers* was not only a weaker novel than *The Metropolis* but a more dangerous one, a calculated roman à clef with J. P. Morgan, E. H. Harriman, William Vanderbilt, Charles M. Schwab, Andrew Carnegie, and other important men appearing as only lightly disguised villains. Allan Montague, the idealistic young lawyer turned investigator, shares many of Sinclair's own qualities of tenacity and abused innocence as well as his conviction that a nefarious conspiracy of capitalists is to blame for every social ill. Ingenious but far-fetched, the charges against Morgan have not even been considered worth dismissing by his many worthy biographers.

Only marginally more persuasive was the novel's description of the armor-plate fraud first mentioned by Sinclair during the inquest into the Helicon Hall fire. Sinclair uses a young naval officer as a character to present the accusation against "Harrison," whom every reader would have recognized as Andrew Carnegie. Many ships of the line, the officer says, were "covered with rotten armour plate that was made by old Harrison, and sold to the Government for four or five times what it cost." Prompted by Sinclair's charges, the *New York American* ran a story on September 6, 1908, in which an admiral admitted that the *Oregon* carried four hundred tons of defective armor plate. Sinclair took the opportunity of the *American* exposé to renew his earlier charge that the "Steel Crowd" had burned Helicon Hall, specifically attacking William E. Corey, the president of the United States Steel Corporation, and E. H. Harriman, the railroad magnate.

Sinclair leaned toward conspiracy theories for much of his life, occasionally with good cause. But he had spent not just the monetary but the psychic and artistic capital he had won from *The Jungle*. He had worked hard, winning a reputation for accuracy and common sense, somewhat compromised by excessive zeal. Now the zeal predominated. He was an American Savonarola, attacking too many evils, too indiscriminately and with too much intensity, to be taken seriously.

His hard-won ties with three reputable publishers were severed. He was estranged from most of his fellow muckrakers, whom he thought too timid. He was disdained by his literary peers, who, in Sinclair's words, thought he had "declassed" himself as a "man of letters" through writing socialist propaganda. And he was ignored by the great middle class of American readers, many of whom were women, as a tedious, often paranoid crank.

His personal life was also a shambles. Repeated efforts on both his part and Meta's to mend their marriage had failed, most recently in Bermuda and at Lake Placid. They discussed divorce but hesitated to follow through, partly because Sinclair still thought he loved Meta, partly because each dreaded the scandal it would cause; divorce at that time in New York required the submission of proof of insanity or adultery.

Frustrated and balked at every turn, Upton Sinclair in September of 1908, about to turn thirty years old, acted out the great American myth of rejuvenation: he bade a temporary farewell to his wife and son and hit the road, heading west for California.

=====

As it had been for the pioneers, Sinclair's progression was a leisurely one. He was still a celebrity in the great populist heartland of the country, where the socialist message of distrust and fear of the capitalist conglomerates headquartered in the East was strong. Eager sympathizers greeted him at every stop. Among his fans was a young man who would later achieve some renown as the "boxcar poet," Harry Kemp.

Born in 1883 to a middle-class family in Ohio, Kemp was inspired to leave high school for a life of adventure by Josiah Flynt's *Tramping with Tramps* (1899) and Richard Henry Dana's classic *Two Years Before the Mast* (1840). He worked as a common seaman on cargo ships that took him to Australia, China, and the Philippines. After spending three months in a Texas jail for vagrancy, Kemp finished high school, lived for a few months at Elbert Hubbard's Roycroft community, and worked briefly as a laborer on Bernarr Macfadden's Physical Culture City. He settled in for a six-year stay at the University of Kansas, in Lawrence, in 1902. Indifferent to formal degree requirements, as Sinclair had been, Kemp was content to curl up in the dusty stacks of the library, devouring obscure works on philosophy and dipping into foreign languages.

Kemp's image was that of the manly aesthete. Six feet tall, square-shouldered and broad-chested, with thick blond hair swept back from a high forehead, scorning coats and hats even in the depths of a Kansas winter, he radiated health and vigor. Like Jack London, he was tough enough to survive hardships beyond any experienced by Sinclair, yet sensitive to the images of beauty within the tattered copies of Keats and Shakespeare that he always carried with him. He was also a writer of great ambition and modest ability.

Sinclair, who liked to encourage new talent, saw one of Kemp's first published poems in 1906 and sent him a complimentary note.

In an amusing echo of Sinclair's own approach to Owen Wister a few years earlier, Kemp responded gratefully to Sinclair as "one of the great men of the world," pleading his own ignorance and need of help. "I have dedicated myself to poetry as a neophyte does to a religious mystery," just as Arthur Stirling had done: "You don't know how true your idea of one's inner living of Art is! Don't think I'm crazy, but if I hadn't lived poetry that way I would have died ere this of very soul-hunger." In 1908 Kemp published a Whitmanesque poem in the *New York American*—the same tabloid newspaper that supported Sinclair's charges against the Steel Trust—one couplet of which clearly owed something to *The Jungle:* "I've seen the mad steer plunge and fall beneath the sledge's stroke / In packing houses by the turbid Kaw."

Kemp recalled Sinclair as a very energetic walker with a head too large for his body; it was a strong head, with a Roman nose, a decisive chin, and a mouth "loose and cruel, like mine." His skin was fair and as smooth as a boy's, so smooth that he hardly needed to waste time shaving once a week just to remove "on each cheek a patch here and there of hair, like the hair on an old maid's face."

An aggressive disciple, Kemp spent a good deal of time during their few days together explaining to his mentor his newly discovered religion of self-fulfillment, according to which people had a "spiritual duty to enjoy life." Sinclair left Lawrence convinced that Kemp could become the new poet of the common man, or at least a worthy rival of Edwin Markham and Edgar Lee Masters. The two men parted with cordial promises to meet again, as soon as possible.

George Sterling, whom Sinclair would also meet for the first time on this trip, was almost as famous in the literary world as Harry Kemp was obscure. Nine years older than Sinclair, Sterling was a gentle, thoughtful man with dark, chiseled features frequently compared to Dante's. He was nicknamed "the Greek," as a kind of Apollonian counterpart to his friend Jack London's Dionysian "Wolf," and for his physicality—tall and lean, he was given to posing nearly naked for the camera on the beaches and rocks of Carmel, joyously waving a speared abalone.

A latter-day Romantic poet with a strong sense of fun, often stoked by whiskey, Sterling was part of the San Francisco literary circle that included London, Joaquin Miller, and the quarrelsome Ambrose Bierce. For the past several years, coincidentally with Sinclair's rise to fame with *The Jungle* and

Upton Beall Sinclair and Priscilla Harden Sinclair, at about the time of Sinclair's birth in 1878. Both parents doted on their precocious son, who later despised his father as a spineless alcoholic and rejected his mother as too conservative.

Upton Sinclair at age eight, in a characteristically assured pose.

Good News

Good News has combined with this publication. The continuation of GOOD NEWS serials will be found in this number. ❧ ❧ ❧ . ❧ ❧

Special Announcement! This Number Contains

FRIENDS AND FOES AT WEST POINT; or, Mark Mallory's Alliance.
By Lieut. Frederick Garrison, U. S. A.

CLIF. FARADAY'S FORBEARANCE; or The Struggle in the Santee's Hold.
By Ensign Clarke Fitch, U. S. N.

ARMY
AND
NAVY
WEEKLY

A WEEKLY
PUBLICATION
FOR OUR BOYS

HOWARD, AINSLEE & CO · · · · · PUBLISHERS · · · · · · · · · · NEW YORK

Vol. 1. No. 7
July 31, 1897

48 Pages

5 CENTS

Issued Weekly.

Subscription Price, $2.50 per year.

By his late teens, Sinclair was a self-described "young shark," ravenous for success. This 1897 magazine cover features some of his earliest published work, though not his name. Using various pseudonyms, including "Frederick Garrison" and "Clarke Fitch," he earned enough money with his patriotic boys' adventure tales to support his parents and put himself through college.

The author in his mid-
twenties aboard a horse
on his Princeton farm;
playing the violin, a lifelong hobby; and playing
tennis in Long Beach in
1917—he won the Gulf
Coast tournament in 1914
and was a ranked player in
southern California for
many years.

The Princeton farmhouse where Sinclair worked on *The Jungle* in 1905; he wrote "incessantly" for months, he said, with "tears and anguish, pouring into the pages all that pain which life had meant to me."

Cover of first edition of *The Jungle*, 1906, published by the Doubleday, Page Company. Sinclair's intent in *The Jungle* was to depict the sorry plight of "wage slaves" in industrial America, but readers responded more to the novel's vivid depiction of bad meat. Ruefully concluding that he had aimed for the nation's heart and hit it in the stomach, Sinclair still took satisfaction in helping to secure passage of the nation's first Pure Food and Drug legislation.

Residents of Helicon Hall gathered around this stone fireplace. The New York press viewed Sinclair's six-month experiment in communal living as a free-love nest. After a disastrous fire in March 1907, the fireplace was all that remained of Helicon Hall.

George Sterling, left, and Sinclair at Carmel, 1908. Sterling was the model for Brissenden, the doomed poet in Jack London's *Martin Eden*. In 1926, Sterling fulfilled London's prophecy by killing himself with cyanide.

Sinclair at Carmel, leaning against tree, was the center of the group though he stayed there only a few months. Others pictured, from left, are Jack London, blowing smoke; Alice MacGowan, a Helicon Hall colonist whose life Sinclair had saved during the fire that destroyed the Hall; an unidentified man; and George Sterling, with cap.

Variously described as "elfin" and sensuous, Upton's first wife, Meta Sinclair, intellectually intimidated by her husband, eventually sought solace in affairs with poets who she regarded as soul mates.

Sinclair with his son, David, Princeton farm, ca. 1904. A reluctant father, Sinclair feared that David's birth threatened his survival as an artist, and the two were later estranged for many years.

Mary Craig Kimbrough at seventeen, upon graduation from finishing school in 1900. Three years younger than Meta, she would become Sinclair's second wife in 1913.

Meta and Craig (Craig is the larger image) together in a typical newspaper photo and story following Sinclair's divorce and remarriage, ca. 1914, during custody battle for David. The coverage made Sinclair feel as if he had been "flayed alive."

MEN TO BALLOT ON VOTES FOR WOMEN AT ELECTION

Equal Suffrage Forces Take Poll Wen Convention Is Decided.

'MY CODE IS MY OWN; I DON'T CARE,' SAYS MRS. SINCLAIR NO. 1

"Woman Always Suffers," Says Plaintiff in Fight for Custody of Son.

(Special to The Item).
GULFPORT, Miss., July 9.—"Do you think, Mr. Gardner, there is any chance for me to see David this morning?" plaintively asked Mrs. Meta Fuller Sinclair, divorced wife of Upton Sinclair, the novelist, who has filed suit in the Harrison county court for the possession of their 13-year-old son, David. She was seated in the rather bleak

Harry Kemp and Sinclair at Arden, 1911. Encouraged and aided in his efforts to be published by Sinclair, the young "boxcar poet's" affair with Meta became front-page news in the summer and fall of 1911.

Craig (now Mrs. Upton Sinclair) with George Sterling (to her left) and Clement Wood in a 1914 Rockefeller protest march, following the Ludlow Massacre in Colorado. Sinclair tried unsuccessfully to serve a personal "indictment" for murder on John D. Rockefeller, Jr.

Sinclair's lifelong interest in film as a means of raising social awareness began with the 1914 film version of *The Jungle*, in which he played the role of a character based on Eugene Debs. The last copy of the film disappeared sometime in the 1930s.

Helicon Hall on the opposite side of the continent, he had been the leading figure of a more hedonistic group of writers in Carmel, where he had a spacious bungalow with a stone fireplace and a wide, comfortable porch. Nothing could be more natural than that Sinclair should seek out Sterling in Carmel when he came west: half a dozen of his Helicon Hall colonists, including Mike and Peggy Williams and the MacGowan sisters, had already done so. Sinclair Lewis would not be far behind; he appeared unannounced on Grace MacGowan's doorstep in January 1909, missing his former boss by days.

When he arrived in Carmel in early November 1908, Upton Sinclair found a world nearly as rustic as his Adirondack campsites. The nearest rail lines were several miles away, in Monterey, and only one or two people owned cars. There were no shops and no markets, just a one-room post office and a haphazard scattering of cabins and bungalows connected by narrow paths. Above the magnificent beach hovered pines and cypress trees, famously twisted by the constant winds off Monterey Bay. There was no electricity, no running water. Oil and kerosene lamps provided light, the water came from wells, and woodstoves were used for heat. When the thick fog rolled in from the ocean, the saturated air felt colder than the north woods in March.

But when the sun came out, as it often did during the winter months, Carmel and its environs could seem the most beautiful place on the planet. One day, Sinclair wrote to Meta, he went for a horseback ride alone on Seventeen Mile Drive. Galloping through the surf, he shouted and sang: "poetry just rolled over me." Everything about the experience was so "enthrallingly beautiful" that he thought he might find a voice teacher: he had "always been hungry to know a lot of beautiful songs, and to use what noise-making power I have . . . for my own pleasure."

Some in Carmel thought Sinclair should let himself go like this more often. Willard Huntington Wright, then the literary editor of the *Los Angeles Times,* described Carmel's writing colony in a feature story headlined "Hotbed of Soulful Culture, Vortex of Erotic Erudition." There were two main groups in the village, Wright said. The "Eminently Respectables," led by the MacGowan sisters, were polite ladies and tame gentlemen who wrote mystery novels and poetry. The merely "Respectables," led by Sterling, devoted themselves to eating and drinking, and sometimes to writing. Upton Sinclair, who was welcomed by both groups, appeared one day at a feast of fried fish and abalone presided over by Sterling. "Running a scornful eye over the steaming dishes," says Wright, Sinclair declined the offer of abalone: " 'Gormandize on poison if you will. As for me, I prefer my health.' And seating himself on a dank rock by the beach, he took a raw tomato from his pocket and consumed it with masticatory unction."

The heavy drinking of Sterling and his friends, who thought of themselves as West Coast bohemians, was no joke to Sinclair. One day, late in the year, the two new friends were traveling by ferry from San Francisco to Oakland, where Sinclair was to give a lecture at the Ruskin Club. Leaning over the side of the boat, Sterling had composed what struck Sinclair as a brilliant impromptu poem inspired by the shimmering iridescence of the bay's oily water. It was only when they walked down the gangplank after they docked that Sinclair realized Sterling was falling-down drunk. When they returned to Carmel, Sinclair delivered an ultimatum to his embarrassed host: he promised to move immediately to San Francisco the next time Sterling took a drink. Much abashed, Sterling swore he would go on the wagon and begged Sinclair to stay. He did, but only for a few more weeks.

Little remembered now as a poet, George Sterling lives on as the flamboyantly gifted Brissenden in Jack London's *Martin Eden;* his "thin lips" could form "mellow phrases of glow and glory, of haunting beauty, reverberant of the mystery and inscrutableness of life," but Brissenden was doomed by his suicidal urge to "squirm my little space in the cosmic dust whence I came." It probably helped Sinclair's effort to stop Sterling from drinking that London, the heaviest drinker of them all and the sun to Sterling's moon, was off sailing in the South Seas on the *Snark;* but it says much for Sinclair's own powerful force of personality that he was able to sway an older man he scarcely knew, especially one with such a potent urge to self-destruction as George Sterling. Their friendship would endure as an important part of Sinclair's life for another eighteen years.

═══

In early January 1909, rested and anxious to get back to work, Sinclair moved to San Francisco, where he would stay for nearly four months. There he tried his hand as a playwright, made a new friend, and confirmed the enmity of an old antagonist: the hated American press.

The three one-act plays that Sinclair wrote and whose production he partly subsidized in San Francisco were earnest explications of socialist complaints, of little general appeal then or now. Another play, however, based on his novel *Prince Hagen,* is of interest for its idealized self-portrait of Sinclair as a dashing young hero who dares to challenge powerful forces with his art: in the opening scene a young man with "wavy auburn hair," wearing "old corduroy trousers and a grey flannel shirt, open at the throat," summons the spirits of the underworld with his impassioned violin rendition of the Nibelungen theme.

One sympathetic spirit who responded to Sinclair's summons was a middle-aged woman named Dell Munger, a recent convert to socialism who had separated from her wealthy husband. She invited Sinclair to stay with her and her several children at their rambling house in Palo Alto. Born in 1862, Dell grew up poor in western Kansas, surviving tornadoes, blizzards, and drought, as described in her 1912 novel, *The Wind Before the Dawn*. The local reviewer emphasized the novel's maternal qualities—it was "a nice, slouchy, comfortable affair, like a mother's lap," infused with a "big-hearted mother love," and reflecting "the moving spirit of modern motherhood." Indeed, her many later letters to Sinclair show that Dell was everything to him, if only briefly, that his own mother had long since ceased to be: warm, generous, and sympathetic to his unorthodox solutions for social problems.

Dell Munger's own offbeat solution to health problems—which she, like Sinclair, connected to social problems—was fasting. According to Sinclair, she took up fasting after years of suffering as a bedridden invalid, with sciatica, acute rheumatism, "a chronic intestinal trouble which the doctors called 'intermittent peritonitis,' " as well as from "intense nervous weakness, melancholy, and chronic catarrh, causing deafness." Now she was capable, after a four-day fast, of riding horseback with Sinclair for twenty-eight miles, up Mount Hamilton, north of San Jose, "in one of the most terrific rain-storms I have ever witnessed."

Sinclair wrote constantly to Meta about his adventures in California, including instructions for David's diet and hers. As he often did, he speculated on the possibility of divorce, which she now wanted and he did not at the moment oppose. They could get a divorce in Reno quickly with "no publicity," he said. But she needed to understand that any scandal would jeopardize his "future existence as a writer": "I know as well as I know my name that any charges you made would be printed in every paper in the U.S." Sinclair signed himself affectionately with Meta's pet name for him: "Mubs" (my husband).

Meta did not respond to Sinclair's suggestions concerning divorce, perhaps because of disturbing signs of mental imbalance in her current off-again, on-again lover, the mercurial Armistead Collier. Collier, working on a newspaper in Tennessee, in April invited his "dear Ole Tiger-Princess" to come to live with him. He envisioned her "lying under the trees, which are cool and full of the sweet, soft music of the winds." Sinclair had given him permission "to make love to you," so why should she resist? Why indeed, other than the fact that Collier also ranted about having to work with "sons of bitches" and vowed revenge upon some unseen enemy: "When a man threatens me, even in conception, because of my devotion to principle, it calls for blood." Meta's absent husband, writing about making yogurt with the motherly Mrs. Munger, must have seemed appealingly placid by comparison with the manic Collier.

Then again, her husband's equilibrium was none too steady. Even as Sinclair was worrying that the press would pillory him for getting a divorce, he was granting an interview to the *San Francisco Examiner,* in the course of which he was asked why he seemed to have such a low opinion of marriage. Off and running, Sinclair said, "You might as well ask me why I am so prejudiced against slavery—or against thievery—or . . . murder. Marriage in this day is nothing but legalized slavery. . . . The average married woman is bought just exactly as much as any horse or any dog is bought. . . . Marriage! Faugh! It really isn't a subject to be discussed at the table."

Despite this outburst, and for all his talk about divorce, Sinclair was no more able to live without Meta than with her. In late April 1909, he went back east, moving with Meta and David into a beach house on Long Island for the summer. He had a new secretary—Dave Howatt, a high school classmate of Harry Kemp's—and a new book to write.

———

Lighter in tone than his earlier works, *Samuel the Seeker* is an allegorical novel; its hero once again suggests Christian in *Pilgrim's Progress,* or the "guileless fool" exemplified by Voltaire's Candide. Like Candide (and like Jurgis in *The Jungle*), Samuel leaves home and is systematically abused and mistreated, until at the end he discovers happiness—as with Jurgis, in the form of socialism. Once again, there was a good deal of Sinclair himself in the character of Samuel—"an Enthusiast," naively inclined to believe what he was told, "especially if it was something beautiful and appealing." (Sinclair's self-image is also reflected in a minor character, a "pale ascetic-looking boy" with "wavy hair and beautiful eyes" who plays the violin.) Samuel, like Sinclair, is "given to having ideals and to accepting theories." No sooner was he "stirred by some broad new principle" than he would "set to work to apply it with fervor." An incorrigible innocent, Samuel is not really a fool. He knew when things "went wrong," and—very much like Sinclair—"according to his religion, he sought the reason, and he sought persistently, and with all his might. If all men would do as much the world might soon be quite a different place."

Samuel the Seeker was too slight to appeal greatly to publishers. Sinclair could get no more than a $200 advance for it, with another $300 upon publication, from B. W. Dodge—it was barely enough to take himself, with Meta and David, back to Battle Creek in late August for another try at healthy living and, perhaps, reconciliation.

≡

Much to Dr. Kellogg's distress, the Sinclair family stayed not at the San but across the street with Bernarr Macfadden—that hateful, "harebrained, posturing, bare-chested, dumbbell-thumping parody" of himself, in T. C. Boyle's phrase. The price was right for Sinclair: he would write a few articles for Macfadden's *Physical Culture* magazine in return for food and free lodging, in two tents once again, on the grounds of the Macfadden Health Home. Sinclair was untroubled by Macfadden's already outlandish reputation as a health fanatic and showman. It was more important that Macfadden had been one of the first to praise "Upton St. Clair" for exposing the Meat Trust.

As the publisher of a string of magazines including *True Story* and *True Crime* and the first of the tabloids, *The Graphic,* Macfadden would later achieve a degree of notoriety matching Rupert Murdoch's today, though he was a much more entertaining personality. Macfadden's motto was "weakness is a crime: don't be a criminal." A former professional wrestler, he often enlivened his popular lectures on fitness by allowing his wife, a sturdy woman wearing pink tights, to leap from a table onto his stomach as he lay beneath her on the stage, wearing only a loincloth. The first issue of his flagship magazine, *Physical Culture,* in 1900, included an article entitled "Why I Adopted Grass as a Diet."

A devout believer in the enjoyment of sex as a natural function, Macfadden invented a device he called a "peniscope" that somehow helped a tired businessman lift his flagging libido. More practically, he advocated "health homes" like his in Battle Creek. Similar in communal principle to Helicon Hall, the Battle Creek program differed in its emphasis on activities relating to the body—special diets, fasting, exercise, and, by implication at least, sex: "Leave your old-fogy" notions of restraint and conventionality at home, he warned his followers. The single object of all their efforts should be to "develop the powers, the intensity and beauties of youth. All sorts of active games will be encouraged."

Macfadden's roguish reputation did not prevent such proper young southern ladies as Mary Craig Kimbrough, then in residence at the San with her ailing mother, from crossing the street to hear a lecture by the celebrated author of *The Jungle,* Upton Sinclair. She liked young Mr. Sinclair's quick stride, his casual attire of flannels and tennis shoes, and his interested response to the book she told him she was writing about Jefferson Davis's daughter. She agreed with the cousin who had introduced them that he was "very sweet-looking when he smiles." And she was entertained by the self-deprecating humor of his lecture on fasting, a quality that she was slightly surprised to find in such a famous social reformer.

Craig, as she was called, also liked Sinclair's pretty young wife, Meta. They were close in age—Craig was then twenty-six, Meta twenty-eight—and both thought of themselves as "new women." For Meta, a New York girl with a spotty education, Craig was something of an exotic bloom. The refined and indulged daughter of a Mississippi judge and plantation owner, she had left home in Greenwood at thirteen to attend the Mississippi State College for Women. At sixteen, she enrolled in the Gardner School for Young Ladies in New York. Craig had been trained to be "serene," and to speak with a low voice that would accentuate her charming accent. ("She could, of course, make nothing of the letter r," Sinclair noted, "and said 'funnichuh' and 'que-ah' and 'befo-ah mawning.' ") She knew and apparently followed all the rules of behavior appropriate for a young lady of good family, but it was a mark of her independence that Craig had rejected several suitors for her hand in marriage. She also had a very good mind, a fact not immediately obvious to Sinclair. ("Take her away," Meta said her husband told her after his first meeting with Craig: "She bores me.")

Into this interesting mix of characters now came the boxcar poet, Harry Kemp, cheerful and hard-muscled after a summer working on the Great Lakes ore boats. Kemp was acquainted not only with Sinclair but with Macfadden, having worked in 1905 as a laborer in the ill-fated Physical Culture City. More inclined at that time to dissipation than discipline, Kemp had been a self-described "ailing, red-eyed wreck" when he showed up in PC City. His spirits were revitalized not by Macfadden's strict rules governing diet and alcohol, but by his nonchalant acceptance of nudity. Finding Macfadden and Sinclair together in Battle Creek struck Kemp as a wonderful conjoining of revolutionaries.

Building on their earlier acquaintance, he now let it be known that he revered Sinclair as America's Rousseau, "more a-flame than ever for the utter reformation of mankind." In the main, Kemp admired Sinclair and agreed with his positions on art and life, particularly his insistence that outdated notions of religion and marriage be abandoned, and that "freedom in every respect be granted to men and women." For Kemp, Sinclair was that rare bird, the dreamer who tried to live out his ideals, not merely to write about them for others.

But Kemp also thought life with such a zealous reformer might be hard on his wife and son, as he explains in his autobiographical novel, *Tramping on Life*. David, called "Dan" in the book, reminded Kemp of Sinclair in appearance, with a large head on a still frail body. The boy, who was then eight years old, took a shine to the brawny adventurer. Because he seemed hungry a good deal of the time, Kemp one day bought him a thick sirloin steak at a restaurant in town. Questioned afterward by his father, David admitted that he had been led astray by Kemp. He was not beaten this time, as he had once been when he allowed a train porter to bring him a tongue sandwich, but Sinclair let Kemp know that his trust had been betrayed. He hoped it would not happen again. Kemp acquiesced, but he was not very repentant. Sinclair "actually kept a vegetarian dog," he noted wonderingly: "It lacked gloss and shine to its coat, and seldom barked."

Meta appears in Kemp's novel as "Hildreth," a languid, sensuous woman with heavy dark hair, a small head, and large, thoughtful brown eyes. She "walked about in bloomers," clearly proud of her lovely legs. As she had done before with Collier and Kuttner, Meta responded warmly to Kemp's poetry and the attention he lavished upon her.

The new friends parted in September 1909, the Sinclairs to travel south for the winter, Kemp, the aging undergraduate, to return to college. Kemp jokingly told a friend that he looked forward to seeing Sinclair and his wife again some time. Meta was a "mighty pretty woman." He thought that maybe he'd go "run away" with her.

CHAPTER SEVEN

THE PILGRIM OF LOVE

(October 1909–February 1912)

Fairhope, Alabama, so promisingly named, was a small artists' community on the eastern shore of Mobile Bay. For Sinclair it met the need for a quiet, warm place to work on his books. For Meta it had the appeal of being only sixty miles from Mary Craig Kimbrough's vacation home in Gulfport. The two women had become close friends at Battle Creek, and Meta spent the month of October with Craig, leaving David with his father.

Few American writers have revealed so much of themselves in their work as Upton Sinclair. But the image that he projected during his earlier years was a paradoxical combination of two selves. The exterior self was that of the warrior who used his art as a means to improve conditions for all Americans. He was the resolutely assertive interpreter and guide who never doubted the wisdom of his many stands. Above all, he was an optimist, a buoyant if often outraged progressive, certain that a fruitful life for all Americans, based on the shared ideals of social justice, could be realized through socialism.

But Sinclair's interior self was still that of the frustrated artist who felt his sensibility was trammeled by an unappreciative family and a materialistic American society. Trapped and harried, he led a life of unquiet desperation. He was often angry, sarcastic, depressed. He was not suicidal, like Arthur Stirling, or any longer a "penniless rat." But he felt that his survival as an artist was threatened by his obligations as a husband and father.

Both selves were fully in evidence for Sinclair's reading public in the two books he wrote or began at Fairhope: *The Fasting Cure,* a self-help guide to better health, and *Love's Pilgrimage,* his lengthy and candid novel about his life with Meta.

The Fasting Cure, consistent with the promise of its title, is Sinclair's effort to persuade his readers that fasting will help them as much as it helped him and others, like Dell Munger. In a related article entitled "A New Helicon

Hall," he praises Bernarr Macfadden for revealing to him "the greatest discovery of my life: the deadly nature of the cooking process, which destroys the health-giving properties, incites to gluttony, and is the cause of 95 per cent of the diseases of the human race."

Dedicated to Macfadden, *The Fasting Cure* first appeared in the form of two long magazine articles in 1910, which were then expanded into book form for publication in May 1911. The book jacket was adorned with before-and-after pictures of the author, intended to illustrate his "really extraordinary recuperation" after taking the cure he recommends. Sinclair blames his own problem on his southern boyhood diet, replete with fried chicken, gravy, mashed potatoes, cakes, candies, and ice cream. If he had a weakness in terms of personal indulgence, Sinclair said many times during his life, it was for this kind of food—he once told Meta he was a "food *drunkard*," capable of gorging himself on "ice cream and cake, chocolates, taffy." Bad food, and lots of it, seemed essential, to the point that when he started earning his own money at fourteen he spent 75 percent of it on food. His health problems, he said, began at the same time, when he started writing for his living. They ended only when Macfadden showed him that unassimilated food in the body produces poisons, "and that in adjusting the quantity of food to the body's exact needs lay the secret of perfect health." Fasting was an essential part of his own dietary regimen, Sinclair said, and he thought it should be for many others as well.

Apparently as incapable of moderation in his newfound nostrum as he had been in his earlier gluttony, Sinclair now praises fasting as "the key to eternal youth, the secret of perfect and permanent health. . . . Nature's safety-valve, an automatic protection against disease." He doesn't pretend that it's useful for smallpox or typhoid, but when he feels the slightest hint of a cold "or a headache, a feeling of depression, or a coated tongue" he turns to the fast immediately. He warns against taking it up casually, but is unmoved by reports of deaths from fasting: "It would be an argument for fasting if it saved any of them. It is no argument against fasting that it fails to save them all." We don't charge the family physician with murder, he concludes, simply because a patient dies.

Sinclair included in *The Fasting Cure* some of the hundreds of letters he said the magazine articles had generated, testimonials swearing that the writers have been cured of syphilis, appendicitis, and cancer, not to mention the common cold. One man felt compelled to testify that when he fasted he realized he must have had "many years of filth" residing in his body, for "the amount of putridity that came from my bowels during the first twenty-five days of the fast was amazing."

Intermittently leavened by flashes of good sense, often irresponsibly exaggerated, *The Fasting Cure* is a curious book. It reveals the side of Sinclair that would cause many, including H. L. Mencken, to reproach him for never meeting a fad he didn't love and, more seriously, for his susceptibility to quackery.

Love's Pilgrimage was a much more interesting exercise in self-revelation. Mencken and others among Sinclair's contemporaries, including Floyd Dell and Robert Herrick, greatly admired it for its frank realism. Dell in particular argued that it was "a masterpiece," one of the "great American novels." The Dutch critic Frederick van Eeden went Dell one better, writing to Sinclair that he thought the novel deserved to be ranked among the great books of the world, and would enhance his already large reputation in Europe. Van Eeden was especially impressed by Sinclair's description of childbirth, which he thought outdid Zola: it was "more human, more poetic." Jack London, to whom Sinclair had sent a prepublication copy of the novel via Harry Kemp, provided the author with a predictably virile reaction: *Love's Pilgrimage* was "the rawest, reddest meat that has been slammed at any American publisher in the last five decades. All I'm afraid of is that you won't find a publisher with guts enough to bring the book out."

Mitchell Kennerley, an adventurous young Irish immigrant who would publish the American edition of D. H. Lawrence's *Sons and Lovers* in 1913, took a chance on Sinclair's novel, which initially sold quite well, more than a thousand copies a week after it appeared in March 1911. While some sections of *Love's Pilgrimage* do have literary power, the novel is, at more than six hundred pages, a bloated *Portrait of the Artist as a Young Man*. Sinclair was no less obsessed with the picture of himself as a confined young genius than James Joyce was, but his self-portrait lacked the objectifying irony and discipline that make Joyce's novel so effective. Sinclair's admirers were swept away by the book's virtues of candor and passion, but also by its message, which appealed to many intellectuals at this time. As William Bloodworth writes in a later analysis, the villain of the novel is "the bondage of love when it is institutionalized in marriage." The section titles of the novel reflect its theme: Thyrsis (Sinclair) is "The Victim," love is "The Snare," sexual intercourse is "The Bait," childbirth is "The Capture Is Completed," and married life is "The Treadmill."

Sinclair was describing the disintegration of his marriage, and reading parts of it to Meta at Fairhope while he wrote it, even as he was trying to hold on to her. As revealing as the lengthy *Love's Pilgrimage* in this regard is a short play, little more than a sketch, that took him only two days to write at Fairhope. He called it *The Naturewoman*. The heroine, raised on a desert island, comes home to Boston to claim her inheritance over the objections of her stuffy relatives. She is a composite of Meta's characteristics as Meta was and as Sinclair wanted her to be: "a girl of twenty-two, superbly formed, dark-skinned, a picture of glowing health. She is clad in a short skirt and a rough sailor's reefer with cap to match; underneath this a knitted garment, tight-fitting and soft—no corsets. . . . Her actions proceed from a continual overflow of animal health. She is like a little child, in that she cannot remain physically still for very long at a time; she moves about the room like an animal in a cage."

Sinclair's repeated insistence that marriage was a trap, even as he tried to keep his wife, naturally confused Meta. So also did his efforts to be generous and understanding, as when, eighteen months earlier, he had suggested that he and Alfred Kuttner and Meta go off to Germany together. There was no reason why he and Alfred couldn't be friends; after all, they both liked to play tennis. "You and Alfred would have music and German and books" and they could all go to the theater and the opera together. That trip had not transpired, but Kuttner was still in the picture. In January 1910, he had come to stay for several weeks in Gulfport with Mary Craig Kimbrough, and to continue his affair with Meta, who had returned to be with her lover. In March, Kuttner came to visit Fairhope for a few days. After he left, Meta told Sinclair she wanted to take David and visit her parents. Sinclair did not object, though it was clear to him that Meta intended to see Kuttner again once they were both back in New York. He stayed in Fairhope for another month, working on the novel that described the collapse of his marriage.

Sinclair's letters during that month reveal the depth of his love for Meta and his distress at her affair with Kuttner. In a "Dear Wiffie" letter he says she "will never know what you did to me," but he can't live without her. He feels "like the man who sat in a furnace shrieking for an iceberg, then after half an hour on the iceberg is dying to get back into the furnace." Was there no halfway point where they could be happy together? If they do reunite, she must understand that "the period of love affairs is past." Or at least, he says—apparently not realizing how he is undercutting himself—if she does have an affair, she has to go away to do it and not return until it's over.

In another letter, Sinclair links company, food, and sex, saying that with each it seems always to be a matter of too much or too little. He understands her own need better now: "You told me that your soul was all eaten thru with cravings; and it is the same with me. And yet I am not naturally sensual, nor are you. Let us not go apart for long periods any more, and let us not indulge in excesses. . . . If you go with A, do not give yourself up to reckless self-indulgence . . . to wanton and undignified things. . . . I will never again try to live near you on the basis of celibacy." He promises "to treat our love as something precious and rare."

Finally, he pleads with Meta to forgive him. He sees now that he has been "clinging to an outworn moral code," the basis of which is David. They will have no more children together. He wants only her happiness: "You may go ahead and do whatever you please. I won't ask and I won't worry. Only don't spend too much money." If Alfred—Erik the sun-god—wants her, it's up to Alfred to pay her expenses. He concludes by saying he's leaving soon for Arden, where he will put up some tents and "be ready for you any time you choose to come there"—but without Alfred, "please—I can't stand any more of that for a while."

═══

In April 1910, Sinclair left Fairhope for Arden, just north of Wilmington, Delaware. Arden sounded like Eden to him, having many of the elements he had liked most about Helicon Hall: bucolic surroundings, easy access to a big city (Philadelphia), and congenial companions, including his old investigative companion, Ella Reeve. Mother Bloor, as she had become known, lived just a block away with her new husband, Lucien Ware, and her son, Hal, who had taken his stepfather's name.

Even more important for Sinclair, Arden had none of Helicon Hall's drawbacks: he didn't have to run the place, invest money in it, or put up with the lack of privacy that living in one building entailed. It did not lessen Arden's appeal that for much of the nearly two-year period that Sinclair lived there, from the spring of 1910 until early in 1912, he was its most important person. Moreover, he seemed to have regained control of his tumultuous marriage, at least during the first months of his stay in Arden; Alfred had finally faded from the picture.

Sinclair had been drawn to Arden through the network of wealthy industrialists who were willing to help social activists. Some, like Wilshire and Wayland, underwrote magazines, or, like King Gillette, the "razor king" who would later be Sinclair's good friend, wrote books arguing for economic and social reform. Some, like Chicago plumbing magnate Charles Crane, gave grants to individuals—one of Crane's beneficiaries was Harry Kemp. A few contributed to experimental communities like Fairhope, funded by Boston paper manufacturer Fiske Warren, and to Arden, whose angel was Joseph Fels, of the Fels Naphtha soap fortune. This web of wealthy supporters tied radicals around the country together; it formed an answer of sorts to the "interlocking directorates" of corporate executives and similar establishment figures about whom Sinclair so often complained.

The single-tax idea on which communities like Fairhope and Arden were based derived from Henry George's economic treatise, *Progress and Poverty* (1879). George argued that inequities in wealth and power grew out of monopolistic ownership of land. He held that land value was a creation of the community, not of the individual; thus all land should be owned by the community and leased to individuals at reasonable cost. Land currently owned by individuals should be taxed so heavily that it would no longer pay them to keep it: that "single tax" could generate all the money needed to reform society.

The political single-tax movement that sprang up after *Progress and Poverty* was published had faded by the early 1890s. Socialists then and later, including Sinclair, thought the single-tax solution did not go far enough, and most Democrats and Republicans thought it went much too far. But its appeal remained strong for idealists like Frank Stephens, a Philadelphia sculptor, and his friend Will Price, a local architect. In 1901 the two men bought a 162-acre farm between Wilmington and Philadelphia for $9,000, about a quarter of what Sinclair paid for Helicon Hall. Joseph Fels secured the mortgage. A key provision of the charter for the new community that was to grow there involved holding all land in common. Rent would be paid to the governing board of trustees, who would use it as needed for community services.

Stephens and Price called their experiment Arden, after the duke's forest in *As You Like It*. The entry side of the town's arched gateway was inscribed "You are welcome hither," from *King Lear*. The reverse side, visible to those leaving the community, read "If we do meet again, why we shall smile," from *Julius Caesar*. By the time Sinclair arrived, Arden had acquired considerable charm, much of which a visitor can observe today. At its heart was the village green, or common, nearly as large as a football field. One end was fenced off and set aside as a clay tennis court, adjoined by a baseball diamond, but most of it was closely trimmed, as though sheep had grazed on it. Around the other end of the green were a forge, several gift shops, a hotel, a community center, an ice cream parlor, a guild hall for traveling players, and an outdoor theater for the inhabitants' own productions and informal meetings.

The theater had three rows of terraced seats, surrounded by a hedge. On summer evenings Frank Stephens might read selections from "Brer Rabbit," or Sinclair would recite anecdotes from a London physician's *Sixpenny Pieces*—so called because the doctor had charged just sixpence for his services. Saturday evenings during the summer were set aside for Shakespeare's lighter plays, *As You Like It* and *A Midsummer Night's Dream* being the favorites.

There was no community kitchen, one of the key departures from Sinclair's Helicon Hall. But the colonists could gather in the community hall for games or sing-alongs, or attend classes in literature, art, economics—and even in Esperanto, which gave Sinclair, as he liked to joke, the ability to say "Mi desiras lo puddingo" when asking for dessert at the inn. Many residents liked to play the game invented in 1903 by Lizzie Magie, a young Quaker from Virginia who had lived at Arden for several years. "Landlord" was a board game that involved buying and selling properties; its purpose was to illustrate the evils of such activities. Thirty years later, in the depths of the Great Depression, Lizzie Magie Phillips needed money for her sick husband's medical care. She sold the rights to her Landlord game for $500 to the Parker Brothers company, which called it Monopoly. Millions of young Americans have since grown up experiencing the joys of growing rich through cut-throat wheeling and dealing for property, thanks to Lizzie Magie's ingenious effort to teach them that such activities are socially destructive.

A dozen or so modest houses lined the remaining areas adjoining the green. One of them was Sinclair's newly completed (in March 1911) two-story cottage, which allowed him to move out of the tent he had been occupying. It had a living room with a fireplace and enough space so that he no longer needed to rent the one-room cabin next door, owned by the young economist, Scott Nearing, as a study. Behind his cottage were two additional tents, one of which Meta stayed in during the warm weather; the other was set aside for David. There was more than enough room for guests; among these were the Sinclairs' new friends, Mary Craig Kimbrough and, a week later, Harry Kemp.

Craig had finished a draft of her book about Winnie Davis, "The Daughter of the Confederacy," the previous autumn. In December, she came to New York to see if she could find a publisher. Meta introduced her to Gaylord Wilshire and his young wife, Mary, whom he had married in 1906, and through them to the growing number of people who liked and admired Sinclair. This was for Craig a time of intellectual awakening. She found delight in visiting the Metropolitan Museum of Art, which "had bored me during my schoolgirl days," and in hearing Paderewski at Carnegie Hall. She attended lectures by John Dewey, Harry Laidler (a founder, with Sinclair, of the Intercollegiate Socialist Society), and Graham Phelps Stokes, Sinclair's old friend, yet another "millionaire Socialist." It was "the opening up of a new world" to her, of serious young people who never—or hardly ever—flirted and rarely smiled.

One such new acquaintance was Walter Lippmann, who asked her about the economic status of Negroes in the delta. She responded innocently that she wasn't aware that they had any. She also met Sinclair Lewis, who talked about his time at Helicon Hall and tried to seduce her, reaching under the table in a Greenwich Village bistro to press her knee. "Is that the way you make love in New York?" she asked politely. He desisted.

By April, Craig was "becoming a radical" through reading Henry George, more excited by selling a "chatty, foolish little story" to Bernarr Macfadden for $25 than by her "prim, sentimental" story of Winnie Davis. Nevertheless, she was willing to hear Upton Sinclair's opinion of it when he called and invited her for a walk on Riverside Drive. He was visiting his mother, who lived nearby. Craig was uncertain as to the propriety of meeting with a married man, but he had nothing on his mind other than to tell her to forget her Winnie book: it was "terrible." She was not hurt by this severe judgment, fully agreeing.

The morning was chilly, and so Sinclair and Craig walked briskly, too quickly for her comfort. Sinclair said he was suffering from poor circulation caused by overwork and needed to keep moving. She had not seen him since Battle Creek, and thought he looked careworn. She took note of his shabby, wrinkled flannel trousers, his tattered coat, his worn tennis shoes (contrasting so strangely with his elegant yellow kid gloves), his uncut light, wavy hair. With the directness that was part of her character, she asked him what had happened to the rest of the money he had made from *The Jungle.* He said he had spent it all on propaganda. She told him about her sale to Macfadden. He said he would be happy to look at whatever else she might write, not so much for her own sake but because she might make "good copy" for him. As they parted, Sinclair told Craig that he would ask his friend George Sterling to call on her. He didn't have time to see Sterling himself because he was "having some marital problems." As he hurried away, Sinclair seemed to Craig to be "small and pathetic."

A few days later, Craig writes in her autobiography, *Southern Belle,* a man appeared at her door, tall and slender, darkly handsome, elegantly dressed. She waited quizzically for him to speak as he stared at her. His first word was "Goddess!" He was George Sterling, he said, dropping to one knee. She was a "star in alabaster"; he was thunderstruck to find "such a heavenly being on this earth." She was his "Bay-ah-tree-chay," she heard him say—the Beatrice to his Dante. She laughed at Sterling's histrionics, but the next day he sent her a poem, a sonnet "To Craig," and invited her to walk with him on Riverside Drive. There they ran into Sinclair, who looked tired and told her she looked terrible, "like a skull." Sterling took offense and Sinclair apologized for his abruptness. The men shook hands and Sinclair walked away. Sterling explained to Craig what she already knew, that Sinclair and his wife had been "on the brink of a smash-up for a long time." Sterling was sorry for Sinclair, he said, but that didn't excuse his unforgivable rudeness to Craig. She answered that she had lost weight; she did look like a skull. "I know it, and if he were not a married man I'd want to marry him. He's the first one who ever told me the real truth."

Craig omitted any mention of Meta in her autobiography. She also implied that she was not present at Arden during the summer of 1911, although Sinclair himself confirms in *American Outpost* that she was there: "Corydon, Thyrsis and Craig settled themselves in the little cottage on the edge of the Forest of Arden," soon to be joined by Harry Kemp, the boxcar poet, "lugging two suitcases full of books and manuscripts, plus an extra blue shirt and a pair of socks." Kemp's own novelized version of the events that followed his arrival suggests that Craig had more than literary affairs on her mind. But Kemp too was describing events and his role in them with an eye to how his readers would regard him. Both Craig and Kemp were imposing meaning after the fact on a series of events that happened more by chance than by design, Craig by means of elision and misdirection, Kemp by invention and exaggeration. Augmented by Sinclair's own accounts, the events at Arden and their aftermath take on a dramatic quality of some intensity. For Sinclair the play would be a tragedy, for his wife and Harry Kemp a comic ménage à trois.

Kemp came to Arden at Sinclair's invitation. After their meeting at Macfadden's two years earlier, he wrote an effusive fan letter to Sinclair ("you great-souled and noble-hearted man") that prompted Sinclair to recommend him to Joseph Fels as deserving of a cash subsidy. He knew Kemp "intimately," Sinclair wrote (on the basis of their two meetings). He was "a man without a vice," who didn't "drink or smoke" or chase women. His whole life was his poetry, which had the "enormous" power needed to match his towering ambition. Although George Bernard Shaw wrote Fels that he thought little of Kemp's talent, the soap magnate agreed to send the young poet $250, based on Sinclair's recommendation. Kemp could hardly find the words to express his gratitude to Sinclair: "How can I ever thank you for this, or repay you?" To have such a friendship was "almost like the love of God."

The two friends had continued to correspond, Kemp sending his mentor manuscripts and asking for advice on his love life. He was still a virgin at twenty-seven, he claimed. Sinclair responded that he was holding out for the wrong kind of woman, the "clinging, tender, delicate" bourgeois maiden who reads the *Ladies' Home Journal.* What Harry needed was "a free, strong, independent spirit"—who would also be willing to take instruction from him.

═══

Arden in mid-July, when Harry Kemp arrived, struck him as a medieval village that had been re-created by William Morris's Arts and Crafts followers. It was as though the Canterbury pilgrims had been settled into toy cottages, painted in various colors, situated among the trees, linked by paths of meticulously placed multicolored pebbles. A "tousle-headed girl in rompers" that she had outgrown directed Kemp to the Sinclair cottage. There was little furniture aside from a Morris chair and a long low shelf beneath the single large window, strewn with cushions. Sinclair greeted Kemp warmly. He seemed to Kemp to have gained some weight. His body was now "stocky," his head "Napoleonic," his "large, luminous eyes like those of the Italian fisher boy" in a painting he recalled seeing.

Sinclair introduced his secretary, Ellen Barrows, a tall, angular, tanned woman with intelligent hazel eyes, an amused expression, and a good mind for poetry. It was clear that Sinclair hoped Ellen and Harry would become more than casual friends.

Meta—"Hildreth" in Kemp's account—was lounging on the cushions beneath the large window when he entered. As she put down her Gorky novel and turned toward him, Kemp was overwhelmed by her sensuousness; she exuded a "sweet aroma" from her "body, bosom, hair—a tumbly black mass—as perfume breathes from a wild flower."

A third woman entered the room as Kemp was staring at Meta: "Mary Darfield Malcolm," i.e. Mary Craig Kimbrough, fresh from a dip in the stream that ran behind the house. Her hair was still wet and wrapped in a towel, and she wore only a filmy yellow negligee with blue ribbons. She had dark brown eyes and her skin was as pure and pale as alabaster. Her cheeks were dimpled. She spoke in a slow drawl that seized each word "by the tail and caressed its back as it came out."

Sinclair recalled Kemp's arrival as a joyous infusion of creative energy: he was a "naive and lovable" young man, a "geyser of poetic activity" who wrote all night and read his poems aloud all day, wandering through the flowery meadows and dells of Arden. He was that rare phenomenon in Sinclair's life: a friend whom he could admire and love. A photo of the two men at Arden shows them with arms companionably draped across each other's shoulders. Sinclair wears a white shirt, sleeves buttoned, tie knotted. One hand is on his hip, the other arm reaches up to Kemp's shoulder, a stretch, for he is nearly a head shorter. Kemp's right hand rests lightly on Sinclair's shoulder. His sleeves are carelessly rolled up, his tie askew, and he is grinning into the camera. Kemp's easy insouciance contrasts vividly with Sinclair's affectionate vulnerability.

The two men took long walks along the stream and through the fields that adjoined Arden, talking about their work, about their plans, about the eternal mysteries revolving around women. The reviews for *Love's Pilgrimage* were just appearing. They augured well for Sinclair as an artist, but he was afraid his chances for personal success in love had passed him by. Harry was younger, he said, and still had a chance. According to Kemp, Sinclair proposed a "love program" for Kemp that included a warning not to be seduced by Meta after she was free—a freedom that seemed uncertain, as she for some reason was still unwilling to agree to a divorce, which Sinclair now said he wanted. Meta, Sinclair warned, was a beautiful trap, "hysterical, parasitic, passionate, [and] desperate." He reminded Kemp of Edward Carpenter's old metaphor of man as the oak and woman as the clinging vine that eventually strangles it; he had been the oak to Meta's vine. Harry should find a "free, strong, independent spirit," a woman with "an intellect as well as sensibility." Ellen Barrows would be an appropriate match for him.

Kemp reacted, he said, with amused bewilderment to Sinclair's earnest advice: "how utterly bookish, how sheerly a literary man" Sinclair was, and "how absurd" in trying to order everything, including human relationships, according to his theories. Coffee, for example, was "poison" to Sinclair. While he had to tolerate its use by Meta and the other women in his household, they took care to keep the pot out of sight when he came down for breakfast and to wave their aprons to disperse its aroma. Sinclair, said Kemp, completely lacked a sense of humor, but often made himself a comic figure by virtue of his extreme rigidity.

The incident that triggered the dissolution of Sinclair's marriage began as a result of Sinclair's impatience with the scatological preachings of an Arden anarchist named George Brown. Brown lived with his wife, a poet, in a shack made of packing crates on the edge of the village. He eked out a living by repairing shoes, badly. He looked like Socrates, bald as a billiard ball, lumpishly ugly, with bushy red eyebrows that twitched when he was excited, which was often. Free speech and free love were Brown's twinned obsessions. Sinclair, among others, objected to Brown's frankness in discussing sexual intercourse with groups that sometimes included small children. When Brown noisily persisted, the villagers, led by Sinclair, complained to the local magistrate. The shoemaker was arrested for disturbing the peace and spent five days in the county workhouse, pounding rocks.

Brown got out of the workhouse in time for the high point of the summer for the villagers, the yearly fund-raiser that they called an old English pageant. There were booths for the ring-toss and the penny-pitch, and events such as an apple-dunking competition and a three-legged race. Some of the villagers dressed up in animal costumes—two men covered by an ox hide were a mule, Frank Stephens appeared as a matador, and a double-jointed girl writhed convincingly as a boa constrictor. Brown, playing the role of a beggar asking for alms, cast a pall on the proceedings. Wearing a burlap potato bag with openings for head, arms, and legs, he complained bitterly to all who came near him about being sent to jail. Many heard him say that two could play at the game of turning people over to the authorities.

According to *The New York Times* a few days later, some of the Ardenites played a joke on Sinclair during the circus that capped the day's entertainment. A clown dressed as a policeman marched into the audience and "arrested" Sinclair, then marched him out of the tent and through the village to the tune of a steam calliope.

Sinclair spent the Sunday morning following the carnival playing tennis with Ella's son, Hal Ware, his favorite opponent. Hal was a tall, well-built boy in his late teens with a booming serve and a slashing crosscourt forehand. Two weeks earlier he and Sinclair had played a five-set match for the village championship that Sinclair finally won. He recalled later with pardonable pride that he probably had no business winning from such a strong opponent at the advanced age of thirty-two.

On Monday afternoon, July 31, two Newcastle County sheriff's deputies appeared at Sinclair's cottage with a warrant for his arrest. He and ten others, including Hal Ware and nine men who had been playing baseball the previous morning, were charged with violating a law that prohibited "gaming on the Sabbath." The infraction of the "blue law," which dated from 1793, had been reported by George Brown. Sinclair argued in vain before the justice of the peace that the law referred to gambling, not sport; he and the others refused to pay the fine of $4 and costs per person and spent the next eighteen hours—that night and all the next day—in the Newcastle County Workhouse.

Though Sinclair did not note the connection, the setting, details, and tone of the Arden festivities, starting with the carnival and ending with the arrests, echo Nathaniel Hawthorne's story "The Maypole of Merry Mount," which describes a breakaway group of fun-seeking Puritans who are chastised by the ecclesiastical authorities. Sinclair and his fellow convicts took their punishment as a lark, treating the constable to an ice cream cone and singing songs on the trolley that took them to the workhouse. But once inside the prison walls—for the first but not the last time in his life—Sinclair took note of the vermin-infested cells and the stinking toilets, the sweatshop clothing factory where the longer-term inmates were forced to work, the lack of exercise space and fresh air. Reluctant to sleep on the cot he was given because it was infested with lice, he spent the night sitting in the middle of the floor, writing a poem to protest the conditions he saw. He gave it to the dozen newspaper reporters who waited to greet him when he was released, a celebrity once again. One couplet prompted a cell mate to shout approvingly, "That's me!" It read, "And then in sudden stillness mark the sound / — Some beast that rasps his vermin-haunted hide."

In Sinclair's absence, according to Kemp's account, tensions between Meta and Craig were growing. Meta complained to Ellen that Craig did nothing but "loaf around" bragging about her social status in the old South, her illustrious ancestors in Boston, and her many handsome beaux. At breakfast, Meta erupted in sudden anger at Craig, throwing a glass of milk in her face.

There were other tensions as well, more appealing ones for Harry and Meta. He had been aware of her exotic presence from the beginning: her dress and manner were enticing. On the evening that Sinclair was in prison they went for a long walk in the woods. She wore bloomers, a white middy blouse, and a blue bow tie, and shyly lowered her long black lashes over her brown eyes, affecting a "pretty droop" to the left corner of her mouth. They played leapfrog in the forest, as Harry put it. A few days after Sinclair returned from jail, he looked through the window of Scott Nearing's adjacent cabin and saw his best friend and his wife making love.

Sinclair now found himself in the first act of what would become a long-running drama. It was the greatest tragedy of his life, not least because for the public at large it was a long-running seriocomic spectacle, a French farce, a scandal almost as juicy as the Harry Thaw / Stanford White / Evelyn Nesbit triangle in 1906.

The immediate upshot of Sinclair's discovery of Meta's adultery was that Craig and Meta, apparently friends again, left for New York to stay at Meta's parents' apartment. Mrs. Fuller came down to look after David while Sinclair and Kemp argued over what would come next.

Harry Kemp had listened attentively to Sinclair's lectures on the need for sexual freedom and openness in marriage, and to Meta's assurances that her marriage was over in all but name. He utterly rejected Sinclair's assertions of betrayal. In his melodramatic yet comic representation of their final meeting at Arden, Kemp says he intends to join Meta in New York. He will "defy the whole damned world—the world of fake radicals that talk about divorces when the shoe pinches them, as well as the world of conservatives." Outraged, Sinclair seizes the coffee pot, pushes it into Kemp's arms, and says, "take this to your goddess, this poisonous machine, and lay it on her altar. Tell her I offered this to you. Tell her that it is a symbol of her never coming back here again." Or so Kemp says. We may doubt the precise words—the supposedly gifted poet had a tin ear for dialogue—but the action suits Sinclair's character.

Meta wrote Sinclair a few days later, after Kemp joined her, to say that she and Harry were the embodiment of the "rightness of free love." They were the "Godwin and Wollstonecraft of the age." (This was an added turn of the screw for Meta to use on her husband, whose first hero had been Shelley; the parents of Shelley's wife, Mary, were the political philosopher William Godwin and Mary Wollstonecraft, whose affair and subsequent marriage had scandalized England in the 1790s.) Meta challenged Sinclair to play by the rules of "the radical game" and not by those of the "conventional world." She reminded him of his own advice to Kemp in a letter the previous summer: when it happens that either a husband or a wife "finds that the other is hindering his or her highest intellectual and spiritual achievements, there will be agreement to part, with the best wishes and noblest unselfishness."

Incensed both by being betrayed and by having his own words thrown back at him, Sinclair wired his lawyer on August 23 that he wanted to file suit for divorce against Meta, charging adultery and naming Harry Kemp as co-respondent. Someone at the telegraph office leaked the information to the press. On August 24, 1911, Sinclair was front-page news again, not just in New York but nationwide, for the first time since the days of *The Jungle.*

The headlines during the ensuing weeks were mortifying: "Sinclair Accuses His Wife"; "Upton Sinclair Says Wife Has Left Him"; "Mrs. Sinclair Now Tells Her Side"; "Kemp's Views on Marriage—Poet Friend of Mrs. Sinclair Pleads for More Freedom"; "Mrs. Sinclair Calls Women Jellyfish"; "What! Kemp Turned Bruiser! New York Hears the Poet Is Going to 'Beat Up' Sinclair' "; "My Code Is My Own—I Don't Care, Says Mrs. Sinclair #1."

The stories below the headlines were even worse. Nothing more excites the public than the sniff of moral hypocrisy on the part of those who presume to tell others how they should behave. "The generally accepted explanation," Sinclair complained, "was that I had married an innocent young girl and taught her 'free love' doctrines, and then, when she practiced these doctrines, I kicked her out of my home." The herd, meaning the press, "had me down and proceeded to trample on my face." He felt "like a hunted animal which seeks refuge in a hole, and is tormented with sharp sticks and smoke and boiling water." He could imagine what being flayed alive felt like. His hair started turning gray. He couldn't sleep.

Yet Sinclair's own actions increased the attention he so longed to escape. He hired a private detective to track down Meta and Harry when they disappeared. Upon learning that they were in Sea Girt, New Jersey, he showed up on their doorstep to have it out with Harry, who threatened to punch him. Instead, Sinclair, Harry, and Meta held a joint news conference, on August 29 at the Imperial Hotel in Manhattan. It was a circus for the reporters, one of whom professed to be shocked that "the three seemed to be on the best of terms." Meta, remembering her Ibsen, had recently told *The New York Sun* that she had "permanently come out of the doll's house." She said now that she was looking for her soul mate, and that trial marriages were a fine idea. Harry concurred, quoting Edward Carpenter. Sinclair predictably called upon "the State" to "endow motherhood" so that a mother could be "free to support herself when she is rearing her child," presumably meaning the father could be left to his own creative devices.

The day after the press conference, Sinclair went back to Arden, while Harry, Meta, and Craig—still surprisingly on the scene—went off to yet another beach town, West Point Pleasant. The two women took one room at a boardinghouse and Harry another, using the name of Arthur Mallory. The three sunbathed together in the nude, reading aloud from Havelock Ellis's *Sex in Relation to Society,* and chatting with a pretty girl named Agnes Boulton, who was there with her mother and her three sisters. Mrs. Boulton regarded Harry, Meta, and Craig as the "play children of the feminist movement." Her own daughter, Agnes, would later marry Eugene O'Neill, the least playful of American playwrights.

Sinclair devoted the autumn months to preparing the statement for the court, the nature of which was dictated by the difficult legal hurdles any couple seeking a divorce in New York had to surmount. Adultery was virtually the only ground for a divorce. Proof of a physical act was required, but the person charged was not allowed to confess, and the married pair could not testify against each other. Moreover, if collusion was established, no divorce would be granted. Painfully aware of how vulnerable he was to charges of collusion, Sinclair tried to establish that Meta was a "depraved and embittered woman"—though not entirely to blame for her actions, coming as she did from a "family of sexual degenerates." For nearly eleven years, Sinclair swore, his marriage had been one long battle to save his wife "from the overwhelming impulses to depravity that were in her."

For her part, Meta delighted in the attention she was getting. Formerly so meek and submissive, she now boasted to reporters that she was a "varietist," while her husband was "an essential monogamist, without having any of the qualities that an essential monogamist ought to possess." She was more explicit about her precise meaning later, in her unpublished novel, saying that in all her years with Sinclair she had never experienced "the joy of a complete sexual expression." Her earlier affairs with Armistead Collier and Alfred Kuttner had offered some pleasure, but it was not until Harry Kemp sailed into her life, the lone sailor on a pirate ship, "full-masted" but "rather raw and bashful," that she had known real sexual fulfillment. Meta was ready for a "full-blooded pagan" and Harry Kemp was happy to oblige. Sinclair had insisted that she be the Corydon to his Thyrsis, after the fashion of the sexless pastoral eclogue. Kemp called himself "Kaa," the caveman, in their love games; Meta, his cave-mistress, was "Naa." Her husband, Sinclair, was on the outside looking in, as he had been when he peered through Scott Nearing's window. With casual cruelty, they called him "Baa."

This was a period of bitter humiliation for Sinclair. Recalling *Pilgrim's Progress* once again, he called it his "slough of despond." On November 19 the New York Supreme Court referee recommended granting the divorce. That recommendation was overturned on December 10 owing to a technicality, however, and in early February 1912 a final judgment was issued denying the divorce on the ground that Sinclair had been complicit in his wife's adultery. The only salve for Sinclair's pain was that the judge had not canceled his temporary custody of David, thereby confirming for Sinclair his charge that Meta was an unfit mother.

Not that Meta seemed to care, having already assured the world via a Christmas Eve press interview that she didn't "give a damn about marriage, divorce," or anything else, presumably including her son, "except being left alone with Harry"—the Harry who, "long-haired and unshorn," fingered a shotgun and suggested to the inquiring reporter that he should hit the road.

Upton Sinclair always thought of himself as a feminist, and indeed he was. But George Herron agreed with Meta that he didn't understand women. Herron had written from his home in Italy in June 1911 to thank Sinclair for the copy he had sent him of *Love's Pilgrimage,* in which Sinclair sympathetically described how Herron and Carrie Rand had been hounded out of the country. He told Sinclair he would have preferred not to see his problems discussed in print, even under a different name. More generally, he disapproved of Sinclair's aggressive and futile proselytizing for his views: Sinclair might "choke the world until it is black in the face," but that was not the way to win arguments. His biggest problem, though, was that he was entirely "befuddled" by women, failing to see their true complexity. Women, Herron said, were not breeding stock, as in Tolstoy, or conniving serpents or vampires, even though he had known some who fit this description. Herron offered no recommendation to Sinclair for overcoming his deficiency, but signed himself "affectionately" and said he hoped to see his old friend in Florence some day.

Herron's judgment was acute: women did "befuddle" Sinclair, who tended to idealize or demonize them. He could also be misled by men, as he had been by Harry Kemp. It's not so much that he failed to pick up on the obvious irony that the big project on which the traitorous Kemp was working during his stay in Arden and afterward, when he was living with Meta in their beach house, was a four-act tragedy depicting Judas as a tragic hero. Nor is being taken in by flattery a terrible fault: many great and not-so-great men have been fooled by sycophancy of the Kempian variety. It's not even a great flaw that Sinclair vastly overvalued Kemp's mediocre talents as a poet.

Sinclair's problem in evaluating human character was more serious. Although he easily saw through and exposed crooked police chiefs or financiers, he was congenitally susceptible to being gulled by a clever pose, a plausible disguise, or an honest idiot. He said as much about himself in *Love's Pilgrimage:* "If by any chance the person was insincere, and used ideas as a blind and a cover," he "might never find him out at all . . . he took people at the face-value of their cultural equipment; and only after long and tragic blunderings could he by any chance get deeper."

Sinclair's greatest handicap was his lack of the psychological sensitivity that all great writers have, not necessarily about themselves but about others. Compare his misperception of Harry Kemp with Theodore Dreiser's astute appraisal. To Dreiser, Kemp was "a disorderly blend of the charlatan, the poseur, the congenital eccentric, and the genius, or honest, sincere thinker," though it was hard to separate the charlatan from the genius. Mostly, Kemp was a "clown or court-jester," Dreiser thought, but sometimes he acted like a boisterous dog that barks and wriggles its behind hoping for a rub. Perhaps Dreiser should have added that Kemp simply didn't have enough character to feel guilty about betraying a friend.

Sinclair's comparative innocence concerning human psychology accounts for his limitations both as a literary artist and as a young husband. Although he would spend most of his career exposing what he thought was wrong with American society, he was constantly being unpleasantly surprised, like Candide, by the human potential for treachery. Yet Sinclair's naïveté afforded him a degree of protection from these disappointments, allowing him to hope, against all evidence to the contrary, for better things to come. The same innocence that helped to cause his troubles was also a renewable resource of energy that let him start anew after every disaster or setback.

But at this particular moment in his history, Upton Sinclair was suffering mightily from his mistakes, and from the actions of those he mistakenly thought he had known and understood. As he had three and a half years earlier, he chose to escape by taking a long journey. This time he would go east, to Europe, not west. And he would go not alone, but with the sole remnant of his marriage to Meta: their ten-year-old son, David.

CHAPTER EIGHT

THE SURVIVOR

(February 1912–December 1915)

S inclair and David crossed the Atlantic in February 1912, traveling "second-class in a third-class Italian steamer." The heaving slate-gray seas and killing cold matched Sinclair's mood of intense melancholy. For six months the nation's newspapers had laid bare his private life. He had been mocked, chastised, and, worst of all, pitied as a cuckold betrayed by his best friend. He felt as if he had been flayed alive, eviscerated, roasted on a hot grill. He was "sick in body and soul," not sure if he would live or die, and not caring much one way or the other. He was thirty-three years old, his marriage was finished, and his career was in ruins.

All that Sinclair had saved from the wreckage of his life, aside from his son, were the friends with whom he had kept up a steady correspondence over the years. Among the most supportive of this group were three men, each old enough to be his father, who had urged him to leave America and visit them in Europe. The first of these to learn of his problems was Frederick van Eeden, the Dutch psychoanalyst, novelist, and playwright, who lived near Amsterdam. The second was Gaylord Wilshire, who had opened his eyes to socialism and introduced him to his chief benefactor, George Herron, so many years ago; still an active socialist, Wilshire was now living in London with his young wife and their son and insisting that Sinclair stay with him as long as he liked. The third was George Herron himself, now writing diplomatic histories in Florence, where he had lived since being driven in disgrace from New York eight years earlier for his adultery with Carrie Rand. For the next ten months, these three men would provide Sinclair with the safe harbors he so desperately needed.

Sinclair's initial visit with Van Eeden was his most important, in practical terms. Its purpose was to begin divorce proceedings against Meta in Holland, where liberal courts required only one party in a divorce suit to be resident and routinely granted petitions for divorce if the second party did not oppose the suit. Van Eeden had written to inform Sinclair of this possibility the previous September, while the scandal was still hot in the press. At the time, Sinclair had believed the New York courts would grant the divorce. Now he had fallen back on Van Eeden's solution as the only one available.

Sinclair had first learned of Van Eeden through reading about his communal farm called Walden, which operated for seven years in Holland until it folded in 1905, and where he now lived on what was left of the grounds. His own Helicon Hall experiment owed something to Van Eeden, just as Van Eeden had been influenced by Thoreau—the waves of influence washed across the Atlantic Ocean in both directions. Van Eeden also tried and failed to establish a colony for Dutch immigrants in North Carolina in 1907, at which time he met Sinclair in New York. Best remembered now for his theory of "lucid dreaming," which he developed in conjunction with Sigmund Freud in 1913, Van Eeden was also deeply interested in mysticism and spiritualism. In 1909, he asked Sinclair to recommend a writer with similar interests who could translate some of his poems and plays. Sinclair put Van Eeden in touch with Harry Kemp at the University of Kansas. In November 1909, Kemp starred in a university theater production of a Van Eeden play that he also translated—appropriately, it was about the plight of a sensitive young poet, alone and scorned in a bourgeois, materialistic world.

Van Eeden thus knew as much as anyone could about the Kemp-Meta-Sinclair affair. He was typical of most European intellectuals in avoiding moral condemnation of something he regarded as a regrettable instance of American sexual immaturity and puritanism, hardly worth the fuss it had caused. He was also typical of most of the writers and social activists whom Sinclair met in his generous bonhomie—Karl Kautsky and Walter Rathenau in Germany, Peter Kropotkin, the exiled Russian anarchist, in Brighton, and dozens of lesser lights. To varying degrees, they were all genial, worldly yet idealistic intellectuals who saw no conflict between creative art and social conscience. Sinclair, Jack London, and Theodore Dreiser were to these Europeans the American writers most in tune with their own sentiments. *The Jungle* in particular had become a fixed point of literary and political reference for those who studied the United States, and Sinclair's subsequent books, up to and including *Love's Pilgrimage,* had been better received in Europe than they were at home.

Sinclair was well educated in political theory; he had read the French and German literary classics in their original tongues, not in translation; and he loved the give-and-take of conversation about ideas with people he respected, regarding it almost as a game, like tennis. This kind of enlivening talk had been one of the great appeals of Helicon Hall and Arden, and he was overjoyed to find it in abundance, especially in England and, later, in Germany. After leaving Van Eeden, he and David spent the last week of February and the first three weeks of March with the Wilshires at their rented house in Hampstead, a suburb of London. David had the Wilshires' precocious six-year-old son, Logan, for company, while Sinclair relaxed with the affable Gaylord, who seemed not to be troubled by the criminal proceedings that had caused him to move to England—he owned a gold mine in the Sierra Nevada mountains of central California, near the town of Bishop, and some disgruntled shareholders had charged him with fraud, forcing him to flee the country while his lawyers at home tried to settle the case.

Mary Wilshire, twenty years younger than her husband, was a lay psychologist from New York who had studied under Carl Jung. She had her own set of friends who welcomed Sinclair. One was an Irish aristocrat, "Mollie" Russell, a writer and friend of George Bernard Shaw and H. G. Wells. Shaw, whom Sinclair revered as the modern Voltaire, "motored" him out to lunch at his country house and talked "an endless stream of wit and laughter, with never a pause or a dull moment." Wells also took him to lunch, at the New Reform Club. Sinclair was disappointed to hear that Wells feared socialism was impossible in England for at least three hundred years. As they left the club he saw "the Grand Khan of Anglo-American literature, Henry James, eating a muttonchop," but decided against introducing himself, even though he revered James for his accomplishment in *The Ambassadors*.

Pleasant though his stay in England was, Sinclair disapproved of the country's rigid class structure, which he saw as leading to the kind of class warfare he feared. The great coal strike of 1912 was under way when he arrived in London, and he eagerly accepted an invitation to witness a debate on the strike in the House of Commons, the seat of modern democracy. He was bitterly disappointed by the performance of both the Laborite leader Arthur James Balfour and the Liberal prime minister Herbert Asquith, who seemed indifferent to the plight of the strikers: their "statesmanship" was a "hodgepodge of cant and cruelty, bundled in a grey fog of dullness." He could barely refrain from rising to his feet to protest at the sight of "rows of savages in silk hats, roaring for what little blood was left in the veins of half-starved miners' families." When he left the debate to visit historic Westminster Abbey, he did not bow his head in veneration of Chaucer, Spenser, Browning, Tennyson, and the other great writers who were buried there. Rather, he was "swept by a storm of horror and loathing" as he wandered "among marble tombs and statues of ruling class killers, and the poets and men of genius who had betrayed the muse to Mammon."

In late March, Sinclair and David went to Italy for a visit with George Herron and his wife. Despite his reservations about *Love's Pilgrimage,* Herron received Sinclair and his son warmly. His timely loan in 1903, which Sinclair credited with allowing his career to flourish, had long since been repaid, and his faith in the young writer amply rewarded. Although Sinclair enjoyed his visit—who, he asked, could "fail to be happy" under "Tuscan skies" in springtime?—he stayed only two weeks. Mrs. Herron was suffering from cancer, and Herron's certainty that war was coming cast a pall over their conversations.

Sinclair would later draw heavily on his memories of Europe to write his successful Lanny Budd novels. Considering that Lanny's cover as a spy is provided by his expertise as an art broker and connoisseur, Sinclair's comments on the art of Florence in *American Outpost* were remarkably limited. All he took away from his afternoons at the Uffizi were images of "multiplied madonnas and crucified martyrs," which reminded him of nothing so much as Tammany Hall and its Catholic machine. What Roman Catholicism meant to him, he said, was Irish Catholic cops beating up socialist strikers, Roman Catholic archbishops getting women who lecture on birth control sent to jail, and Polish Catholic judges preventing him from getting his divorce.

Sinclair had hoped to leave David with the Herrons in Florence for a few months. Herron regretfully said no. His wife was too ill, and his own health too uncertain, for them to look after a young boy for so long a time. In search of an alternative for David, father and son traveled in mid-April through Switzerland to central Germany. There they visited an experimental school that Sinclair had read about: "a lovely spot on the edge of the Harz Mountains, with a troop of merry youngsters living the outdoor life." He enrolled David in the experimental school and returned to England.

Sinclair did not reveal why he chose to leave his young son, who was undoubtedly suffering from the trauma of his parents' extended and acrimonious separation, alone in the middle of Europe—a Europe that Herron correctly thought was marching toward war. One possible explanation was provided by Craig's sister Dollie. Dollie, who was born in 1896, was thirteen years younger than Craig. In the early 1970s, many years after Craig's death, Dollie told a Sinclair biographer, Leon Harris, that Craig was pregnant by Sinclair in the spring of 1912. She came to England in late March in order to get an abortion. Dollie said her information came from Mary Wilshire, at some unspecified time.

If Dollie's account is true, then Sinclair presumably left David in Germany in order to keep him from learning the true circumstances of Craig's trip to England, and of his own relationship with Craig. There is no way of knowing how much David had observed and understood of the events at Arden the previous summer. Harris, unfortunately, never followed up on Dollie's story by asking David what he remembered. But David, who would later become a physicist, was an intelligent boy who would have been capable of putting two and two together if he had been on the scene—which, thanks to his father, he was not.

Craig claimed in *Southern Belle* that she saw nothing of Sinclair from August 1911 until the following April, when she met him, purely by chance, at Gaylord Wilshire's house in England. She simply "stayed on quietly in New York" during the period, following the counsel of her mother and an aunt, who warned her that she "must not see Mr. Sinclair while the reporters were on his trail!" Her real suitor during the fall of 1911, Craig wrote, was not Sinclair but George Sterling, the romantic San Francisco poet. Sterling asked her to marry him but Craig refused him because of his bohemian ways, even though he swore he had not taken a drink since he met her.

Craig followed Sterling's advice "not to get anywhere near" Sinclair that fall, she said, and continued to work quietly at her own writing in New York through the winter of 1912. In early March, Mary Wilshire invited her to come to England for a visit, and to meet Mollie Russell, who wanted to use Craig's life as a "Southern belle" in a novel. Craig accepted Mary's invitation. In mid-April, upon returning from a walk on Hampstead Heath, she was surprised and delighted to see that "there in the Wilshire drawing room sat Upton Sinclair, debating Socialism versus Syndicalism" with Wilshire. Their romance blossomed forthwith, in large part because, Craig wrote, Mollie Russell was "a born match-maker, and she picked me out as the future Mrs. Upton Sinclair."

Much of Craig's account is accurate enough: Sterling was indeed very fond of her, she did stay in New York as she said, she did get an invitation to come to England from Mary Wilshire. Where it is misleading, according to Dollie, is in its understandable omission of the pregnancy and consequent abortion, and in its assertion that she did not see Sinclair during the fall of 1911. No letters or documents exist to confirm Dollie's assertion. But if it is true, as seems likely from subsequent events, it would appear that what happened is this: Craig discovered she was pregnant some time after Sinclair left New York, in February 1912. She wrote to him at the Wilshires' to tell him the bad news. Sinclair asked Mary Wilshire for advice, knowing of her medical training and her familiarity with the laws governing abortion in England. Mary made the necessary arrangements and invited Craig to visit her, using Mollie Russell as a cover story. Craig arrived in March, had the abortion, and remained with the Wilshires during her recuperation. Sinclair returned to England in April without David, and met Craig at the Wilshire home. In May, the divorce from Meta was final. Craig and Sinclair could now travel openly together, in the company of Dr. van Eeden, to Germany. In August, they brought David back with them to England. David was then enrolled at a boarding school in Highgate, near the Wilshires' home in Hampstead, and would remain there for nearly two years.

Mary Craig Kimbrough and Upton Sinclair returned to the United States in December 1912—on separate ships, in order to frustrate the speculations of prying New York reporters. They were married in Fredericksburg, Virginia, on April 21, 1913. In May, they returned to Europe for a honeymoon trip of four months, bringing both David and Craig's sixteen-year-old sister, Dollie, with them. Their life together, for the next half-century, is a relatively open book—Sinclair referred often and admiringly to Craig, both directly in his nonfiction and indirectly in his fiction, and she to him in her many letters.

But there was an underlying tension between them that was never resolved. Despite his natural introversion, Sinclair was a public figure from 1906 forward. Both his ego and his sense of mission required him to be. Craig's temperament, even before she met Sinclair, inclined her toward privacy. After their marriage, in part because of the events that preceded it, she became increasingly guarded and secretive with strangers, especially those who wanted to dig into her husband's past, and her own. As late as 1938, she listened uneasily as Irving Stone, who was hoping to write a biography of Sinclair, asked him some pointed questions about his earlier relations with women. Craig had disliked Stone's approach to Jack London's complicated love affairs in his biography *Sailor on Horseback,* which had appeared earlier that year. When she heard Stone ask what "sins" Sinclair could recall committing, she abruptly canceled the interview. Sinclair reproached Stone the next day in a long letter, saying "You came and started immediately upon the subject of what you called 'sin'—my sins, to be exact." Sinclair, sensing Craig's discomfort, had tried to change the subject. "But you would not have it, and kept coming back to the same question—'What about sin?' Naturally, it made my wife extremely angry."

By the 1950s Craig's insistence on privacy was such that Western Union had to deliver its telegrams to Sinclair by throwing them over his locked gate because his wife refused to answer the doorbell or the telephone. Sinclair found his social life increasingly restricted, and many of his friends pitied him for being married to a hypochondriacal hermit. The possibly traumatic circumstances of Craig's premarital relationship with Sinclair seem to offer at least a partial explanation for her neurotic insistence on privacy. They also help to explain her uncomfortable relationship with her stepson, and even why she engineered her husband's long estrangement from David, that unwelcome reminder of a period she preferred to forget.

Craig's actions then and later need to be understood in the context of the crushing weight of public opinion on young women in 1912, especially for those who came from prominent families in the deep South. Despite her intellectual flirtation with radicalism, Craig was not an early flower child, like Meta. It took courage for her to try to make her way as a writer, and honesty to recognize that she had no calling in that respect.

Much more important than the circumstances of Craig's life before she married Upton Sinclair are the qualities that made him regard her as the single most important person in his life. It was not just that she devoted herself to advancing his career, that she ran their household efficiently, that she was highly intelligent, or that she had a lively sense of humor. It was her deeply felt sense of Sinclair's *vulnerability*.

Craig's perceptiveness is evident in an unpublished short story, written at some point before 1911, in which a young woman has a "remarkable vision" of a writer, clearly Sinclair. Her vision was "so vivid in every detail that she could have put him on canvas if she had had a painter's skill. She saw him in a sun-lit garden, where there were rose trellises and borders of pink and yellow flowers, and also paths of sharp rocks and thorn hedges, and he was a beautiful child—his face in reality was often that of a child in its wetness and openness of expression. And the beautiful child in the garden was blindfolded and stumbling along the rocky paths, wounding his bare feet on the stones, tearing his outstretched hands on the thorn trees, but always smiling with that exquisite wonder and hurt surprise with which a very sweet child meets suffering, that wonderment as to why he who meant no harm to anyone should be tormented."

Craig saw not only Sinclair's vulnerability but the essential innocence of his character. She understood him better than anyone else did, and she comforted him. Coming as he had from a near-death experience with the Meta affair, it is no wonder that he turned to Craig. In her last years, Sinclair would repay her with devoted care that seemed little short of saintly to his friends.

Craig was a good companion for Sinclair, lively and witty. On their return trip to Germany, in 1913, with Dollie and David, they had lunch in a Berlin restaurant. Sinclair quarreled with the pompous waiter, who insisted on bringing them all a huge order of pancakes that they did not want. As the waiter waddled away, Dollie shocked Sinclair by muttering "Damn his hide!" and complaining that there wasn't a good-looking German man anywhere in the room. They all looked like the murals on the walls and ceiling of fat, round dolphins, but they weren't leaping, just overflowing their spindly chairs. To "dispel the gloom," Craig made up a verse on the spot: "There are Adolphs and Rudolphs and dolphins, galore / Those on the ceiling like those on the floor."

Craig was also a significant part of what would turn out to be Sinclair's single most important experience in Europe and the touchstone for his greatest artistic achievement, the Lanny Budd novels. This was the music festival at Hellerau, near Dresden, in June 1913. The group went to Hellerau because Dollie Kimbrough was interested in dance, and would remain in England that fall with the Wilshires to study the new dance discipline called "Eurythmics." The highlight of the Hellerau festival was Gluck's *Orpheus and Eurydice,* which was being staged by Emile Jaques-Dalcroze, the inventor of Eurythmics. For Sinclair an added attraction of the Hellerau festival was a chance to meet once again with George Bernard Shaw, and to introduce him to his new wife.

Sinclair later used the memory of his meeting with Shaw at Hellerau as the opening scene for his first Lanny Budd novel, *World's End,* published in 1940: The thirteen-year-old Lanny stands with two friends before a "tall white temple with smooth round pillars in front of it," watching for the "king of celebrities" to appear. When Shaw, the "king," does step forward, his whiskers glow like gold, his eyes are "as gay as the bluebells of the meadow" and his teeth "like the petals of the daisies." He "wore an English tweed suit of brown with reddish threads in it, and when he threw his head back and laughed . . . all the flowers on the bright meadow danced."

Sinclair was showing in this scene how the sunny optimism inherent in the person of Shaw was about to be destroyed by the ugly reality of looming war: like Orpheus, Europe in 1913 was about to descend into hell. The scene became the touchstone for the series that would take Lanny through World War II and into the Cold War. It also introduced Sinclair's dominant, central question, the one that gives coherence to his life and to most of his work, both literary and political: "What part do moral forces play in history?"

Sinclair's greatest strength as a writer, however, was not so much in grand themes or theories as it was in closely observed details. In order to re-create the *Orpheus* premiere, Sinclair wrote to Jaques-Dalcroze in 1938 to confirm some of the details of the production. As he often did, he balanced his own impressions against Craig's, in a way that shows how precise and sensitive hers were. His own "most vivid recollection" was of the "bare white arms and limbs of those masked figures." Craig, Sinclair continued, "has a very keen sensibility for external beauty, [and] recalls the lighting as of a dark blue twilight or moonlight. She recalls the woodwork in the auditorium as golden oak, and I wonder if that is correct memory after twenty-five years." Jaques-Dalcroze wrote back to confirm that Craig's impressions were correct.

Mary Craig Kimbrough Sinclair was, then, much more than the whining neurotic whom her detractors condemn—with good cause—for mistreating David or for isolating Sinclair. She was also a highly intelligent, witty, and sensitive soul mate for an often difficult man: a man who never doubted that she had rescued him when he was drowning in despair or that he was reborn as a writer following their marriage.

═══

The Sinclair entourage returned to England in July, after the Hellerau festival. David was enrolled again in the Highgate school for the coming year, and Dollie took up her studies with a Eurythmics instructor in London. Sinclair and Craig returned to the United States in October 1913 and spent the next six months in Bermuda.

This was a period of continuing recovery for them both, now more essential for Craig than for Sinclair. During her first voyage home from Europe before their marriage, she had injured her spine in a shipboard fall, and she continued to complain, as she would for the rest of her life, of various unspecified ailments. They lived in a small cottage on the beach, luxuriating in the cool ocean waters, the warm sun, and lazy afternoons on the veranda of the Princess Hotel, where Sinclair frequently played tennis. He soon resumed his active correspondence and his work on a second novel drawn from Craig's stories of the deep South.

The first of these two novels, called *Sylvia,* was published by the John C. Winston Company in 1913. Its sequel, published by Winston in 1914, would be *Sylvia's Marriage.* The character of Sylvia Castleman is lovingly modeled after Craig, as are some of the incidents in the novels. Craig's home was the same Mississippi that William Faulkner would immortalize with his often grotesque stories of race and class and sex, entangled like the roots of a mangrove tree. She grew up hearing similar stories, and passed them along to Sinclair. He then wove them into a lengthy two-part narrative about a strong-minded, beautiful young woman who suffers cruelly from the ignorance and conventions of her society.

A central theme in the Sylvia novels concerns the causes and effects of sexually transmitted diseases. Sinclair believed that the only way to eliminate evils such as wage slavery in the meatpacking industry or the conspiracy of silence about sexually transmitted diseases was to expose them to public scrutiny. He knew from his own experience how the press could manipulate its readers into thinking the worst of good, though fallible, people. But he also knew that, properly handled, the press could serve a useful purpose in arousing outrage: "Public opinion is a terrible agent," he notes in *Sylvia*, "which has driven mighty princes to madness, and captains of predatory finance to suicide." Socially aware fiction could also serve that purpose.

But sometimes only direct personal involvement would do. In April 1914, shortly after returning from Bermuda to New York, Sinclair revived the issue of wage slavery that had first made him famous. His new target would be John D. Rockefeller, Jr., the son and heir of the greatest of all "captains of predatory finance."

Back home briefly during the spring of 1913, Sinclair had supported the striking silkworkers in Paterson, New Jersey. Lasting for six months, from January through June 1913, the strike idled twenty-five thousand workers. Bill Haywood and the Wobblies—the Industrial Workers of the World—were actively involved, as were Elizabeth Gurley Flynn and Carlo Tresca. Sinclair and Craig had to miss the high point of the strike, which coincided with their visit to Hellerau. In June the radical young journalist John Reed—assisted by Meta's old flame, and Reed's classmate at Harvard, Alfred Kuttner—organized a fund-raising pageant at Madison Square Garden, featuring speeches by the IWW leaders and a spectacular reenactment of the strike's most dramatic moments by nearly a thousand workers. An early example of what would be called agitprop, the spectacle heartened its advocates and dismayed the press, which viewed it as an incitement to violence and anarchy.

The most recent locale for industrial strife had been in eastern Colorado, where some three thousand miners had gone on strike against the Colorado Fuel and Iron Company. The strike had begun the previous September; by the spring of 1914 tensions between strikers and scab workers brought in to replace them had grown, and many workers and their families were living in tent cities, having been evicted from their company housing. On April 20 the governor of Colorado, responding to reports of violence in Ludlow, south of Colorado Springs, dispatched the state militia to restore order.

On April 27, Laura Cannon, whose husband was the president of the Western Federation of Miners, spoke about the terrible events of April 20 to a Carnegie Hall audience that included Upton Sinclair. The story was stark: a confrontation between the miners and the militia erupted in gunfire. The soldiers torched some of the miners' tents. Two women and eleven children died of asphyxiation. Two other children and five strikers died during the fighting, as did four soldiers.

Sinclair returned to his apartment on Morningside Heights after Laura Cannon's speech, more shaken than Craig had ever seen him. Almost as bad as the story he had just heard, he told Craig, was the scanty newspaper coverage it had received. He was certain that the public, if they knew what had happened, would be as outraged as he was. But the Colorado Fuel and Iron Company was a Rockefeller holding. Its president reported directly to John D. Rockefeller, Jr., who had been vocal in his support of previous actions taken against the strikers. Sinclair believed the press barons had clearly decided to protect their fellow capitalist from embarrassment—another instance, for him, of the power of the interlocking directorates.

The younger Rockefeller's more famous father had learned to his sorrow how destructive public opinion could be after Ida Tarbell's book *The History of the Standard Oil Company* began as a series for *McClure's* in 1902. Tarbell's exposé helped President Theodore Roosevelt in his effort to target Rockefeller as the most rapacious of robber barons; Rockefeller himself blamed Tarbell for the antitrust suits that ultimately resulted in the dissolution of the company as a stand-alone monopoly. Now Rockefeller was virtually retired, at seventy-four, and the burden of running his many enterprises had fallen on the shoulders of his son.

John D. Jr. was, according to Ron Chernow's massive biography of the father, *Titan,* a thoughtful and decent man, and a good deal more sensitive to public opprobrium than his father had been. "Reeling from the Ludlow Massacre," Chernow writes, Rockefeller Jr. turned for advice to Sinclair's old friend, Hearst editor Arthur Brisbane, who suggested that he hire the famous publicist Ivy Lee to "burnish the family image."

Aware—probably through Brisbane—of the Rockefellers' new resolve to shape public opinion, Sinclair determined to mount his own publicity campaign. He would undermine the benign image that Ivy Lee, whom he dubbed "Poison Ivy," had created, forcing the younger Rockefeller to recognize the union that his Colorado company was resisting so violently. His lever would be the Ludlow Massacre. What followed over the next weeks was Sinclair's most vigorous venture into public protest since the days of *The Jungle.*

The first act of the extended drama began the morning after Laura Cannon's talk, when she, Sinclair, and Craig tried to confront Rockefeller in his office at the Standard Oil Building, at 26 Broadway. Refused entry, Sinclair left a letter for Rockefeller, a "solemn warning" that he intended to "indict" him for "murder" that very evening, at a meeting of the Liberal Club. He thought it was only "fair play" to let Rockefeller know what lay in store for him.

The meeting was sparsely attended, by about thirty people. Among them, however, were Lincoln Steffens and Sinclair's old friend Leonard Abbott, as well as a dozen reporters who had been given copies of Sinclair's "indictment" and whose papers gave the story some attention the following day. Sinclair did his best to arouse the group to a fever pitch of indignation. One reporter thought the slight, "blue-eyed, fair-haired" writer, who claimed he was within inches of using a horsewhip on Rockefeller, was nearly out of control. Sinclair certainly confused his listeners, whom he had done his best to inflame, when he told them to offer only passive resistance if they were arrested for protesting. One of the men in the audience, a former leader in the Paterson silkworkers strike, scoffed at the idea of passive resistance. He urged stronger tactics, involving guns and clubs, and walked out of the meeting, taking with him the sympathetic Lincoln Steffens.

The next morning, Sinclair joined with about twenty other people, all wearing black mourning armbands, to walk a picket line in front of the Rockefeller offices at 26 Broadway. By the time Craig arrived—she had delayed in order to buy what Sinclair called "an elegant white cape" for her first public appearance as a rabble-rouser—Sinclair and four women supporters, all self-described suffragists, had been arrested for disorderly conduct and hauled away to adjacent cells in the Tombs, the city prison. Released on bail in the early afternoon after promising to appear in court the following day for sentencing, they returned to the demonstration. In court the following morning, April 30, the arresting officer testified that Sinclair's conduct had been that of "a perfect gentleman," but the magistrate pronounced him and the women guilty of disorderly conduct. Declining to pay the fine of $3, they were taken back to prison to serve their three-day sentence.

Sinclair spent two days fasting rather than eat prison food. His entertaining cell mate was a young thief who said he stole because he enjoyed outsmarting "the owners of property in the great metropolis," as well as the police, who never bothered to check his fingerprint records and would undoubtedly let him go in a few days. Meanwhile, Craig was on the picket line, marching with Leonard Abbott and George Sterling, who happened to be in town. She also tried to console another visitor: her mother, who had come from Mississippi to rescue her daughter from public shame. "My God Mary Craig," Mrs. Kimbrough complained, "what have you brought us to. I am almost crazy to think of you causing us such mortification! I wish I was dead, a thousand times dead! . . . *my* child in jail for disturbing the peace and breaking the law!! What shall we do!!"

Craig, who was never charged or jailed, ignored her mother's protests. On the third day of Sinclair's imprisonment she paid his remaining $1 fine, which entitled him to appeal the sentence and seek restitution, and the two left the Tombs to find a horde of inquisitive reporters waiting for them.

Closer so far to farce than drama, the tone of the protest now began to change. On the morning that Sinclair was in court, a young woman was arrested for entering the Standard Oil Building with a loaded pistol and shouting that she was there to kill Rockefeller, a threat she repeated several times while she was in custody. She was following the model established by another protester, Alexander Berkman, the notorious anarchist who had spent fourteen years in prison for shooting and seriously wounding Henry Clay Frick, president of Andrew Carnegie's Homestead Steel Works, in 1892 during the Homestead Strike. Berkman was now out of jail and living in New York. So too were his lover, Emma Goldman, then editing the anarchist magazine *Mother Earth,* and a hotheaded young French Canadian named Arthur Caron. Caron and several Wobblies had picketed in front of Rockefeller's home on West Forty-fifth Street, against Sinclair's wishes.

On May 2, Sinclair tried to calm the waters he had already roiled at another meeting, this one at the Socialist Club on West 125th Street. A much bigger crowd was on hand for this affair. The room was "packed to suffocation," according to one reporter, with supporters eager to hear the answer to the question posed by Sinclair's talk. His title—"Shall We Murder Rockefeller?"—sounded anything but calming. The reporter noted that "police stenographers were visibly nervous" and a burly officer "shot his cuffs preparatory to making an impressive showing when he placed the bloodthirsty Sinclair under arrest."

But Sinclair insisted he was not after blood. His answer to the idea that Rockefeller should be murdered was a resounding "No!" There were two Rockefellers, he explained. One was an ordinary human being, "an inoffensive and possibly likeable person." It was the "phantom" Rockefeller who had to die, that "specter of power, of predatory force, of murderous inspiration." Not the man but the symbol must die, with the system that spawned him.

Thomas Carlyle had made the same argument in *The French Revolution:*

kingship, not the king's head, was the issue. The possibility that the modern Jacobins—Berkman, the *Mother Earth* anarchists, and the Wobblies—could hijack his nonviolent protest against Rockefeller and destroy it was certainly on Sinclair's mind. On Saturday, May 9, he attended but did not speak at another meeting. This one was organized by Berkman and featured the radical Protestant minister and author Bouck White, who had recently founded his own Church of the Social Revolution. To wild applause, White read aloud the letter he had just delivered to "the Rockefeller pastor," the minister at Calvary Baptist Church on Fifth Avenue, which was attended and supported by the Rockefellers. In the letter, White vowed to address Rockefeller directly in his church at services the next morning. He warned that if he were turned away, "the wilder spirits in the revolutionary movement" would be unleashed.

On Sunday morning, May 10, as Sinclair boarded the train in Grand Central Terminal for a three-week research trip to Colorado, Bouck White appeared with several followers at Calvary Baptist. He pointed to the Rockefeller family and shouted that he had come to tell the worshippers "about one member of your congregation who is guilty of the murder of women and children in Colorado." Following a brief scuffle, White was arrested with ten of his supporters, one of them a woman who had physically assaulted John D. Rockefeller, Jr. All would serve several months in prison.

The Rockefellers had retreated after this incident to their country estate of some four thousand acres at Pocantico Hills, in the picturesque village of Tarrytown, made famous by Washington Irving in his tales about Rip Van Winkle and Sleepy Hollow. On May 30, the day before Sinclair's return from Colorado, Berkman and a loose coalition of *Mother Earth* supporters and other radicals met in Tarrytown. When they found that the Rockefeller estate was walled and well guarded by a private police force of about sixty men, they tried to hold a rally in a local park. Lacking a permit to speak, they were arrested until the small jail was filled to capacity, then clubbed and shoved onto trains leaving for Manhattan. A few days later Sinclair persuaded a local sympathizer to let her land be used for an outdoor gathering on Sunday, June 14.

That meeting began smoothly enough, with Sinclair describing his trip to Colorado. But as he had earlier, he both incited the crowd and pleaded for restraint. He asserted that Rockefeller was a killer: "We must establish the principle . . . that a capitalist is guilty of murder if he hires gunmen to go out and kill people to increase his dividends." At the same time, he warned against violence. The meeting dissolved in chaos when Adolf Wolff, an anarchist sculptor, loudly objected to the idea of compromise or negotiation: "We shouldn't plead, we should take!" The people of Tarrytown were "cowards, curs, and traitors."

Sinclair did not attend the next meeting in Tarrytown, on June 22, no doubt because it was led by the troublesome Alexander Berkman, who was intent on provoking a violent reaction from the local villagers. Berkman succeeded: the anarchists were pelted first with eggs, then rocks, and chased to the train station, with the aid of half a dozen mounted aqueduct policemen. One young woman had two black eyes, and several men, including Arthur Caron, suffered concussions from being clubbed on the head.

On the morning of July 4, the top three floors of a seven-story tenement on Lexington Avenue blew up in a dynamite explosion that shattered windows a mile away and obscured the skies above New York with billowing black smoke. Miraculously, only four people were killed: an innocent woman in an apartment adjoining the one where the bomb accidentally exploded, and the three men who were building it to use against the Rockefeller family. One of the three was the nineteen-year-old Canadian Arthur Caron.

The Sinclairs learned what had happened a few hours later when Craig answered the telephone in their apartment. A policeman asked if she would come to the morgue and identify Caron's body. The would-be bomber had plummeted, along with shattered concrete, plaster, and glass, to a fire escape landing two floors below his room. She declined. Sinclair did not volunteer to go in her place.

A few days later Sinclair sent copies to the newspapers of an open letter addressed to "My Friends in Tarrytown." It was their fault, he said, that "three men and one woman have been blown into eternity." Arthur Caron's "frank laughing face haunts me terribly." If this nineteen-year-old boy was "a plotter of violence," he was driven to it by the merciless beatings he had suffered numerous times at the hands of the police, and at the hands of a mob in Tarrytown. "His clothing filthy with eggs, his eyes full of sand, his face streaming with blood," Caron had been pursued by the aqueduct police at a gallop. Like "avenging Cossacks," the police followed him onto the station platform and into the train. There the boy was clubbed into unconsciousness as he cowered in his seat. Sinclair concluded by saying that he was "not a man of violence, I do not deal in violence. I would die before I would sanction violence." But as "a student of history," he understood what happens when men are deprived of their rights.

Sinclair had an entirely different message for his socialist audience in *Appeal to Reason,* warning that such violence as Caron's would only invite further repression. The temptation to dynamite one's enemies "out of existence" must be "resisted at all hazards. For our enemies are not men" but, as he had said many times, systems and ideas. "If Caron was himself the bomb maker, then it is better that he died as he did. It would be better that all bomb makers should blow up themselves, for they can do nothing but harm to the cause they would serve."

As Sinclair suspected, there was no question about Caron's guilt. Berkman said six months later, with the certainty of a man who had been closely involved, that Caron and his friends planned "to wait for an opportunity and hurl [the bomb] into the carriage or automobile of the Rockefellers when they were leaving the Tarrytown estate. They wanted to get both of them together, but would have taken the life of either one."

Sinclair later argued that the violence, however reprehensible, probably forced Rockefeller to the negotiating table. Inasmuch as the strike had already been broken by the time Sinclair returned from his trip to Colorado, well before the July 4 explosion, this seems unlikely. But it is true that Rockefeller himself traveled to Pueblo in October 1915 to talk to the miners about the need for a new partnership between capital and labor. He pointed to a table in front of him, saying the modern corporation was like that table, supported by four legs: employees, stockholders, directors, and management. He placed a pile of coins on the table and lifted one end of it. The coins slid to the floor. He said, "Men, only when every man connected with that square corporation" is "on the level" will both workers and employers thrive.

The Colorado coal strike, writes labor historian John Graham in his introduction to Sinclair's *The Coal War* (1976), stands out as a "remarkable illustration of the transformation of the American political economy from laissez-faire capitalism to the corporate capitalism of the twentieth century." Sinclair spent nearly three years on the events leading up to and following the Ludlow Massacre, writing two long novels about it in addition to organizing the picket march and the protests against Rockefeller. He thought he was there in spirit—and that he deserved to be—when "John D. Jr." went out to Pueblo and "danced with the miners' wives and made friends with the angry old Mother Jones"—and, more significantly, recognized the unions and vowed to improve conditions in the mines.

In fact, Sinclair's legacy in the Rockefeller adventure is more ambiguous than it was with Ogden Armour and *The Jungle*. He certainly contributed to public indignation over mistreatment of the miners, but the two novels that he would write out of his experience lacked the insight, the control, and the power of *The Jungle*. More troubling, though, was his apparent willingness to stir his listeners to violence even as he said, with undoubted sincerity, that he deplored it. He had yet to regain the precarious balance between activism and art that he had found in *The Jungle.*

======

Sinclair's financial balance was also shaky. His divorce from Meta had not been costly, largely because he had succeeded in portraying her as a loose woman in the custody battle for David, and he was not required to pay for her support. But the royalties from the Sylvia novels were nonexistent in the United States, where the books sold poorly, and slim even from England, where they were better received.

Early in the summer of 1914, Sinclair broached the idea of an anthology of socialist writings to be called *The Cry for Justice* with John C. Winston, who agreed to advance him $1,000 (about $18,000 in today's dollars). In early July, after the Caron disaster, Sinclair withdrew from active involvement with the coal strike protests and rented a cheap but charming cottage at Croton-on-Hudson, sixty miles north of the Rockefeller estate. Though money would be tight, Sinclair was buoyed by the expectation that *The Jungle* would once again make him rich—this time in the form of a movie, with himself as one of the characters.

Sinclair had chosen Croton as his new residence in part because it was a watering hole for radical artists and intellectuals, including, a few years later, John Reed and Louise Bryant. Now it was a bucolic retreat for colleagues like Floyd Dell, Robert Minor, and Max Eastman, and an appealing place for friends like George Sterling and Lincoln Steffens to visit him.

Another reason was that his close neighbors and tennis partners were Edgar Selwyn and his wife, Margaret Mayo, the former actress who, years earlier, had tried to seduce Sinclair at the Princeton farm. But Mayo was no longer a temptress, she was a businesswoman who, with her husband, had formed the All-Star Feature Company. Still intrigued by the dramatic possibilities of Sinclair's novel, she and Selwyn produced a six-reel film (about sixty minutes), which received its premiere in New York on June 1, 1914. Another Croton friend and neighbor, and fellow Rockefeller protester, Clement Wood, provided a rave review of the film in *Appeal to Reason*. He said it was the "most effective Socialist propaganda" yet seen, singling out for special attention the scenes in which a man falls "into a vat of boiling lard" and Jurgis hurls Connor "into a bellowing stampede of cattle." (Neither scene occurs in the novel, though the first is based on its most notorious but unproved allegation.)

Sinclair himself played the role of Eugene Debs, the speaker who converts Jurgis to socialism. His performance, if one sympathetic viewer is to be credited, was not a complete success. Some years later Joseph Cannon, whose wife had so excited the Carnegie Hall crowd with her account of the Ludlow Massacre, had moved from organizing miners to making propaganda films. He suggested to "comrade Sinclair" that if, as he hoped, the film could be remade, they should consider hiring a professional actor to replace him. That plan never came to fruition. Sinclair did not comment on his own attempt to act, but he was disappointed in the movie. The last surviving copy of the film disappeared some time in the 1930s.

Sinclair's most interesting reference to the film in his *Autobiography* turns around the comment of a fellow writer who attended the premiere and who congratulated Sinclair warmly. It was Richard Harding Davis, still more handsome than most matinee idols though past his prime as the dashing foreign correspondent whose adventure novels, especially *Soldiers of Fortune* (1897), had made him one of the most celebrated popular authors of his day. Sinclair had never met Davis, but had read a few of his books and thought of him as "the prince of snobs." Now, though, the great man, dressed in khaki as though he had just stepped in from the veldt, shook his hand and murmured, "Ah, now, *you* are a *real* writer. I only write for money."

Sinclair still prided himself, as this rather self-righteous recollection indicates, on his indifference to money. It was true that he did not lust after luxuries, property, or expensive vacations. He didn't even mind living in tents. But he did understand the power and the appeal of money, and its necessity for letting him do what he wanted to do. As a younger man he had been shameless in asking relatives, friends, and even strangers for money, and he sensibly did not object to being paid for his honest labor. He would have been happy to make the money from the film version of *The Jungle* that Davis made from one of his bestsellers. But most ordinary viewers appeared to agree that the movie was six reels of gloom "laid down with a shovel," and it soon vanished. He held out better hope for his real work, the anthology that would take up nearly two years of his life.

As would become increasingly evident during his career, Sinclair's literary sensibility was much subtler than those of his fellow muckrakers. A fair number of the contemporary selections he chose to include in his anthology, including half a dozen from his own work, hold up well today. Some, like Sylvia Pankhurst's "Forced Feeding of a Suffragette," still have the power to shock. Those he took from earlier writers, including Dickens, Tennyson, and Voltaire, are equally effective.

Sinclair worked hard at securing permissions from about thirty publishers for the material still in copyright. He was candid about his intention to make the anthology a bible for socialist true believers, even to the point of having Winston bring out a limited number of copies in a special edition, bound in limp black morocco, with rounded corners and the edges stained red. When Harper's refused to let Sinclair use "The Two Reigns of Terror" from *A Connecticut Yankee in King Arthur's Court,* Sinclair replied indignantly. He "had the honor of knowing the late Mr. Clemons" [*sic*], who had told him when they met in Bermuda that he had a deep interest in social justice. The passage had already been quoted in an anarchist press publication, Sinclair noted, probably without permission; he at least was requesting permission! He understood perfectly well that Harper's "disapproved of myself and my writings," which he could accept "very pleasantly," being accustomed to such attitudes. But this was a free speech issue: he thought it was hardly fair for a publisher to prevent the distribution of its authors' works when they were somehow deemed offensive. Harper's did not relent, and Sinclair had to paraphrase the selection as well as Twain's posthumous "A War Prayer"—the latter found today in virtually every college anthology of American literature.

As an editor-advocate for the selections he had chosen, Sinclair sometimes let his enthusiasm get the best of him. Jack London, who granted free permission to use five selections, had to warn him that calling every single one of his writers "great" was not only silly but "invidious." London ordered Sinclair to drop all the adjectives: "You are not a society reporter." When the anthology finally appeared, in September 1915, the war and its overwhelming impact had crowded out interest in social protest, and *The Cry for Justice* did not make back its advance for Winston. It was another respectable failure for Sinclair.

By that time, though, at least the financial pressure on Sinclair was less than it had been; he and his wife were living rent-free in Mississippi. Craig's father, Judge Allan McCaskill Kimbrough, was a southern gentleman of the old school, gaunt and erect at six feet four inches tall, with a small white beard and brooding, deeply set eyes. He presided over a chancery court and owned a plantation in Greenwood. His second house, in Gulfport, about a hundred miles to the south, was a rambling wooden structure called Ashton Hall. In 1913, when the judge learned that his daughter planned to marry Upton Sinclair, the notorious socialist, he had turned her portrait to the wall and refused to attend the wedding.

But in the late spring of 1915 Judge Kimbrough, prompted by a pleading letter from Craig, invited her and her husband to come to stay in Gulfport, for as long as they liked. His large family—Craig was the eldest of eight children—used Ashton Hall only during the four hottest months of the year, from June through September or mid-October. Craig and Sinclair could have it to themselves the rest of the time. Within a week of their arrival, Sinclair assembled a platform tent near the beach, as far from the teeming house with its summer crowd as possible, and began to work on the first of his two long novels about the coal strike.

Judge Kimbrough offered his son-in-law a cool handshake upon their first meeting, but was soon won over as Sinclair "thanked him for the most precious gift I had ever received. He had hated to give it, of course, but all the same I had it, and for keeps." Craig later said, "Well, Papa, what do you think of him?" The judge offered the first apology she had ever heard him utter: "I guess I overspoke myself."

David Sinclair had returned from England in August 1914, when the war started, and gone directly to a prep school in North Carolina. Now thirteen, he came to Gulfport to join his father and stepmother. He would spend much of his time with Hunter Kimbrough, one year his senior. Hunter was eighteen years younger than Craig, more like a son to her than a brother. Perhaps aware of Hunter's privileged position with his stepmother, David did not react as enthusiastically as might be expected of a boy with a new playmate and freedom to explore the beaches and bayous of Gulfport.

No doubt confirming Craig's continuing sense that David meant trouble for her was the news in mid-July that Meta had checked in to a Gulfport hotel in order to visit her son. Meta had grown increasingly erratic since the divorce. In late 1913, Harry Kemp, seeing that she was tired of him, had traveled to England to stay with the Wilshires. He wrote to Meta, as "Kaa" to "Naa," vowing to remember her as one who would "always be a sort of dream-woman to me, my first love, who taught me how exquisite and spiritual sex and sexual love can be." But Meta's behavior after dismissing Harry had been neither exquisite nor spiritual. Most recently, she had been involved in another divorce scandal, reported in *The New York Times* in late June 1915. She may have felt that by persuading the Mississippi courts to award her total custody of David, she could restore her good name.

Even Meta's parents acknowledged that she had little real interest in her son. It is difficult to understand why she thought she could somehow persuade the judicial colleagues of her ex-husband's new father-in-law to give her custody of David. She particularly enraged Sinclair by resurrecting the claim that he had burned down Helicon Hall for the insurance. He hit back violently in a widely circulated "Letter to My Friends," also sent to the judges considering his case, which enumerated Meta's alleged and admitted infidelities in great detail. On July 19, he wrote Meta that when he had taken David from her three and a half years earlier, the boy was "a perfect little monster of selfishness and trickery" as a result of living with her. He said he had rescued David then, with the help of Craig and Dollie. They still had a chance, he said, of "making him into a sound and useful man."

But, Sinclair went on, he had mistakenly allowed David to spend the previous Christmas with Meta, who had undone all of his good work. Now David was "rebellious, distracted, moody—and above all, *filled with lies to tell his father.*" Meta, Sinclair declared, had overplayed her hand when she accused him of indifference toward David: "I have loved this boy as few fathers I have ever known have loved a child. I have been to him father, mother, nurse, servant, teacher and playmate." He planned to devote the rest of his life to "repairing in the soul of the child the ravages you have wrought there."

Sinclair was a professional at controversy, Meta a rank amateur. She failed to argue effectively that Sinclair's claim of filial love was more than open to challenge, it was preposterous: he had hardly seen David in the past three years, at least partly because Craig did not want the boy around. The judicial outcome was predictable. Because her own behavior had become notorious, Meta was not only refused custody, but she lost the right to have her son visit her in New York. The court limited her to one visit of two weeks each year, in Gulfport or Greenwood, Mississippi.

Through all his travels, troubles, and books, Sinclair had returned as often as he could to his two early loves, the violin and tennis—especially tennis. Even as he was quarreling with Meta and writing about the coal strike during the summer of 1915, he was spending three or four mornings a week on the carefully tended clay courts of the Great Southern Hotel. He never lacked for opponents, as the hotel was a favorite resort for young army officers on leave from nearby bases.

Sinclair occasionally used tennis to make an ideological point: a socialist in *Sylvia's Marriage* recalls watching a match between doctors at an insane asylum, with the inmates let out of their padded cells to serve as ballboys. This was for Sinclair a "perfect simile" of modern civilization: "Some people wear white and play tennis all day, while other people chase the balls, or howl in dungeons in the background!" On a more personal level, George Sterling thought Sinclair used tennis to satisfy his puritanical need for self-discipline, but Sinclair disagreed. While he approved of the emperor Cyrus for making his soldiers work up a sweat once daily, he said, he didn't play tennis for the exercise or the discipline, or because it provided useful literary similes. So quick on the court that he was nicknamed "the rabbit," he loved tennis for the "keen competition" it offered. It was a "clean game" that he "played with the utmost delight," but only, when possible, with opponents of his own caliber. Otherwise he found his mind wandering back to whatever book he was working on. The odd thing was, he said, that the more he had on his mind, the better he played, given strong opposition. That summer, when he did have a lot on his mind, Sinclair beat a dozen superbly fit officers, young men who viewed the game as a means of social and professional advancement and worked hard at it, and won the Gulf States Tennis Championship for 1915.

In November, Sinclair left Craig behind in Mississippi while he headed west once again, to scout out the possibilities for them of life in southern California. He had been attracted by the state for years, ever since his first visit to Carmel in 1908. It was three thousand miles away from Meta, and blessed with a warm climate that would let him play tennis to his heart's content. His grasshopper days, as Mike Williams had called them, would soon be at an end.

CHAPTER NINE

THE HOMESTEADER

(January 1916–December 1919)

I n January 1916, Sinclair wrote in sunny spirits to Craig from Coronado Island, near San Diego, where he had rented a small house on J Street a few blocks from the Pacific Ocean. "You're never going to have any more cares. I am going to be very good to you," he promised. She would have no mundane housekeeping chores, no duties other than to be his "guest and read me poetry." She could join him in his morning stroll along the beach to the beautiful Hotel del Coronado and watch him play tennis from the porch that overlooked the clay courts, with the shining sand and the broad blue ocean as a backdrop. They would be happy, just the two of them, far from their troubles with Meta and her friends. Although his chance meeting in Los Angeles a few days earlier with that bad penny Armistead Collier had provoked unpleasant memories of Meta and her affairs, it also "made me realize what a hell we have got out of."

By the time Craig joined her husband, in late February, he knew that he had to find a warmer climate. The damp ocean air made him cough and the cold wind ruined his tennis. In March, young Bobby Scripps, the son of the newspaper magnate, wrote to Sinclair, reminding him that they had met in San Francisco in 1909 and inviting him for a visit in Pasadena. The tennis pro at the Del assured Sinclair that he would find the weather there to his liking.

For Sinclair, who had always lived in or near a big city, Pasadena was perfect. Only fifteen miles east of downtown Los Angeles, nestled against the San Gabriel Mountains, it was famous as "the millionaires' retreat." But it also had its modest neighborhoods of bungalows on dusty streets lined with eucalyptus and pepper trees. By the end of the year the Sinclairs had bought a tiny house on a large lot on Sunset Avenue, about a mile from the Rose Bowl in the Arroyo Seco. Although Sinclair had promised Craig that she would be free from the drudgery of housekeeping, she soon revealed a latent talent for real estate and home construction that complemented her husband's artistic abilities. Within just two years of their arrival, Craig created the home that she and Sinclair would live in for the next twenty-five years. It was, as Irving Stone said, "a little mad, but it worked for him."

The Sinclair house was an ingenious amalgam of their original bungalow plus four small wood-frame houses that Craig found and had moved to their lot. The conjoined structures of various sizes, colors, and rooflines shocked Sinclair's neighbors, who, like those at Helicon Hall, regarded his new experiment in housing as part of a "Socialist circus." Sinclair joked that the house looked like a camouflaged battleship until a few years later, when Craig had it painted pink. Then the long covered veranda with its Ionic-capped pillars, rocking chairs, and climbing roses managed to suggest something like the Mississippi mansion where she had been raised.

Despite the modified facade, the dominant effect inside and out remained curiously asymmetrical. No two floor levels or ceiling heights were the same, and there were half a dozen different sizes and styles and locations for the windows. Anchoring one end of this maze, Sinclair's office was comfortably spacious—the second floor of a former tailor's shop had been removed to create a cathedral ceiling—but austerely furnished with thrift shop furniture, metal file cabinets, and worn Oriental rugs. His desk and typewriter, and the old couch where he often napped, were in the center of the room. A back door led to a small porch with a long table for packaging his self-published books and the magazine he began in 1918, *Upton Sinclair's*.

Determined as ever both to be independent and to join with others who were similarly inclined, Sinclair quickly persuaded eight new friends to form the Workers Co-operative Association of Pasadena. The members traded everything from magazines and books to clothing, shoes, food, and "coal, coke, wood and fuel oil." The group had disbanded by the time David joined the household during the summer of 1917, but Sinclair and Craig were still buying in bulk—thirty pounds of Japanese persimmons, ten pounds of dates, twenty pounds of grapes, five-pound boxes of oatmeal. David ate oatmeal until it was coming out of his ears, he remembered. One day he found an old box of the cereal crawling with weevils and showed it to his father, hoping to persuade him to change his buying habits, but Sinclair simply nodded and said, "Well, son, you don't need to eat any more" from that box.

The twenty-month period when David lived in Pasadena, until he returned in January 1919 to Mississippi to finish high school there, would be the longest that he ever spent with his father after his parents' divorce. Craig, never fond of her stepson, eventually persuaded Sinclair that the boy would be better off with her family in Mississippi, and David's virtual estrangement from the father who had fought so hard to keep him becomes a continuing motif in Sinclair's life. For a time, though, the three lived in relative harmony. David confirmed in his reminiscences of this period what Sinclair wrote about his love of the climate: "I live where the sun shines most all of most days, and in the morning I can take my typewriter out into the garden. I can wear a pair of bathing trunks and a white canvas hat while I walk up and down behind jasmine and rose hedges with the people of my books." So intense was his concentration, David said, that his father would wear a rut several inches deep. Every so often he would stop to shovel dirt into the ruts, then resume his endless pacing. Once at his desk, his study door was never closed, but not because Sinclair welcomed interruption. Rather, he knew that his family understood he was not to be disturbed while he was working.

Although he had stepped away from the center of cultural and intellectual life in New York, Sinclair soon found that Los Angeles had its own attractions—not least that it was an arena for radical and conservative contention of every imaginable type. As Sinclair saw the local scene, its far-right business and political establishment suggested the banana republics of Central America. The growing movie industry was a lowbrow affair, dominated by a few big studios and run by men who catered to common if not degraded tastes. Religion was the purview of rabid fundamentalists like Billy Sunday and the Roman Catholics, who imposed their ideas on nonbelievers through political manipulation and pressure. Higher education was a joke, particularly at the University of Southern California, funded by oil millionaire Edward Doheny. And the press, as represented by the *Los Angeles Times* under Harrison G. Otis, was a reactionary nightmare. Such, at least, were Sinclair's impressions of his new home. It was perfect for him.

For his first year in California, Sinclair's life was relatively placid. While he worried, like everyone else, about the war in Europe, America would stay out of it until April 1917. He worked on his novel about the coal strike; George Brett at Macmillan had taken Sinclair back into the fold after ten years, and was pressing him to finish the book soon. Simply keeping up with his correspondence took an hour or two out of each day. George Bernard Shaw wrote to say that lecture circuit entrepreneurs kept offering to bring him to America, under the impression he was a revivalist preacher. He promised to try to locate Pasadena if he did come. From Holland, Frederick van Eeden asked if the Wilshires' son, Logan, then eleven years old, was well; he was concerned because he had received a telepathic message that the boy was sick, and he was worried about him. And in mid-August 1916, Sinclair received a tempting though cryptic letter from Jack London, inviting him to visit for as long as he liked at his ranch in Glen Ellen, just north of San Francisco. London promised to let him work all he wanted, but said it was time they had a "straight-from-the-shoulder" talk with each other. Rather ominously, London said "It is coming to you, it may be coming to me. It may illuminate one or the other or both of us."

There is no record of a response to Van Eeden concerning Logan Wilshire, perhaps because the boy was healthy enough but also because Sinclair was too irritated by his father's gold mine machinations to worry about Logan. The legal proceedings that had forced Wilshire to move to England had been dropped, and he had relocated the company's headquarters from London back to Bishop after the war began. He was now engaged in building a house for himself and his family in the Sierra Nevada foothills, near the mine. On May 12, Sinclair, against his better judgment, bought $750 worth of stock in Wilshire's enterprise. Three weeks later he was complaining furiously because Wilshire, without his permission, had listed him as a de facto company officer, authorized to receive proxies from stockholders wishing to vote. Sinclair told Wilshire that he was sorry if he sounded "cross"—one of his favorite words—but added, "you know very well that a matter of business sends me up in the air like a thousand hornets."

Sinclair also wrote to both London and Wilshire that he was too busy to visit them. A few months later, on November 22, 1916, London was dead. He was only forty—two years older than Sinclair. Newspaper accounts tantalized the public with speculations on the circumstances of his death— uremic poisoning according to the coroner, suicide according to George Sterling, who wrote (incorrectly) to Sinclair that London took cyanide "so death must have been swift and painless." Most of the obituary notices called attention to London's youthful, photogenic appearance in his prime, and to his international celebrity. They also noted London's role as the central figure of the West Coast literary world, and contrasted him as a socialist reformer with Sinclair—the brawling street fighter as opposed to the intellectual theorist–investigative reporter.

London had boosted Sinclair's career with his praise of *The Jungle,* and Sinclair respected and admired him—with serious reservations. Although Sinclair would later claim that he regarded him as a close friend, the two men met only three times, over a period of ten years. Sinclair was repelled by the deep streak of violence in London's makeup, and by his conviction, as shown in books like *The Iron Heel,* that only violence would achieve the goals of socialism. He may also have envied London's greater talent as a novelist, clearly seen in a comparison of their two autobiographical novels about frustrated young writers, *Martin Eden* and *The Journal of Arthur Stirling*. But what most separated them was Sinclair's conviction that London had abused his great gifts and destroyed himself through alcohol, drugs, and debauchery. London, for his part, never wearied of teasing Sinclair for his fear of giving in to physical appetites. His invitation to come visit him for a man-to-man talk had probably been issued with the intent of trying one last time to show Sinclair the error of his puritan ways.

Craig later said that she had had a premonition of London's death, which might have been suggested by the presence of the troubled George Sterling during his stay with them earlier that fall in Pasadena. The years of dissipation had taken their toll on Sterling, who was living a hand-to-mouth existence as a freelance writer in San Francisco. He had a free room at the Bohemian Club, favorite haunt of writers, artists, and roisterers, who encouraged him to drink himself into an amusing stupor. Sinclair now saw in London's death a way to save Sterling from himself. On December 8 he sent Sterling an impassioned plea to write a biography of London, his good friend.

Sinclair told Sterling that Jack London had been a great man, for all his flaws: "no more striking and vivid personality has ever appeared in American literature." Only Whitman deserved to be "named in the same breath with him." Sterling's long and intimate association with London made him "the possessor of a treasure of priceless value." He was also honest enough to know that Jack was "the last man that would ever wish to be set up in a stained glass window." Sterling would be able to avoid the error of so many biographies that offer "canonized images for us to worship—they so seldom give us a friend, that we can live in a house with."

Sinclair didn't bother waiting for a reply from Sterling before writing about his idea to London's widow, Charmian, and to George Brett at Macmillan. He promised Brett, who knew something of Sterling's indolent temperament, that he and Craig, as Sterling's "closest friends," would do all they could to help the project along. The London book should not be a formal biography, which Sterling probably lacked the discipline to pull off, but a "true and vital" account of a "great and noble friendship." Brett responded quickly, saying the book might sell if it could be done soon. Since the war had started, "events in the great world" now came so fast that they overshadowed the memories of even the most illustrious figures. Unfortunately, Brett wrote, he could not offer Sterling an advance. The proposed Sterling biography of Jack London went nowhere.

Sinclair now returned in earnest to *King Coal,* the first half of his massive two-volume novel on the Colorado coal strike, on which he had been working for more than two years. He had reviewed thousands of pages of testimony before congressional committees and visited Colorado three times. The events and the real-life characters involved seemed so vivid to Sinclair that he thought it unnecessary to expend much energy on creating a persuasively realistic protagonist—a critical error.

For months Brett had been trying to persuade Sinclair that the general public preferred entertainment to instruction or propaganda: "Bear in mind that it is a novel you are writing and not a work of history or controversy." Sinclair showed Craig Brett's letters, and she reminded him that she had anticipated his editor's objections. Then, without Sinclair's knowledge, she wrote a personal note to Brett, apologizing for such a breach of protocol but assuring him that she fully agreed with his criticism of *King Coal.* Craig was sure that part of her husband's stubbornness was simply due to his "physical and emotional fatigue" after so much hard work. She said he respected her literary judgment and would listen to her. She implored Brett not to give up on Sinclair, impulsively scrawling "Return this and tell me I'm an idiot!," then adding a plea not to respond in any fashion.

Later, Sinclair acknowledged Craig's help with *King Coal,* saying he had forced his beautiful young heroine, Mary Burke, to run around "naked"— lacking psychology and personality. For many years afterward, "put some clothes on Mary Burke" was Craig's shorthand for telling Sinclair to write stories about people rather than ideas.

King Coal's theme may again owe something, as did Sinclair's earlier *Prince Hagen,* to the cannibalistic underground creatures—formerly miners—of H. G. Wells's *The Time Machine,* as well as to Wagner's Nibelungen, which had figured earlier in *Prince Hagen.* Here Sinclair describes the miners as "a separate race of creatures, subterranean gnomes, pent up by society for purposes of its own." Unlike *The Jungle,* which has as its protagonist a member of the lower class, *King Coal*'s Hal Warner is much like Sinclair, a handsome young aristocrat, slightly built, with wavy brown hair and an engaging manner. Hal's conversion from privileged scion of the coal company owner to active supporter of the strikers requires him to try to overcome his Anglo-Saxon bourgeois values, but he has trouble dealing with "what was repulsive in these people—their barbarous, jabbering speech, their vermin-ridden homes, their bare-bottomed babies."

When *King Coal* was published in September 1917, Mary Burke and Hal Warner were themselves too bare-bottomed, still too scantily clothed with human attributes to appeal to many readers. This did not matter for the distinguished Danish critic Georg Brandes, who provided a slapdash introduction for Sinclair, comparing the novel to Zola's *Germinal,* the touchstone for strike fiction in Europe. But Brandes was overly generous. Though Sinclair's vivid depictions of work in the mines and the mechanics of mounting a strike against difficult odds are effective, *King Coal* is too thin to be good fiction and too one-sided to be acceptable history. It sold poorly, and Brett declined to publish the sequel that Sinclair wrote the following year, *The Coal War,* which suffered from the same faults as its predecessor. It remained unpublished during Sinclair's lifetime.

=====

King Coal's failure to reach a wide audience was due in part to bad timing beyond its author's control. The crowding "events in the great world" to which Brett had referred had plunged America into the European war that would shape the twentieth century. The two critical challenges to Western democracy, fascism and communism, were slouching toward Bethlehem, as Yeats had prophesied. Sinclair's literary career from this point forward would largely be an effort to define, describe, and respond to these challenges, both abroad and at home.

In 1907, as a recent convert to socialism, Sinclair had written "War: A Manifesto Against It," arguing that "under no circumstances will we be led out to slaughter our fellow-men." He assumed that advanced nations should have no need to resort to war to solve their disputes. But he was willing even then, as Lewis A. Fretz remarks, "to justify the use of force against underdeveloped nations where the people were too 'ignorant and helpless' to restrain the aggressive ambitions of their rulers." By 1916, the second year of the war in Europe, Sinclair was certain that Germany, the most advanced of nations in many ways, was a threat to civilization. He wrote with alarm to Graham Phelps Stokes from Coronado in early February 1916, arguing that they had to awaken the country "for the final struggle on behalf of Democracy" despite socialist opposition. He made the same point more forcefully eight months later, in September, in a letter to the Committee of the Anti-Enlistment League. Germany, he said, was a "civilized nation" in the thrall of a "barbarian caste." There would be no peace in the world until that caste was overthrown. The Allies deserved American support, in whatever form it might take. He ended by arguing that wars can and do solve social problems: if the South had won the Civil War, "we in America should have had militarism saddled upon us for centuries." If the Germans were to win the current war, the result would be similar.

Sinclair was at the center of a debate relatively new to his time but familiar to ours: what is the proper use of America's power beyond its own shores? The terms of the debate were remarkably like those we hear today. Was it, as Sinclair often said, a battle for civilization, or was it, as some of his former allies in the Socialist Party of America said, a capitalist plot for imperial domination? Both the political hierarchy and the membership of the ASP, following the logic that war was simply squabbling between controlling capitalistic interests, resolutely opposed joining what they saw as the hordes of brainless automatons swarming to their doom, to no discernible effect.

On April 2, 1917, President Woodrow Wilson won approval from Congress for American soldiers to join the battle in Europe. Sinclair wrote and spoke vigorously in Wilson's support, despite charges from fellow socialists that he was a Judas and a Benedict Arnold. On May 16, his life was threatened for his "betrayal" of the socialist cause. The incident, as recounted by Sinclair's friend Frank Bohm, occurred after a speech Bohm gave in Hollywood. Among the audience was an Austrian anarchist named Otto Fleischman, who introduced himself to Bohm, saying he had been a war correspondent. Bohm told Fleischman he could not stay to talk; he had invited both Sinclair and Armistead Collier, who was living in Hollywood, to join him for dinner at the Clark Hotel, where he was staying. Sinclair, overcoming his aversion to Collier, had agreed to meet them both at the hotel.

Bohm boarded the streetcar with Fleischman tagging along, picking up Collier on his way. When Fleischman learned that the two men were meeting Sinclair, he excitedly announced that he intended to challenge Sinclair to a duel: he would "call him out." "If he wants war, I'll give him war!" Trying to ignore Fleischman, Bohm and Collier entered the lobby of the Clark Hotel. When Sinclair stepped forward to greet Bohm, Fleischman pushed himself between them and yelled in Sinclair's face that he would "give you all the war you want." Bohm said Fleischman's countenance was "red and distorted," and he was cursing wildly, using the "vilest imaginable epithets." Bohm tried to take Fleischman's arm to lead him away. Fleischman said he had as much right to be in the hotel as anyone; he intended to sit at the table next to theirs and take notes and then to publish what they said. Bohm asked another guest to take Sinclair and Collier to the dining room, saying he would join them soon. Fleischman, his eyes "bulging," said he wasn't so easy to get rid of—"I am going to *get* Sinclair—and if you butt in, I'll get *you,* too."

Bohm thought Fleischman was dangerous and that his threats should not be lightly dismissed. Craig Sinclair agreed. In January 1911, a madman had shot and killed Sinclair's friend and fellow muckraker David Graham Phillips, and Craig would worry for the rest of her life that Sinclair might be assassinated.

Sinclair, who admired the military virtue of physical courage, joked about such dangers. During their winter in Bermuda he even placed a notice in the local newspaper addressed to a burglar he had frightened off a few nights earlier. (Only Sinclair would assume that a burglar read the newspaper!) If the intruder was hungry, he should stop by during the daytime and they would give him whatever he needed in the way of food. Sinclair added that he kept a revolver by his bedside, but had pretended the burglar was a cat, not wishing to shoot him. However, the burglar was on notice: not even the most ardent socialist could be expected to let "strangers prowl about in his bedroom after midnight."

Sinclair now wrote lightly to George Bernard Shaw that he had been having "an entertaining time" avoiding an "anarchist lunatic" who was trying to shoot him. "We have to keep all the curtains in the house drawn and steal out the back way, as if we were in the Indian country." But he also applied to the Los Angeles chief of police for a concealed weapon permit. On the day that he picked up the permit, May 30, he ate lunch with Harry Carr, the managing editor of the *Los Angeles Times,* who afterward went with him to a nearby gun store where he bought a new revolver and some ammunition.

It was a chilly day, so Sinclair was wearing a light topcoat. He slipped the revolver into a large pocket and returned with Carr to the *Times*—the lion's den, as he thought of it, the lair of its infamous publisher, General Harrison Otis. Though they had never met, Otis conceived a violent dislike for Sinclair after his talk the previous year to a ladies' club. Craig had urged Sinclair to get a haircut en route to the luncheon, but he didn't, he joked to the ladies, because he couldn't pick out the barbershop's striped pole for all the patriotic, war-whooping bunting along the streets. Alma Whitaker, the young reporter on the scene for the *Times,* wrote the story up with Sinclair's joke represented as a slur on the flag. Otis blasted Sinclair editorially the next day as "an effeminate young man with a fatuous smile, a weak chin, and a sloping forehead." He was a "slim, beflannelled example of perverted masculinity," guilty of advocating "anarchy, destruction, lawlessness [and] revolution," who would never have dared to say the things he did before an audience of real men.

As Sinclair was perusing the books on Carr's shelf, General Otis came into Carr's office and chatted briefly with his managing editor. Carr apologized to Sinclair after Otis left for not introducing them, but he was sure the old man would have made an ugly scene. Greatly amused, Sinclair considered Otis's reaction if he ever learned that such a dangerous anarchist and sexual pervert had been lurking in the shadows of his own offices with a gun in his pocket. As it happened, Otis was only a year away from death—by natural causes.

On July 22, 1917, Sinclair's letter of resignation from the American Socialist Party was published in the *Chicago Sunday Tribune*. He had not gone over "bag and baggage to the capitalist system," he said, and he was hardly alone in his support of the Wilson administration's war policy. Others among the intellectual leadership of the ASP, including Stokes, John Spargo, and William English Walling, took the same position as he did.

But Sinclair was uniquely vulnerable. As a writer already shut out from many of the nation's mainstream newspapers like the *Los Angeles Times,* his primary source of income had been from socialist publications. Now these were closed to him. Even magazines whose editors were more tolerant of his apostasy, particularly Max Eastman at the *New Masses* and Frank Harris at *Pearson's Magazine,* were having trouble getting U.S. postal permits. The newly passed Espionage Act allowed the reactionary postmaster general Albert Burleson unprecedented latitude in barring virtually any publication from equitable treatment by the post office.

Consequently, Sinclair launched his own monthly magazine, modestly called *Upton Sinclair's,* in April 1918. He ran it out of his house, hiring part-time secretarial help but doing much of the routine labor himself, with Craig's invaluable aid. Unable to buy mailing lists from socialist organizations, he had to compile his own, which took months, by which time, lacking any advertising base, he was severely in debt. In addition, although he was actively supporting Woodrow Wilson's war policy rather than opposing it, he was initially denied the essential second-class mailing permit for magazines. The refusal, he learned, stemmed from his involvement with Arthur Caron, the young man who had blown himself up with the bomb he was preparing for the Rockefellers. An influential Mississippi cousin of Craig's father's chastised W. H. Lamar, the postal official who had cited Sinclair's account of Caron's death as the reason for effectively killing his magazine: "The part that you blue penciled saying, 'The young man became frenzied, and in his bitter fury he went to making bombs,' you seem to think is an expression of approbation by Mr. Sinclair for making bombs. It is just exactly the opposite." Bobby Scripps also helped, using his father's prestige to contact the journalist George Creel, who was working for Woodrow Wilson as his director of propaganda—officially, he was in charge of the Committee on Public Information. Creel was a famously combative man, a former boxer; he "got in some pretty good licks" at the post office for Sinclair, according to Bobby. The necessary permit was quickly granted.

Sinclair wrote most of each sixteen-page issue himself, though he also included letters from subscribers, sometimes supportive, often abusive. A few of the titles will serve to suggest *Upton Sinclair's* tone and content: "A Clean Peace"; "Our Smiles to the Censor"; "Socialism and War"; "Sherlock Holmes and War"; "A Telegram for Russia." Lighter selections included a description of his home office, an account of his operation for appendicitis (in August 1918), and book reviews. His primary concern during the brief but intense lifespan of the magazine—a total of just ten issues—was the war, which he addressed in the form of frequent open letters to President Wilson and, more substantially, in a novel he called *Jimmie Higgins.*

George Brett, always willing to entertain Sinclair's ideas for new novels, had liked the opening chapters of *Jimmie Higgins* that Sinclair sent him in the spring of 1918. The novel's premise was intriguing: "Jimmie Higgins" was socialist slang for what today would be called a gofer, a hardworking underling who does all the grunt work and gets none of the glory. Sinclair intended to show how his hero, a true socialist, could switch from opposing the war to supporting it, eventually giving up his life as a soldier in France. Though he reflects Sinclair's own struggle to reconcile his opposing impulses, Jimmie is a poor, unlettered, good-hearted lower-class hero like Jurgis in *The Jungle,* suggesting to Brett that Sinclair might be returning to the kind of story that had been his greatest success.

But Brett was still wary of Sinclair's insistence on preaching the socialist gospel in his fiction, and declined to offer an advance. After reading the first eleven chapters in October and Sinclair's plan for the rest of the novel, he turned it down, saying it was "overloaded" with propaganda. And so it is. But much of the propaganda in *Jimmie Higgins* is in support of the war rather than a pitch for socialism; the second half of the novel is a compendium of German atrocity stories, including the discredited one about the Allied soldier crucified on a barn door by the beastly Huns. Sinclair even wrote to Woodrow Wilson, through George Creel, to propose that *Jimmie Higgins* be published and distributed by the government in support of its war effort. Creel saw only the first half of the book, in which Jimmie's socialist credentials, including a worshipful scene with Eugene Debs, are set forth. He told Sinclair that his office was restricted to publishing pamphlets, not full-length novels, which was true; but he cannot have been impressed by what he had read. As Sinclair would learn some years later, Creel regarded socialism as anathema, and those who supported it as fools.

Beginning in April 1918 and concluding in August 1919, Sinclair was writing chapters of *Jimmie Higgins* in much the same way as a journalist covers a breaking story: like the daily newspapers during the period when it was written, the novel is full of action but lacks a plot, as the conclusion to the epic battle between nations was still unknown. As for Jimmie's fate, all Sinclair knew for sure was that he would die fighting nobly for the Allied cause in France.

Beginning in June 1918, however, events conspired in such a way that Sinclair sent Jimmie not to France but to Siberia. His young hero was one of the thousands of soldiers—British, French, and American—dispatched by their governments to overthrow the Bolsheviks and restore the deposed Russian czar to power.

Sinclair, like everyone on the left, had greeted the Russian Revolution with the same enthusiasm that Wordsworth felt in 1789 after the French Revolution: "Bliss was it in that dawn to be alive!" The Allied intervention was roundly condemned by the left as a capitalist plot to destroy the new Russia and reinstate the old, evil order, but Sinclair's more thoughtful ambivalence is reflected in the tennis simile he used to describe Jimmie's feelings: he was "battered back and forth, like a tennis ball, between the two forces of Militarism and Revolution." Jimmie's terrible fate, perhaps the bleakest in any of Sinclair's works, reflects the philosophical paralysis of Sinclair and other liberals at the time, caught as they were between two evils: arrested and interrogated by the American military police for helping Red friends distribute Bolshevik propaganda, Jimmie is so brutally tortured that he loses his mind.

Considering how quickly Sinclair wrote *Jimmie Higgins,* and how busy he was with his magazine, the writing is often surprisingly good. He always had the ability to coin a phrase—the kaiser's Germany was "the Beast with the Brains of an Engineer"—and many of the novel's scenes, particularly those describing trench warfare and Jimmie's martyrdom (as it is represented) are compelling.

Nevertheless, *Jimmie Higgins* was published by Boni & Liveright in May 1919 to unenthusiastic reviews. Liberals and socialists disliked it for letting Jimmie go to war, the communists hated it for trying to represent more or less fairly the Allied arguments for invading Russia even while disputing them, and the Establishment press dismissed it as propaganda. Sinclair himself grew bitter about his support of the war in the face of Wilson's failure to secure a nonpunitive peace at Versailles and the growing repression of civil liberties at home: "If at the beginning of 1917 I had known what I know today," he said a few years later, "I would have opposed the war and gone to jail with the pacifist radicals. I cannot forgive him [Wilson]; it is not merely that he made a fool of himself, but he made a fool of me!"

Sinclair was also disappointed by the failure of his magazine to lure more than ten thousand subscribers, not enough to pay the bills. The last issue appeared in February 1919. In April, Sinclair struck a deal with Emanuel Haldeman-Julius, an energetic young journalist and editor who was now publishing the successor to *Appeal to Reason* as *The New Appeal,* still based in Girard, Kansas. Haldeman-Julius absorbed *Upton Sinclair's* and provided Sinclair's subscribers with *The New Appeal.* He also bought the serial rights to *Jimmie Higgins* and another book that Sinclair called *The Profits of Religion.* As a final sweetener, he guaranteed Sinclair $30 per week—about $300 in today's currency—to write on any subject he chose, for an audience of more than a quarter-million readers.

It was an ideal solution to Sinclair's problems, getting him out from under his backbreaking publishing labor and giving him both money and a large continuing audience. Once again, he was bouncing back.

A few days after he signed his magazine over to Haldeman-Julius, Sinclair hopped on his bicycle to visit a new neighbor who was also an entrepreneur, though on a rather larger and more successful scale. His name was Henry Ford, and he was tinkering in the garage of the house he had rented for the winter with Mrs. Ford and their son, Edsel. Ford was then in his mid-fifties, a tall, slender man, gray-haired, with "sensitive features" and a kind, unassuming manner. He was puzzled, he said to his visitor, by what appeared to be an extra hole in the carburetor he was holding. Did Sinclair have any idea what it could be for? Sinclair laughed and pointed out that he was traveling by bicycle. He could *drive* a car, he said, but that was the limit of his mechanical knowledge. In any case, he said, he preferred to walk. If Mr. Ford and Edsel were interested, he could show them some splendid hikes in the San Gabriel Mountains that loomed above his house.

Over the next weeks Sinclair and Henry Ford, sometimes accompanied by Edsel, took several long hikes, chatting as they walked, lunching in shady groves of sycamore and oak. Sinclair liked Ford, perhaps because one of the richest capitalists in the world seemed unoffended by challenges from a sincere but polite socialist. Ford was a genius at what he knew, Sinclair thought, but remarkably, almost endearingly, ignorant of almost everything else. When Sinclair asked what Ford thought of the profit system and Ford responded that he didn't know what it was, Sinclair was reminded of the Molière character who was surprised to learn that he had been speaking prose all his life.

But Ford was not dense. What he meant was that to him "profit" was not a system, it was a fact of life, like photosynthesis, or gravity. Well, Sinclair argued, Ford had offered to give up his profits during the war, letting the government run his plant free of charge. Why not "have public service in time of peace?" Why not the same enthusiasm "for feeding and clothing men as for killing them?" Ford said the war was a special circumstance. In peacetime nobody except a few "artists and engineers and inventors did their work for the love of it. They were not the money-making type." Maybe poets, too, though he didn't know any poets. Sinclair puckishly suggested that it might be a good idea if the government—"the people"—could own the automobile industry and "put Henry in charge of it." Ford said that idea didn't appeal to him very much. In fact, he said, he saw no reason why the Pasadena fire department should not be privately owned: "Let some competent business man attend to putting out fires."

On another occasion Ford again advocated what today would be called "privatizing" government functions rather than socializing industrial ones. Sinclair conceded that business barons might indeed do a good job at whatever they were assigned, but they were like kings—fine when you had a good one, but when they went bad there was no way to get rid of them. "That was why," he said, sounding very like Mark Twain, "the king business had broken down in the end." Now, in the twentieth century, the "industrial king business was breaking down because there were so few Henry Fords." Ford modestly disagreed, saying he was hardly one of a kind.

Opening another line of attack, Sinclair said not every tycoon agreed with Ford's ideas on capitalism and socialism. Would Ford be interested in meeting a friend of his, also a very successful entrepreneur, who had his own ideas about social justice? Ford said he would indeed.

Sinclair's friend was King Gillette, "the razor king." Now in his late sixties, Gillette was, like Ford, a midwesterner, born in Wisconsin and raised in Chicago. A traveling salesman of hardware supplies in his early years, Gillette was a large, friendly, extroverted man, handsome and blessed with what his biographer, Tim Dowling, calls "an almost hypnotic cloak of easygoing, clubbable charm." He sounds much like Dreiser's appealing salesman Drouet in *Sister Carrie,* but blessed with a gift for tinkering and a social conscience. The tinkering led to the disposable razor and blade at the turn of the century that made Gillette, in Dowling's words, "the inventor of the disposable culture," as well as a sizable fortune. The social conscience derived from Gillette's early reading of Bellamy's *Looking Backward,* and it impelled him to devise his own scheme for remedying the evils of the very system that had made him rich. He was determined to write his own book, but he knew he needed help. When Gillette heard of Sinclair's arrival in Pasadena, he drove out to visit him. His chauffeur knocked on the door and was informed by Sinclair's recently hired secretary that Sinclair was busy and did not wish to be disturbed. When Gillette persisted, sending in his business card with a $100 bill wrapped around it, Sinclair consented to be disturbed.

Their collaboration extended over a period of several months in 1916. Gillette paid Sinclair $500 a month for their twice-weekly editing sessions of the book that Gillette finally published in 1924 as *The People's Corporation*. Gillette was not an easy client. For one thing, he was horrified by the word "socialism," even though his ideas, Sinclair said, were those of a man "who apparently had never read a Socialist book in his life but had thought it out all for himself." Moreover, like many amateurs with money, Gillette was willing to pay a professional for advice but unable to understand or accept it. Sinclair bowed out of their joint project, but the two men remained on cordial terms, meeting frequently at the salon gatherings of another Pasadena millionaire, Kate Crane Gartz. Gillette responded eagerly to Sinclair's invitation to meet Henry Ford.

"The flivver king and the razor king," as Sinclair called them, relaxed before the fire in Sinclair's study on a cool April afternoon and swapped ideas. Craig sat by her husband as the two kings discoursed, and left an entertaining account of their conversation. Ford suggested that what the world needed most was more of what he had already developed in his automated factories—efficient ways to avoid waste. He pointed to the poker with which Sinclair had stirred the fire, saying, "If it stays where it is it will soon be too hot to pick up." What it needed was a heatproof handle, which would avoid the inconvenience of waiting until it was cool enough to pick up, by which time the fire would have died. "It's the same wherever you look—some labor-wasting device where a labor-saving device is needed." He concluded, "We must invent more and better things, and sell them at lower prices." Gillette agreed on the need for better products, but lamented "the waste of competition" involved in persuading people to buy one version of the same thing over another. He wanted "a People's Corporation," which would not charge itself higher prices than needed and would not "waste time and money and brains in competitive selling." Sinclair smiled as the flivver king, "lean and spry," and the razor king, "large and ponderous," bounced off each other like billiard balls: "they hit and then flew apart, and neither made the slightest impression upon the other."

Sinclair would see a good deal more of Gillette in the coming years, but nothing of Henry Ford, who did not return to Pasadena. He did manage to persuade Ford before he went home to Detroit to start his own magazine, since Ford was dissatisfied with the way his ideas were represented in the popular press, which Ford in fact proceeded to do. Unfortunately, Sinclair said later, in the context of his 1938 novel about Ford and his empire, *The Flivver King,* the *Dearborn Independent* was from its first days of publication "the most reactionary magazine in America."

———

Sinclair's earnest hope that Henry Ford would begin a progressive newspaper grew out of his accurate perception that magazine and newspaper journalism did much to shape American public opinion. He was in his own right a born pundit, as his recent experience with *Upton Sinclair's* had shown. With his phenomenal energy, his ability to work on half a dozen different projects at the same time, and his certainty that what he had to say was important, Sinclair would prosper as a columnist for Haldeman-Julius and *The New Appeal* from 1919 through 1925.

Sinclair's topics for discussion in *The New Appeal* and elsewhere were timely and provocative. For several years following his move to California he had considered doing a series of social critiques on American institutions and attitudes. Moving beyond the relatively narrower confines of business and government that had been the chief targets of the muckrakers before the war, he now aimed for the biggest game possible: religion, journalism, education, and—strangely—the art of literature. Collectively, he said, the institutions, individuals, and values associated with each of these composed a "dead hand" around the throat of free men and women in America.

The first of his attacks, and the most controversial, was *The Profits of Religion,* published serially in his magazine and then as a book, in October 1918, which Sinclair self-published when he couldn't find a commercial publisher. Like the other books in the series, *Profits* was deliberately incendiary and intensely autobiographical. It reflected both the advantages and the disadvantages of its original publication as a series of articles—each dependent on an attention-getting hook, each capable of being read apart from the others. When read today as a book, the arguments in *The Profits of Religion,* as in its successors, seem repetitive rather than fully developed. The pitch is too high for comfort and many of the specific targets, familiar to Sinclair's readers at the time, are now remote.

But the Dead Hand books overflow with vivid, and often very funny, passages that reveal Sinclair's insufficiently recognized strengths as a literary stylist. Many of his aphorisms, like this one recycled from *Prince Hagen,* are still arresting: "If you can once get a man to believing in immortality, there is no more left for you to desire; you can take everything he owns—you can skin him alive if it pleases you—and he will bear it all with perfect good humor." And his opening scene for *The Profits of Religion* is a tour de force worthy of Voltaire or Swift.

Picture, Sinclair says, an inquiring stranger wandering across a broad plain among dense clusters of men and women, all of whom are bending over and busily tugging at their bootstraps. At the same time, their eyes are fixed upon the sky with "a look of rapture upon their faces" as they howl ecstatic cries of triumph "amid grunts and groans." The stranger asks one man what he is doing. "I am performing spiritual exercises," the man responds. "See how I rise?" When the stranger remarks that so far as he can see the man remains firmly fixed to the earth, the worshippers dismiss him as a "materialist," fatally lacking in "spiritual vision."

The bemused stranger moves on. Another figure glides through the crowd, lightly lifting the wallets from the conveniently hoisted rear ends of the bootstrap-uplifters; his badge identifies him as an officer of the "Wholesale Pickpockets' Association." A nobler, "stately figure, clad in scarlet and purple robes," then appears, intoning "It is more blessed to give than to receive" and "Blessed are the Bootstrap-lifters, for theirs is the kingdom of Heaven." When the traveler asks by what right the priest and his agent collect the money, the Bootstrap-lifters he seeks to defend call the police and send him packing.

As a parable, this scene suggests not only Swift and Voltaire but Sinclair's early favorite, *Pilgrim's Progress.* In a world full of fools and knaves, among the worst knaves for Sinclair were those who shared his own great gifts of expression and persuasion but who abused those gifts for their own profit—witness "Poison Ivy" Lee, who grew rich persuading the public that John D. Rockefeller, Sr., was a saint.

Sinclair's stated purpose in *The Profits of Religion* was to show that religion was in the hands of clever exploiters working not in God's behalf but as agents of capitalism. The rest of the book fills in the blanks in terms of particulars, arraigning with equal gusto every belief from Roman Catholicism to Mormonism to southern California cults, which he groups under the heading "The Church of the Quacks."

Sinclair couched his argument as coming from an affronted Christian. He was not an atheist or even an agnostic, he said. He was raised as a devout Episcopalian and he still wanted, as he had written to Edwin Markham in 1901, "to give every second of my time and of my thought, every ounce of my energy, to the worship of my God and to the uttering of the unspeakable message that I know he has given me." He discounted, however, the unexplainable or supernatural elements of Christianity—in a word, everything that had to be taken on faith was not only unprovable but unimportant. Sinclair did believe that man was more than merely "a worm that perishes, a stirring in the slime." But his faith at base was a kind of Transcendentalism, reflected in his admiration of the Emerson who asserted

> I am owner of the sphere,
> Of the seven stars and the solar year,
> Of Caesar's hand, and Plato's brain,
> Of Lord Christ's heart, and Shakspeare's strain.

The core of Sinclair's Christian doctrine was the image of Jesus as a revolutionary leader who worked for the poor—the same idea that underlies what radical Catholics today call liberation theology. His personal experiences also loom large in *The Profits of Religion*. His disgust with the Protestant blue laws that got him thrown into jail for playing tennis on Sunday at Arden, and his fury with the Catholic-dominated legislature in New York for impeding his divorce, are frequently stated in this and his other books. Because he was such a true believer in the rightness of his cause, Sinclair seems not to have understood that he mirrored his adversaries in an important way. Belief in a personal God demands that one accept as true an unprovable abstraction. Sinclair's belief was essentially a negative certainty: All religion *not* based on opposition to the established order must be fraudulent and complicit in the maintenance of that order, which in modern times is capitalism.

Entertaining in places but demonstrably overstated and unfair, *The Profits of Religion* earned Sinclair a host of enemies who would not forget or forgive his scattergun indictment of religious faiths and practices. Sinclair Lewis, who had his own problems with his former employer, read the book carefully twice in preparation for writing *Elmer Gantry*, itself attacked as antireligious but comparatively much more temperate and certainly a greater book than its partial source.

For all its flaws—or because of them—by 1926 *Profits* had provided Sinclair a comfortable economic validation. It was in its fifth edition and had sold sixty thousand copies. It was also widely translated, into twelve languages. But its success would pale in comparison to that of the second book in Sinclair's Dead Hand series, in 1920. This would be his gleefully vindictive attack on the one institution that had plagued him from the earliest days of his career: the American press.

CHAPTER TEN

THE CIVIL LIBERTARIAN

(January 1920–December 1923)

A sympathetic editor wisely advised Upton Sinclair as a young man that he needed "a good stiff course in plain, every-day newspaper reporting. Newspaper reporters have many deficiencies, but at least they learn to keep in touch with their audiences, and to write in a way that takes hold of the people." Sinclair never worked as a reporter, but he obviously learned how to "take hold" of his audience. He used this ability to spectacular effect in 1920 with an attack on the press itself in the second book of his Dead Hand series, *The Brass Check*.

The Brass Check owed its success in part to the fact that Sinclair was writing about something he knew from professional as well as intensely personal experience. *The Profits of Religion* had been written from the outside looking in. He knew a great deal about religion, but the religious temperament was alien to him except as it could be practically applied to social problems. The reportorial temperament, on the other hand, was one that Sinclair shared. But because he subordinated everything to what he saw as the need to work for social justice, the institution that should have been Sinclair's natural ally, the press, became his deadliest enemy, bent on destroying him. Or so he said, using his familiar martial metaphor: "You are listening to a man who for fourteen years has been in a battle, and has seen his cause suffering daily wounds from a cruel and treacherous foe."

Sinclair's paranoia about the press ("I have been persecuted for twenty years by prostitute Journalism") resulted in a book that is best seen as two parts personal pique and one part tendentious argument, leavened by glimmers of objective analysis. The title itself comes from the old practice in New York City whorehouses of requiring a customer to pay a cashier for a brass token, which he then gave to the prostitute he had selected.

So intermixed are Sinclair's pique and his analysis in *The Brass Check* that it is hard to pry them apart, but the structure of the book is clear enough, as are its main points. The first half, which Sinclair calls "The Evidence," is an often bitter personal memoir. It is casual and anecdotal, reflecting the method of its original publication in *The New Appeal* as a series of weekly columns. Many readers reproached Sinclair for overstatement, but he was psychologically incapable, it appears, of doing otherwise. He once explained his perspective on controversial topics in terms of a psychological picture puzzle. At first the puzzle reveals nothing, but closer inspection shows the outline of a cat. Those who come to perceive the cat can see nothing else but the cat. Those who do not see it cannot be convinced, even with instruction, that the cat is there at all.

In a wild mélange of metaphor, Sinclair describes the newspapers' attacks on his integrity after *The Jungle* appeared and their refusal to print his rebuttals: he had become, he said, a dangerous beast, "an animal in a cage" whose "bars were newspapers." He paced furiously inside the cage, finding the bars "impossible to break." Worst of all was what happened during his divorce proceedings, when he was "caught upon the hook of an unhappy marriage, gutted, skinned alive, and laid quivering on the red-hot griddle" of the daily press.

Sinclair introduces the second half of *The Brass Check,* "The Explanation," with a favorite quote from Virgil: "Happy is he who knows the causes of things." Although they are exaggerated in Sinclair's telling, both the causes and the effects of the problems he describes will be as familiar to readers today as they were a century ago, especially when extrapolated to include what we call "the media." Simply stated, Sinclair argues that "American newspapers as a whole represent private interests and not public interests" and that they are largely owned or controlled, like everything else in America, by "perhaps a score of powerful individuals." The newspapers, their owners, and those who work for them are all parts of "the great stream of capitalist prosperity." The stream "may flow irregularly, it may have eddies and counter-currents, stagnant places which deceive you for a while; but if you study this great stream long enough, you find that it all moves in one direction, and that everything upon its surface moves with it."

The postwar shortage of paper forced Sinclair to print his first edition of *The Brass Check* on coarse brown kraft paper. The book was ignored or condemned by the newspapers he maligned, and Sinclair was chastised by journalism professors and by Associated Press spokesmen. Friends warned him that he had set himself up for innumerable libel suits (none of which developed). Yet he had clearly struck a nerve with a public that, then as now, harbored deep suspicions about the press: *The Brass Check* was Sinclair's biggest hit since *The Jungle,* selling 155,000 copies in a dozen printings in the United States alone. For journalism students, it became a cult classic. As late as 1933, one student assured Sinclair that no other book had been "read more earnestly and thoroughly" by him and his friends: "We refer to it on many occasions, first because we believe in it and second because our department head does not believe in it."

Some historians credit Sinclair with helping to stimulate reforms that would justify referring to journalism as a profession. Others, as the introduction to a 2003 University of Illinois Press edition of *The Brass Check* argues, see little improvement: the "dawn of the twenty-first century finds us in a position not entirely unlike the one Sinclair and his compatriots were in more than eighty years ago. The media are exceptionally concentrated, journalism is of dubious integrity, and the political system is awash in corruption."

═══

Sinclair interrupted his pursuit of his next Dead Hand target, American education, to toss off a novel in six weeks that he called *100%,* ironically subtitled "The Story of a Patriot." He published it himself in October 1920 as a cautionary tale about the evil effects of the government's campaign against the "Red Terror" following the war. Louis Untermeyer, one of the few critics to comment on *100%,* called it a "cumulative record of blackmail, espionage, intimidation, intrigue, unwarranted assaults, invasions, property destructions, paid witnesses, illegal jailings, horse-whippings, lynchings, frame-ups, 'patriotic' murders; an orgy of confiscation, Bolshevik-baiting, mad hysteria, mad fear, and a madder frenzy."

Somewhat more substantial was Sinclair's collection of columns from *The New Appeal* called *The Book of Life,* also self-published, in September 1921. Many of his readers had come to regard Sinclair not merely as a political guide but as an expert in all fields, including mental, physical, and spiritual health. He responded to their many letters eagerly, pleased to tell them "how to live, how to find health and happiness and success, how to work and how to play"—everything up to and including "what books to read." He poked fun at himself for taking on such "a large order, as the boys phrase it!"—but he was serious about his advice, much of it stemming from his own experience, and some of it recycled from his correspondence with his son, David, now a college student at the University of Wisconsin.

David had graduated from high school in Greenwood, Mississippi, in June 1920. During that summer he wrote to ask his father's advice on choosing a college. Sinclair thought David was too immature to leave Mississippi and the security represented by Craig's family. He urged him to attend a local agricultural or trade tech school. David was desperate to get out of Mississippi and to win his father's approval by taking on a more challenging course of study. He suggested that he might attend Stanford, less than four hundred miles from Los Angeles. He even added a note to Craig, touchingly insincere. He was sorry to hear she had injured herself in a fall: "you are a mighty unlucky person, as well as a very kind and unselfish person."

Sinclair vetoed Stanford on the laughable ground that it was too dangerous: some of its heavy stone buildings had tumbled into dust during the 1906 San Francisco earthquake. Besides, if David were to fall ill again with the "flue," as he had earlier, Craig would feel compelled to come up and care for him. Her own health was still precarious, undermined by constant stresses—she had been up half the night trying to catch a horse that had broken into the orchard. David should consider attending college "somewhere in the Midwest" (where any distant illness presumably would not trouble Craig). Sinclair suggested Kansas or Wisconsin. Wherever David went, of course, he would have "to work and fight your way as I did myself," with no financial support from Sinclair: it built character when a young man put himself through college. He reminded David in closing to be sure and tell him "what kind of training you have in mind."

Sinclair, who had fought Meta so hard over David, had apparently made a Faustian bargain with Craig—who was capable of making his life miserable if he didn't agree to keep David at a considerable physical and emotional distance. In *100%* Sinclair's protagonist Peter Gudge's rueful awakening after his marriage offers some insight into Sinclair's own situation with Craig: Gudge "suddenly discovered who was going to be top dog in that family. He was shown his place once for all, and he took it—alongside that husband who described his domestic arrangements by saying that he and his wife got along beautifully together, they had come to an arrangement by which he was to have his way on all major issues, and she was to have her way on all minor issues, and so far no major issues had arisen." Forty years later, in a play about Cicero, Sinclair has the Roman orator voicing the cliché, in connection with his imperious wife, that men "can't live with them and can't live without them." Craig herself is quoted in *Mammonart,* Sinclair's 1925 book about literature: "In our family the men have a traditional saying: 'It's all right to be henpecked, but be sure you get the right hen!' "

As a lonely freshman who was obviously relegated to the category of a "minor" rather than "major" problem for his father, David wrote often to his mother for consolation. In late September he indiscreetly told Sinclair that Meta thought he was not treating their son fairly, especially in denying him financial support for college. An irritated Sinclair responded to David that he couldn't be "drawn into this maelstrom again." Meta had been an "endless waste of my life and my energy and my time and money." Be wary of the "born parasite" when you come to marry, he warned David; don't let Meta "win you from me, to punish me for taking you from her. When you were a little fellow, she would give you candy to get her way with you. She will give you mental candy now," saying it is "shocking that you should scrub floors for an education" instead of living like a gentleman in a fraternity, as she would wish. He reminded David that until he was twenty-one, he would hold Meta to her agreement that she could see him only two weeks out of the year, in Mississippi. He was "not a vindictive person," Sinclair assured David; rather, he was "foolishly easy-going and generous," but Meta had "drain[ed] my blood drop by drop," possessed as she was by such "poisonous venom—." He broke off with a promise that some day he would show David Meta's letters and "affidavits" that would reveal her for what she really was.

─────

Perhaps because of the tensions between David and his father, there is no record of a meeting between them during the several days that Sinclair spent at the University of Wisconsin in May 1922 while researching his exposé of higher education, *The Goose-Step,* the third book in his Dead Hand series. Sinclair's comments on this visit are limited to his extended confrontation with the president of the university and his triumphs over the tennis team— seriatim and each dispatched in straight sets, he boasted.

Sinclair had far fewer personal grounds for complaining about American education than he had concerning journalism or religion. Whatever its deficiencies, the system had given him a variety of useful skills and an enormous fund of knowledge, both esoteric and practical. His gripes about his years at Columbia, which allowed him to range freely through the curriculum, seem especially petty: it was "a hollow shell, a body without a soul, a mass of brick and stone held together by red tape." Why? In large part because it wouldn't let him submit a novel as a master's thesis, unwilling, like all universities then, to entertain "the possibility that there might be a man of genius actually alive in America at the beginning of the twentieth century."

Sinclair augmented his personal reminiscences with interviews conducted on the road, his longest journey in six years. He left Craig in Pasadena on April 5—she felt too ill to travel—and returned at the end of June 1922. Selecting names from his extensive mailing list, he had set up interviews at a score of colleges and universities, including Stanford, Oregon, Montana, and Pittsburgh, as well as at Wisconsin and Columbia. He also spoke to teachers on the lower levels, especially in the high schools, believing at the time that he would write just one book instead of the two that he eventually did.

Sinclair approached his topic with the certainty that education was the tool of the business establishment, designed to train obedient, submissive servants rather than to educate independent thinkers. He solicited opinions from those who agreed with him, men and occasionally women who were often at war with their institutions. The complaints will sound familiar to a modern audience, many more of whom have firsthand acquaintance with college, either as students or as instructors, than did most of Sinclair's readers in 1920. He targeted excessive regimentation, rote learning, subsidized and quasi-professional student athletics, authoritarian administrations, ignorant trustees, stingy state legislators, party-mad students and their fraternities, and the general failure to distinguish training for work from education for life.

Sinclair intended his provocative title, *The Goose-Step,* to suggest more than "merely a physical thing, the drilling of a whole population for the aggrandizement of a military caste; it was a spiritual thing, a regimen of autocratic dogmatism." He blamed the arbitrary lockstep indoctrination characteristic of modern education, as he saw it, on the eighteenth-century philosopher Johann Gottlieb Fichte, who said "To compel men to a state of right, to put them under the yoke of right by force, is not only the right but the sacred duty of every man who has the knowledge and the power. . . . He is the master, armed with compulsion and appointed by God."

Sinclair's admirers have often praised him for avoiding mean-spirited attacks on individuals. In fact, he frequently pilloried individuals as representative and symbolic instances of personal corruption. The bigger the target, the more uncompromising the assault. In the world of higher education, the prime target was Nicholas Murray Butler, the noted philosopher, scholar, and teacher who was both president of Columbia University and a respected adviser to Republican presidents. Sinclair had studied Kant with Butler, and remembered him as a cold, impersonal teacher who read from prepared notes twice a week, took a few questions, closed his books, and left without a word of farewell. What particularly disturbed him about Butler, Sinclair said later, was that he probably had "the greatest mind in America"; but like the president of every university, even of those land-grant institutions supposedly funded by the states, he was in thrall to the great banks and corporations that run the country. Columbia was in reality, said Sinclair, the

University of the House of Morgan, with its endowment invested in holdings "under the supervision of the interlocking directors," including several of the fourteen railroads on which Sinclair traveled to do his research.

Consistent with the tyrannical nature of the regimes they had to serve, as they saw it, Sinclair's confidants were mostly professors who often begged him to conceal their identities thoroughly ("Please let me know that you will spare me"). Typically, they complained about college administrators. Columbia under Butler, one anonymous source said, was a "twilight zone of mediocrity" where most faculty were cowed and terrorized. But some of Sinclair's respondents from other institutions said the faculty had themselves to blame for their problems. "We are good cows," said one. "We stand quietly in our stanchions, and give down our milk at regular hours. We are free, because we have no desire to do anything but what we are told we ought to do. And we die of premature senility." "The young instructors are weaklings, selected as such," said another. "They seek a comfortable berth, sheltered from the storms of the world." Professors are like actors, said a third: each one "thinks of himself as something impossible to duplicate."

Sinclair's favorite quote went directly to the heart of the problem, as he saw it: lack of common cause, or solidarity. The average professor, his respondent said, will watch a college president abuse a colleague with the same indifference as a rabbit observes a ferret chase down another rabbit and drink its blood. "We know, of course, that it would cost the non-attacked rabbit his place to express sympathy for the martyr; and the non-attacked is poor, and has offspring, and hopes of advancement."

The Goose-Step sold well enough under Sinclair's own imprint, approximately sixteen thousand copies. Its impact was narrower than that of *The Profits of Religion* or *The Brass Check,* and the world of American higher education is far too complicated for *The Goose-Step* to be of more than minor interest today. Sinclair's basic problem in his analysis of education in the United States was that, as he so often did, he largely ignored the great and compensating benefits provided by the system, for all its flaws.

In September 1922 appeared yet another fictional *esprit,* a break between Sinclair's Dead Hand books. *They Call Me Carpenter,* published by Boni & Liveright, develops his idea, first voiced in *The Jungle,* of Jesus as a revolutionary. Ten months earlier, uniformed veterans celebrating Armistice Day in Los Angeles had noisily protested showings of the avant-garde German film *The Cabinet of Dr. Caligari.* Sinclair's novel begins with that event. The mob beats the novel's narrator, who finds refuge in a Roman Catholic church. The stained-glass image of Jesus looks down upon the desperate fugitive as he collapses, unconscious. The narrator awakens to a comforting voice. Opening his eyes, he is amazed to see the real Jesus before him. The sequence of events that follows reenacts those leading up to the Crucifixion, with particular attention given to Christ's teachings and the conversions of Mary Magdalene (a sluttish movie star named "Mary Magna") and Paul, a repulsive movie director. Jesus himself is called "Mr. Carpenter."

Mr. Carpenter's sermons are a mix of Sinclair's socialism and the words of Jesus as taken from the Bible, as in this passage: "The days of the exploiter are numbered. The thrones of the mighty are tottering, and the earth shall belong to them that labor. He that toils not, neither shall he eat, and they that grow fat upon the blood of the people—they shall grow lean again." The leading newspaper—i.e., the *Los Angeles Times*—responds, in a passage that shows Sinclair's talent for broad parody: "the order-loving and patriotic people of our Christian community" will "stamp their heel upon this vile viper before its venom shall have poisoned the air we breathe."

The idea of Christ returning only to be crucified again, showing how little mankind has progressed during his absence, was hardly new—Dostoevsky had used it to great effect in the best part of *The Brothers Karamazov,* "The Grand Inquisitor"—but Sinclair developed it with considerable ingenuity in *They Call Me Carpenter.* He erred badly, though, in his effort to make the Jewish movie producer as obnoxious as possible, hoping to show how Jesus could work miracles of conversion. Some of Sinclair's critics have found in this and other instances convincing evidence that Sinclair was anti-Semitic.

It is true that Sinclair offered frequent observations about Jews that will offend most readers today, often having to do with business acumen, sexuality, and behavior. In his defense, it may be noted that he did the same for virtually every group that he took the time to examine, including Mormons, the English upper classes, and American Legionnaires. More to the point, admirable Jews figure prominently in Sinclair's best work, the Lanny Budd novels, especially the Robin family. Lanny himself is taken under the protective wing of a Hungarian Jew whose model was Sinclair's high school friend Martin Birnbaum.

Sinclair's slurs when they do occur—such as naming a character Abey Tszchniczklefritzsch—probably grew out of his quasi-aristocratic background, and are reminiscent of his distaste for the boardinghouse denizens he grew up with, or the old ladies who infuriated Arthur Stirling. Even so, he was concerned enough about charges of anti-Semitism to deny them earnestly, and there is no question that he did not endear himself to those

Hollywood producers who collectively provided Sinclair with the model for his caricature.

They Call Me Carpenter was a success for Sinclair. Despite his attacks on Hearst and his papers in *The Brass Check, Hearst's International Magazine* had serialized the novel for $2,500 from July to October 1922—about $27,000 in today's dollars. He entertained himself late in the year by writing a blank-verse drama called *Hell,* a complicated antiwar fantasy that he sent to Eugene O'Neill for the Provincetown Players. O'Neill diplomatically responded that that the play would present an interesting challenge for the theater that chose to stage it. And that, other than a serial run in *The New Appeal* in April 1923, was the end of *Hell.*

Sinclair's amusingly titled sequel to *The Goose-Step,* begun in the fall of 1923, was *The Goslings,* a study of secondary and high school education. When it appeared in February 1924, it stirred some controversy for its charges that local school boards were often paid off by construction interests in return for lucrative building contracts. But the best part of *The Goslings* has nothing to do with education, except in the broadest sense of the word. It describes how Sinclair wound up in jail yet again, as an indirect consequence of actions involving his old antagonist, General Harrison Otis of the *Los Angeles Times.*

Sinclair's lighthearted memory of the day in 1917 when he briefly saw Otis in Harry Carr's office suggests that Carr shared his own dislike of the old publisher. In fact, Carr, like many in southern California, revered Otis as a heroic master builder, one of a handful of titans who had turned a barren wasteland on the far edge of the continent into an oasis, and very nearly a paradise. A "rugged, strong character," in Carr's words, Otis was "bitter in his hatreds and loyal in his friendships." His bitterest hatred had been directed toward the men who blew up the *Times* building in 1910 as a protest against his closed-shop, anti-union stance. Twenty-three of Otis's employees had died, and the two prime suspects, James and John McNamara, had pleaded guilty in order to avoid execution for the crime. The general was now dead, but during the years since the bombing the tensions between business and labor in Los Angeles had continued to grow. The extremes of opposition were represented on the right by the Merchants and Manufacturers Association—the M&M, as it was generally known—and its hard core, the Better America Federation, composed of men as righteous as Otis, and more ruthless. The M&M's most resolute antagonists on the far left were the Industrial Workers of the World, the IWW—the Wobblies.

Most of the members of the IWW were tough but honest workingmen, but their public image had long been tarnished by violence. Wobbly leaders were instrumental in the 1905 murder of Idaho's governor Frank Steunenberg, as J. Anthony Lukas, a sympathizer, reluctantly concluded in his book *Big Trouble* (1997). Joe Hill was executed by a Utah firing squad in 1915 for murder, thus becoming an IWW martyr. And the McNamara brothers had been defended by Wobbly lawyers. By the early 1920s the Wobblies' reputation for violence had brought them to the edge of extinction, barely holding their own in such areas as the logging camps of the Northwest and on the West Coast docks.

The Wobblies and anyone else inclined to protest were especially hindered by the new federal Sedition Act, passed during the last months of the war. Later overturned, the Sedition Act provided for "a fine of not more than $10,000 or imprisonment for not more than twenty years, or both" for anyone disposed to "utter, print, write, or publish any disloyal, profane, scurrilous, or abusive language about the form of government of the United States." In 1919, California passed its own law, the Criminal Syndicalism Act, which allowed those who "advocated or taught the commission of crime, sabotage, force, violence, or terrorism to effect change in industrial or political control" to be jailed for periods ranging from one to fourteen years. Los Angeles went even further than did the federal government or the state, authorizing a special enforcement unit of the police called the "Red Squad." One hardly had to be a radical in those years to be afraid that the right to speak freely was in danger of vanishing entirely.

Sinclair had long been infatuated with the Wobblies. Like Jack London and Harry Kemp, he saw in them a compound of rebellion and romance; they were criminals and poets, murderers and martyrs, and they held the same risky fascination for radical intellectuals that Genet would later have for Sartre, or the Black Panthers for Leonard Bernstein. Sinclair's life had been relatively protected. He knew only vicariously the kind of adventures lived by London and Kemp, which may have increased what one writer calls his "boundless affection" for the Wobblies' "romantic individualism, their lack of organization, and above all, their position at the bottom of the heap."

But Sinclair knew from his experience during the Rockefeller protests in 1915 that the Wobblies drew violence to them, even when they did not initiate it. Out of deference to Craig's fears for his safety, he declined an invitation in January 1923 to speak on behalf of the waterfront workers. He also merely watched from the sidelines as, on April 25, the Wobbly-dominated Marine Transport Workers Industrial Union No. 510 called a strike. Its work-related goal was to shut down the company-controlled hiring hall, the

Sea Service Bureau, disparagingly known as "Fink Hall." Another major goal with which many citizens, workers or not, could agree was the repeal of the Criminal Syndicalism Act. But the union raised the ante and lost public support by including among its demands the release of all those inmates at San Quentin and Folsom whom it regarded as "political and class war prisoners." The International Longshoremen's Association and the American Federation of Labor refused to join the strike, but enough men did during the next two weeks to paralyze the Los Angeles port at San Pedro. Estimates ranged from fifteen hundred to three thousand striking workers.

On May Day, speakers roused a crowd of some two thousand sympathizers with red flowers in their lapels as an airplane, painted a bright red, circled overhead dropping leaflets. A motorboat cruised the harbor, passing out strike literature to the curious crews of as many of the ninety idled ships as they could reach. But on May 2 the *Times* reported in a story headlined "Reds' Confidence Oozing" that the strike was collapsing. On May 4, strikebreakers were brought in and cargo began to move onto the docks, though slowly.

Sinclair became involved in the strike by chance three days later. He had been invited to give a talk on *The Goose-Step* in late April at Pasadena's University Club. The president of the club, an "ex–naval officer who would have faced the guns of a foreign foe, but dared not face a new idea," then blushingly withdrew the invitation because William J. Burns, the head of the U.S. Secret Service, had reportedly called Sinclair "a dangerous enemy of the United States government."

William Burns was a formidable opponent. It was Burns who had crushed the Molly Maguires, and who later helped to catch and prosecute both the Steunenberg murder suspects and the McNamara brothers. In response to a telegram from Sinclair, Burns denied making any remarks about him. A subsequent United Press story, however, quoted the famous detective as saying his opinion of Sinclair had been uttered as "a private individual," not as a government official. Sinclair protested to Burns that anyone hearing such a comment from the head of the Secret Service would assume he must have cause for it. Burns assured Sinclair in a succeeding telegram that he had never made any such statement about him, period. By threatening the University Club with a lawsuit for slander, Sinclair learned that the source of the supposed Burns quote was Irwin Hays Rice, the president of the Merchants and Manufacturers Association.

On Monday, May 7, according to Sinclair's account in *The Goslings,* he waited outside Rice's office to ask him about the Burns remark. With him was Craig's brother, Hunter Kimbrough. Now twenty-four years old,

Hunter had come to live with the Sinclairs after a checkered academic career in several different southern colleges. Good-natured and hardy, an inch or two over six feet and weighing close to two hundred pounds, Hunter did odd jobs around the house and frequently accompanied "Mr. Sinclair," as he always called his brother-in-law, on his travels around the city. Mr. Rice, a refreshingly "two-fisted man of action," told Sinclair that Burns had indeed called him "a parlor pink and a dangerous enemy of the United States government." Sinclair thanked Rice for confirming his statement and showed him the telegram in which Burns flatly denied making any such accusation. Rice was satisfyingly nonplussed, but for Sinclair it hardly mattered which of his two antagonists was lying, as one of them had to be. His certainty of a conspiracy to smear him was confirmed, and it was coincidentally linked to the strike that he now decided, against Craig's wishes, to support actively.

We have no confirming evidence for Sinclair's account, which seems almost too tidy, anticipating his later hero Lanny Budd's ability to be always on the spot at the critical moment. But subsequent events do suggest an intricate web of influence, power, and deception consistent with the impressions he took away from his dispute with Rice and Burns.

When street meetings of the strikers were outlawed by the city, a local sympathizer, Minnie Davis, said the protesters could meet on her vacant waterfront lot, which was quickly dubbed "Liberty Hill." Twenty men were nevertheless arrested when they tried to meet there on May 9. On the following day, an estimated five thousand marchers paraded for five hours around the city jail. Chief of Police Louis Oaks assumed command of the Harbor Police and vowed to jail anyone participating in street demonstrations. In addition, he said, "All idle men at the harbor must explain their loafing and show they are not I.W.W.'s or go to jail." The *Times* story on Oaks's follow-up to his threat was headlined "Raids on Wobbly Nest at Harbor Net 300 Reds."

On Saturday, May 12, strikers raised the Soviet Union's flag—along with those of the United States and several other nations—on Liberty Hill as Captain Plummer of the Los Angeles police looked on. Plummer shouted, "You've lost your constitutional rights!" and arrested twenty-eight men for raising the hammer and sickle flag in violation of a city ordinance. Several hundred more men were plucked off the streets and arrested over the course of the next three days, among them an Episcopal priest from Philadelphia and a restaurant owner charged with prolonging public disorder because he had fed the strikers.

On the afternoon of Tuesday, May 15, Sinclair and a group of citizens met with Mayor George Cryer for an hour to protest the crackdown. Cryer, according to Sinclair, cited the city's law against raising the Communist flag—soon to be declared unconstitutional by the State Supreme Court—and added that he couldn't tolerate strikers calling Plummer a "fat prostitute." Sinclair said he intended to go to Liberty Hill that afternoon to speak to the workers. He would read the Constitution to them and explain the Bill of Rights. Cryer agreed to call Plummer and tell him that Sinclair should not be molested so long as he did not incite the crowd to violence. (Cryer, Sinclair notes, subsequently denied making this promise.)

Sinclair and his group of "a dozen ladies and gentlemen" then "repaired to the harbor," as he drolly recounts, where Chief of Police Oaks said he would arrest and hold them without bail if they tried to go ahead with their incitement. It was now dark, so Sinclair had to use a candle as he read the First Amendment—"Congress shall make no law . . . abridging the freedom of speech, or of the press; or the right of the people peaceably to assemble, and to petition the government for a redress of grievances"—after which he was arrested. Hunter, too excited to think straight, shouted, "You have just heard the first Article of the Declaration of Independence," and was led away by the police. A friend from Santa Barbara, Pryns Hopkins, got no further than "We did not come here to incite violence." Hugh Hardyman, a young Englishman then visiting the Sinclairs, said only "This is a most delightful climate" before he was arrested. The charge against all of them? "Obstructing traffic."

The farcical elements of this, Sinclair's third arrest, echo those of his first two, at Arden and in New York. But Elmer Belt, Sinclair's doctor, thought there was real danger involved, and not just from the police. He said the Wobblies "were angry, they had guns, and they threatened to shoot anyone who approached them." Sinclair "took off his coat, handed it to someone and walked up" to the strikers, who "didn't shoot him" but instead agreed "to abandon their warlike attitude and to talk sense with the authorities." Louis Adamic, a recent Serbian immigrant and an aspiring writer, remembered standing a few feet from Sinclair. Adamic's account points up the emotional tension of the scene: Sinclair's slender frame looked "rather meager and quite unheroic; and his voice, trembling a little with the tenseness of indignation, could scarcely be heard above the clatter of a passing train." He held a candle whose "fluttering flame" revealed his intense, boyish face. He read a few lines; then a puff of wind blew out the candle and he walked between two policeman to face Chief Oaks, who stared coldly at the offender and growled, " 'None of the Constitution stuff here, see?' and put him in the jug."

Los Angeles at this time had an extensive rail network, the Pacific Electric

Railway, which was famous for its red trolley cars. Special "Red Cars" were called into service to take several hundred strikers to the jails. When the two city jails were filled, a stockade was constructed in Griffith Park, Los Angeles's equivalent of New York's Central Park, for the overflow. Sinclair warranted special attention. Two police cars took him, along with Pryns Hopkins, Hugh Hardyman, and Hunter Kimbrough, to the nearest police station. Chief Oaks followed in another car and stepped in as Sinclair was being booked, according to Craig's account in *Southern Belle*. He herded Sinclair, Hopkins, and Hardyman into a large black sedan waiting outside. When Hunter tried to get into the car, the chief told him, "You're clear. Beat it—skidoo!" Hunter insisted on being arrested and was allowed to stand on the running board as the police car drove in a meandering fashion for an hour or more, through orange groves and wheat fields. At some point, according to Hunter, the car stopped: "The officers pretended they were lost. They argued for a moment, then turned the car around. We were quite satisfied with our lot and talked about other matters. A discussion of psychoanalysis got under way. The officers listened at first," but turned away, bored, as the "discussion shifted to Coué; then to the jail system, Herbert Spencer, the Renaissance, the Ruhr situation, H. G. Wells, Ibañez, the Plumb Plan and so on."

The four prisoners were finally delivered to the Wilmington jail, less than a mile from San Pedro. The police had been driving in circles, stalling for time to allow Oaks to prepare the much more serious charge of "criminal syndicalism." Sinclair and the others were booked and locked in their cell. Their requests to telephone attorneys and families were denied. Craig, who had stayed home during the protests because of illness, knew only that Sinclair and the others had been arrested. She was awakened from a restless sleep at three o'clock Wednesday morning by a phone call from a sympathetic reporter who said he was alarmed because neither he nor other reporters on the scene in San Pedro had been able to find out which jail Sinclair and the others were in. Craig then called everyone she could think of for help, including her old friend Kate Crane Gartz, who she knew had been one of the "ladies and gentlemen" with her husband in the mayor's office, and in San Pedro when he was arrested. As part—though a mildly disreputable part—of the Pasadena nobility and the Los Angeles business hierarchy, Kate Gartz wielded more influence than anyone else she knew.

Kate Gartz was yet another example of the intricate and far-flung network of socialists and their sympathizers to which Sinclair belonged. She was the daughter of the millionaire Chicago plumbing magnate Charles Crane, who many years earlier had given Harry Kemp a grant to write his poetry. Her

German-born husband, Adolf Gartz, wealthy in his own right, had no sympathy with her radical ideas, but he understood that her emotional state was precarious. In 1903, when he and Kate and their five children were still living in Chicago, their young daughters Mary and Barbara were among the six hundred people killed in the Iroquois Theater fire, still the worst such disaster in American history. The family moved to Los Angeles in 1907, and Gartz built a magnificent house in the hills above Altadena, the most exclusive part of Pasadena, which they called the Cloister. Kate recovered gradually but her behavior continued to be unpredictable. During the First World War, despite having two sons in the army, she proclaimed her socialist and antiwar sympathies by fixing a German flag to her limousine. Her new friend, Craig Sinclair, was not too surprised when an FBI agent asked her if Mrs. Gartz was "a German sympathizer or just a plain fool." Craig assured the agent that Kate was not disloyal, agreeing that she was a "plain fool" as the only way of protecting her.

By the early 1920s Kate Gartz had achieved a fame rivaling that of Mabel Dodge in New York for her literary salon. She held Sunday afternoon gatherings where writers, artists, "socialists, anarchists, single taxers, pacifists, [and] famous or would-be famous people from India, China, Mexico might be heard," as the writer Paul Jordan-Smith recalled. Over the years, Sinclair would meet writers as various as Gertrude Stein, his old friend Charlotte Perkins Gilman, and Edna Ferber at the Cloister. In an admiring portrait of Kate in *100%,* Sinclair presents her as "Mrs. Godd," whose proper home should be on Mount Olympus. In fact, though, he never took her very seriously. Kate was a "parlour provocateur," he said, and in later years her strong communist sympathies would strain their friendship.

For all her eccentricities, Kate Gartz was a formidable ally, a "massively handsome woman, almost regal in appearance," as Jordon-Smith said, with wide-open "great liquid eyes" that caused considerable discomfort for those who earned her disapproval. On the Wednesday afternoon after Sinclair's arrest, Kate took Craig with her to Los Angeles, where they waited together at the Gartzes' attorney's office, with a handful of supporters, for further news of Sinclair's whereabouts. At 4:30 Craig took a call from a police reporter who said Sinclair was in the city jail. Chief Oaks planned to hold him overnight without bail and to give him the "third degree." Craig had less than a half-hour to get to the police court and arrange for her husband's bail.

The police court was a few blocks away. Kate's chauffeur was not in sight, nor were any taxis. Craig ran, a lawyer on each side to catch her if she fell, while the ponderous Kate shouted for her chauffeur. The police court judge tried at first to say that Craig was too late, setting bail for Sinclair and the others at $500 each, more than Craig or the lawyers with her could summon up immediately. In the nick of time, the breathless Kate Gartz arrived, cowed the judge, and guaranteed the bail.

Craig's dramatic account of her late arrival, and of her friend's, may be somewhat embroidered. According to a *Times* story (itself not above suspicion) on May 17, "a heavily veiled woman, said to be Mrs. Upton Sinclair, loitered all day around the police station to speak with the prisoner." But Craig's brother's report of a conversation that same day with Captain Plummer seems plausible enough. An admiring clergyman said of Hunter Kimbrough at the time that he was a "splendid" young man whose "wholesome, straight-forward, almost boyish honesty won everybody" over to him. His amiable manner certainly drew Captain Plummer into some damaging admissions.

Plummer had greeted Hunter cordially when he stopped by the San Pedro station the day after his release, and asked him how he felt about being thrown in jail. Hunter said he didn't understand how the captain could have violated constitutional law as he did. Plummer retorted that he had acted in the face of an emergency: Wobblies were on the scene, waving the red flag and yelling that this was not a strike, it was a revolution. Ninety percent of the men on the scene were foreigners, Plummer said, with no constitutional rights, unable even to speak English. Well, Hunter replied, what about the 10 percent, like himself and Sinclair, who were citizens? Didn't they have those rights? No, Plummer said. "Sinclair is a good sport," but he had no right to be on the scene of the strike, nor did his friends. What about the charge of blocking traffic—the original complaint on which they had been booked? "They had to have something to charge you with," Plummer responded.

In a separate statement, a Detective Wyckoff confirmed that the decision to charge Sinclair and the others with blocking traffic had been made even before they appeared on the scene. He added that he knew there would be no real trouble because he was dealing with ladies and gentlemen, not criminals.

═══

There were several consequences to the dock strike, which ended in defeat soon after the Liberty Hill adventure. For the Wobblies, it was a disaster. Forty of the protesters were quickly dispatched to San Quentin or Folsom. Two brutal attacks the following year, one involving the Ku Klux Klan working with the police and another allegedly paid for by northern California shipping interests, effectively destroyed the Wobblies as a force in southern California.

Also destroyed was the career of the Los Angeles police chief Louis Oaks, who had gone too far and embarrassed his masters. Unlike Captain Plummer, Oaks disliked Sinclair intensely, calling him "the worst radical in the country," a man "more dangerous than 4,000 Wobblies," and demanding that he be imprisoned. Sinclair responded in an open letter to Oaks on May 17, the day of his release from jail, which was widely distributed as a leaflet. He charged Oaks with brutality and linked his actions with the Merchants and Manufacturers, and vowed that he intended to do "what little one man can do to awaken the public conscience." He was "not a giant physically," Sinclair wrote, and he found it unnerving to see "a hundred policemen with drawn revolvers flung across a street to keep anyone from coming onto private property to hear my feeble voice." But he had received a telegram from the American Civil Liberties Union asking him to give a speech in Los Angeles a few days hence, and he intended to do so. He invited Oaks to come and hear "what the citizens of this community think of your efforts to introduce the legal proceedings of Czarist Russia into our free Republic."

In early July, Hunter wrote a satirical squib for the ACLU newspaper, *The Call*, in which he portrayed himself and a former Princeton tackle chasing the chief around his office as they tried to serve him with a subpoena. By mid-August the chief was gone. According to an August 17 *Los Angeles Times* story, his own officers had discovered Oaks and a "very nice looking" young woman in the back seat of his Cadillac touring car with a half-gallon of whiskey. They were just getting some fresh air, the chief explained, though in another version he claimed he was "gathering evidence." Sinclair's belief that he had forced the M&M to get rid of Oaks was not quite correct, according to Martin Zanger's thorough account of this incident. Other civic activists had been after Oaks's hide for several years, and even the *Times* was obviously happy to see him go. But it was probably the Sinclair imbroglio that gave the chief the final nudge out the door.

Sinclair's own reputation, on the other hand, was enhanced by the Liberty Hill incident. George Sterling teased him in a letter on May 18 for "having the time of your life" and "wallowing in the joys of martyrdom," and many editorial pages in newspapers around the country agreed with the *Los Angeles Times* that Sinclair was a publicity hound. At the same time, virtually everyone also agreed that Los Angeles had made itself a laughingstock by arresting Upton Sinclair, an American citizen in good standing, for trying to read the Constitution in public.

Sinclair shrugged off criticism of his actions as grandstanding, saying Abraham Lincoln would have been arrested by the Los Angeles police, as would Jesus. He denied having serious political ambitions, though the speech to which he invited Oaks (who failed to attend) revealed to Craig, and perhaps to Sinclair himself, a growing ability to communicate effectively with a large audience. He began quietly, Craig wrote, "as if he were talking with two or three in our living room. Somehow his voice seemed to reach the farthest edges. He quoted the guarantees of freedom of speech and assemblage—he knew them all by heart. And he told the story of the past eight days, turning it into a hilarious farce, which I suppose it was if you never know fear. He ridiculed his captors, and got the crowd laughing so that he could hardly finish a sentence. He asked the crowd questions and they shouted their answers; all of them just had a grand time for an hour or so."

In the weeks that followed, Sinclair worked with others toward the founding of the Southern California chapter of the ACLU. In August, Clinton Taft, pastor of the Plymouth Congregational Church in Los Angeles, was persuaded after several hours of earnest talk "on a sunny slope back of Upton's literary workshop" to become the permanent director of the new branch. "I came to my decision then and there," Taft wrote later, because "Upton said that he would stand by me, and he promised to get some financial backing from well known liberals in Southern California."

In 1976 the Los Angeles ACLU formed a new foundation to fill what it saw as a "gaping hole" in local philanthropy for groups promoting civil liberties. It chose to call the foundation "Liberty Hill." In 1983 the foundation sponsored the first of a continuing series of Upton Sinclair Award Dinners. Its high-profile honorees have since included Gregory Peck, Martin Sheen, and Harry Belafonte. John Ahouse suggests that Sinclair "rightly considered" his role with initiating the ACLU in his new home town as "one of his great accomplishments." There is no doubt that he would be pleased with the results of his failed attempt to read the Constitution on Liberty Hill.

CHAPTER ELEVEN

THE MAN OF LETTERS

(January 1924–December 1928)

In April 1924 Sinclair sent George Sterling a copy of *Singing Jailbirds,* the play he had recently finished about the San Pedro strike. Sterling dismissed it out of hand: "It bears no relation to literature—why should it, since it cannot be staged, or at least won't be except by some Socialist club? For me, I can't see the use of writing such things for folk already of your form of persuasion."

Inspired by his third arrest and imprisonment, *Singing Jailbirds* had occupied Sinclair for several months after the San Pedro incident, an unusually long time for such a short work. Its deceptively perky title reflects the Wobblies' famous penchant for expressing themselves in song—in this case as their heroic leader, "Red" Adams, is interrogated for his role in the strike, tried and convicted by a kangaroo court, thrown into "the hole," and finally killed. After Red's death, his spirit consoles those who remain: "even in the blackest dungeon" there is unity and brotherhood. Echoing the conclusion of *The Jungle*—"We will take Chicago!"—the prisoners sing "Solidarity forever!"

Both Sterling's remarks and the agitprop flavor of the play misleadingly suggest that, at forty-six, Sinclair had matured very little in terms of literary sophistication. In fact, he was poised at the edge of the most substantial period of his literary career so far. Within the next five years, he would publish *Oil!* (1927) and *Boston* (1928), two novels far superior to anything he had done since *The Jungle*. He would also write a sweepingly magisterial though eccentric two-part overview of Western literature: *Mammonart* (1925) on the writers who had preceded him, and *Money Writes!* (1927) on his contemporaries. If there was ever a time in Sinclair's life for his admirers to argue that he was more than merely a political gadfly with a gift for words, that he was indeed a wide-ranging "man of letters," this was it.

That case was easier to make for the novels than it was for the literary overviews, which were based on a provocative but perverse premise. Having shown the complicity of religion, the press, and education in frustrating social reform, Sinclair now proposed to demonstrate that Western art, especially literary art, had served throughout history to reinforce the status quo and to inhibit progress. All art was propaganda: the word itself was neutral rather than pejorative, in Sinclair's view, meaning simply that every artist consciously or subconsciously advanced a view of the world. Those artists who prospered did so because they portrayed the world as its rulers wanted it to be seen. Thus "Mammon" and "art" were yoked together for the title of the first book, and *Money Writes!*—a takeoff on the slang expression "money talks"—carried the idea forward. A heroic handful of writers, either outcasts or rebels, resisted the corruption of money and power in every age: Cervantes, Swift, and Shelley among those in the past, Frank Norris, Theodore Dreiser, and, of course, Upton Sinclair in the present.

Sinclair began writing the first of the articles that would grow into *Mammonart* immediately after finishing *Singing Jailbirds*. It was published serially in *The New Appeal,* beginning on August 9, 1924, and issued as a book under Sinclair's imprint in mid-February 1925. George Sterling, always candid, didn't like the sections of the book that Sinclair sent him in July any more than he had *Singing Jailbirds*. He said that "by all means" he wanted to see the rest of *Mammonart* before it was published: "When I see a friend about to make a world-ass of himself, I feel that I should do what I can to lessen the infliction." He didn't want to hurt Sinclair's feelings, Sterling said, "but you are such a colossal egoist that one has to hit hard" in order to make an impression.

There is no question that *Mammonart* offered Sinclair's enemies an easy target. He praised his wife's mediocre sonnets and dismissed Coleridge's "Kubla Khan" as pointless fantasy—while revealing that he thought "Xanadu" was pronounced "Kanadu." Even worse was his attempt to show that Clement Wood's sonnet about the Ludlow Massacre was superior to John Milton's "On the Late Massacre in Piedmont" (1673), in part because the world, and therefore the mastery of poetry, had progressed since the seventeenth century. Herbert Read, an influential English scholar, savaged Sinclair's comparison of Milton and Wood. Sinclair, he said, spitefully denigrated great writers because "no critic of importance has ever mistaken [him] for an artist. He is the *poète manqué,* the cock without a comb. The midden he crows on is immense, but it is muck."

A reviewer in distant Sydney, Australia, accurately noted the key problem with *Mammonart* but concentrated on its merits: "If you drop entirely his theory," Sinclair's book was often informative and amusing. Sinclair's readers in *The New Appeal* were much closer in their level of sophistication to the Australian reviewer than they were to Sterling's or Read's aestheticism; they understood that his strength had never been in constructing theories but in close observation and explanation of details and processes.

Once himself the Arthur Stirling aesthete who scorned public taste, Sinclair now persuaded his readers that he read literature as they did, for instruction, persuasion, and entertainment. He was the common reader, unconcerned lest he be dismissed as a philistine or a lowbrow. Confused by Robert Browning's *The Ring and the Book*? So was Sinclair, who wondered why a reader should have to work so hard to decipher a poem. Find it hard to take *The Scarlet Letter* seriously? Sinclair was with you, seeing Hawthorne's world as "entirely archaic, an object of curiosity mingled with repugnance." Fond of unfashionable poets like Longfellow and puzzled by the mockery of his famous lines, "Life is real, life is earnest / And the grave is not its goal"? Sinclair too preferred Longfellow's "incitement to diligence and sobriety" to those modern writers who think "art is incitement toward going to hell in a hurry."

Sinclair's readers liked him because he did not talk down to them and he seemed to share their attitudes. He also entertained them with provocative illustrations that their English teachers might not have made. Flaubert's *Madame Bovary,* for example, resembled Sinclair Lewis's *Main Street:* both authors were realists, but Lewis "proceeds upon the assumption that it is possible to restrain passion, and on the whole, better to try," while Flaubert assumes "that it is impossible to restrain passion, and that if you pretend to do it, you are a Puritan, and what is worse, a hypocrite." Carol Kennicott's story ends with her "still trying to introduce a little light into Gopher Prairie," but Emma Bovary dies miserably and her town remains the bleak, soul-destroying place it always was. More positively, *Don Quixote,* Sinclair suggests, asks a critical question that is obviously close to his own heart: "What shall be the relation of the idealist, the dreamer of good and beautiful things, to the world of ugliness and greed in which he finds himself?" If he tries to apply his vision of the good, "the world will treat him so badly that before he gets through he may be really crazy."

Sinclair's easy rapport with his readers came partly from making Craig into a levelheaded, patient, and humorous partner in his narrative. *Mammonart* begins with a clever, if slightly labored, allegory of the first artist, the Neanderthal "Ogi," who finds meaning in his life by scratching crude images on his cave wall of the beasts he eats and who try to eat him. Ogi's mate—Mrs. Ogi—supports him, but the tribe, dominated by early members of the Los Angeles Merchants and Manufacturers Association, expels him because he alone, among all the other painters, refuses to make the images they want. Finding refuge in another cave, Ogi continues his work, poor and isolated but honest. His more pliable fellow artists remain in the big cave, well fed and honored. Thus we see, Sinclair says, that "from the dawn of human history, the path to honor and success in the arts has been through the service and glorification of the ruling classes; entertaining them, making them pleasant to themselves, and teaching their subjects and slaves to stand in awe of them."

Sinclair as the modern Mr. Ogi and Craig as Mrs. Ogi trade quips and barbs throughout *Mammonart,* sometimes more revealingly than Sinclair intended. Apparently he forgot that Harry Kemp and Meta had used the Neanderthal ploy back in 1911, calling themselves "Kaa" and "Naa"—and him "Baa." And he seems not to have noticed the points of connection between himself and Rousseau when he excuses the French philosopher for leaving his children in an orphanage, on the grounds that such magnificent efforts on behalf of "liberty, equality, and fraternity" far outweigh the great writer's personal weaknesses.

Sinclair's life with Craig was a good deal more complicated than his references to her in *Mammonart* suggest, in part because of her continuing aversion to his son. David had been at loose ends after finishing his studies at the University of Wisconsin in 1924. Sinclair did not attend his son's graduation, but David's grandmother did. Priscilla impressed a society reporter in Madison as "a very dignified and aristocratic old lady with such a fashionable Parisian hat," and a simple gown set off by an "unusual jet brooch," who enjoyed playing bridge and talking about her famous son: "Do you know he sends me his manuscripts before he shows them to anyone else? I will always tell him, and I am pretty nearly always right, whether his books will sell or not." When he earned his first money at fourteen, she was alarmed. "I really didn't care to encourage a child prodigy, but I knew Upton was doomed to be a writer, and I couldn't stop him."

By May 1925, David was living in New York and trying to fashion a career as a musician. He wrote to his father and said he would like to visit him in Pasadena; they had not seen each other since 1922, and he wanted to have the benefit of his father's advice and experience. Sinclair wrote in early June to tell David that his letter put him "in a painful position," because "Craig is close to a complete nervous breakdown, she has been at death's door more than once, and hard as it may [be] for me to make it clear to you, any visit will have to be at a later time." Among other things, Craig "has had the flue [*sic*], and her heart almost stopped beating." Her "change of life" was upon her and "she may be in this same more or less hysteria for years." David had to try to understand Craig's "neurasthenia," as well as his father's "seemingly unnatural attitude." Sinclair hoped that he and David might get together "after I have written this oil novel, which I know will be the best thing I have ever done. . . . Please believe that I love you. Father."

As Sinclair's terminology—"hysteria," "neurasthenia," "change of life"—suggests, both he and Craig were proper Victorians, for whom illness was a way of life as well as a major literary theme. Edith Wharton's novel *Ethan Frome,* published in 1911, the same year as *Love's Pilgrimage,* offers a useful gloss on Craig's situation, and on Sinclair's. Ethan's wife, Zeena, maintains her hold on him by exploiting her illnesses, which she describes as "troubles." When he shows signs of restiveness, she graduates to "complications." While everyone had "troubles" and could live with them for years, to have "complications" was "a death-warrant," meaning that Ethan would be responsible for her death if he opposed her wishes. Sinclair's concern for Craig's well-being was sincere. Though he may well have thought her illnesses were psychosomatic—just "troubles"—he did everything he could to keep them from becoming real "complications." This included keeping his son at continued arm's length.

It also meant, in late 1926, leaving the comfortable nest that Craig had created for him in Pasadena in the hands of her sister Dollie and Dollie's invalid husband, Robert Irwin. Craig believed that one source of her ailments was the constant invasion of her privacy by Sinclair's eager disciples, who thought nothing of banging on their door in the middle of the night. (One such visitor came with geometrical drafts of the Fourth Dimension, the most important advance, he said, since the invention of mathematics.) Fortunately, her health did not interfere with her active pursuit of good bargains in real estate. Early in 1924 she purchased two narrow lots, part of a block of eight, on the west slope of Signal Hill, near where oil had been struck three years earlier (and only about five miles inland from the scene of Sinclair's recent arrest in San Pedro). Her intent had been to hold the lots until the expanding oil field operations made them valuable; but when offers were made by the oil interests, they were contingent on agreements by all of the property owners to sell at the same price. Some owners, greedy for more than their lots were worth, stalled the sale.

During the next two years, through the autumn of 1926, Craig and Sinclair attended many disputatious meetings, effectively compressed into an early scene in *Oil!,* the novel they inspired. As Sinclair worked on his new novel, Craig abandoned her dream of becoming an oil millionaire. Instead, she decided that Long Beach would become their new home. In November

1926, by means of a complicated trade, she gave up the would-be oil lots in return for a cottage and a nearby garage on Alamitos Bay, just south of the city of Long Beach—plus, as she says in *Southern Belle,* "several thousand dollars."

Sinclair was relatively contented during the fall of 1926. The upcoming move, scheduled for late December, did not trouble him. So inflexible in other ways, he had been happy in the past with his various platform tents, and he still cared little where he lived. Ernest Greene, the efficient young man who had been his secretary for several years, could continue to look after his business affairs in Pasadena, and he would have his own new office in the two finished rooms above the garage—with the added attraction of a sundeck on the roof where he could relax. There were tennis courts at the elegant Virginia Hotel in downtown Long Beach, and a good vegetarian restaurant nearby that featured a Battle Creek menu. Craig's health had finally taken a turn for the better, and he was nearly finished with *Oil!* He had even managed to publish three slight works under his own imprint during the period from September 1925 to August 1926. The first was a play based on the life of O. Henry, called *Bill Porter,* the second a useful elementary explanation of economic concepts to a workingman, *Letters to Judd,* and the third a labored satire on Calvin Coolidge, *The Spokesman's Secretary.*

In September 1926, Sinclair's combined interests in economics and politics found expression in his nomination for governor of California on the American Socialist Party ticket. He had stood for office twice before as an ASP candidate since moving to California, running for Congress in 1920 and for the U.S. Senate in 1922. Largely symbolic, these candidacies had been virtually ignored by the hostile mainstream press. In the 1926 race he gained more attention than previously by virtue of his platform attacking the "water monopoly," but he still would win only a relative handful of votes: 46,000 compared to the Republican candidate, who won the election with 815,000 votes. A rerun of the campaign in 1930 would earn him similar results.

His heaviest writing tasks finished, the move to Long Beach agreed upon, and his candidacy for governor little more than a formality, Sinclair had ample time to contemplate the visit to Los Angeles in late October of his longtime friendly antagonist H. L. Mencken. He even proposed that Mencken stay with him and Craig in Pasadena, but Mencken, undoubtedly much to Craig's relief, responded that the novelist Joseph Hergesheimer had already booked him into the Ambassador Hotel.

Henry Louis Mencken was just two years younger than Sinclair. They had passed their earlier years within less than a mile of each other in Baltimore, but did not meet until 1922, when Sinclair was researching *The Goose-Step.* Their correspondence, which would continue until 1951, began in 1918 when Mencken congratulated Sinclair on his new magazine. As the editor and publisher of the iconoclastic *American Mercury,* Mencken knew what a difficult task it was to write and edit an honest journal of opinion. The fact that his own opinions were almost always the exact opposite of Sinclair's did not lessen either man's pleasure in their verbal combat—not yet, at least. Mencken rejected the occasional articles that Sinclair submitted, except for his affectionate reminiscence about his Columbia music teacher, Edward MacDowell, as too doctrinaire and likely to offend the *Mercury*'s many liquor and tobacco advertisers. He did publish a number of writers whom Sinclair recommended, so many, indeed, that William Manchester, an early Mencken biographer, called Sinclair one of the magazine's "greatest bene-factors." Convicts, laborers, dockworkers, immigrants like Louis Adamic, even communists like Mike Gold, all of whom Sinclair championed, saw print in the *Mercury* as a result of Sinclair's generous intercession with the editor who rejected his own work.

Sinclair tried valiantly to match Mencken in the area of clever riposte in their correspondence. In late September, Mencken joked that he would be arriving in town soon to play Pontius Pilate in a new DeMille biblical epic. He looked forward to getting Sinclair royally drunk. In return, Sinclair sent Mencken an article from the *Pasadena Record* in which he denied arranging for Mencken to address the local Rotary Club; he also vowed to convert Mencken to socialism and to celebrate the conversion by firing off a "salute of 21 bombs under the Rotarians of Pasadena." (*Times* editor and Rotarian Harry Carr gave thanks for Mencken's absence, saying "we timid gentlemen of ordinary mental equipment can take heart once more." Mencken was an undeniably "brilliant man," but he had "a naughty little boy's fondness for stirring up the animals.")

Soon after Mencken arrived in town, on October 27, he spoke to a group only marginally less conservative than the Pasadena Rotarians: the Los An-geles Women's Athletic Club. Sinclair was present, and he wrote an affec-tionate account of the guest of honor sitting on a plush sofa before the ladies, "short and solidly made," with the "bright china-blue eyes and the round rosy face of a cherub." He admired Mencken's "rage against stupidity, full-ness and sham," Sinclair said in *Money Writes!,* employing his familiar mili-tary metaphors: Mencken was "a whole army, horse, foot, artillery, aviation and general staff all in one, mobilized in a war upon his enemies," the hordes of "boobus Americanus." Beneath the joy of combat, though, Sinclair detected fatigue and self-deception. Mencken did not see that he was himself a crusader, "a Christian Anti-Christ, a tireless propagandist of no-propaganda." The basis of his faith was the abolition of "every kind of restriction upon thought and expression, and to reduce restrictions upon action to the absolute minimum." Mencken was a libertarian, with "very little regard for facts," hoping to "amuse and startle." He and his followers perfectly matched "the mood of the time," a compound of "cynicism, ridicule, and contempt for democratic bungling."

Mencken's epistolary challenges to Sinclair were often teasing, particularly concerning the ability of any government to do anything competently. He claimed that in 1904, the Baltimore fire department let half the town burn down, costing him "a suit of clothes, the works of Richard Harding Davis, and a gross of condoms." On the federal scale, "it took years of effort to induce the government to fight mosquitoes, and it does the work very badly today. There is malaria everywhere in the South. It is mainly responsible for the prevalence of religion down there."

Mencken's published remarks on Sinclair's books and ideas were often more pointed than his letters. Concerning *The Brass Check,* he genially wrote to Sinclair that the "common people" he was trying to protect were "due to be diddled forever. You are fighting a vain fight. But you must be having a lot of fun." His actual review of the book in *The Smart Set* was more dismissive: "Dr. Sinclair's" diagnosis of the ills of American journalism was accurate but, if anything, too generous: the newspaper business was "ten times" as "devious, hypocritical, pusillanimous, pharisaical, pecksniffian," and so on as Sinclair said it was. What could be done about it? Nothing. There were no wise men to sit on the high court of review for our newspapers that Sinclair proposed; his solution was "simple, bold, clear, and idiotic," based on his faith "in the wisdom of the incurably imbecilic, the virtue of the congenitally dishonest, the lofty idealism of the incorrigibly sordid."

Opposites in most ways, Mencken and Sinclair shared a work ethic and a commitment to their positions that aroused mutual respect. When Mencken overheard some friends disparage Sinclair's latest book, he silenced them with, "Well, he sat down and wrote it, didn't he?" Sinclair for his part once said that Mencken was "a much more solid man than people realize. If, for example, you will read his book, *The American Language,* you will see that on a subject in which he is really interested he has made himself a real authority." They were also similar in their literary traditionalism, disdaining experimentalists like James Joyce and T. S. Eliot, while praising realists like Dreiser and romantic idealists like George Sterling.

Indeed, Mencken even proposed that Sterling should be the American poet laureate, if such a post were ever established. He disagreed with Sinclair's contention, based on his eighteen-year friendship with Sterling and the poet's occasional visits to Pasadena since they had been living in California, that Sterling was yet another example of a potentially great writer who had ruined himself through alcohol.

Mencken planned to see Sterling after he left Los Angeles, in San Francisco, where he would be the guest of honor at a Bohemian Club banquet on Tuesday, November 16. Still in residence at the Bohemian Club, Sterling was to be his personal host. Mencken planned to persuade Sterling to write about Jack London for the *Mercury*—reviving a version of Sinclair's similar biography attempt eleven years earlier. Given Sinclair's own connection with all three writers, as well as his long friendship with Sterling, he and Craig might have been tempted to attend the Bohemian Club dinner. As it happened, Craig had to sign the contract for the Long Beach house that same day.

On Wednesday, November 17, the late-afternoon papers in Los Angeles carried a wire story from San Francisco that contained a terrible shock for Craig and Sinclair: George Sterling, fifty-seven years of age, had been found dead shortly after noon in his room at the Bohemian Club. He had killed himself by taking cyanide. Mencken was quoted as saying he was greatly saddened by Sterling's death; he had been "a great poet," "one of the few men of letters" who never "yielded to present-day fashions. He always adhered to classical traditions."

Mencken, Sinclair learned afterward, had knocked on Sterling's door shortly after arriving at the Bohemian Club on Tuesday afternoon. Sterling responded through the closed door, but he was clearly too drunk to talk. Mencken said he would go to the dinner party and return in the morning. When he did return, there was no answer. The hotel manager opened the door and found Sterling dead. Charles Malamuth, a local writer who attended the dinner, wrote a few days later to Sinclair, still shaken by what had happened. Malamuth was "really knocked out" to think that even as Sterling was writhing "in the throes of cyanide poisoning," he and his friends were all "listening to Mencken's discourse on chamber music, or, tired of that, exchanging predictions that George's chagrin at being too drunk to entertain Mencken would drive him to suicide."

Mencken returned to Baltimore in late November to find a letter waiting for him from Sinclair about "poor George," who was the "most interesting man" he had ever known. "All my life," Sinclair wrote, "I have watched a melancholy procession of beautiful men going to their graves because of liquor. I am wondering how many such cases it will take to make you begin to revise your views on the subject." He offered to write an article about Sterling for the *Mercury*. Mencken's reply was remarkably obtuse: "Whatever George told you in moments of katzenjammer, I am sure that he got a great deal more fun out of alcohol than woe. It was his best friend for many years and made life tolerable. He committed suicide in the end, not because he wanted to get rid of drink, but simply because he could no longer drink enough to give him any pleasure." If Sinclair wanted to write a piece about Sterling without preaching against alcohol, Mencken concluded, he might consider publishing it.

Sinclair responded temperately enough, even joking that the subject of Sterling without liquor was like *Hamlet* without the ghost. He reminded Mencken that Sterling had actually voted for Prohibition, "even though he had not the strength of will to practice it." The issue to be addressed, Sinclair said, was the irrationality of self-destruction that was revealed in Sterling's drinking: "You say that he committed suicide because he could no longer drink enough liquor to get a kick out of it," but the "rational pleasures of life do not bring a man to this condition." In the end, Sinclair wrote nothing for Mencken, who instead published Mary Austin's reminiscence of her days at Carmel with Sterling. The *Mercury*'s advertisers could not have objected to Austin's conclusion that Sterling was an intensely emotional poet who used liquor as "the apparatus by which all his energies were stepped up to the creative level."

———

On the morning of the day that Sterling was setting out to kill himself in San Francisco, Upton Sinclair was in Pasadena, typing a note to Floyd Dell that he had just written "The End" for *Oil!*

Oil! was a long novel, at two hundred thousand words. It had also been, for Sinclair, relatively long in the writing, interrupted by his solicitous care for Craig during her periods of ill health. Inspired by the Teapot Dome and Elk Hill scandals of 1922, and by his and Craig's experiences with the oil lots, Sinclair had started gathering material in early 1924. By early January 1925, he envisioned a novel about the petroleum industry that would also reflect his growing interest in southern California as a literary setting.

The early oil strikes by wildcat operators in Long Beach had turned out to be huge, rivaling those of Texas in quality and output. But whereas most oil fields were found in remote areas, these were crowded into a fifteen-square-mile urban area, itself only a short streetcar ride from Los Angeles. Sinclair's novel would deal not just with oil and politics, but with such distinctly local subjects as Hollywood and the film industry, Aimee Semple McPherson and the excesses of religious fundamentalism, the defining elements of the new automobile culture, and the repression of radical students and faculty at the University of Southern California. As sprawling, lively, and idiosyncratic as Los Angeles itself, *Oil!* would restore Sinclair's long-dormant reputation as a novelist. The admiring and influential librarian-critic Lawrence Clark Powell later said *Oil!* was Sinclair's "most sustained and best writing," indeed, "the largest scale of all California novels."

Sinclair was certain that *Oil!* was good, but he always felt that way when he was in the midst of a project. His publisher, Boni & Liveright, held out only modest hopes for it when they offered Sinclair a contract in January 1927 that provided for a $1,000 advance (about $10,600 today) and 15 percent royalties. Sinclair had for several years relied on William Conkey, a printer in Indiana, for cheap and quickly produced copies of books like *The Brass Check* that he published himself. Now he directed Conkey, in an unusual move that shows how involved Sinclair was in the business of publishing, to provide five thousand copies for Boni & Liveright and three thousand for Sinclair to issue under his own imprint. The novel was released in March 1927.

The plot and characters of *Oil!* resembled Sinclair's earlier works in which a naive, idealistic young man, born to privilege, becomes converted by degrees to a position of radical activism. His young hero, nicknamed "Bunny," admires his father for having transformed himself from Jim Ross, teamster, to J. Arnold Ross, rising oilman in southern California. Ross, called "Dad" throughout, buys a ranch at distress-sale prices (as Sinclair almost did, in exchange for Craig's oil lots). The rancher's son, Paul Watkins, a few years older than Bunny, becomes his friend and intellectual guide. Following army service in 1918 that requires him, like Jimmie Higgins, to fight in Russia against the Bolsheviks, Paul joins the Communist Party of America. He returns to the oil fields as a union organizer, bringing him into conflict with Bunny's father. As a former workingman, Dad Ross has been unusually solicitous of his employees, but the more powerful oilmen pressure him to resist Paul's union efforts. Bunny's loyalties are split between his friend and his father.

Oil! ends with Paul murdered by a right-wing mob, Dad Ross ruined by the oil cabal and dead of a heart attack, and Bunny torn between his opposition both to capitalism and to the intransigence and advocacy of violence that led Paul Watkins to his death. He speculates vaguely that socialism will offer him and the country a way out, but the conclusion of *Oil!* is distinctly less than hopeful.

Energy and life suffuse the work nevertheless, largely through Sinclair's descriptions of how the oil business works and the relatively well-developed character of Dad Ross. In the opening scene of the novel, Sinclair effectively captures the appeal of Bunny's father as the two drive through the night in an open touring car toward Beach City (Long Beach). As a beginning, the scene anticipates both the famous first scene of Steinbeck's *The Grapes of Wrath* and the opening sequence of Robert Penn Warren's *All the King's Men*. The point of view is Bunny's: "The road ran, smooth and flawless, precisely fourteen feet wide, the edges trimmed as if by shears, a ribbon of grey concrete, rolled out over the valley by a giant hand. The ground went in long waves, a slow ascent and then a sudden dip; you climbed, and went swiftly over—but you had no fear, for you knew the magic ribbon would be there, clear of obstructions, unmarred by bump or scar, waiting the passage of inflated rubber wheels revolving seven times a second. The cold wind of morning whistled by, a storm of motion, a humming and roaring with ever-shifting overtones." Sinclair, once such a restless traveler himself, was still closely in touch with one of the most basic and compelling motifs of American literature: the lure of the open road.

He had also retained, and perhaps even improved, his ability to describe events and vividly bring them to life, as in this account of an oil fire: "there was a tower of flame, and the most amazing spectacle—the burning oil would hit the ground, and bounce up, and explode and leap again and fall again, and great red masses of flame would unfold, and burst, and yield black masses of smoke, and these in turn red. Mountains of smoke rose to the sky, and mountains of flame came seething down to the earth; every jet that struck the ground turned into a volcano, and rose again, higher than before; the whole mass, boiling and bursting, became a river of fire, a lava flood that went streaming down the valley, turning everything it touched into flame, then swallowing it up and hiding the flames in a cloud of smoke."

Oil! was completed in time for Floyd Dell to include a discussion of it in the culminating chapter of his admiring biography of Sinclair, which appeared in 1927. Dell, born near Chicago in 1887, was the author of *Moon-Calf*, a semiautobiographical portrait of the artist as a young man that was published to considerable acclaim in 1920. Among its admirers was Upton Sinclair, whose angry young poet Arthur Stirling had been one of Dell's early heroes. Dell was added to Sinclair's huge list of regular correspondents. In 1926, Sinclair, responding to repeated requests from his readers in Europe for biographical information, suggested to Dell that he would make himself available for a biography if Dell was interested in writing it. The result was a brief but useful book called *Upton Sinclair: A Study in Social Protest*.

Dell ended his study with a prescient prediction concerning Sinclair's longevity and his later success as a novelist: "Upton Sinclair is at this point in his career forty-eight years old; he intends to live to be as old as Bernard Shaw, and he probably will. His future literary career may bring surprises; the poet in him may yet overwhelm the propagandist."

Dell wrote at a time when Freud's theory of art and neurosis was at its peak of influence. He corresponded at some length with Sinclair, who was generous with his time and candid about his experiences, particularly those concerning his parents and his first marriage. Dell's reading of Sinclair's early novels, especially *The Journal of Arthur Stirling* and *Love's Pilgrimage,* confirmed his sense of the conflict in Sinclair. The drama of his life had been the transformation from a sensitive, withdrawn poet into a "Voltairean" literary warrior "against wrong." The price that Sinclair had paid, however, was considerable: his "Puritanism" with regard to sex, and to a lesser degree with all other forms of self-indulgence such as smoking and drinking, had hobbled his creative gift as a novelist. Dell told Sinclair that he "must therefore permit me to regard you as a neurotic in certain respects, and to deplore that fact."

Sinclair disagreed that his psychological makeup had been distorted by his earlier experience or that his alleged puritanism diminished the quality of his work. At the same time, he did not want to be discarded as old-fashioned by a new generation of readers that had become used to the sexual candor of the postwar writers. In *Oil!,* perhaps as a result of Dell's observations, Sinclair introduced a new frankness (for him) concerning sex, including several references to abortion.

The relevant passages hardly challenged those in *Lady Chatterley's Lover,* consisting mostly of some mildly racy scenes of Bunny being seduced by a movie star, though one episode was memorable: a beautiful young woman steals Bunny's clothes while he goes skinny-dipping in the Pacific near what appears to be the Hearst estate at San Simeon. He sees her disappearing down the beach on her horse, with his clothes, and pursues her—naked, and successfully. It's an amusing scene, lightly handled, which Sinclair later said he had simply imagined, rather than hearing about as Hollywood gossip.

In April 1927, when sales of *Oil!* were lagging, Sinclair asked a friend whose book had been banned in Boston to use his influence with the censors there: a good banning would do his book sales a world of good. He was joking, but his concern about sales figures was justified. The book had started off well, as a major selection of the Literary Guild. It had also been helped by the coincidental collapse of the Julian Petroleum Company in San Diego County, which, as Jules Tygiel explains in his introduction to a 1997 edition of *Oil!,* cost shareholders an estimated $150 million, equivalent to $1.5 billion today.

But in early May, Mencken, whose contacts were wide-ranging and well placed, wrote to Sinclair about a rumor he had heard: J. P. Morgan and Co. was supposedly pressuring magazines, by means of a circular letter, to avoid mentioning Sinclair's novel. *The Atlantic Monthly* had, as a result, killed a review of *Oil!* that was already set in type.

There is no way to verify Mencken's suspicion. It seems unlikely that Sinclair's attack in *The Moneychangers* on old J.P., who died in 1913, lingered within the institutional memory of his company. Much fresher, though, was the memory of the bomb in front of the Morgan building in October 1920 that killed thirty-three people and injured hundreds. A note found nearby said, "Remember we will not tolerate any longer. Free the political prisoners or it will be sure death for all of you. American Anarchists Fighters." Several years of efforts to solve the mystery of the bomb attack had failed. Sinclair, in his own voice as the omniscient author in *Oil!,* clearly distorted the facts of the case. The explosion stemmed, he claimed, from an accident involving "a wagon loaded with blasting material, making its way through Wall Street with customary indifference to municipal ordinances." In Sinclair's version, only "about a dozen people were killed. A few minutes after the accident, the bankers called in America's sleuth-celebrity [his old enemy William Burns] to solve the mystery; and this able business man, facing the situation that if it was just an accident it was nothing, while if it was a Bolshevik plot it was several hundred thousand dollars, took three minutes to look about him, and then pronounced it a plot." According to Sinclair, the famous "wave of witch-hunting" that characterized the period, including the Palmer raids, soon followed. (In fact, that sad period in American history had nearly ended by the date of the attack.) The Morgan company, which had been the victim of a murderous attack, found itself blamed in *Oil!* for unleashing civil disorder. Whether or not Morgan executives tried to sabotage the novel, their distaste for Sinclair's revisionist history, if they knew about it, would be understandable.

In mid-May, Sinclair got his wish to be banned in Boston—a quaint custom born of the conservative Irish Catholic bishopric's belief that it had the right to tell not only Catholics but everybody else in Boston what they should be allowed to read. Though the law was widely mocked and often ignored, a bookstore clerk who sold a copy of *Oil!* had been arrested and was scheduled to go on trial in June. Sinclair was soon on the scene, having stopped first in New York to visit with David—who confirmed, Sinclair told *The New York Times* on June 8, his assertions that college students frequently "went all the way" at "petting parties" of the kind the Boston censors deplored in *Oil!*, which condemned such activities.

David was still only intermittently employed, but he was soon to marry Bettina Mikol, the daughter of a socialist and union organizer, who worked as an editor at Columbia University for an academic journal, *Political Science Quarterly*. Neither he nor his father, who had not seen each other for the past five years, left a record of their reunion in New York. Sinclair's account of his adventure with the Boston police and censors, by contrast, is amusingly detailed in the book that would soon follow, *Money Writes!*

Personalizing the dispute once again, Sinclair concentrated on his encounters with the Boston police superintendent, "a large Catholic gentleman by the name of Mike Crowley," and the police court judge, appropriately named Creed. Crowley told Sinclair that he "would personally appear to prosecute" him if he tried to sell a copy of *Oil!* in Boston. Sinclair set Crowley up as a fool, having him say "You don't find any of these bedroom-scenes in Shakespeare," and himself as an impish provocateur—the following day he sold what appeared to be a copy of *Oil!* to a policeman, then revealed that the offending book was really a Bible. Judge Creed dismissed the case with a reprimand, saying, "We think, Mr. Sinclair, you've had your share of book-advertising."

Sinclair returned to his hotel, where he picked up a few of the 150 special paperback copies of *Oil!* that he had instructed Conkey in Indiana to prepare and ship to him in Boston. For each of the nine pages (out of 527) that the Boston censor had identified as offensive, he had substituted the image of a fig leaf. He included a frontispiece explanation for his "Fig Leaf Edition," pointing out that most of the "political and social information which is the real cause of the attack upon the book" remained intact. He also noted that "the greater part of the material" in one passage comes from the "Song of Solomon," "which you may read in any copy of the Old Testament."

Conkey had prepared two poster-sized images of a fig leaf, prominently featuring Sinclair's name and the title of his notorious book. After alerting the local press, Sinclair marched to the edge of Boston Common, the traditional ground for protest in the city, donned the two fig-leaf posters fore and aft, like sandwich boards, and announced that he was offering special copies of *Oil!* for sale. Within days, photographs of the diminutive, neatly dressed author handing a copy of *Oil!* to a Boston matron had hit the front pages of newspapers everywhere, including Europe. In the United States, sales shot up from slightly more than two thousand for the first quarter to more than six thousand per month through the summer, ultimately reaching 75,000 in the United States and an astounding 125,000 copies in Germany.

At one point in *Oil!* Sinclair compares his young hero to Siddhartha, the Indian prince who gave up "his land and his treasures, and went out to wander with a beggar's bowl, in the hope of finding some truth about life that was not known at court." In *Money Writes!*, published under his imprint in November 1927, just seven months after *Oil!*, Sinclair presents himself as a kind of Siddhartha, the last honest seeker after truth, disappointed in most of his fellow writers for having forsaken the quest. Fresh from fighting with the Boston censors, who said he was immoral, he now found himself condemned by the writers who should have been his natural allies for arrogance, egotism, and self-righteousness.

Sinclair had deliberately set out to stir the pot in *Money Writes!*, telling Mencken that he looked forward to "dealing with" their contemporaries: "I am going to tear the hides off a great many of them." His method of attack had been part of his arsenal as far back as *The Metropolis,* where he used the same violent metaphor: like the Roman satirist Juvenal, he "flayed the aristocracy of the empire for their vileness and materialism." As a critic, Sinclair was the opposite of amiable; he was a conservative prosecutor rather than a liberal defense attorney. Aside from generous and lengthy comments on George Sterling, London, and Norris, he had relatively little to say in either book about writers he liked, such as Dickens, Ruskin, and Dreiser. The rest he denounced, as Edmund Wilson noted, when they failed to affirm "his own particular moral stated in his own particular terms."

Broadly speaking, Sinclair had three large targets, all of which are still recognizable today. The first was the idea of "art for art's sake" as it was associated with Oscar Wilde. The second was the mix of pessimism, nihilism, and hedonism that Sinclair, with good reason, thought defined the social and intellectual climate of the 1920s. The third was America's "celebrity culture," as it was already beginning to be defined, and the ways in which it degraded popular taste.

Sinclair knew he was out of step with intellectual fashion. He was, as he said later of Lanny Budd, "conservative in his taste in the arts. He liked a writer to have something to say, and to say it with clarity and precision; he liked a musician to reveal his ideas in music, and not in program notes; he liked a painter to produce works that bore some resemblance to something. He disliked loud noises and confusion, and obscurity cultivated as a form of exclusiveness."

In both *Mammonart* and *Money Writes!* Sinclair was writing about literature for a nonliterary audience: the bulk of his readers were still those who thought of him as a social activist rather than a novelist or critic, and many were rebellious teenagers drawn to iconoclasm. Who else but Sinclair would say, as he does of *The Importance of Being Earnest,* that he never was "more bored" by a night at the theater? Oscar Wilde's celebrated aphorisms are for Sinclair nothing more than a parlor trick that anyone could master "in two minutes."

Worse than merely trivial, Wilde was dangerously wrong, Sinclair argues, in saying "There is no such thing as a moral or an immoral book. Books are well written or badly written," and "The sphere of art and the sphere of ethics are absolutely distinct and separate." As proof of the folly of separating art and morality, Sinclair cites Wilde's story of Salome, as adapted in the Richard Strauss opera. The scene in which Salome fondles and kisses the bloody severed head of John the Baptist seems to Sinclair "the most cruel, cold, and disgusting piece of lewdness in the English language." He recalls his feeling upon seeing this play before the war, in 1913. The audience consisted of "bedizened and bejewelled fat beasts, male and female, having their sick nerves thrilled by this 'grand' opera," and he had been certain that "European capitalism was ready for the slaughterman's ax."

For Sinclair, Wilde was also the perfect example of the writer as intellectual celebrity, famous for the wrong reasons. His only "excuse for having lived" at all is found in works where he sees that his life was a tragic waste, *De Profundis* and "The Ballad of Reading Gaol," "a supremely eloquent and noble poem." Sinclair's more recent contemporaries, he argues in *Money Writes!,* have abdicated their responsibility in a manner sometimes different from Wilde's but no less destructive. They have become celebrities because they exalt and personify the meretricious, even as they ignore the significant. Categories are confused, distinctions rendered meaningless: the man who flies across the North Pole and the "scientist who discovers a cosmic ray" must compete for the public's attention with "the man who eats a gallon of beans in eleven minutes" and "the movie star who marries her seventeenth husband." Each has his day—his fifteen minutes, as we now say—"or perhaps his week" on the front pages of the newspapers, and is then forgotten.

Literary elitism also displeases Sinclair in *Money Writes!* He boasts that he is not a part of the literary scene. He lives in "the wilds of the west, where the only art centre is Hollywood, so I do not attend the poetical tea-parties and gather the gossip of the salons." (Kate Gartz, whose literary salon Sinclair regularly attended, apparently did not count.) Unfortunately, Sinclair woefully betrays his ignorance of more than just salon gossip, saying not a word about Pound, Eliot, Joyce, Hemingway, Fitzgerald, Frost, or any of a dozen other writers of incalculably more interest than those he does talk about: Gertrude Atherton, James Branch Cabell, Floyd Dell.

Rather, he settles for a vicious poke at an easy target, the imagist poet Amy Lowell. Modern poetry, he jokes, is best defined as lines that don't run all the way to the right margin. Lowell, a very modern poet, is the prime example of how "a woman with no trace of inspiration [could] fool all the critics and editors." Sinclair cruelly describes Lowell as fat, crippled, ugly, talentless, and given to smoking smelly black cigars, famous only because she is a Lowell in Boston, living proof that "if you have money and social prestige, you can get away with murder in America."

Critics who should know better than to be fooled by Oscar Wilde or Amy Lowell are responsible for misleading readers, Sinclair says. They emphasize technique, a "code of artificialities" designed to impress readers. "The sophisticated critic accumulates a vast complex of technical and historical knowledge, and overwhelms us with this apparatus of learning, and with his ability to appreciate work in which we can see no sense whatever." His standards have "no relationship to beauty, kindness, or wisdom." They raise new writers up, using the same clichés for all of them. The most influential critics are those who, like Van Wyck Brooks, belong to "the highbrow school, fastidious and aloof," with "a serenity so lofty that it scorns to be aware of opposition."

Sinclair's position in *Money Writes!* was an awkward one in several respects. For one thing, much of his success derived from his own celebrity. As the sandwich-board caper indicates, he was a gifted and shameless self-promoter—shameless because he justified his actions as selfless, for a cause greater than himself. He had also sometimes made a great deal of money from his books, again justified, in his eyes, by the fact that he poured it all back into his work. Finally, there was a strong element of payback in some of his remarks; Brooks had condescendingly dismissed Sinclair as a propagandist, and George Horace Lorimer of *The Saturday Evening Post,* another target, had opened his pages to Ogden Armour's attacks on *The Jungle.*

Sinclair also took aim in *Money Writes!* at his former protégé and accidental namesake, Sinclair Lewis. He begins by referring obliquely to the satiric newspaper article his "ex-furnaceman" wrote about Helicon Hall: young Hal Lewis was "red-headed and talkative, merry, and as we learned later, observant." He then credits himself with helping to make Lewis the good writer that he became: he "sat around our four-sided fireplace in the evenings and got a complete education in every aspect of the radical movement, which was far more useful to him than anything he could have got at

Yale." Unfortunately, Sinclair concludes, Lewis now seems to have forgotten what he learned, partially from him, and practiced so well in *Main Street* and *Babbitt.* He needs to "displease a million or two of his readers" and tell the truth better than he has in his more recent books, *Elmer Gantry* and *Arrowsmith.*

Sinclair's comments on his "pupil" were relatively mild, but Lewis was famously touchy. According to his friend George Seldes, Lewis was "almost weeping" when he said, "I love Upton," but "look what he writes about me." Lewis wrote a long, outraged letter to Sinclair, recommending that he withdraw his book from the market. Sinclair suffered mightily from twin delusions, Lewis charged: that his critics were all capitalist toadies, and that he could somehow master in a matter of weeks complicated subjects that took others years of study. As for those of his own books that Sinclair had criticized, including *Arrowsmith* and *Babbitt,* Lewis said Sinclair not only misunderstood but misrepresented them. He knew that Sinclair would dismiss his complaint as coming from a corrupted millionaire, but Lewis hoped he had made some impression: "My God, Upton, go and pray for forgiveness, honesty, and humility!"

On August 5, 1927, Sinclair took a break from reading the galley proofs for *Money Writes!* to drop a note to Kate Gartz. He would soon return to Boston, he said, on a more serious mission than simply "making a fuss about *Oil!*" The situation there with regard to the ongoing Sacco and Vanzetti case, concerning the two Italian anarchists who had been convicted of armed robbery and murder, was "too tense" for "that kind of joking." He planned to go there soon to gather material "very quietly" for a big novel centering on Sacco and Vanzetti that would take him a couple of years to write. On August 22, the two Italians were electrocuted, and Sinclair's relatively leisurely plan was scrapped. Only fifteen months later, in November 1928, he brought out the longest of all his works so far, a two-volume behemoth of more than 750 pages, twice the length of *The Jungle.* It was called, simply enough, *Boston.*

Half as long would have been twice as good. The Sacco-Vanzetti case had been a continuing story for seven years, and there was little new to be said about it until its implications had been fully considered. Virtually everyone in the intellectual community, from left to center-right, agreed that the conviction of the two men was a miscarriage of justice, based on tainted evidence and prejudice against immigrants and radicals. Even in the legal community, few could dispute the charge of Felix Frankfurter, the Harvard law school professor who would later be appointed to the U.S. Supreme Court by President Franklin D. Roosevelt, that Judge Webster Thayer's handling of the case was characterized by "misquotations, misrepresentations, suppressions, and mutilations." The drama of the doomed men, however, was so overwhelming for Sinclair, especially after their execution, that he became possessed by it, as he had not been possessed since the days of *The Jungle.* His greatest problem in telling the story would be that he came to doubt the innocence of the men whose story he had set out to tell. Sacco, he felt, was almost certainly guilty of the crime with which he was charged, and Vanzetti probably knew about it.

Boston remains of interest today as an overview of the major events of those seven years. It is surprisingly objective and relatively free from propaganda, as Sinclair had pledged it would be to Albert and Charles Boni, who had parted company with Horace Liveright to establish their own company. In terms of his own fiction, the novel is remarkable for Sinclair's choice of an elderly Boston matron as his central character, rather than a young man. Cornelia Thornwell, whose husband had been the governor of the state, decides to begin a new life after his death. Much to the horror of her proper children, she becomes a "runaway grandmother," going to work in a cordage factory and rooming with an Italian family. She meets Bartolomeo Vanzetti several years before his arrest; certain that no man with such qualities of intelligence and humanity could be guilty of murder, Cornelia works hard to free Vanzetti and his friend Nicola Sacco, using her money as well as her connections in high places.

Though too long, *Boston* represents an estimable fusion of Sinclair's talents with a subject that was perfect for him. It also offers, in the form of his extensive correspondence and documentation, an unusually detailed insight into his method of dealing with such a mass of material in so short a time. One of these documents is a vivid description by an anonymous observer in whose home Sinclair was questioning a politician and a psychiatrist about the case: Sinclair is astonishing to watch, the observer says, a "super-reporter," swiftly jotting down what is said, interrupting with pointed questions, "tracking down every scent." He is not "a partisan spirit." His "mind is open. Open, but direct; there are no side-paths. No detours. This is a one-way thoroughfare leading from purpose to achievement." This phrase could be his "coat of arms": "he is a cause in action, a living Crusade." He is like his hero, Shelley, "a man of purpose, of program, of humorless addiction." No, the writer corrects himself, Sinclair is not humorless in the ordinary way; he knows and appreciates a good joke, though not when it's off-color, and he can laugh heartily, though with "a dry, intellectual quality that connotes release rather than acceptance." His laughter is unlike his friend Mencken's—it's "do I make myself clear?" Sinclair is "a pilgrim, not a wayfarer. There is little joy in the man; he has too much soul."

Sinclair spent six weeks in Boston during the late summer of 1927, meeting people connected with the case and pursuing leads, much as he had done twenty-three years earlier in Chicago, but he did most of the writing back in Long Beach and relied on his many contacts to send him the material he needed. His correspondence bears out the anonymous observer's sense of him as a tireless researcher, as a brief look at just a few of the hundreds of letters he wrote and received during this period will show. On February 27, 1928, he wrote to Michael Musmanno, later an eminent judge but now a young Italian-American volunteer attorney for the defense team, to ask how the courtroom was decorated. On February 28 he wrote to Floyd Dell about the problem of using dialect to characterize Vanzetti: "Do you get tired of it or find it difficult reading, and do you think it cheapens his character?" He was deliberately lessening the heavy Italian accent as the novel progressed because Vanzetti's English was improving as the result of his conscientious effort to study the language. On February 29 Sinclair commented to another friend, Porter Sargent, that he wanted "to follow the account of the police strike strictly according to fact," but the "trouble is that the authorities all differ. I want to do the best I can to reconcile the differences."

Simply getting hold of a copy of the trial transcript was a problem for Sinclair. On March 14, H. B. Ehrmann, an attorney in New York, regretted that he could not send Sinclair his firm's transcript because he needed it himself, though "it is hard to resist anyone as winsome as you." Two days later, Sinclair asked Felix Frankfurter for a copy, pleading that he couldn't wait for it to be published and noting that "perhaps a thousand times as many people will read my novel as will ever look" at the published record. Still no luck. On March 19 he succeeded in persuading Bernard Flexner, the legal publisher in New York that had contracted to print the transcript, to let him see the galley proofs immediately.

Sinclair also worked hard to keep his sources in line. George Thompson, one of the defense team lawyers, worried that it was improper for him to help Sinclair write a novel that some might consider propaganda. Sinclair responded that anything written about the case, including Frankfurter's recent *Atlantic Monthly* article, would be construed as propaganda. Thompson owed it to himself to help Sinclair make his novel as good as it could be, since "the obvious fact" was "that nobody is going to have as much to do with making the truth about the Sacco-Vanzetti case known from now on as I am." He apologized for sounding egotistical, but noted that "half a dozen translators" were already at work on the completed portions, which were appearing serially in Germany, Czechoslovakia, and Great Britain. He concluded by assuring Thompson on March 14 that he had never violated the confidence of any of the "hundreds of lawyers" who had helped him write "dangerous books" over the past twenty-five years.

Among Sinclair's more interesting letters are those he wrote to Mrs. Elizabeth Glendower Evans, whose social position in Boston and active support of the accused pair made her a partial model for his heroine. Was she serious, he asked on March 15, in asking to have her name left out of *Boston* entirely? He wanted to include a passage about her so that readers outside Boston would assume that she was *not* the model for Cornelia. He reminded Mrs. Evans that he was, of course, within his rights to use her name, even without her permission: "when a man is writing an account of a public event he should be free to use all those facts which have been published in the newspapers about the matter," meaning her involvement—an amusing stricture, given Sinclair's own distrust of the newspapers. He then added what must have struck Mrs. Evans as a cheeky postscript: "Please let me know as near as possible, the exact date when you first became interested in the Sacco-Vanzetti case."

At about the same time, on March 13, Sinclair was writing to Fred Moore, one of the lead attorneys for the defense, to explain how he intended to use Cornelia to advance his story. She "begins naively, as she would have done, and we all actually do. Then, little by little, things will begin to occur to her, and she will wonder and doubt, and the reader will be left to wonder and doubt at the end, just as I do now. So I want Cornelia to be completely fooled" about the purported innocence of the accused men: "she would have been, would she not?"

It was Fred Moore, Sinclair said later, who confirmed his own growing doubts about Sacco's and Vanzetti's innocence. Meeting in a hotel room in Denver on his way home from Boston, he and Moore talked about the case. Moore said neither man ever admitted it to him, but he was certain of Sacco's guilt and fairly sure of Vanzetti's knowledge of the crime if not his complicity in it. This knowledge had not prevented Moore from doing whatever he could to save the two men, perhaps including illegal activities. The entire legal system was corrupt, Moore insisted, assuring Sinclair that "there is no criminal lawyer who has attained to fame in America except by inventing alibis and hiring witnesses. There is no other way to be a great criminal lawyer in America."

Sinclair's decision to end *Boston* on a note of ambiguity concerning the guilt or innocence of the Italian anarchists—as distinct from his treatment in

Oil! of the Morgan bombing—subjected him to a torrent of abuse from the left. His old friend Robert Minor learned of Sinclair's intentions and called him in California, saying "You will ruin the movement! It will be treason!" Sinclair told Minor that he intended to tell the story "objectively," not omitting the existence of "direct actionists"—"direct action" being the left's euphemism for violence—in both the anarchist movement and the Communist Party.

Minor then did charge Sinclair with treason to the socialist cause, with cowardice, and with outright lying. But Sinclair's refusal to bend the truth as he saw it won him unusual praise from less biased observers, even those who were sympathetic to Sacco and Vanzetti. The novel was widely reviewed as his best yet, with even *The New York Times* lauding it on November 18, 1928, for its "literary achievement." It was "full of sharp observation and savage characterization," demonstrating a new "craftsmanship in the technique of the novel"—sweet words indeed to a man who had often been charged with lacking both craft and characterization, whatever his other virtues.

Sinclair had optimistically hoped to see *Boston* published on his fiftieth birthday, September 20. That had proved impossible. But now, after years of being scorned by the literary establishment as a propagandist if not a hack, a different kind of impossible goal had apparently been achieved. As the year ended, Sinclair learned that *Boston* was a serious contender for the Pulitzer Prize for the Novel for 1928. He felt, rightly, that there were no other novels in the running that were comparable in both heft and quality to *Boston*. Sinclair hungered after the honor, certain that it would be his reward for finally transcending the limitations of propaganda—and blissfully unaware that he would be denied the prize for precisely that reason.

CHAPTER TWELVE

THE VENTURE CAPITALIST

(January 1929–December 1931)

Thornton Wilder, not Upton Sinclair, won the 1928 Pulitzer Prize for the Novel, for the admirable but slight novella *The Bridge of San Luis Rey*. *Boston* "only missed winning," said the chairman of the selection committee, Dr. Richard Burton, "because of its socialist tone." Burton deplored what *Boston* represented, the *Minneapolis Star* reported—namely, "the confusion that exists as to what is and what is not a novel, claiming that he has encountered people who consider biography, autobiography, pathological analysis, travel books and even poetry as fiction." In response to an indignant query from Sinclair, Burton said "your novel was rated high among the books of fiction of the year" by the jury, but "the artistic value of the book was, in my personal opinion, injured by its effect of special pleading."

Boston did include instances of "special pleading" for social justice as it would be achieved through socialism, but Sinclair had made a conscientious effort to deal honestly with the ambiguity he felt was inherent in the Sacco-Vanzetti story. A more intelligent reader than Burton, though unfortunately one with no influence on the selection committee, was the English translator of Proust: C. K. Scott Moncrieff wrote to Sinclair's publisher to say that not only were American novelists in general "immensely superior" to those in England, but *Boston* was "perhaps the greatest American novel" yet. Felix Frankfurter, among the many whose help Sinclair solicited in an effort to revise the Pulitzer nomination and selection process after his loss, tried to console him: "What a gusto you have for life, and with what abundance your energy flows!" But he wondered why Sinclair should care so much about a prize which seems "partly irrelevance and partly absurdity . . . the whole modern tendency of having small groups of people tell us what to read and what not to read, what is great and what is not great, runs counter to my individualistic fibre."

Sinclair was no less an individualist than Frankfurter, but he had good reasons for caring about the honor he had been denied. He believed that every serious writer was a double personality: by nature generous, eager to share, "a naive and trusting creature—half a child, or the make-believe impulse would not survive in him." But he also needed food and shelter, and his only means for attaining those was to sell what he wrote as "merchandise." The world was a Darwinian jungle where those who did not fight were doomed. A writer's reputation was his best weapon; when it was attacked, he had to respond effectively or die—at least figuratively.

Both aspects of Sinclair's own authorial persona are vividly illustrated by the alternatives he considered for the title of his autobiography. The first, "Speaking Through a Smile," came from Charlie Chaplin's description of his characteristic manner, and reflected, Sinclair said, the "light and anecdotic" manner in which it was written. The second choice was more revealing: "American Outpost," redolent with implications of intrepid, solitary pioneering on behalf of the nation. Sometimes Sinclair deflected attacks with self-deprecating humor, "speaking through a smile," as in his responses to Mencken. On other occasions, he struck back, as a lonely soldier attacked far from home must do, with all the force he could muster.

American Outpost, as the autobiography would finally be called, was finished during the first half of 1929, but would not appear until three years later, after Priscilla Sinclair's death. His mother had objected to some parts that Sinclair showed her, and he chose to wait until she was gone rather than change what he had written. When it did appear, in 1932, the jacket description, which sounds as though it was written by Sinclair, accurately reflected the book's mild charm and suggested its limitations: "Frankly and engagingly he traces from his strange childhood the dramatic incidents and moods that have made him a social novelist and propagandist, loving mankind, hating drink and lust—that extraordinary combination: a Revolutionary and a Puritan!" In fact, the book is much less frank, and a good deal less intellectually and emotionally engaging, than the segments drawn from Sinclair's life in *Love's Pilgrimage, The Journal of Arthur Stirling, The Brass Check,* and other works. That Priscilla could object to it confirms Sinclair's more acerbic private remarks concerning her inability to understand him or his work. Those who study Sinclair's life have, of course, found *American Outpost* essential, given the loss of most original documents for his first twenty-eight years in the Helicon Hall fire. But far more significant material is omitted than is included, particularly with regard to Meta and Craig. More important still, "speaking through a smile" was Sinclair's manner, not his nature. It was protective coloration that he adopted as a means for survival.

Both the amiable and the combative sides of Sinclair were in evidence during the early summer of 1929, when he spent six weeks in Denver. He used the time, or much of it, to write a novel called *Mountain City*. The novel itself is little more than a winding-down diversion after the heavy labor required for *Oil!* and *Boston*. Its German title, *So Macht Man Dollars,* "says it all," John Ahouse explains: *Mountain City* is a "How to Get Rich in America" handbook, an oddly sympathetic look at a young entrepreneur's rise to wealth that shows how "Sinclair had mellowed over the years." In the course of telling the story of his genial hero, Jed Rusher, Sinclair draws on an obvious allusion to Owen Wister's *The Virginian,* which he had once greatly admired: there is an "old tradition of the West," the narrator recalls, "that you may call people certain bad names, provided you smile while you say it."

But Sinclair was feeling far from mellow during his stay in Denver. He was there because the *Rocky Mountain News* had called him "certain bad names," and he had sued the newspaper for libel. The occasion for the suit was the paper's negative review, in August 1927, of Sinclair's character as it was reflected in Floyd Dell's biography earlier that year. The review was illustrated by a caricature of Sinclair holding a spotlight on himself. It made him appear to be, as Sinclair summarized in his own words, "a snob and a publicity-seeker, a popinjay and a renegade, a man ashamed of his ancestry, a pseudo-rebel, a pseudo-Socialist, and various other kinds of falsifier and poseur." Sinclair claimed that the reviewer quoted him as making statements he never made; he demanded $200,000 to compensate for the damage done to his reputation.

In Sinclair's indignant summary of the trial and his defeat, published later that summer in *The New Leader,* he objected that the defense attorneys had turned him into the offender, grilling him for three days straight, for a total of eighteen hours. Sometimes their maneuvers involved strategic omissions, as in, "Did Dell state that 'Upton Sinclair is a guide conspicuously lacking in tolerance'?" He could only answer yes, not being permitted to add the rest of Dell's line: "for drunkenness or debauchery." Another defense tactic was to bring out "blunders I had made at the age of thirteen, and recorded in semi-fictional form"—these were now "set forth as evidence of my character at fifty." Words that Sinclair had quoted from persons with whom he disagreed were read back to him, and "I was asked, with a menacing finger thrust when I sought to explain why and how I had written that, I was commanded: 'Answer yes or no!' " Most damaging of all, he had, over "thirty years of effort to be honest with the public," provided his enemies with a huge mass of material that was easily "taken out of context and twisted into terrible meanings." In particular, all of his scathing comments about Colorado in *The Coal War* made him as "helpless as a hog on ice."

———

Sinclair's failed suit revealed that he was a tenacious fighter, but also one with an Achilles' heel of unusual tenderness. His vulnerability lay not only in his long history of published remarks on virtually every conceivable subject of controversy; he had also for many years given those who were unsympathetic to his ideas abundant reason to dismiss him as an eccentric, a faddist, or a crank. Idealistic communes, conspiracy theories, diet and health fads like fasting—and, more recently, experiments with mediums, séances, and mental telepathy—prompted many to agree with Mencken that Sinclair had a "credulity complex."

Sinclair's willingness to believe the unbelievable, the unlikely, or at best, the unprovable, may have stemmed from the childlike willingness to indulge in make-believe that he thought was part of being a writer. It certainly coincided with the inclination of radicals, whatever their persuasion, to shock bourgeois sensibilities. Most likely, what Sinclair thought of as an openness to daring ideas derived from two seemingly opposed characteristics. On the one hand, he maintained a justified confidence in his rational, objective capacity to sift and examine evidence, as he had done so effectively in *The Jungle* and in many other works. On the other, he had a lifelong tendency to believe in the ineffable—first in Christianity, later in mysticism, spiritualism, and extrasensory perception, and always, to varying degrees, in his own special gifts as a seer.

Craig too had come to believe that she had a special gift, in her case for mental telepathy. She was encouraged by a handsome young Polish immigrant who claimed to be a count named Roman Ostoja, who was with them so much that Sinclair, in a letter in February 1929 to *The New Republic,* said he was "practically a member of our family." Sinclair explained that Ostoja was a medium who could enter a trance and stick pins in his body without visible pain or injury; he could "induce in himself a cataleptic trance, in which his body becomes completely rigid, and can be placed between two chairs on the heels and head, and a hundred and fifty pound rock can be broken with sledge hammers." Sinclair had himself "stood upon his body." On another occasion he watched Ostoja make a table weighing thirty pounds "rise four feet in the air and move slowly eight feet to one side."

Sinclair knew that he was dabbling in a field rife with fraud, and he tried to take precautions against being cheated. Every experiment he undertook or observed involved elaborate controls, supposedly foolproof. Even before meeting Ostoja he had read widely in the field and corresponded with Harry Houdini, who was ruthless in tracking down and exposing hoaxes. He even queried the Polish embassy in Washington, in 1927, about the count's claims to nobility; these were never verified, and Sinclair was finally persuaded to discard Ostoja in 1930.

Ostoja had encouraged Craig's interest in mental telepathy, which became intense during her stay in Long Beach. In their most significant collaboration aside from her later autobiography, she agreed to let Sinclair gather material for a book on spiritualism and mental telepathy. Although his publisher, Charles Boni, initially discouraged the idea, Sinclair persisted, and the book, called *Mental Radio,* appeared in March 1930. In it, Sinclair summarized Boni's objections, admitting that he stood to lose more than he gained by writing such a book; his friends might say "Sinclair has gone in for occultism; he is turning into a mystic in his old age." He could only respond, "if what I publish here is mysticism, then I do not know how there can be such a thing as science about the human mind."

In any event, Sinclair said, the book was not about him, it was about Craig. Except for including some of Ostoja's unbelievable feats, such as the floating table, *Mental Radio* was relatively restrained, even plausible for many readers. Sinclair's evidence was modest and tangible, consisting of communications between Craig in her Long Beach house and her sister Dollie's husband, Robert Irwin, in their Pasadena house. These telepathic communications were images of various objects—a chair, a water glass, a coathook, a star, an elephant—that Irwin, or sometimes Sinclair, would sketch and then "send" to Craig, thirty miles away. No talent was required on the part of the sender, just the ability to concentrate sufficiently so that the receiver could tune in. Craig would "receive" and sketch the images, not always completely or correctly but enough to make the case that some kind of mental communication was happening.

In *Mental Radio* Sinclair adroitly disarms his readers' skepticism even while assuring them "Telepathy is real; it does happen. Whatever may be the nature of the force, it has nothing to do with distance, for it works exactly as well over forty miles as over thirty feet." It appeals to Sinclair the socialist that telepathy is not restricted to an elite few; everybody has some capacity for it, meaning that it can be learned and enhanced. He admits that he has not been able to develop any such gift himself, and that his readers are entitled to be wary: he is like the wandering peddler "who taps on your door and gets you to open it, and has to speak quickly and persuasively. . . . Your prejudice is against this idea; and if you are one of my old-time readers, you are a little shocked to find me taking up a new and unexpected line of activity.

You have come, after thirty years, to the position where you allow me to be one kind of 'crank,' but you won't stand for two kinds."

Mental Radio turned out to be a likable book, one that sold well over the years and continues in print today. In it the smiling Sinclair tries to charm the reader into buying his wares, and he's a good salesman. Reviews were generally friendly. Even Mencken let him off lightly in his *American Mercury* review: "materialists will greet his evidence with ribald winks, but it will probably be convincing enough to his fellow Socialists." Albert Einstein, one of those socialists, thanked Sinclair warmly for the gift copy of *Mental Radio* he had received and said he would be happy to write an introduction for a German edition. Sinclair wrote back in November 1930 to say he had "just read that you are coming to Pasadena," for a two-month teaching post at California Institute of Technology. Though they had never met, Sinclair said that if Einstein wanted "a quiet garden to come to and be let alone in, we will provide it. You had better bring your fiddle along, and we will play duets if you don't mind my being out of tune occasionally."

Sinclair's dismissal of Ostoja did not mean that he had lost interest in spiritualism, which many of his friends and correspondents shared to some degree, among them Arthur Conan Doyle, Theodore Dreiser, and Charlie Chaplin, as well as Einstein. He and Craig turned during the summer of 1930 to a young Englishman named Arthur Ford, who on July 16 conducted a séance for the Sinclairs at the People's Spiritualist Church of Los Angeles. Sinclair described the séance shortly afterward in an article for *The Occult Review*, entitled "Is This Jack London?" Ford's supposed channel to the spirit world was a French Canadian called Fletcher. Following previously agreed-upon instructions, Sinclair handed Ford some letters he had received in the past from friends, each sealed within a thick manila envelope. Ford had no way of knowing whose letters Sinclair had selected. They were from Eugene Debs, George Sterling, Arthur Conan Doyle, Georg Brandes, and Jack London.

Ford tied a handkerchief over his eyes and went into a trance; "Fletcher" appeared, speaking with a French Canadian accent. Fletcher/Ford said, "There is a person here you knew in life—John, called Jack. He talks about writing. His name is London. He is the nearest to you. . . . He calls you Upton, no, something shorter, like Uppie. He says that you have a letter from him here. Is that so?" Sinclair had selected a letter written by London during the 1908 cruise of the *Snark,* when he was in Carmel. The letter had been mailed from Tasmania; it was an apology for not writing, and included a reference to picking up a new novel of Sinclair's in Hobart. Fletcher said, with reasonable accuracy, that London's letter was "a short note, some plan not finished, a bread and butter note, you understand? Thanking you." After a few more minutes Fletcher said "Jack London again." Jack's message, as paraphrased by Sinclair, was that "he was helping me, and gave that as the reason why I was writing more fiction of late years. I thanked him and told him to go on helping me." Jack's visit concluded with his assertion that "when history is written fifty years from now there will be only three living American writers who will be remembered, and Upton is one of them. He's the only one they read in Europe now. Say what you please, the squareheads do think."

"This last sentence sounds like Jack London," Sinclair assured his readers. "I won't say the rest is Jack; it will be better if I say it is Jack as the subconscious mind of Upton would have him!" London's last words concerned his suicide. Sinclair told him, through Fletcher, that Craig had known he was about to die. Jack exclaimed, "Why didn't you tell me, Mary?" Craig replied, "I didn't know if you'd want me to." Jack signed off: "I'm sorry I did it, but now I'm out of it."

Ford was later exposed as a fraud, but not until the 1950s. He was industrious and clever: it was a safe bet that Sinclair would have wanted to hear from London, and Ford would have known enough about Sinclair's friendship with London to construct a plausible scenario. Minor errors such as calling Craig "Mary" could be ascribed to static in the ether. Sinclair was willing to be persuaded; he was flirting with spiritualism as far back as 1907 in *The Metropolis,* where Allan Montague found it appealing.

As becomes clear in the Lanny Budd books, where he involves his hero in a score of melodramatic scenes with spiritualists, Sinclair loved the theatrical elements of séances like those in which Jack London came to visit. In his own tidy fashion, he was himself a dramatic personality whose success as a writer had always benefited from a vivid sense of public performance, from the *Arthur Stirling* hoax through the fig-leaf sandwich boards for *Oil!* In addition, not only had he written a dozen plays, he had been involved from its early years with the world of film entertainment. His participation in the 1913 production of *The Jungle* whetted his interest in movies and may well have been a contributing factor in his move to Los Angeles. Within months of his arrival in 1916 he had offered several stories to the U.S. Amusement Corporation, one of which, "The Adventurer," was produced in 1917. In 1918 he sent a sketch he called "The Hypnotist" to Charlie Chaplin, who was then churning out weekly two-reel comedies. "In the beginning," Sinclair's pitch begins, "you are running a hypnotist and spiritualist parlor." After three double-spaced pages of elaborate scenario, Sinclair concludes that in his eyes the sketch "contains the requisite amount of fun, and also so-cial criticism. How does it strike you?"

Chaplin declined Sinclair's idea, but the two became friendly. Chaplin was eleven years younger than Sinclair, whom he later referred to as one of his "two mentors" in Hollywood. (Chaplin's other mentor was Rob Wagner, the editor of *Script,* the influential Hollywood trade magazine, who was also a Sinclair friend.) Sinclair frequently visited the sets of Chaplin's films while they were being shot, and later treasured the memory of Chaplin giving him a solo performance of his "little tramp" routine in his dressing room. Chap-lin participated in several séances at Sinclair's home, they had dinner fre-quently at Rob Wagner's home in Beverly Hills, and Craig later become close to Chaplin's second wife, the actress Paulette Goddard.

Chaplin shared Sinclair's radical political sentiments, in part from having grown up poor in London. But by 1930 he was near the zenith of his popu-larity, his fame and fortune immensely greater than Sinclair's. He was un-derstandably amused when Sinclair asked him, as he had earlier asked Henry Ford, if he truly believed in the profit system. Chaplin not only be-lieved in the profit system, he believed in holding on to what he had earned. When the Russian film director Sergei Eisenstein came to Hollywood in 1930 and approached him for funding to make a documentary film about Mexico, Chaplin declined and suggested that he ask Upton Sinclair for sup-port. Thus was set in motion the series of events that Sinclair would come to regret for the rest of his long life.

Sergei Eisenstein was a prodigy. Just thirty-three years old when he met Sin-clair, in November 1930, he was famous as the director of the 1925 film about the Russian navy's mutiny against the czar, *Battleship Potemkin.* His next film, *Ten Days That Shook the World,* in 1927, was based on the 1919 book by John Reed. In the spring of 1930, Paramount Studio's chief, Jesse Lasky, met Eisenstein in Paris. After long conversations—Eisenstein's command of spoken and written English was unusually fluent—Lasky invited him to come to Hollywood for six months, along with his cameraman, Eduard Tissé, and his assistant director, G. V. "Grisha" Alexandrov. The three men would receive a total of $900 a week. If Eisenstein came up with a script that went into production, the combined salary would jump to $3,000 a week.

Eisenstein arrived in mid-June, found a house in the Hollywood Hills, and tried without success to provide a script acceptable to Paramount. His most promising idea was a dramatization of Theodore Dreiser's recent best-selling novel *An American Tragedy* (1926), but while he wanted a psychological drama of crime and punishment that reflected the ills of American society, the studio wanted, as Eisenstein put it, nothing more than "a good stiff police story!" Paramount canceled the contract on October 23 and gave the Russians their return tickets to Moscow.

Eisenstein was happy to be unshackled from posing for publicity stills with Rin Tin Tin and Jean Harlow, and from the need to be polite to executives like Sam Goldwyn, who thought he might be interested in producing something like *Potemkin,* but "rather cheaper, for Ronald Colman." But he was not eager to return to Stalin's Russia so soon. Several years earlier his interest in Mexico had been stimulated by his experience in adapting for the stage Jack London's short story "The Mexican." Now, at loose ends, he was encouraged by the Mexican painter and convert to communism Diego Rivera to make a documentary film about the Indians in Mexico. Other sources told him he could probably do the job with about $25,000.

Sinclair later wondered grumpily why Chaplin, "the proud possessor of seven million dollars," sent Eisenstein to ask him for money, but there was good reason for Chaplin to assume that the Russian's project would interest him. Sinclair's novels as well as his nonfiction were hugely popular in the Soviet Union. In 1927, Eisenstein had written to express interest in filming Sinclair's *King Coal.* Nothing had come of that idea, but Sinclair wrote a letter to *Izvestia* describing how deeply he had been moved upon seeing *Potemkin.* The two men met briefly when Eisenstein arrived in California. When Sinclair heard of the Russian's troubles with Paramount he wrote him a sympathetic letter, saying "Do drop me a note and tell me what you are planning to do. Let us not lose touch with each other."

They met for the second time shortly afterward, during the first week of November, to discuss Eisenstein's Mexican film plans. Sinclair and Craig agreed to sponsor him, and contract negotiations were concluded by the end of the month. Sinclair's name and connections were invaluable from the start in securing an extension of Eisenstein's American visa, in negotiating the Russians' entry into Mexico, and in winning promises of cooperation from the Mexican authorities. He asked his friends and acquaintances to invest in the project, promising a healthy return, but he and Craig would bear most of the burden—and realize, they hoped, most of the anticipated profit as well. They took out loans on several of the properties that Craig had accumulated; the contract, accordingly, was in Craig's name. It obligated her to provide $25,000 (about $300,000 in today's dollars) to Eisenstein, who was to work on site in Mexico with Alexandrov and Tissé for a maximum of four months. The film would be Craig's property insofar as American showings were concerned. Once her costs were recouped, Eisenstein was to receive 10 percent of any additional profits. The film would be made available to the Soviet Union at no charge.

Written into the contract was an important stipulation, assuring Eisenstein the right to make "a picture according to his own ideas of what a Mexican picture should be, and in full faith in Eisenstein's artistic integrity, and in consideration of his promise that the picture will be non-political, and worthy of his reputation and genius." No less important was a separate agreement concerning the appointment of Craig's brother, Hunter Kimbrough, now a sturdily built and widely traveled man of thirty-two, to act as the Sinclairs' business manager. Hunter's base of operations was to be in Mexico City, but he would also travel frequently with the Eisenstein party to locations around the country. Hunter left for Mexico City on December 1 to arrange for accommodations and government permits for filming; the Eisenstein party left to join him a few days later, on December 5—after first viewing, with Sinclair, an early version of what would become one of Charlie Chaplin's finest films, *City Lights*.

The ensuing three-year saga involved swirling charges of manipulation, fraud, and betrayal. Illnesses caused by nervous tension sent both Eisenstein and Sinclair to the hospital, and Craig at one point threatened to leave her husband. The story is immensely complicated, as revealed by Harry Geduld and Ronald Gottesman's exhaustive study, *Sergei Eisenstein and Upton Sinclair: The Making and Unmaking of Que Viva Mexico!* That said, what happened is relatively straightforward in its basic outlines: after a few weeks of initial shooting around Mexico City, Eisenstein expanded the original intent of the contract, changing the focus of the film from a simple documentary travelogue to an epic narrative of Mexico's past and present. Sinclair was excited by the new plan, vague though it was (and would remain) in its details. Despite Craig's nominal importance in terms of the contract, he was calling the shots. He agreed to let Eisenstein stay beyond the original contract term of four months, which expired April 1, 1931, and to raise the necessary added funds.

The film as now envisioned was to consist of four episodes—Eisenstein called them "novels"—drawn from the country's past, framed by a prologue and an epilogue. In the opening scene a funeral procession would be intercut with images of Mayan ruins in the Yucatan, dramatizing the interrelated themes of death and immortality, and of the ancient coexisting side by side with the modern. The four "novels" would describe oppression and revolution in various phases. The penultimate section, on the role of courageous women in the revolution, was to be called "La Soldadera." An epilogue would feature the traditional carnival known as Day of the Dead, in which the native marchers wear death masks. In the final scene a young boy, smiling broadly, would tear off his mask, representing, in Eisenstein's words, "the new, growing Mexico"—hence Eisenstein's optimistic and uplifting title for the film, "¡Que viva México!"

His advocates have since argued that Eisenstein's planned film, given this prospectus, would have rivaled the greatest of his earlier successes, including *Potemkin*. Given Sinclair's own fondness for epic similes and heroic projects, Eisenstein could be excused for thinking that his sponsor should have shown more comprehension of the difficulties that he faced, and of the achievement that would result from mastering them.

But even the relatively simple travelogue that Sinclair originally thought he had approved would have been hard to finish in the time originally allowed. Now, with the more ambitious plan, the four months grew to be fifteen. Eisenstein and his team stayed in Mexico until February 1932, supported entirely by Sinclair's money. At least some of the money and the time were well spent: miles of raw footage were shipped from Mexico to Los Angeles for development. Tissé was an extraordinarily gifted photographer and cameraman, and much of what Sinclair saw was brilliant. But because he had no understanding of the film editing process, Sinclair could not envision a coherent narrative emerging from what he saw: tangled sequences of palm trees swaying in sunset breezes, rebozos and agaves and cacti, cockfights, bullfights, and religious pilgrims crawling on their hands and knees, peasants in the fields, rebels killing soldiers and in turn being buried alive and beheaded. Despite his vast experience in winnowing out stories from mountains of data, Sinclair could not comprehend that the miles of film footage were the filmmaker's research materials, not evidence of wasted effort.

Although he was confused and anxious at having so little control over a process that he barely understood, Sinclair resisted Hunter's continued warnings that Eisenstein was dragging his feet because he was unwilling, perhaps afraid, to go back to Russia. Sinclair had assured his Russian contact with Amkino in New York that Eisenstein fully intended to return to Russia when the film was finished. (Amkino was the American arm of a Soviet film company that had promised to provide $25,000 toward the costs of "¡Que viva México!")

But on November 21, 1931, Sinclair was alarmed to receive a telegram from Stalin himself concerning Eisenstein. It read, in part,

EISENSTEIN LOOSE [*sic*] HIS COMRADES CONFIDENCE IN
SOVIET UNION STOP HE IS THOUGHT TO BE DESERTER WHO

BROKE OFF WITH HIS OWN COUNTRY STOP AM AFRAID THE
PEOPLE HERE WOULD HAVE NO INTEREST IN HIM SOON STOP
AM VERY SORRY BUT ALL ASSERT IT IS THE FACT STOP WISH
YOU TO BE WELL AND TO FULFILL YOUR PLAN OF COMING TO
SEE US STOP MY REGARDS STOP STALIN.

Sinclair's noncommittal public reaction to Stalin's key role in turning the
Soviet Union into a tyranny based on fear and trembling had already provoked complaints from his fellow socialists. He justified his silence by arguing that undermining the Soviet Union would not serve the cause of
socialism. Now his policy of restraint at least gained him a hearing: Sinclair
responded immediately in a letter to "My Dear Comrade Stalin," generously
and at considerable length defending Eisenstein from any hint of disloyalty.
He also assured Stalin that the "many delays" that had kept Eisenstein in
Mexico for so long were not the director's fault but due to physical infirmity,
including having seven teeth pulled, and to incompetence and foot-dragging
by Mexican authorities. Sinclair ended with the hope that the rumors about
Eisenstein's disloyalty would "die away" once he returned with a film that
would certainly be "crowned by the applause of art lovers throughout the
world."

But Stalin, incited by Eisenstein's enemies within the Soviet film bureaucracy, seems not to have been mollified by Sinclair's letter. Amkino soon re-
neged on its promise of funds for Eisenstein. Sinclair also failed to persuade
the Soviet Union, in yet another try, to send him his royalties, which he
promised to apply toward the film. (Stalin's regime ignored international
copyrights. It deposited token royalties for authors it approved of, like Sinclair and Dreiser, in Russian banks. Such authors could come to the Soviet
Union, withdraw their rubles, and spend them in Russia, but otherwise received nothing for their books.) Wealthy friends like Kate Gartz, oil heiress
Aline Barnsdall, King Gillette, and Charlie Chaplin declined to get involved.
Sinclair must have been feeling like poor Christian in *Pilgrim's Progress,* in
need and unable to find succor, when two men came through for him—
Morris Hillquit, an old Socialist Party leader and friend, who put up $1,000,
and New York banker Otto Kahn, whose $10,000 investment later won him
loving mention in the Lanny Budd novels.

Hunter eventually persuaded his sister and Sinclair that although Eisenstein was serious about making a film, he was indeed deliberately dragging
out the process, happy to tour Mexico on their money in lieu of going back
to Russia. Sinclair canceled all further funding in February 1932. Eisenstein
went home, leaving Mexico by way of Texas, never to see Los Angeles or

Sinclair again. Sinclair was left with his debts and miles of Eisenstein's unedited film footage. He turned it over to Sol Lesser, a Hollywood producer of western movies and a Tarzan adventure. Lesser said he could make a profitable commercial film of about ninety minutes, using a portion of the Eisenstein footage, and recoup at least a part of Sinclair's expenses.

It would be another year and a half before the rest of the Eisenstein story would be played out, but at least the immediate crisis had finally ended.

====

Sinclair suffered a loss of another kind as the expedition in Mexico unraveled, but this one had at least been anticipated, and he accepted it with a coolness that shocked his son. Priscilla Sinclair died of heart disease at the age of seventy-five, on October 19, 1931, after a lengthy illness. Mother and son had grown increasingly distant in recent years. Sinclair wrote Priscilla infrequent and dutiful letters, but she never visited him in California—nor is there any indication that she was ever invited. In March 1929, Sinclair dictated a letter saying he hadn't heard from Priscilla for a while. He had finished "the book which you don't like," Sinclair said—his autobiography, which he then shelved for her sake—"and will hope for better luck next time."

No correspondence of interest follows for more than two years, until their letters of late August 1931, which crossed: Priscilla said she would like very much to read the copy of his new novel, *The Wet Parade,* that Sinclair had sent her, but she was too ill to sit up for more than an hour a day. Perhaps he could send a copy to a young minister who had been kind to her. "Love to see you," she concluded: "Many thoughts of you. Love from Mother." Sinclair's letter expressed concern that he had not heard from Priscilla "for some time. I hope it is not because you are worse. We have been having very hot weather here."

Sinclair wrote to David shortly after his mother's death to say that it was of course a "shock" for him. But it was "impossible to grieve much when life had sunk to such a low ebb as it had with Mother." He directed David to search Priscilla's apartment for the manuscript of *The Jungle*—the single remaining copy that he had so carefully wrapped in oilskin and found unharmed after the fire at Helicon Hall, and then entrusted to his mother for safekeeping; he understood it might be worth $25,000. (The copy was never found.) David should also sell or give away whatever he and Betty didn't want of the furniture and other possessions, and "not fall a victim to the graft of funeral directors and undertakers. My guess is that Aunt Maria [Priscilla's sister] will want to have the burial in the family plot in Baltimore." David shouldn't think his father was "unsentimental"—Sinclair put the word within quotation marks—about "poor Mother. She was the best of mothers" until he was about sixteen. "Then I grew beyond her, and she wouldn't follow, or couldn't. If she'd let me alone, it would have been all right; but she still thought I was a child and stubbornly fought to direct my life and *mind*." For forty years they hadn't met without quarreling.

Responding to David's apparent reproach for having refused to send Priscilla any money for support, Sinclair said, "I paid her $25 a month until a few years ago; then I hardened my heart—simply because [Aunt Maria] was so rich, it seemed I could use the money more sensibly." Remember too, Sinclair said, that Priscilla had always been blindly jealous of Craig, and could not even bring herself to be polite to her. Whereas "my mother never had a gleam of interest in any of my ideals," Craig "ruined her health fighting with me for my ideals, through poverty and other things too painful to mention." All Priscilla could say to Craig was, "You're a fool to ruin your health. Make him behave himself."

More than thirty years later, when he was in his mid-eighties, Sinclair said that his emotional identification was with those who deserved it. He had received as a young man "absolutely no sympathy from any member of my family," including his parents, who had consequently earned their dismissal.

═══

In 1930, when he won the Nobel Prize for Literature, Sinclair Lewis generously conceded that there were other American writers who were at least as deserving as he of the award, including Theodore Dreiser, Eugene O'Neill, and Upton Sinclair, "of whom you must say, whether you admire or detest his aggressive socialism, that he is internationally better known than any other American artist whosoever, be he novelist, poet, painter, sculptor, musician, architect."

Upton Sinclair fully agreed that he deserved the prize. Beginning in late 1930 and intensifying throughout 1931, he mounted a campaign fronted by his former secretary, Ernest Greene, now living in New York, to get it. Greene assembled, at Sinclair's direction, a committee that included some famous, and even a few illustrious, names: Albert Einstein, John Dewey, Bertrand Russell, Harold J. Laski, Robert Morss Lovett, Edwin Markham, Robert Herrick, and the future senator from Illinois, Paul Douglas. Greene wrote an "Argument for Awarding the Nobel Prize to Upton Sinclair" that included financial need, an unusual approach. He noted that in the past the prize money, recently increased to about $40,000, had gone to writers who didn't need it (like Sinclair Lewis?)—and asserted that Upton Sinclair was living "in poverty." Greene praised Sinclair as "the Tolstoi of the stockyards," comparable to Rousseau and Voltaire. Signatures from nearly eight hundred supporters in fifty-five countries came in, including those of George Bernard Shaw, Romain Rolland, and Siegfried Sassoon—along with a great many assistant professors of German, political science, and freshman English in obscure state colleges and foreign universities whose authority as judges of great literature was not self-evident.

Greene's pitch also drew negative responses from many, including a figure from Sinclair's past, Owen Wister, and an influential literary historian and professor, Arthur Hobson Quinn. Wister, soured by his experience with Sinclair in 1903, had later included him, in 1915, in an attack on "quack novelists"—writers who, like quack doctors, might look like the real thing but who prescribe dangerous nostrums instead of useful medicine. Wister now wrote to Greene concerning Sinclair's candidacy. Sinclair read the letter and responded to it, complaining that Wister had maligned him as a communist and a failed idealist who had never been the same since his ideas about marriage "blew up when he tried them out in Arden." In a follow-up letter to Wister, Sinclair accused him of perpetrating a "personal slur upon my private life."

"For Wister," according to his biographer, Darwin Payne, "this impassioned letter only indicated anew Sinclair's perfidy, and he told him so bluntly in a rejoinder." But Wister was by now an old man whose own literary contributions were regarded as minor. His opposition to Sinclair mattered little when compared to that of Professor Quinn, who represented the mainstream consensus of academic opinion. Quinn told Greene of his strong conviction as a professor of American literature for many years that "Sinclair's works are not literature," and he subsequently mounted a campaign to deny Sinclair the prize. Sinclair was still bitter in his eighties, claiming that Quinn's opposition derived from his devout Catholicism: "I suppose he's now up in heaven, perhaps singing hymns with the angels and being congratulated upon his having achieved the task of keeping me from being a Nobel Prize–winning author."

The Nobel Prize for Literature has always had a spotty record for quality; Sinclair probably deserved the award as much as did the winner for 1932, John Galsworthy, but the crassness of the poverty pitch could not have done him any good. In fact, he was hardly lining up at soup kitchens. Despite the drain from financing the Eisenstein film, his net income for 1931, after deducting expenses, was $21,386, or a quarter of a million dollars today. But it was true that he had lived in poverty in the past, and he had reason to fear that Sergei Eisenstein might spend him into bankruptcy in the near future. Forty thousand dollars in Nobel Prize money—the precise value in 1932 was $46,350, worth $625,764 today—would greatly have eased his financial situation.

Fortunately for Sinclair, he had other sources of income in the form of several books, either finished or in the works. While none was likely to make those who had opposed his selection for the Nobel Prize regret their decision, at least one of them would show Sinclair's uncanny resilience as well as his shrewd business sense—so at variance with the public's image of him as a simple idealist, a credulous enthusiast, or a dreamy habitué of mediums and séances.

CHAPTER THIRTEEN

THE INSIDER

(January 1932–September 1933)

W hen *American Outpost* finally appeared, in 1932, Upton Sinclair was fifty-four years old. He had written one epochal novel, *The Jungle,* and two others of considerable merit, *Oil!* and *Boston,* plus half a dozen works of nonfiction that, taken together, constituted an impressive critique of American institutions as a collective "dead hand." The moment was right for a summing-up, if not a valedictory—and for a corrective reshaping of the impression that Floyd Dell had left with his 1927 biography. Dell's Freudian interpretation of Sinclair's life was admiring and sympathetic, but too narrowly grounded in the notion that Sinclair was a puritan and a neurotic.

The most perceptive response to Dell's book had been that of Walter Lippmann, whose association with Sinclair went back to the early days of the Intercollegiate Socialist Society. Dell was trying to show, Lippmann said, that Sinclair had gone from despising and rejecting the world he lived in to becoming "the greatest American reporter of actuality," as seen in *The Jungle* as well as in the Dead Hand series. Lippmann argued that Sinclair had not changed, he had simply shifted from rebelling against the wiles of women—as in *Love's Pilgrimage*—to attacking materialism, or capitalism. Lippmann's most striking assertion was, in effect, that the scales did not fall from the eyes of the isolated young artist when he was converted to socialism. Rather, he constructed even higher barricades between himself and the corrupt and degraded world outside.

Lippmann went on to praise Sinclair as an "apocalyptic socialist" who was searching for the "Messianic Kingdom," not the real America that Dell thought he was defining. Sinclair was a visionary, one of that long list of figures throughout history who hate the times they live in and who flee from their world into dreams of perfection. He was a "saint" and a "hero," one of that select band who "by the contagion of their ardor for righteousness, manage to stir men somewhat out of their lethargy, and to set their eyes on distant goals."

Lippmann's apparent admiration for Sinclair obscured the fact that he was sidelining him as an estimable freak, just as Dell made him a neurotic. *American Outpost* is Sinclair's version of himself as a representative man—though he is compelled to acknowledge his extraordinary accomplishments and his gifts. But Sinclair, who said many times that he really was much less interested in people than in ideas, remains resolutely unreflective about himself in his autobiography. Undeniably an egotist, he seldom questioned his actions or ideas, and was constantly being surprised when friends complained that he had somehow offended them. When writing about himself, rather than about adventures in which he was involved, Sinclair could seem both callow and shallow. William Bloodworth usefully captures the puzzling quality of *American Outpost:* it conveys an image of Sinclair as "not sufficiently *serious* . . . that he could parade around the streets of Boston, sandwiched between oversized fig leaves while gathering information on the tragedy of Sacco and Vanzetti is compelling support for such an expression." Perhaps, Bloodworth suggests, "the lightheartedness, the nonchalance, the lack of seriousness, and facetiousness, the tendency towards fantasy in Sinclair, were all part of a defense system of a sensitive personality that had been extensively and painfully shocked by both personal and social reality."

A less sentimental reading of Sinclair's motives for erecting a barrier between his inner self and the public in *American Outpost* suggests that he was simply trying to preempt the kind of psychological analysis so common in modern biography—or, even more simply, that he had reached a point in his life where he was at last able to view it with a hard-won degree of balance and equanimity. Certainly the direct and forthright actions he took to recover his fortunes as a consequence of the Eisenstein disaster suggest that he was a good deal more assertive than Dell's neurotic or Lippmann's otherworldly ascetic could have been.

Indeed, between 1931 and 1933 Upton Sinclair wrote and published two books—a novel about Prohibition and a commissioned biography of a studio executive—that show he was becoming a Hollywood insider of some stature. In the fall of 1932, he and Craig bought a house in Beverly Hills, a move that brought him closer to the centers of power in Los Angeles. A year later, in September 1933, he would shock all who knew him by leaving the American Socialist Party to become a Democrat, joining the mainstream of American politics. On the heels of that surprising turnabout, Upton Sinclair, Hollywood producer, would attend the New York premiere of *Thunder Over Mexico,* the conventional thriller that Sol Lesser had made using Sergei

Eisenstein's Mexican film footage. Film enthusiasts and leftists who had been hoping to see another *Potemkin* would stridently argue that Sinclair, in an effort to recapture some of the money he had lost on Eisenstein, had turned into a card-carrying capitalist philistine.

Given all of these developments, even old friends began to think that the arch-rebel, now in his mid-fifties, was joining the Establishment he had so long scorned.

The Wet Parade, the only novel by a major American writer in praise of Prohibition, was begun in July 1930 and published by Farrar, Straus, Sinclair's eager new publisher, on September 12, 1931. This was just five weeks before Priscilla's death and nine weeks before Sinclair's fateful first encounter with Eisenstein. Only seven months later, in March 1932, the *Los Angeles Times* featured a story about the sure-to-be-brilliant premiere at Grauman's Chinese Theatre of MGM's new film, *The Wet Parade,* starring Walter Huston, Jimmy Durante, and Robert Young. The *Times* noted smugly that the novel by Upton Sinclair had been "unquestionably revised and freed from radicalism."

It was true that Irving Thalberg, the brilliant young head of production at MGM who had overseen the production of *The Wet Parade,* was anything but a left-winger. He had at first resisted the recommendation of his story editor, Sam Marx, to buy Sinclair's novel, saying he did not want "that Bolshevik inside this studio!" Thalberg's sentiments were shared by his boss, Louis B. Mayer, who said "that bum" Sinclair would probably show up at the studio with a bomb. But Marx liked Sinclair and finally persuaded Thalberg of *The Wet Parade*'s merits as a good dramatic vehicle. Thalberg offered Sinclair a generous option fee of $20,000 for his book. Sinclair signed the option over to Craig, at her request, easing the pain from the continuing hemorrhaging of their funds in the "¡Que viva México!" expedition.

Sinclair's *Wet Parade* was "radical" only in the sense that he saw capitalism, in the form of the liquor industry, as to blame for ruining so many lives. He also believed that alcohol abuse was a social problem, and therefore solvable by social action, not an illness or disease to be treated through medical intervention. His odd title for the book came from a New York protest march by thousands of "wets"—those who opposed the "dry" advocates of Prohibition, and who seemed to be gaining force in their repeal efforts by the late 1920s. Sinclair's own "wet parade" is thus a procession of folly and viciousness whose progress is impeded by his hero, Kip Tarleton, and Kip's wife, Maggie Mae. Both of their fathers having been killed by alcohol, the young couple dedicate their lives to doing what they can to fight it, Maggie Mae as a temperance lecturer and Kip as a government prohibition agent. The novel ends with Kip's murder, in the line of duty, and Maggie Mae's rise to national influence as a charismatic advocate for continued prohibition.

The Wet Parade offers useful insights into Sinclair's childhood, much of the action taking place in a New York boardinghouse like that described in *American Outpost*. It also suggests an idealized picture of Craig—Maggie Mae Tarleton comes from Mississippi, and Sinclair's account of her life there owes much to his own experiences in Gulfport. Kip's father's name is Powhatan, the name of one of Sinclair's uncles, a drunk who shot himself. Clearly modeled after Upton Beall Sr. as well as Sinclair's uncle, Powhatan Tarleton had been a delightful playmate when his son was small; he had an Indian costume and "knew how to dance war-dances and whoop war-whoops." But now that Kip was a man he could see that "the costume was full of moth-holes, and felt only scorn for his father." Like the elder Sinclair, Kip's father is "the 'professional Southerner,' full of large, expansive phrases, of noble ideals derived from a vanished past, and wholly out of relation to a despised present; generous with things he did not earn, and even with those he did not own; a gambler and 'game sport,' free with whisky as with words; the soul of gallantry to ladies, and of bonhomie to men; delightful to those who had only to listen to him, and did not expect any real service or effort."

On another level, *The Wet Parade* proves once again how Sinclair's intellectual independence could lead him in useful directions as well as eccentric ones. As a primer on the causes and effects of Prohibition, it succeeds admirably, forcing the reader to think seriously about a topic usually dismissed without thought. Kip's wife, for example, ponders the cliché about Prohibition—its ends were noble, its means questionable—and asks a challenging question: what else justified any means, other than the end to which they were directed?

The Wet Parade also contains some pointed satire of literary fashions, elaborating on similar observations in *Money Writes!* Kip's friend, the handsome playwright Roger Chilcote, seems from his physical description and his moral deterioration to owe something to Harry Kemp, but his real-life equivalent is obviously Eugene O'Neill. Roger writes fashionable plays, meaning depressing and dirty—"written with the phallus," as Sinclair has one critic say admiringly. They last for three hours, and all the principal characters kill themselves or go crazy by the final curtain. Roger's newest play is a particularly "grim and ghastly thing," a "great success with the high-brow critics, who compared it with Strindberg, and Dostoievski, and other names which were passwords to glory."

The movie version of *The Wet Parade* was a straightforward adaptation of the novel, faithful to its tone, characterization, plot, and message. It was particularly effective in its attempt to show that inadequate enforcement, rather than lack of wide public support for Prohibition, was causing its failure. But the film, like the novel, was completely out of step with the taste of sophisticates who, in the 1920s, preferred the hard-drinking heroes and heroines of Hemingway's and Fitzgerald's fiction, and, a little later in the 1930s, the insouciant badinage of the always-drinking Nick and Nora Charles in the *Thin Man* movies. The death in *The Wet Parade* of the straight-arrow hero, Kip Tarleton, aroused only joy in H. L. Mencken, who joked to Sinclair that all he wanted for Kip was a longer funeral.

Hollywood's *Wet Parade* allowed Sinclair's hero, played by Robert Young, to live, killing off his buddy Jimmy Durante instead. But the movie itself soon died at the box office, the repeal of Prohibition in 1933 rendering moot the issue that it addressed. Sinclair's experience with Hollywood in connection with the dramatization of his novel was nevertheless a gratifying one. His conscientious effort to do something about a social problem at least as serious as any of the others he had tackled had paid off. *The Wet Parade* remains useful as an effective exposition of the moral, social, and political questions raised by "the great experiment."

───

Irving Thalberg was sufficiently impressed by *The Wet Parade* to give Sinclair $10,000—$135,000 in today's currency—to propose a new film project in August 1932. The eleven-page outline that resulted was called "The Gold-Spangled Banner," revised by Sinclair from Thalberg's original title, "The Star-Spangled Banner." Nothing further came of that effort, no doubt because of the shift of emphasis from celebration to criticism implicit in Sinclair's change of titles. But the money earned from *The Wet Parade* film and the aborted Thalberg project encouraged Craig to follow up on a friend's suggestion that houses could be bought for virtually no money down in Beverly Hills during these trying times. A buyer merely had to assume the mortgage. On October 4, 1932, the Sinclairs moved into a comfortable house at 614 North Arden Drive, and Sinclair rented office space a few blocks away at 663 North La Pere Drive. They kept the Pasadena house and used the one in Beverly Hills more as a pied-à-terre than as their primary residence. Sinclair was slightly embarrassed at capitalizing on the misfortunes of others during the Depression, admitting in a letter to David that he would probably come in "for some teasing over having moved into such a fashionable place," but he thought he could "live it down."

Sinclair had yet another reason to be living closer to Hollywood. During the summer he had finished a commissioned biography of the legendary film pioneer William Fox for the considerable sum of $25,000. Inasmuch as Fox was by this time a pariah in the film industry, the book came to be regarded by many of Fox's fellow moguls as another Sinclair exposé. He needed to be on hand to answer those charges, an effort that turned out to be less than entirely successful.

William Fox saw the entertainment potential in the nickelodeon while in his teens, and by 1915 had become a successful film distributor. In the years that followed, the Fox Film Corporation, the progenitor of Twentieth Century–Fox studios, thrived, but in the late 1920s Fox ran into financial difficulties as the result of converting his eleven hundred theaters to sound. As Fox told the story, he was attacked and undermined by jealous rivals in Hollywood, including Louis B. Mayer. Suits and countersuits, accompanied by various charges of bribery, extortion, and larceny, had reduced Fox to a shadow of his former power by 1932. He hired Sinclair to help him make his case, as Sinclair understood his assignment.

Sinclair was candid later, though not at the time, about taking on the Fox biography for the money. Perhaps because he had little in common with his subject, he begins his book with a cozy picture of the two of them sitting together, Fox in Sinclair's favorite "old-fashioned walnut rocking-chair," before a fire in his study—just as the earlier titans Henry Ford and King Gillette had done. Formerly stout, now somewhat shrunken, Fox is "a tired and stricken man," but still natty in his golf clothes: he wears white flannel trousers and a white sweater underneath a light blue sport coat, with white socks. In his jacket pocket is a row of long brown cigars, wrapped in cellophane; he peels the cellophane carefully from a cigar, rolls it into a tight little ball, and drops it into an ashtray—which Sinclair the nonsmoker has thoughtfully provided.

Fox and Sinclair, it turned out, were the same age, and grew up in lower Manhattan at the same time. But Fox was a Hungarian Jew, born Wilhelm Fried, and spent his early years pushing carts in the garment district, eight blocks—and a world—away from Sinclair's boardinghouse with its failed southern aristocrats. Their real point of contact lay in the fact that Fox, like Sinclair, was an independent entrepreneur who had to do battle with the ruling establishment in order to succeed.

Such at least seems to have been Sinclair's way of coping with the fact that he was making a hero out of a capitalist, an enterprise that David chided him for, as did Lincoln Steffens, who warned him that Fox was a shady character. Sinclair, however, saw Fox's story as a natural stage in "the evolution of

American industrial affairs," where size had become the critical issue. He said it was important to set this story before readers because "in our country is a great machine of business and money which governs the lives of the plain people, and they do not often get a look into the insides of it. Here they have a chance."

A workman worthy of his hire, Sinclair devised an ingenious method of writing Fox's story as a Hollywood "thriller." He, Upton Sinclair, was now a "producer and director"; the chapters were "reels," the book jacket showed a proscenium, and the "movie" was called *Upton Sinclair Presents William Fox.* It was subtitled "A Feature Picture of Wall Street and High Finance," and it was hyped by a parody of Hollywood promotional prose ("A melodrama of fortune, conflict and triumph . . . Never in screen history has there been a feature so stupendous as this.")

Sinclair's hero and most of his villains were almost all first-generation eastern European or Russian Jews, and his unrestrained use of religious and racial epithets associated with these immigrant entrepreneurs exposed him once again to charges of anti-Semitism. Kevin Starr, in his history of the Depression in California, *Endangered Dreams,* chastises Sinclair for portraying "Hollywood as the Cosa Nostra of American Jewry." Sinclair insisted, as he often had occasion to do, that many of his friends were Jews, and that he had simply represented Fox's story as it was told to him. But Mayer among other influential Hollywood producers felt Sinclair was more prejudiced than he admitted, and he vowed revenge.

Sinclair may have stressed what he considered the more entertaining peculiarities of Jews in Hollywood in an effort to make Fox's complicated business history interesting, leading readers expertly through thickets of charge and countercharge. Some of these readers found his insights into the world of movie moguls exciting; one wrote to offer his own insight into the secret of Sinclair's success as a writer: it lay in the fact that he was "wise enough to keep a direct current with the reader." Sinclair was like a high-flyer on the trapeze, the admirer continued, doing his death-defying act in front of the "estheticians"—the literary establishment that failed to appreciate the way he took command of a subject and made it his own.

This perceptive reader had put his finger on a key point, too seldom noted by Sinclair's critics. He was successful because his books did create that peculiar "current" with his readers, in part because he was on the same wavelength as they were, but also because they appreciated the effort he put forth to make them feel plugged in. Despite his intimate connections with the rich and the powerful, in Hollywood and elsewhere, he persuaded his readers that he was one of them, and like them, in his tastes and attitudes;

among these were, on occasion, a midwestern populist condescension for foreigners and recent immigrants, including but not limited to Jews. Frequently Sinclair became so caught up in establishing the mystical connection with his less sophisticated readers that he crossed over the line of taste and discretion, forcing him subsequently to backpedal and apologize. But he was never less than certain of his own integrity and his good intentions.

Imagine Sinclair's chagrin and anger, then, when he learned after completing the manuscript and delivering it to Fox that the producer had no intention of releasing his biography to the public: he thought of it simply as a weapon to use in his ongoing wars with his fellow moguls. The money he had paid to Sinclair to write it was of no significance to Fox, who said he was welcome to it. Sinclair now understood why Fox had generously declined to request a share of the royalties from the book sales: he had known there would be no royalties.

Sinclair retaliated by ignoring Fox's wishes: it was *his* book to do with as he chose. He sent his carbon copy of the manuscript to William Conkey, his printer in Indiana, telling him to set the type, run off page proofs for him, and make plans to print twenty-five thousand copies. Despite Fox's protests when he learned that Sinclair had sent review copies around the country, the book sold out of its first edition, published in February 1933, at $3 a copy, and then sold another twenty-five thousand copies. Sinclair thus made a healthy profit out of his encounter with a devious Hollywood mogul. He advised his readers in a preface to the book that Fox had declined to share in the royalties. Sinclair's own royalties, he added, with breathtaking egotism, "will be used for the purpose of putting a set of twelve volumes of my books into public libraries throughout the world." Fox later went to jail for trying to bribe a judge, and was bankrupt by 1936. He died in 1952.

During the first three months of 1933 the Sinclairs spent more time in Pasadena than in Beverly Hills because their friend Albert Einstein would soon finish his third ten-week appointment as a visiting professor at the California Institute of Technology. Shortly after Einstein and Sinclair had exchanged letters concerning *Mental Radio,* two years earlier, Craig's sister, Dollie, told her that there was "an old man walking up and down the street" and peering into the yard. The visitor identified himself as Albert Einstein and said he was looking for Upton Sinclair. "Such was the beginning of as lovely a friendship as anyone could have in this world," Sinclair wrote later; Einstein was "the kindest, gentlest, sweetest of men."

Sinclair took Einstein to dinner in Hollywood, to concerts in Los Angeles, to an early showing of some footage from Eisenstein's film. Einstein played Mozart for Sinclair on his violin. Sinclair begged off joining him in a duet when he saw that his playing skills were not up to Einstein's, but he was an appreciative audience. They also shared an interest in spiritualism, and on one occasion Einstein participated in a séance with Roman Ostoja (surprisingly reinstated for the occasion) at Sinclair's Pasadena house. According to Helen Dukas, Einstein's secretary, who was with him, they were warned by Sinclair before the séance that "we shouldn't be afraid if suddenly the piano starts to play and flowers come from above. I was frightened to death. It was a really scary atmosphere. And, oh my gosh, suddenly the doorbell rang and I nearly jumped out of my skin." It was only a telegram, but Ostoja "went into catalepsy and made mumbling noises" and the séance ended in failure. Sinclair said "hostile forces" had ruined the experiment.

The strongest point of contact between Einstein and Sinclair was radical politics, as the physicist was a longtime and committed socialist. Robert Millikan, the Nobel Prize–winning physicist who was then the president of Caltech, worried that Sinclair was leading his innocent star professor off into the political wilderness. "Dourly conservative, faintly militarist, and with more than a touch of right-wing enthusiasm," in the words of Einstein's biographer Ronald Clark, Millikan was unhappy with Einstein's unguarded comments on world affairs in his frequent newspaper and film interviews. Sinclair had warned Einstein, "I am considered a very dangerous person," an opinion in which Millikan concurred. Responding to a Caltech benefactor who complained about his hiring foreign communists, Millikan explained that Einstein was not a communist but a naive do-gooder who was being "exploited" by various people, some of them "the Charlie Chaplin type" and some "the Upton Sinclair type," especially the latter.

A few days before Einstein's scheduled departure from Pasadena on March 11, 1933—he had agreed to take a permanent position at the competing Princeton Institute for Advanced Studies—Sinclair stopped by his house to say goodbye. Millikan was also present, and Einstein made a point of introducing the two men, who shook hands awkwardly. Einstein had also given Sinclair a signed photograph of himself, with an affectionately teasing poetic inscription in German that Sinclair was proud to include in his *Autobiography*. It reads, in John Ahouse's translation:

> Who scrapes from grimy pots and pans a certain kind of truth?
> Who tells the world to "Open Wide" and spots a hollow tooth?
> Who disavows the Here and Now and swears by what's ahead?
> Who thinks the word "undignified" is better left unsaid?

Sinclair is that most valiant man—
If anyone's to vouch for it, then I'm the one who can.

⸻

Sinclair's gift to the departing Einstein was an advance copy of his latest book, published in May 1933, called *The Way Out: What Lies Ahead for America*. His promising title was prompted in part by the recent triumph of Franklin Delano Roosevelt over Herbert Hoover in the November 1932 election. Roosevelt's first hundred days, and the innovative programs for industrial and economic rejuvenation that they had produced, held out hope for a start on the kind of radical change that Sinclair had been advocating for the past three decades. The Great Depression that had swept Hoover out of office had not harmed Sinclair unduly—needless to say, he had no money in the stock market—but he feared the possibility of fascism similar to that in Germany and Italy erupting in the United States. Roosevelt's solutions were well intended but did not go far enough, Sinclair felt, in addressing the root causes of economic dislocation. In *The Way Out,* presented as a series of letters to a wealthy businessman named Perry, Sinclair set the stage for his own entry into politics later that year. He also signaled that he was ready to give up on the idea that socialists, so identified, could ever achieve real political power in the United States. Equally significant, he showed that he could make the same argument effectively to different and opposed constituencies, an essential gift for a politician.

Sinclair's earlier primer on economics, *Letters to Judd,* had been addressed to a local handyman who did odd jobs for him. *The Way Out* (originally called "Letters to Perry" before Farrar asked for a better title) covers much the same ground, with lucid explanations of inflation, the gold standard, tariffs, taxes, and the growing gap between rich and poor. In both books, Sinclair's voice is that of sweet reason, reflecting his stance that once the facts are known, his audience will have no choice but to agree. In *The Way Out* he concedes that some needed reforms carry their own price: going off the gold standard and jailing people for keeping some gold under the mattress punishes the value of thrift he learned as a boy, for example. He even concedes the tendency to "stagnation" in government bureaucracies, as well as in business offices. The answer for that would be to stimulate the idealism and "the imaginations of our young people," to persuade them that public service is honorable and good, and to reward their efforts with "prizes and medals, trips abroad and scholarships."

In *Letters to Judd,* Sinclair referred often to his conversations with the handyman as they repaired a roof together. In *The Way Out,* he assures his executive correspondent that he too is "a business man, engaged in publishing his own books—purchasing paper, paying the printer, advertising and marketing, looking for a loan from the Reconstruction Finance Corporation in order to survive. . . . We capitalists must stand together, Perry!" Sinclair is no more a revolutionary than Perry: "For thirty years I have been crying out in public places," he says, for changes in the economic system that would let the country avert the calamity of violent revolution: "bloody insurrection, mobs invading our homes," and "years of chaos and misery."

The communists, Sinclair says, have called him a "social fascist" for trying to persuade men like Perry to change their ways, but he rejects their doctrines. What Sinclair wants instead is a resurgence of Jeffersonian idealism. At the same time, Sinclair recognizes that the United States is now an industrial power, not the nation of sturdy farmers that Jefferson had envisioned. He cites the Tennessee Valley Authority and the New York Port Authority as admirable examples of what can be achieved by a forward-looking government inspired by progressive ideas.

Sinclair also addresses once again the question of human nature and its relation to social change, using a poker analogy, as he had earlier for Judd. But now his focus has shifted from the suffering workers to the man who ended up with all the chips: "the game was fine for him" and the few other winners at other tables, but "the room is crowded with those who have lost"—i.e., the Judds—"and who no longer like the game, but clamor that the cards were stacked, or that they never had their fair share of chips. So menacing do they become that the successful players look at one another in anxiety, and whisper that perhaps it might be the part of wisdom to restore to the losers a part of their consumer capacity."

Sinclair has made the same argument to different audiences—it's the same argument, in essence, that he had been making since *The Industrial Republic* in 1907. But to Judd he had emphasized victimization at the hand of incomprehensible forces. To Perry, he concentrates on the fear that the victims might combine to take away his winnings unless he agrees to share with them. Interestingly, Sinclair does not claim the game was rigged. The winners may well have been smart as well as lucky, and the losers dumb as well as unlucky. Human nature, he now seems willing to concede—if only by implication—may indeed be unalterable, along with human capability. But such squabbling over theory and over labels like "socialist," "fascist," and "capitalist" no longer mattered. Even the winners of the poker game now admitted that the current crisis required not ideological but pragmatic solutions.

Sinclair gave no indication in May 1933, when the first edition of his new book was published, that he personally intended to show Californians "the way out" of their economic troubles. But by mid-August, when the second edition appeared, he was willing to tell a group of southern California Democrats why he would, if asked, run for governor of California in 1934 on the Democratic ticket.

The meeting occurred in a small, cheap hotel in Santa Monica, across the street from the much grander Miramar Hotel, which a businessman and Democratic power broker named Gilbert Stevenson had recently lost due to bankruptcy. Stevenson's problems were shared widely in southern California, where more than half of the state's nine hundred thousand unemployed workers lived. City and county relief efforts were strained to the point that people were threatened with starvation, even as, along the eight-hundred-mile length of California, the results of overproduction were daily visible: milk was poured into the sewers, pigs were slaughtered and covered with kerosene to make their carcasses inedible, and tons of fruits and vegetables were plowed under in the fields. The Republicans, who had dominated state government for fifty years, had no program to alleviate the suffering, and the desperate efforts of the federal government to reduce overproduction, combined with the ineffective programs proposed by the badly split state Democrats, were only creating further havoc. What, Stevenson asked Sinclair, would he suggest needed to be done?

Sinclair's response to Stevenson that August afternoon was elaborated in the following weeks in a short new work of fiction that he called *I, Governor of California, and How I Ended Poverty.* As fiction, *I, Governor* would not begin to challenge the work that most directly inspired it, Edward Bellamy's *Looking Backward,* and it would also fail as prophecy. But as an instrument of rhetorical persuasion, it would have an influence comparable to that of *The Jungle,* and greater than any other single work by Sinclair during his lifetime.

Sinclair's core idea was what it had always been: production for use and not for profit. The arguments concerning various elements of the plan were spelled out in *Letters to Judd* and *The Way Out,* and in dozens of other works. Sinclair had run for office previously as a socialist, trying despite the certainty of losing to educate the voters as to the merits of socialism. Now he saw the possibility of applying his ideas in earnest. California was a live test, a laboratory experiment in the making, an emergency operation on a dying patient.

All Sinclair had to do was to renounce the very faith that had formed the basis for his belief—that is, to desert the American Socialist Party and become a Democrat. He did so without leaving behind any evidence of soul-shattering doubt. On September 1, absent any of the fanfare that he knew how to arouse, he quietly entered the Beverly Hills city hall and signed the papers that would make him, for the first time in his life, a member of the Democratic Party. An outsider for most of his fifty-four years, he had now not only joined the Establishment; he was about to become, if his plans worked out, one of its leaders. He had, he said, "lost interest in novels."

But there was one final item of unfinished business to attend to before he began campaigning: the New York premiere of the ninety-minute feature film that Sol Lesser had made from Eisenstein's film footage, *Thunder Over Mexico*. The Hollywood premiere of *Thunder* in May had been a disaster, disrupted by local communists who rolled stink bombs down the aisles, but the major opening at the Rialto Theatre in Manhattan was to be a much bigger affair. If it went well, the Lesser film could help Sinclair recoup a major portion of the money he had lost. It was essential for him to be there to introduce *Thunder Over Mexico* to the influential New York critics. On September 17 he and Craig, and Sol Lesser, left Los Angeles for New York.

═══

Though it began well, the eastern trip ended badly for Sinclair, on both the personal and professional levels. He finished the text of *I, Governor,* by the time the train reached Chicago, on September 19, and he spent an entertaining hour there with the visiting mayor of New York, Fiorello La Guardia—whose father, a soldier during the Spanish-American war, had died from eating the "embalmed beef" that Teddy Roosevelt and Upton Sinclair had so vigorously condemned.

It pleased Sinclair that he was once again big news in what amounted to his home town, New York, as the gathering of reporters greeting his train at Grand Central Terminal suggested. Also on hand were David Sinclair and David's wife, Betty, with their three-month-old baby, Diana. The family reunion, however, was strained. Sinclair and David had not met since 1927, and Craig had not seen her stepson since sending him back to Mississippi in 1918. One of her few efforts at communication had been a backhanded congratulatory note upon David's graduation from Wisconsin in 1924, in which she said she had never thought he would make it through college. Neither Sinclair nor Craig had met Betty, who took offense when Craig's only comment about her baby was that she probably needed an operation for adenoids.

David Sinclair was now thirty-one years old, living on research grants at Columbia while he worked on his Ph.D. in physics, and on Betty's small editorial salary at Columbia's *Political Science Quarterly*. Sinclair had sent David a generous monthly check for $250 ($3,500 today) for the first year of his graduate studies, but had ceased to do so when David said he could get along without it. In 1931 David and Betty had spent two months in England, France, and Germany, where Sinclair's letters of introduction had proved useful. David had also visited the Soviet Union for a month and tried unsuccessfully on his father's behalf to persuade the authorities to release some of the funds that had accrued there from sales of his books.

Both David and Betty were disillusioned by their observations of corruption, tyranny, and matchless inefficiency in Russia, but they remained staunch socialists. They were disappointed by what they regarded as Sinclair's artistic affront to Eisenstein, as represented by Sol Lesser's Hollywood movie. Even worse in their eyes was Sinclair's desertion of his true party and his principles in the quest for mainstream political power. David and his wife blamed Craig for instigating Sinclair's artistic and political defections. According to a letter several years later from Sinclair to his son, they let Craig know their feelings even before the group had left the platform at Grand Central.

These recriminations, and Craig's angry denials, were at least conducted out of earshot of the assembled reporters. But David continued the political argument in the presence of a *Herald Tribune* reporter who accepted Sinclair's invitation to meet with him at the Algonquin Hotel, where he was staying while in New York.

According to the reporter, Sinclair was "talking rapidly, with a pair of spectacles perched precariously on his aggressive nose, explaining enthusiastically to two newspaper men" how he had made his decision to run for governor of California. When David, "a tall young man with an earnest manner," appeared, Sinclair said, "Hello, there, son," and continued his story. "Aw, Dad," David "groaned," "I wish you'd wait." " 'Now, son,' said the father, 'you sit here and listen.' " David said, " 'Well, I'm sorry. I didn't mean to break in like this.' And with another groan, the younger Sinclair leaned back in his chair, placed his hands behind his head with a gesture of resignation, and looked at the ceiling of the Algonquin lobby." David suffered in silence for some time as Sinclair talked, then asked "derisively" how his father expected to accomplish his goals under capitalism: " 'I wish you'd go back and read all your books again and become converted by them!' " Sinclair "frowned, then smiled tolerantly." He reminded the reporters and David that he had addressed these questions as far back as 1907.

As Sinclair launched into the details of his plan in *The Industrial Republic,* the reporter ended his account with a condescending ellipsis, and a reminder that the famous writer was in town for the premiere of *Thunder Over*

Mexico. The story that appeared the following day carried the headline "Son Reproves Upton Sinclair as Backslider." The subhead continued, "Chides Him for His Plan to Run for Governor of California as Democrat"; "Just Can't Do It, Dad."

———

Thunder Over Mexico was never intended to be high art. To save money, it was made as a silent film, one of the last. The plot was merely a device to string scenes together: during the corrupt regime of Porfirio Díaz, a noble peasant lad suffers terribly because he reports the rape of a maiden by a wealthy landowner. But the movie served its purpose, according to Lesser, making enough money for Sinclair to pay back most of his expenses—though Sinclair always said he had lost money even with the *Thunder Over Mexico* revenues.

As had always been the case with both Eisenstein's films and Sinclair's writing, the line between politics and art was blurred. In this instance, Sinclair's alleged mutilation of Eisenstein's work was aggravated by the false charge that he had also placed the gifted director in harm's way by complaining to Stalin about his behavior—when in fact Sinclair had eloquently defended Eisenstein's loyalty to the Soviet Union. Additionally, Sinclair was mocked as a puritan for taking offense at some pornographic drawings that Eisenstein had included with materials that he returned to Sinclair before he left New York for Russia. The American Communist Party created a front organization, led by the young New York dance critic and *Hound and Horn* editor Lincoln Kirstein, called the International Defense Committee for Eisenstein's Mexican Film. A Mexican friend warned Sinclair that the communists were accusing him of being an "oil man and movies enterpriser," a "Mecenas" who hoped to get a million dollars from each of several pieces cut out of Eisenstein's footage. Kirstein followed this line of attack, describing Sinclair as an exponent of his own "mammon art" in a flyer that said "Upton Sinclair, you have butchered a great work of art," and that swirled with words like "duped," "capitalist sabotage," and "double-crossed."

On September 18 Kirstein passed around his flyer before the first showing of the film in New York, at the New School for Social Research. According to an account in *Variety* the following day, the leaflet, "despite its heated phrases, did not excite the audience in the well filled theater, and Helen Woodward, advertising woman and a friend of Mr. Sinclair, spoke briefly before the picture was to start." Kirstein rose to question her and was quickly "deposited" on West Twelfth Street by "hands trained in ejecting unmannerly persons" who disrupt performances.

The Rialto Theatre premiere on September 24 was even more contentious. Sinclair took questions from the audience at some length before the showing, denying that he had allowed Lesser to make a "reactionary" film—a charge based on Lesser's deletion of several satirical scenes of Mexican government officials. Eisenstein's contract, Sinclair said, stipulated that the film he would make be "non-political." Any cuts had been made in accordance with that agreement. An unidentified questioner demanded to know why Sinclair allowed his "name and prestige" to be used in connection with such "horror and treason." "That's enough now," Sinclair responded heatedly. "I have said there were to be no speeches from the floor." But, according to the edited transcript of the fracas, "the speaker had a lusty voice and kept on raising it and outshouting Sinclair until he had finished, for until that point, whenever Mr. Sinclair wished to, he shouted down questioners at certain points and then took the floor himself."

Richard Watts caught the mood at the time of the nondoctrinaire, neutral majority of film enthusiasts: "Mr. Sinclair's foes," Watts said, were probably correct in their charge that Sinclair was guilty of preventing Eisenstein's film from being properly edited. Eisenstein may have been something of a "poseur and a faker," Watts admitted, but he wondered if Sinclair too was not "the great idealist that, for all of these years, he has been insisting he is," but just another businessman. Watts had difficulty in seeing Sinclair as he presented himself, "the victim of an unfortunate train of events and not the despoiler of what should have been a masterpiece." He had had a chance "to play a splendid, if perhaps difficult, part in a great esthetic adventure and then proceeded to fail those who depended upon him."

Sinclair returned to California in late September, embittered by the communists' attacks on his integrity and relieved to be once again among people who prized him for that very quality. For the rest of his life, he regarded the Eisenstein fiasco as his worst professional mistake, though not on the grounds of artistic mutilation or political cowardice. He had, he believed, been victimized by those who exploited his own idealism.

In 1953, Sinclair generously donated the bulk of the Eisenstein footage that he still owned to the Museum of Modern Art. That same year, he was attacked yet again as a traitorous philistine in a new biography of Eisenstein by Anya Seton. Responding to a *Manchester Guardian* review of Seton's book, he indignantly defended himself. In the process, he exaggerated Eisenstein's culpability, charging that the Russian's behavior had been marked by "pure rascality from the beginning, but it was done in the name of Art": there was no question, Sinclair wrote, that Eisenstein had been "moving heaven and earth to avoid having to go back to his beloved Soviet Union," or that he "broke his word to me systematically and continuously over a period of fifteen months."

Not everyone in the film world condemned Sinclair, either at the time or later. The noted critic Stanley Kauffman, writing in the 1960s, thought Eisenstein had been overpraised in the matter of "¡Que viva México!" he cited with approval the opinion of Otis Ferguson, an earlier critic, that "Sinclair took a villainous drubbing" from zealots who had their own axes to grind: "A way to be a film critic for years was to holler about this sort of great art."

But passions over the Eisenstein affair continued to flame even after Sinclair's death. Lincoln Kirstein, one of his most bitter critics, responded with contemptuous dismissal to Leon Harris's 1970 letter asking for his final thoughts on Sinclair's contribution to American history. Kirstein said, in effect, that Sinclair's contribution was worse than worthless, and that he still regarded him with contempt and loathing.

Mrs. Upton Sinclair had her own quarrel with her husband: "poor, forthright, psychologically obtuse Upton," as Craig described him to Helen Woodward in 1933, was partly to blame for their being "hunted and driven" by the communists. The whole affair had been "our worst adventure," she wrote to another friend. She could only hope that from it "Upton has learned his lesson. He can write—but nothing else! Oh yes, he can cook a beefsteak."

CHAPTER FOURTEEN

THE POLITICIAN

(September 1933–November 1934)

The notion that a celebrity could seriously hope to become the governor of a major state like California seemed more outlandish to Upton Sinclair's contemporaries in 1933 than it does today, after Ronald Reagan and Arnold Schwarzenegger. No actors or sports stars had achieved prominence in the United States as governors or on the national level; only a clutch of military heroes, from George Washington through Theodore Roosevelt, and certainly no novelists. So it was understandable that Sinclair's opponents at first scornfully dismissed his long campaign to win the Democratic primary, a marathon that stretched from September 1933 to August 1934. By the time they understood what was happening, Sinclair had not only won the nomination but had single-handedly taken charge of the state party he had just joined. It was a monumental achievement for a writer, unprecedented in American history, and most of the credit for its success goes to Sinclair. So too does much of the blame for his failure to win the general election in November, just three months later.

Sinclair's disadvantages as a candidate were varied and obvious. He was mocked as a food faddist who had tried eating a spoonful of sand each day for his digestion, a spook-chasing spiritualist, a publicity hound. It was said that although he looked like an elderly bank clerk and talked like a Sunday school teacher, he was an egomaniac with a Messiah complex, a divorced man who wrote about free love and had attacked the institution of marriage as legalized prostitution. Even his friends admitted that he had insulted, in print and in person, over a period of thirty-five years, every conceivable vested interest, especially those associated with organized religion, with education, and with the engines of national prosperity, its businesses and corporations. He was a socialist at heart in a country whose citizens generally saw few distinctions between socialism, communism, and anarchism, and loathed all equally. Paradoxically, he was viewed as at once both dangerous and irrelevant, a former leader of a party that had only two thousand active members in California.

Worst of all for the professional politicians whom he now presumed to lead to victory, Sinclair was a five-time loser in his races for elective office, four of those in California; in addition to his early bid for Congress in New Jersey, in 1906, he had run for Congress in 1920, for the U.S. Senate in 1922, and for governor in 1926 and 1930. He had never won more than 46,000 votes, out of more than a million votes cast. Now he was charged with lacking even the decency to stay with his own Socialist Party; his new baptism as a Democrat was not a sign of conversion but proof of unprincipled, opportunistic ambition and lust for power, coming just as the Democrats in California were finally beginning to challenge the Republican supremacy that had prevailed there for a generation.

Offsetting Sinclair's disadvantages, as they were perceived, were several critical strengths. These included his fame, the weak and fragmented political opposition of both major parties to his candidacy, and the widely shared feeling in the state that *something* had to be done.

His fame was what had first attracted the Democratic insurgents in Santa Monica. If Sinclair's writing exposed him to attack, it also gave him a degree of what is today called "name recognition" far beyond the reach of his various opponents—an American journalist traveling across the vast Gobi desert sent a dispatch to the *New York Herald Tribune* during the campaign to say that he had just had a nice chat with a young Mongolian and asked him who his favorite authors were. Mostly "Dostoievski and Sinclair," was the response. Closer to home, hundreds of Sinclair's key campaign activists as well as ordinary voters indicated that they had grown up reading his books and were attracted by precisely those qualities of independent thinking and iconoclasm that his enemies thought would disqualify him.

The weakness of Sinclair's political opposition derived mainly from the long dominance of the Republicans in every aspect of the state's government, which had made them fat and lazy. Their incumbent governor, James Rolph, was mortally ill; the lieutenant governor who would succeed Rolph in June 1934, Frank Merriam, was a mediocrity. The powerless Democrats were split into quarrelsome factions, unable to agree which of their several candidates to run for governor and thereby to exploit the Republicans' weakness. Sinclair was able to take the high road in the primary, for the most part avoiding attacks on his opponents in either party in favor of a sustained and vigorous assault on "the system" and its life force, capitalism. Politicians were virtually irrelevant, he said, aiming instead at that "little band of 'insiders,' the masters of our chain banks, railroads, and public service corporations," i.e., his old antagonists, the "interlocking directorates."

More important than either his fame or his opponents' weakness was the tidal wave of popular discontent with the status quo that Sinclair was riding. Many thousands of Californians less radical than he had already joined movements, some new and eccentric, some rooted in American tradition, that also promised a "way out" of the Depression. Sinclair's sudden conversion to the Democratic Party provided these different groups with an unexpected opportunity to see some of their ideas put into practice. In turn, Sinclair gained a huge ready-made support base of passionate advocates for change.

One of the most interesting of these groups was the Technocracy movement, which grew out of a Columbia University consultant's proposal that engineers and technicians should run the economy along scientific grounds. The Technocrats were strongly influenced by Thorstein Veblen's arguments that poverty in the midst of plenty was simply irrational—besides, as Sinclair said, being morally wrong. Therefore, applied reason would solve any problems. A friend of Sinclair's, Manchester Boddy, was the chief advocate for Technocracy in southern California, arguing vigorously for its merits in the pages of his Los Angeles *Daily News* in 1932 and 1933.

The weakness of the Technocrats was that they had no program as such. They simply argued that the logic of "production for use"—Sinclair's favorite formula from his first days as a socialist—was so obvious that all they had to do was educate the wider public as to its meaning. The movement's momentum faded quickly, for the same reason that most programs based solely on reason fail: it made no deep emotional connection with its audience. Sinclair admired both the Technocrats' original point of inspiration, Thorstein Veblen, as well as the intellectual rigor of their arguments; he made his first campaign appearance before the Santa Barbara Technocracy Club, and later brought many of Technocracy's members into his own campaign.

A peculiar offshoot of Technocracy, founded by three of its former members in September 1933, was the Utopian Society, a semisecret fraternal organization that took its new members through a complicated initiation, swearing them to secrecy and fidelity to the order. Its use of arcane rituals apparently satisfied the emotional needs of the nearly half a million members who signed on within a year of its founding—the society "grew like a gourd in the night" in the hothouse of southern California, according to the political writer Carey McWilliams, before being laughed out of existence for its "mumbo-jumbo" by more orthodox politicians. Like the Technocrats, most of the Utopians ended up supporting Sinclair.

Sinclair's biggest competition, though on its face the program closest to parts of his own, was the Old Age Revolving Pension plan promoted by a retired physician from Long Beach, Dr. Francis E. Townsend. Townsend proposed that the federal government raise money through a special sales tax and use it to give $200 per month (about $2,800 today) to everyone over sixty years old. The money would have to be spent within thirty days, thereby stimulating the economy. Townsend Clubs with several hundred thousand members were scattered across the country by August 1934.

Sinclair opposed sales taxes on principle as regressive, and made the abolition of the existing state sales tax one of his key goals. Even so, Townsend fielded no candidates for office in the coming election, which meant that his thousands of mostly elderly supporters should have been receptive to Sinclair's appeal. But Sinclair regarded Townsend, with good cause, as an economic illiterate, undiplomatically said so, and made an enemy of him and his followers.

Far more important than Townsend for Sinclair, and more sensible, were the cooperatives that had sprung up throughout the state in the early 1930s. California offered fertile ground for cooperatives. There was a huge surplus of goods, especially agricultural products, and too little cash or credit with which to buy them. The idea of people helping themselves by bartering goods and services, rather than relying on charity or welfare, was widely appealing; Sinclair had tried it himself when he moved to California, and even the Republican administration of Governor Rolph had recently agreed to encourage its possible development.

═══

Sinclair had other advantages, related directly to his gifts as a writer and to his character. His best books, from *The Jungle* through *Boston,* grew out of his ability to write clearly and persuasively about complicated matters, gracefully fusing emotion and fact. Using those long-honed skills, he now incorporated ideas from a dozen different sources, including his own books, into a plan that he called EPIC, or End Poverty in California. His twelve-point program was simple enough to be understood by anybody—and radical enough to assure his supporters that he did represent something new and different in American politics. Among its key elements was a provision to seize all idle agricultural land and turn it over to unemployed farmworkers, who would live on it and return it to productive use. Sinclair also proposed that the state buy or rent factories and businesses—everything from fish hatcheries to laundries—to employ non-farmworkers.

A gigantic statewide cooperative would result, eventually becoming self-supporting. The cash for fueling this new machine would come from an Authority for Money, which would design a scrip to use for currency. Other EPIC provisions included eliminating taxes on properties worth less than $3,000, in addition to repealing the sales tax. The budget shortfall would be made up by introducing a graduated income tax and by increasing inheritance taxes to the point of confiscating everything over $50,000 (about $700,000 in today's currency). Sinclair also hoped to tax wealthy landholders out of existence and to greatly increase public utility taxes. Finally, he wanted to provide monthly pensions of $50 for three-year residents over sixty and those who were needy or blind, with a similar amount for widowed women with dependent children.

Sinclair's campaign would be a campaign of ideas; but because they were ideas that he had been advocating for so long, and frequently tried to put into practice in his own life, much of what he said and wrote during his fourteen-month run for governor reflected his own personality—and his ego. The title of his signature book for the campaign, *I, Governor of California,* harked back, no doubt unconsciously, to his angry demand for attention in 1903, "I, Upton Sinclair, Penniless Rat." In *Manassas,* he had represented himself as a Homeric singer of the great American epic, the Civil War. Now he had transformed himself into an EPIC hero. Like Walt Whitman, he was singing a song of himself as the personification of what he thought America should be. "So far as I know," he said, "this is the first time an historian has set out to make his history true." He apologized for what might appear to be unseemly ambition, assuring his audience that he had no need for money or fame, and for talking about himself so much. But, he said, "In the nature of the case, this is the only material I have."

Sinclair's irrepressible egotism, far from being a handicap, was the source of his appeal for many Democrats and independents: he had so thoroughly integrated his private self with his social ideas that he struck them as a man incapable of subterfuge or hypocrisy. Equally appealing for many who had grown tired of hearing that their problems defied solution was his optimistic assurance that he could accomplish everything he said must be done, easily and quickly. Not only would he "construct a complete industrial system, a new and self-maintaining world for our unemployed," but he would do this in "no more than one or two years" of the single four-year term to which he was limiting himself in office. Moreover, his administration would operate with the openness of a fishbowl; every conversation with anyone concerning state matters would be "in a public reception room, with a stenographer present to make a record of it, and with the public, including the press, invited to be present."

═════

Sinclair's integrity was indeed his greatest strength. His program, his organizational skills, his eloquence both in writing and in speech, and the currents of the times were all essential, but it was his reputation as a selfless and sincere man that prompted a groundswell of enthusiasm across all lines of class and education. Though he had so much support among the poor that EPIC was thought by some analysts to be a lower-class mass movement, Sinclair's most valuable adherents were idealistic young men and women who had already known him through his books. Many were college-trained professionals, and not a few were small-businessmen.

Chief among these was a young real estate developer from San Luis Obispo named Richard Otto. Born in 1897 in East Orange, New Jersey, into a wealthy family, Dick Otto grew up in Europe, looked after by governesses and privately tutored. His mastery of French was so complete that his American friends teased him as a "froggie," and his knowledge of German allowed him to study engineering in German at the University of Zurich. A gifted amateur carpenter who made fine furniture, an expert sailor who would later take an eighty-six-foot schooner on a four-year voyage around the world, Otto was so handsome that he was frequently likened to the English statesman Anthony Eden. By nature and training an aristocrat, he was nonetheless repelled by the class snobbery he had observed in Europe and by the excessive materialism he saw in America. He became a Bellamy fan after reading *Looking Backward,* and it was at a Bellamy Club meeting in Los Angeles that he met Upton Sinclair during the summer of 1933. He then read *The Way Out* and sent Sinclair an article he had written on Bellamy's story "The Parable of the Water Tower." When Otto learned of Sinclair's candidacy in September, he offered to serve as his campaign manager—an offer, Sinclair later said, that took him all of five minutes to accept.

He and Otto began their operation, Sinclair recalled, with "one old lady" as their secretary, in one room of the cottage in Beverly Hills that had been his office. Before long there were two rooms and two secretaries, then a larger cottage, then "a whole office building." The EPIC headquarters was a virtual beehive of activity—the cliché fits because the campaign symbol approved by Sinclair was the bee: "she not only works hard but has means to defend herself and is willing to use them on behalf of the young." The campaign motto thus became "I produce, I defend."

There were hundreds of EPIC beehives around the state. Dick Otto appointed each chapter's secretary, and he plotted campaign strategy with EPIC's Los Angeles directors, but it was left to the local storefront chapters to conduct their own fund-raising activities in support of what would turn out to be a large slate of EPIC candidates for the state legislature. From November forward, the campaign took on the air of a gigantic festival, a ten-month-long statewide block party or barn-raising, an endless succession of picnics, dances, rodeos, yard sales, and bake sales. All these were designed to raise money, in dimes and dollars rather than by means of the usual corporate and fat-cat donations. Otto even established a policy of charging admission to rallies and selling campaign materials rather than giving them away, a clever innovation, inconceivable today, that showed how deep and how widespread Sinclair's appeal was.

Sinclair managed to establish with many previously uninvolved voters—whom some called the "little people"—the same kind of "current" that an admiring reader had once found in his writing. Some of those people were little indeed: Lincoln Haynes, whose father was a laid-off carpenter, was only ten years old when he organized a puppet show in his Silver Lake neighborhood of Los Angeles to raise money for Sinclair. Gordon Haskell was just sixteen; he did his part by singing in a barbershop quartet at EPIC rallies. La Rue McCormick, a nurse, remembered how wide Sinclair's support was among mechanics, mill workers, and hospital technicians. Morton Newman, who earned 25 cents an hour delivering print jobs for a devout Republican, pasted a Sinclair sticker on the windshield of his van as soon as he pulled onto the street—right over the Merriam sticker of his boss.

Sinclair's own time during these long months was divided between writing campaign materials, alone in his study, and trips to EPIC chapters, where he spoke to increasingly large audiences in public halls. With little money to buy radio time and billboards, and virtually shut out by the state's mainstream newspapers, personal appearances were vitally important. So too was the *EPIC News,* the campaign's weekly newspaper, edited by Reuben Borough with great flair, and distributed door-to-door by volunteers.

Because Sinclair's base of support was in southern California, Otto was able to invite delegations to visit the candidate at his homes in Beverly Hills and Pasadena. Jerry Voorhis, who would turn out to be one of Sinclair's key volunteers, was, like Otto, typical of the EPIC cadres. Voorhis left a vivid record of his impressions of Sinclair that helps to explain his appeal to skeptical intellectuals who inherently distrusted all politicians—a group to which Sinclair himself had long belonged.

Voorhis is best remembered today as Richard Nixon's first opponent for

Congress in 1946, when he was mercilessly smeared as a communist and lost the Democratic seat that he had held since 1938. (Nixon would defeat Helen Gahagan Douglas, another EPIC volunteer, in similar fashion during the race for the Senate in 1948.) Voorhis was the same age as Sinclair's son, David. A graduate of Yale, he founded a school for homeless boys in San Dimas, twenty miles east of Pasadena, where he acted as both teacher and headmaster. In 1933, Voorhis was a member of the American Socialist Party, active in a local cooperative, and distressed because his boys were told, when they looked for work, that they were "unwanted, unneeded, useless." He did not share the visceral sense of betrayal that many individual socialists felt toward Sinclair for leaving the party, just as they had when he left it to support the war effort in 1917, but Voorhis was uncertain about supporting him if he prevailed in the primaries and ran in the general election. In mid-September 1933, Voorhis attended an informational meeting organized by John C. Packard, an old ACLU friend of Sinclair's, at Sinclair's home in Pasadena. He immediately signed on as an EPIC volunteer and as a state congressional candidate himself on the EPIC ticket.

Voorhis did not support Sinclair out of personal affection. Unlike many who in later years stressed Sinclair's warmth and cordiality, Voorhis found the candidate emotionally remote. He was a "dedicated, determined, somewhat proud man," Voorhis said. "He lacked the personal warmth of most successful politicians. His intellect and the logic of his plan were to carry his campaign." Sinclair's small size "seemed only to accentuate the piercing power of his eyes, and reinforce the finality of his decisions. Through his spectacles he looked clear through you, as if he were undressing you, at least, intellectually. He was austere and puritanical in his personal habits. He was the friend of all who joined him in his fiery zeal to expose all the wrongs of society. But hardly a warm friend or one with whom one looked forward to spending a relaxed evening over Coca-Cola."

Sinclair was a man, Voorhis thought, with whom one "did not contend easily." He was then at the peak of "a life-long crusade to rout out wrong and reveal its perpetrators with all the skill and merciless resourcefulness of a writer with a purpose to which every literary art was made a servant." His "razor-sharp mind" left no room for gray areas of doubt. "Even as his mind shot, bullet-like, from one point to the next, so his very lithe body seemed to jump and pulsate with his ideas." He expected his lieutenants to accept his ideas and to follow his "grand strategy" without question. He was not interested now in the give-and-take of intellectual debate; he was trying to create a society that was "altogether good," and only those who fully shared his vision earned his total trust.

This was the Sinclair that Meta had once said was "all mind," a "thinking machine." Paradoxically, when speaking to large groups of people, ranging from farmers to factory workers to college students, he was remarkably patient in responding to not only their questions but their challenges. To Voorhis, who introduced him to many such gatherings in southern California, it was obvious that Sinclair preferred writing to public speaking: "He was, like so many other great and nearly great men, a natural introvert." But he always responded on the platform with such "complete and transparent candor and honesty" that it was impossible for voters not to be favorably impressed. Other than his greater patience in public than in private, there was never any suggestion of Sinclair's trying to shape an "image"; the very idea offended him, he testily told an interviewer many years after the election. He had simply said what he thought.

Sinclair's public actions often seemed intended to prove that he was his own man. The most dramatic gesture he made in this regard was his trip to San Quentin in February 1934 to see one of the state's most notorious prisoners, Tom Mooney. Two decades earlier, Mooney had been a socialist antiwar labor organizer; in 1916 he was convicted of setting off a bomb that killed ten people in San Francisco, and sentenced to death. The sentence had been commuted to life in prison, in part because there were grounds for suspecting that some of the testimony against him was perjured. Sinclair had portrayed Mooney as a martyr in his novel *100%*. He now promised Tom Mooney personally that his first official act as governor would be to pardon him—a vow that both endeared Sinclair to his radical base and would cost him during the general election.

Sinclair also attended productions in Los Angeles of his own agitprop play *Depression Island*. On the platform, however, he was determinedly low-key. He spoke in a conversational, often humorous tone, never using notes or material prepared by speechwriters. His responses to questions, even when prepared, sounded fresh, as in the case of the rumor that unemployed hoboes and bums would flock to California if the welfare state he proposed were to be realized. "Well, you see," he would answer, "there are two kinds of bums, those who come to California riding the brake rods and those who come riding in Pullman cars. The brake-rod bums are no problem whatever. We'll just put those who want to work on some job in an EPIC colony and those who do not want to work will go hungry. Those who cannot work will be cared for." It was "the bums who come in Pullman cars" that were the real problem," he continued, at least if you accepted his definition of a bum as "anybody who can work and will not work and who compels other people to support him."

It was no small part of Sinclair's appeal that he was capable of poking fun both at himself and at his audience. He once tricked a group of listeners with a series of rhetorical questions requiring them to shout "Yes!" by tossing in this question: "All who want to starve, say 'yes!' " After hearing a resounding chorus of "yesses," he quickly ordered, "All those who want to eat, say 'no!' " The crowd, seeing the joke, burst into appreciative laughter. (It's hard to imagine a candidate for office today taking that kind of risk, pointing up as Sinclair did both the speaker's capacity for manipulation and the crowd's mindless assent to absurd propositions in the heat of the moment.) Finally, he could take questions from the audience and rely on his quick wit to disarm attacks and slurs. When told that one of his opponents, George Creel, said he had "the brains of a pigeon," Sinclair said he was no expert on "pigeon anatomy," but he did know that "nobody ever saw ten million pigeons starving to death while the ground was covered with corn and the trees loaded with cherries."

The key to Sinclair's effectiveness as a speaker is provided by a student of rhetoric, Albert Albrecht, who wrote his doctoral dissertation on Sinclair's platform performance during the EPIC campaign. Albrecht goes back to Aristotle's *Rhetoric* for the earliest classic definition of a persuasive speaker. Such a man, said Aristotle, must "make his own character look right" through his "good sense, good moral character, and goodwill." Cicero, a favorite of Sinclair's, said much the same thing: the feelings of an audience "are won over by a man's merit, achievements or reputable life." It is worth noting in this regard that H. L. Mencken, who disagreed with Sinclair about almost everything, also generously compared him with Aristotle. But the most touching tribute to Sinclair's platform appeal, and one that he later valued the most, came from an ancient observer who as a boy had seen the Lincoln-Douglas debates, and who claimed that Sinclair was like Lincoln in seizing and holding his respectful attention.

Arrayed against Sinclair, the anti-Establishment candidate, was the formidable combination of forces representing that establishment: the career politicians, the big-businessmen and industrialists, the press, and the churches, along with patriotic, social, and charitable organizations such as the American Legion, the Elks, and the YMCA. Many of his opponents were convinced that Sinclair had to be defeated, by fair means or foul—the fair generally attacking his ideas, the foul concentrating on his character. Some margin of his appeal is provided by the overwhelming predominance of the foul as it became clear that Sinclair actually had a chance of being elected.

His most principled opposition in the primary campaign came from an old acquaintance, George Creel. Creel was now the West Coast director of the National Recovery Administration, better known as the NRA. He was based in San Francisco, and was regarded by northern California Democrats as the best man to stop Sinclair, though, like Sinclair, he had never run for elective office. The two novices had much else in common, for Creel's adventurous life as a reformer and writer had coincided at various points with Sinclair's. Two years Sinclair's senior, and an inch shorter, he had also grown up in relative poverty, in Independence, Missouri, later to become famous as Harry Truman's home town. Creel's father, a hopeless though kindly alcoholic, had died the same year as Sinclair's father, in 1907, and Creel, like Sinclair, had been supported and encouraged by his long-suffering mother. Less interested in books than in earning money as an amateur boxer and semipro baseball player, Creel didn't get started in his newspaper career until he was in his early twenties. When he did, it was through writing jingles and jokes, as Sinclair had done, first for the *Kansas City World* and then for some of the same magazines that had published Sinclair's first efforts. By 1912 Creel was working as an editorial writer for *The Denver Post,* championing the crusades of his friend (and Sinclair's), the famed juvenile court judge Ben Lindsey. In 1913 he filled the editorial columns of the *Post* with invective against John D. Rockefeller after the Ludlow Massacre, a year before Sinclair began his own campaign against the Rockefellers. Perhaps their most interesting points of association arose when Creel was President Wilson's director of the Committee on Public Information and helped Sinclair secure the second-class mailing permit for his magazine—and, less favorably, when he declined to circulate *Jimmie Higgins* to the American troops.

Creel knew and had once admired many of Sinclair's fellow muckrakers, including Lincoln Steffens, Ray Stannard Baker, and Ida Tarbell. As a young man he had been favorably impressed by the humane socialism of the English Fabians, particularly with regard to public ownership of such natural monopolies as utilities and mineral resources, and later he was attracted by the single-tax arguments of Henry George that had led to the founding of Arden and Fairhope. But by the mid-1930s Creel viewed socialism as the first step on the road to communism. He never doubted that "the American form of government is the best system ever devised by man," and warned that reforms had to "stop short of a deadening level that did away with the incentive motive and denied proper rewards for initiative, industry, and ability"—i.e., capitalism.

Creel was a dangerous opponent, especially in print: witty and pugnacious, he came across as a realist who knew how the world turned. He ridiculed Sinclair as one of those "swarms of self-anointed saviors [who] poured out of every pecan grove" with plans to end "every social and economic ill." He admitted later that Sinclair presented a hard target: "The worst of it was that I could not attack Sinclair's sincerity," Creel said; he was no "cheap demagogue," but a "starry-eyed and ecstatic" true believer, "like Peter the Hermit leading the Children's Crusade." But Sinclair's plan was more intellectually epileptic than epic, Creel joked. He regarded facts and figures as "noise," and closed his ears to them. As an example of Sinclair's carelessness with figures, Creel noted that his proposal to repeal the sales tax and replace it with a transfer tax on stock purchases and sales was hopelessly wrong: the sales tax generated $46 million a year, while the proposed 4 percent tax on stock transfers would bring in at most $2 million. As for Sinclair's proposal to exempt houses assessed at less than $3,000 from property tax, "Did he not know that property was assessed on a 40-per-cent valuation," meaning that he "would strip 55 of California's 58 counties of almost every cent of revenue?"

Surprisingly, given his scrappy nature and sharp tongue, Creel was a wooden speaker—H. G. Wells had teased him for talking through clenched teeth, like Teddy Roosevelt, but to less effect—and his attacks on Sinclair, who largely ignored them, made him look cynical and mean-spirited. When the votes were counted after the Democratic primary on August 28, 1934, Sinclair had won nearly 52 percent of the 844,000 votes cast for him and his seven opponents. Creel, the favorite of the party establishment and the smartest, most experienced political operator of Sinclair's six opponents, came in second, with 34 percent. Sinclair, the rank amateur with, in Creel's words, "the brains of a pigeon," had crushed him.

Sinclair defeated the party regulars by going over their heads to the people. Now, rather than gathering the bruised leaders together and soothing their wounds, he left the state immediately, on August 30, 1934, for a self-invited visit with Franklin D. Roosevelt in Hyde Park, New York. In his shrewdest move of the general campaign, Sinclair would solicit the imprimatur of the president himself; if he could get that, the rest of the leadership in California would have no choice but to support him vigorously against Frank Merriam, who had recently replaced the ailing incumbent, James Rolph. Merriam was derisively nicknamed "Old Baldy" and considered a reactionary incompetent even by most Republicans, who in the GOP primary gave him a hundred thousand fewer votes than Sinclair had won. A third candidate in the general election would be the young Republican Raymond

Haight, who had bolted the party and was running as a Progressive. Though he would draw some votes from Sinclair, his strength was in the San Joaquin Valley and he was not considered a threat. The statehouse was in his grasp, Sinclair felt, and greater triumphs beyond that: he was already planning to revise the EPIC acronym to signify not just End Poverty in California but End Poverty in Civilization.

Memories of his distant past accompanied Sinclair on his drive up the east shore of the Hudson River to Hyde Park. It was only September 4, but the sumac was already turning red, as it had on the autumn bicycle and hunting trips he had made almost forty years earlier there and in the Adirondacks. It was in this same vicinity that his career as a writer had begun, across the river and a few miles north, researching his cadet novels at West Point. And it was his visit in 1906 to FDR's second cousin Theodore that had been instrumental in the launching of his career as, for a time at least, perhaps the most famous writer in the world.

Sinclair's account of his interview with FDR is the only one available, since the president chose to meet privately with his guest and kept no record of the occasion himself. The day was cool, and a small fire was blazing in the library fireplace. Roosevelt sat behind his desk in a large leather chair beside a table stacked with papers and said to Sinclair, in his genial way, "You see how far behind I am in my work." Sinclair, who knew the time for his visit with the president was limited to thirty minutes, said that, like everyone, he "marveled that he was so far ahead with it." The two men chatted—or rather, FDR talked while Sinclair listened, telling stories "with gusto" about overcoming opponents who were trying to frustrate his New Deal programs. Sinclair laughed at the stories and said, "I have met two Presidents named Roosevelt in my life. The other was Theodore, and I don't know which of you is the more indiscreet." FDR "threw his head back and laughed" in the dramatically hearty manner that had already become famous. Speaking of Theodore and Sinclair's visit to the White House, Roosevelt recalled his mother reading *The Jungle* to him at the breakfast table when he was just a boy.

Sinclair had vowed not to be "taken in by personal charm, or the honor of being cordially received" by FDR. He wanted to determine how much the president knew about EPIC and how likely he was to come out in support of it. Sinclair did not say that he regarded the Civilian Conservation Corps as so much useless leaf-raking, as he did. Instead, he emphasized the need to put the millions of unemployed around the country "at productive labor and let them produce what they were going to consume." The president "understood all that clearly," Sinclair wrote later, and said that his advisers had persuaded him to give a two-part radio talk: "The first will deal with general problems, and the second will deal with unemployment." Roosevelt added, "I am coming out in favor of production for use." "If you do that," Sinclair responded, hardly able to contain his joy, "it will elect me." Roosevelt said, "That is what I am going to do. It will be somewhere about the 25th of October."

Sinclair was in high spirits as he left Hyde Park for an interview with reporters at the Nelson Hotel in nearby Poughkeepsie. Though he was forbidden to speak in any detail about his meeting with FDR by the terms of their meeting, as set up by the president's cautious staff, he felt free to say that his brief chat had been extended by FDR to a full two hours, and that he found Roosevelt "open-minded and loveable," a "very cheerful-hearted man and a tonic" for the country. He assured the people of California that "the President knows what we are doing," implying strongly that FDR approved of the EPIC plan.

That evening the New Hampshire newspaper publisher William Loeb—whose father had been Theodore Roosevelt's secretary when Sinclair was invited to the White House—drove Sinclair at breakneck speed down the same Riverside Drive where he had ridden his pony en route to Arthur Brisbane's Long Island estate in 1906. He arrived a few minutes late for an interview at WMCA, broadcast nationwide—because, he said apologetically, the president had kept him for such a long time. A midnight interview with Jim Farley, the burly chairman of the Democratic National Committee and a key Roosevelt aide, followed, the upshot of which was that Farley, according to Sinclair, said "Call me Jim."

The following morning, September 5, Sinclair traveled to Washington for two days. He addressed a warmly receptive overflow crowd of reporters at the National Press Club. He then met with many of Roosevelt's key program directors, including those in charge of the Surplus Relief Corporation, the Home Owners' Loan Corporation, the Farm Credit Administration, and the Reconstruction Finance Corporation. He thought he heard Harold Ickes, who headed the Public Works Administration, promise to provide federal support to a farm aid program that Sinclair called the Central Valley Project, and Secretary of the Treasury Henry Morgenthau, Jr., urged him to "ask for anything I wanted." He also met with Harry Hopkins, director of the Federal Emergency Relief Administration, telling him that he expected an influx of the unemployed from other states to come to California when he was elected, and that he would need federal funds to care for them.

Sinclair arrived in San Francisco on September 12, serenely confident that he had secured the full support of FDR and the national Democratic establishment. But he still had to win the formal nomination of the Democratic Party in Sacramento on September 20—by no means a sure thing. Despite his overwhelming primary victory, many of the regulars were dead set against Sinclair as a radical interloper, a cuckoo pushing them out of their nest. Some vowed to sit out the election, even though that would ensure victory for Frank Merriam. Sheridan Downey and Culbert Olson, both able politicians who had signed on with EPIC, did their best to heal the party's wounds. Downey was Sinclair's running mate as the candidate for lieutenant governor, which prompted the inevitable campaign slogan, "Uppie and Downey," and Olson was the State Senate candidate from Los Angeles who would himself become governor in 1938. Downey and Olson worked to persuade U.S. Senator William Gibbs McAdoo, the state's most powerful Democrat, that Sinclair's old-age and widows' pension would not bankrupt the state, and to assuage George Creel's similar fears regarding the repeal of the sales tax and the institution of Sinclair's property tax reforms.

Sinclair's negotiating position was strengthened by his long coattails in Los Angeles County, where EPIC owned 177 out of 210 votes on the county Democratic committee, and by similar strength in other southern California counties. After extended negotiations with Creel, McAdoo, and other party regulars in both San Francisco and Los Angeles, a compromise platform was hammered out for presentation to the convention on September 20. The compromise retained the principles of EPIC, such as production for use, while scaling back some of the specific means of realizing its goals, such as the elimination of the sales tax—only food would be exempt. Both sides could reasonably claim victory, and the platform, with its candidates, was accepted unanimously by the convention delegates. In his acceptance speech, his first as the acknowledged leader of the Democratic ticket, Sinclair described his visit with President Roosevelt and vowed to send Frank Merriam out to pasture with Herbert Hoover. George Creel followed and announced that the Democratic Party was now united behind Sinclair, and Senator McAdoo, who had recently blasted Sinclair as a socialist "interloper," addressed him respectfully as "Governor." Creel and Sinclair then sent a telegram to President Roosevelt, assuring him that they were now in "complete harmony."

Sinclair could not have asked for a better birthday present: he was fifty-six years old on the day of the nominating convention, which represented the pinnacle of his achievement, the coalescence of everything he had worked for since 1903. He would have similar moments over the next twelve weeks, buoyed by the formal support of the party he had captured, but not many; the opposing forces that had thus far largely ignored him, assuming he had no chance to win the nomination, wasted no time in launching a series of devastating attacks on Sinclair. As Greg Mitchell demonstrates in his comprehensive account, *The Campaign of the Century,* probably nobody could have survived the combination of fraud, chicanery, and manipulation of public opinion marshaled against Upton Sinclair. What is remarkable is not Sinclair's defeat, but the desperate measures required to achieve it—for there were elements of his plan, and especially of his rhetoric, that many voters would finally have rejected on their own, along with their author, as much too extreme.

═══

Consistent with Sinclair's fondness for military metaphors, he may be said to have directed so far a brilliant insurgency, a kind of audacious guerrilla warfare that had depended on passionate language and daring thrusts such as his trip to Hyde Park. Now, in the pitched battle of the general campaign, the arguments and tactics that he had used so successfully to inspire his followers came back to haunt him.

Sinclair's chief weapon had been his pen, as always—in this case the fantasy of the future that would follow his election in *I, Governor.* In practical terms, *I, Governor* was enormously successful, ultimately selling well over a million copies, winning adherents and contributing mightily to EPIC's treasury. But the book had been hastily written and did not stand up well under close examination. Sinclair's promise to revise the American industrial and economic system within the first two years after his election was foolish, though perhaps excusable because of his lack of experience in government. But he must have known from his days as the autocratic ruler— "the czar"—of Helicon Hall, that anything resembling the "fishbowl" government he proposed for Sacramento was impossible. On purely pragmatic terms, what Sinclair was proposing often seemed unrealistic at best, silly at worst—and sometimes even dangerous to democratic ideals.

Other parts of *I, Governor* provided additional ammunition for opponents who charged Sinclair with trying to destroy, not merely reform, the system. In his vision of the future, Sinclair compared the progress of EPIC to a "swiftly flowing river eating into a sand bank. Private industry began to crumble; and as quickly as any productive enterprise failed, it was made over into a public institution. Nothing could withstand the current of cooperation." It was also possible to see personal resentment behind some of Sinclair's proposals. For example, the problem of corrupt and irresponsible newspapers that he complained about in *The Brass Check* was solved in his imagined new order because there was "no private business to provide them with advertising subsidies." Newspapers were run by "governing boards" that included "the employees of the paper" as well as two appointed college professors and one other member appointed by the governor. Radio stations no longer made any money because "the advertisers of cigarettes and soaps and hair-tonics no longer subsidized them. They were socialized, and the trash was cut out of their programs."

Careful readers noted the passive voice in these formulations and asked who would be running the show in Sinclair's Sacramento. His ideal state sounded more like Plato's *Republic* than a democracy. Was this the way the arch-apostle of free speech would solve the problem of its abuse by the fourth estate—by establishing a board, led by a philosopher-king called Sinclair, to make it behave? No less frightening to many was Sinclair's vision of the new society, which to modern ears sounds suspiciously like the reeducation camps so popular with communist dictatorships: "Every land colony will become a cultural center, with a branch library, a motion picture theatre, a lecture hall where we can explain the principles of co-operation."

On a less serious level, Sinclair sometimes mislaid the common sense that Albrecht, the scholar of rhetoric, said was a part of his appeal. Consider, for example, FDR's story about his mother reading *The Jungle* to him at the breakfast table. A moment's reflection should have told the proud writer, before he passed it on to the reporters in Hyde Park, that this was not just unlikely (what mother would read such a book to her son?) but absurd: Roosevelt was only four years younger than Sinclair; in 1906 he was a twenty-four-year-old law student at Columbia, already married to Eleanor. If any "Jungle" book was being read to Roosevelt when he was a boy, it must have been Rudyard Kipling's—and even that, published as it was in 1894, when FDR was twelve, is unlikely. Sinclair, dizzy with excitement at having been received by the great man, must have misheard what Roosevelt said, in a way that flattered him immensely. So wedded was Sinclair to this ludicrous error that he not only repeated it throughout the campaign but included it later that year in his book *I, Candidate for Governor, and How I Got Licked.*

What this mistake revealed was Sinclair's fatal willingness to hear what he wanted to hear: the flip side of what George Creel said was his obliviousness to bothersome facts and figures. From FDR on down through "Call me Jim" Farley, Sinclair was dealing with politicians whose first rule was never to offend anyone needlessly, who thought it was far better to nod in seeming agreement to whatever a petitioner wanted than to say no. But when pushed, they could be ruthlessly clear as to their meaning. While Sinclair could tell reporters "I've been welcomed into the family," the New Dealers covered themselves by denying that they had made any promises to him. They were waiting for a clear signal from FDR, who was typically opaque.

The president's own status with the electorate was still unclear: hindsight shows that his strength in the summer and early fall of 1934 was immense and growing, but he was still only a year and a half into his first term. He knew, as all successful American politicians have known, that to wander far from the political mainstream or middle ground was to court disaster. While he sympathized with some of Sinclair's positions and his goals, FDR sincerely wanted to save capitalism, not to destroy it; he did not agree with the far left wing of his party on this issue, and dared not be seen as catering to it. On the other hand, it was that left wing, personified by Sinclair at its most radical, that had energized his party and promised to be his most faithful shock troops in the coming battles with Congress. A clever cartoonist for *The Washington Post* captured FDR's dilemma with a telling sketch and an even better caption: "This is the question that's / Thinning my hair; / What'll I do / About Upton Sinclair?"

=====

But Sinclair's weaknesses in early and mid-September were much less obvious than his strengths, to which the panicked over-reactions of his various opponents offered a kind of tribute. These ranged from the communist left to the evangelical Christian right. The communists, including his old friend Robert Minor, assailed him as a capitalist lackey, and Aimee Semple McPherson, Billy Sunday, and Robert Shuler, a prominent preacher in Los Angeles, quoted extensively from *The Profits of Religion* to show that Sinclair was an atheist bent on undermining all churches.

No less fervent in their opposition to Sinclair were the business interests in Los Angeles and San Francisco that he had attacked for so many years. All of the major newspapers predicted disaster if Sinclair became governor, particularly his longtime enemy the *Los Angeles Times,* but also the *San Francisco Examiner* of William Randolph Hearst, the man he had once thought of as a reformer and predicted would be president in 1912. Finally, the heads of the movie studios, most notably Louis B. Mayer, vowed to destroy Sinclair for his past affronts to them and, they said, because he would destroy the film industry.

The Republican politicians were by and large the creatures of these ruling powers. The San Francisco public relations firm of Clem Whitaker and Leone Baxter, hired to promote the candidacy of Frank Merriam, concentrated its efforts on undercutting Sinclair. When the indignant acting governor complained to Asa Call, the president of the Bank of California, that all anybody heard was "what a stinker Upton Sinclair" was and nothing about why he, Frank Merriam, would be a good governor, Call told him to face the facts: "You're a tough guy to sell, and we're going to do it our way. We're going to continue to say that Upton Sinclair is a no good son-of-a-bitch, and we're going to spend a lot of money for that. In the last ten days of the campaign we'll promote you with billboards. . . . That's what we have planned, and *that's* that."

Call and his associates had no trouble lining up allies, ranging from the Standard Oil Company of California, which warned stockholders that their holdings would be in peril if Sinclair were elected, to the Wholesale Grocers' Association of Northern California, the California Insurance Producers' Association, the California Hotel Association, and the California Real Estate Association. Every triumph achieved by interests sympathetic to Merriam was trumpeted in the press, as was every error, or perceived error, by the Sinclair campaign.

On September 26, the morning after returning from his triumphal week in San Francisco, tired but in high spirits, Sinclair bantered with a group of reporters on the porch of his Pasadena house. As Craig looked on, he made a casual remark that the press, he later said, distorted so ruthlessly that it cost him the election.

Sinclair should have been forewarned: the knives were clearly out. But when asked about the fear that poor workers from around the country would flood across the borders of the state if he were elected, Sinclair sought to mock the danger by exaggerating it, and to display his closeness to the powers in Washington. He smiled knowingly and said he had just recently told Harry Hopkins that "if I am elected half the unemployed of the United States will come to California, and he will have to make plans to take care of them." He was just making a "sales talk" to Hopkins, Sinclair continued, making sure he knew the federal government was aware of a problem that they already knew existed in California. The only way to keep people away was to make conditions as miserable as the Republican candidate apparently wanted to make them.

Sinclair's attempt to dismiss danger with humor backfired. The next morning a front-page headline in the *Times* warned, "Heavy Rush of Idle Seen by Sinclair." He was reported as saying, "If I'm elected Governor, I expect one-half of the unemployed in the United States will hop aboard the first freights for California." The accompanying lead editorial interpreted Sinclair's figures as amounting to five million indigents, since there were ten million unemployed in the country; how would "bringing in fifteen times as many poverty-stricken, jobless indigents as we have already" end poverty in California? Among these, the *Times* noted darkly, "would come a horde of radical Communists, agitators and anarchists—the Red offscourings of the country."

Harry Chandler, the publisher of the *Times*, had been opposed to Sinclair from the start, sharing fully the repugnance his father-in-law, General Otis, had felt for the upstart socialist. The *Times* at first dismissed Sinclair himself as a starry-eyed idealist, harmless because he had no chance, though it did warn that his supporters included "a maggot-like horde of Reds," termites that were "secretly and darkly eating into the foundations and the roof beams of everything that the American heart has held dear and sacred." After Sinclair's return from Washington, however, and especially as his strength seemed to increase during September and October, Sinclair became a "literary dynamiter," an "apostle of hatred." Boxed quotes from Sinclair's works, some but not all taken out of context, appeared on the front page of the *Times* each day: Methodists were "children of hell," bankers were "legalized counterfeiters," the Elks were "primitive lowbrows," the movie studios were "honey-pots which gather the feminine beauty and youth charm of the country for the convenience of rich men's lust," San Francisco was "a city without order, dignity or charm, whose standards of truth are those of a horse trader," the American Legion wanted to "take your schools and make 100,000 little West Points," and so on, ad infinitum. The quotes and accompanying caricatures of "Uppie and Downey" by *Times* caricaturist Bruce Russell continued "day after day with devastating effect," according to Ed Ainsworth, a *Times* reporter involved in the process. They turned the tide against Sinclair, Ainsworth said: "By mid-October we knew we had won."

The *Times* did not stop there; it closed its pages to any semblance of objective reporting about Sinclair's campaign, running only negative stories. Even Sinclair's old friend Harry Carr attacked Sinclair in his popular column for the *Times*, "The Lancer." Sinclair sadly recalled in a letter to Carr how, many years ago, "a half-insane anarchist threatened my life and I sought and received your friendly advice about the matter." He said he hoped "to keep bitterness out of this dispute," but he did not interfere when Reuben Borough blasted Carr in the *EPIC News* as a mercenary hatchet man whose nickname was "Fat Boy."

Kyle Palmer, the chief political correspondent then for the *Times*, laughed when Turner Catledge, a *New York Times* reporter, talked about covering a forthcoming speech by Sinclair. "Turner, forget it," Palmer said. "We don't go in for that kind of crap that you have back in New York of being obliged to print both sides. We're going to beat this son of a bitch Sinclair any way we can. We're going to kill him."

=====

Another former associate who turned on Sinclair was Irving Thalberg, who thought neither Sinclair nor his wife, those southern aristocrats, knew how to behave. It was bad enough that he had thrown away $10,000 on Sinclair's rabble-rousing and unusable "Gold-Spangled Banner." Worse still was Sinclair's showing up in a business suit for *The Wet Parade*'s premiere at the Grauman Theater; when the audience called for the author to make a few remarks, Sid Grauman prohibited him from taking the stage because he was not in formal attire (Sinclair never would own a tuxedo). As for Craig, her first remark to Thalberg when she and Sinclair were finally introduced to him, after the movie was a success, was to ask if he was indeed the famous Boy Wonder, an epithet that Thalberg despised. "If so, I never heard it," he replied icily, ending the meeting.

Thalberg was only thirty-seven years old when he died of pneumonia in 1936. The movie industry continues to honor his genius each year with an Oscar awarded in his name, and F. Scott Fitzgerald depicts him in *The Last Tycoon* as the admirable Monroe Stahr, sensitive, principled, and brave. But it was Irving Thalberg who did as much as anyone to destroy Sinclair, using trickery and deceit without regret. In mid-October, at the suggestion of Kyle Palmer and encouraged by Louis B. Mayer, Thalberg commissioned a three-part series of phony newsreels, called the *California Election News* and anchored by a supposedly objective "inquiring reporter." Newsreels at this time were popular as fillers between movie double features, lasting as long as twenty to thirty minutes. They were more widely seen, and with much greater interest, than most television news shows are today. Only the readers of Manchester Boddy's *Daily News* even knew that Dick Otto had vigorously protested the rigged newscasts, frozen out as Sinclair was from the state's other papers. One of these showed an army of hoboes supposedly California-bound. Another featured a bearded, frothing immigrant who proclaimed that since Sinclair's system "vorked vell in Russia, vy can't it vork here?" The third sequence relied on outtake film footage from a 1933 Warner Bros. movie called *Wild Boys of the Road,* the "wild boys" a raggedy mob of vagrants waiting at the border for Sinclair's victory. Perhaps the most shameless image was that of an old lady sitting on the front porch of her tiny house in a rocking chair: "For whom are you voting?" the inquiring phony reporter asks. "I'm voting for Governor Merriam." "Why, mother?" "Be-

Sinclair and his friend Charlie Chaplin, ca. 1923; Chaplin said Sinclair always "spoke through a smile."

Craig in middle age, ca. 1925.

All images courtesy Lilly Library, Indiana University, Bloomington, Indiana, except where noted.

When Sinclair's 1927 novel *Oil!* was banned in Boston for obscenity, he prepared a special "Fig Leaf" edition of the book, with the offending pages replaced by fig leaves. This image of a startled Boston matron receiving a copy from the author in sandwich boards gained Sinclair worldwide publicity, as intended.

Sinclair with Russian filmmaker Sergei Eisenstein, on left, in 1931, about to make what he regarded as the worst professional mistake of his life: sending Eisenstein with a film crew to Mexico for over a year to make *¡Que viva Mexico!*, a documentary film celebrating the Mexican revolution.

As this image of Eisenstein sporting with a skeleton on the set in Mexico suggests, he was a mischievous and playful revolutionary, qualities that troubled both the Mexican authorities and his patrons, the Sinclairs.

At ease with large crowds, like this one at Inglewood's Centinella Bowl in July 1934, Sinclair even charged a nominal admission fee, invited hecklers onto the stage with him, and almost always spoke without notes—habits that sometimes got him in trouble.

I, GOVERNOR OF CALIFORNIA

And How I Ended Poverty

A True Story of the Future
By UPTON SINCLAIR

This is not just a pamphlet.

This is the beginning of a Crusade.

A Two-Year Plan to make over a State.

To capture the Democratic primaries and use an old party for a new job.

The EPIC plan:

(E)nd (P)overty (I)n (C)alifornia!

PRICE 20 CENTS

UPTON SINCLAIR, LOS ANGELES, CALIFORNIA
(West Branch)
(ADDRESS ALL LETTERS AS ABOVE)

I, Governor was Sinclair's bestselling book other than *The Jungle*. More than most candidates for higher office, he wrote his own material, drawing on arguments he had been honing for decades. Much of his appeal derived from voters' certainty that he was an independent man of principle, even when he was in error.

"Mother Bloor" at an American Communist Party rally in 1937; she assisted Sinclair with *The Jungle* in 1906 and was his neighbor in Arden. By the mid-1950s Sinclair regarded her faith in communism as deluded and treasonous.

A family friend of President Roosevelt and a famous playboy, Cornelius "Neil" Vanderbilt (left), ca. 1950, provided Sinclair with tall tales and vivid anecdotes for the later Lanny Budd novels.

Albert Birnbaum, Sinclair's boyhood friend, also provided him with the sophisticated background and knowledge that Lanny's character needed. *Photo ca. 1940, courtesy of the Martin Birnbaum Collection, 1862–1979, Archives of American Art, Smithsonian Institution.*

Dragon's Teeth, the third of the eleven Lanny Budd novels, won the Pulitzer Prize in 1943 for its description of Hitler's rise to power. Denied an earlier Pulitzer Prize for *Boston*, in 1929, because it was deemed "propaganda," Sinclair now felt that he had at last achieved artistic respectability.

Sinclair's securely gated Monrovia house, where he moved from Pasadena in 1943. Craig Sinclair feared assassination attempts (and disliked visitors generally) and made herself and her husband into virtual recluses, refusing even to answer the telephone. Western Union delivered its messages attached to rocks tossed over the gate.

For most of Craig Sinclair's last fifteen years, she was a virtual invalid. Upton devoted himself to her care, prompting an admiring friend to say that "in a time of great talents with small hearts," Sinclair had "a particularly large one." *Photo 1956, courtesy of the Leigh A. Weiner Archive.*

Sinclair in October 1963, at Indiana University's Lilly Library. With him are his son, David, a physicist finally reconciled with his father, on his left; his third wife, May; and David Randall, director of the Lilly Library who bought Sinclair's massive archives in 1957 for the Lilly.

Sinclair in his favorite rocking chair, around 1962. The picture of his friend Albert Einstein behind him was signed and inscribed with a poem in which Einstein praised Sinclair as a "valiant man" who "tells the world to 'Open Wide' and spots a hollow tooth."

Sinclair and his third wife, Mary Elizabeth Willis, or "May," on their wedding day, October 16, 1961, six months after Craig's death. A seventy-nine-year-old recently widowed grandmother, May was indeed a breath of spring for her eighty-three-year-old bridegroom. She joked that she would put the "rove" in "Monrovia" and the "sin" in "Sinclair," and get him back into circulation after years as a near-recluse. She succeeded. *Courtesy of John Ahouse.*

cause," she answers, "I want to save my little home. It's all I have left in this world."

Thalberg confirmed his part in the deceptive newsreel features after the election in a conversation with the actor Fredric March, who said it was a "dirty trick." Thalberg said there was no such thing as fairness in politics; it was "a contradiction in terms." They could all sit there and figure out "dirty things" to do for the rest of the night, "and every one of them would be all right in a political campaign."

MGM and the other major studios also pressed their employees, including screenwriters, directors, and actors, to contribute financially to the campaign against Sinclair. Many of these resented being dunned to defeat a man they admired, and with whom they identified as a creative spirit. But of the major stars said to be in Sinclair's camp—including Katharine Hepburn, Douglas Fairbanks, Will Rogers, Clark Gable, James Cagney, and Charlie Chaplin—only Cagney and Chaplin were able to defy the studio bosses and openly support him. Even so, Cagney was finally forced to back off, and Chaplin's involvement was not extensive; on June 27, 1934, an EPIC fundraising event at the Shrine Auditorium in Los Angeles featured a showing of selections from Eisenstein's film footage, called *Death Day,* and a performance of Sinclair's one-act play *Depression Island.* Chaplin delivered the only partisan speech of his career for Sinclair that day. Years later, in a review of Chaplin's autobiography, Sinclair said, "He was my friend, and I tested him, and he did not fail me."

Sinclair's real support in Hollywood, as Greg Mitchell explains, came from its screenwriters, and from writers there and elsewhere who had admired him. Chief among these was Frank Scully, a longtime fan who formed an Authors' League for Sinclair (ALFS), enlisting, among others, Groucho Marx, Dorothy Parker, and Lillian Hellman. Theodore Dreiser was persuaded to write a laudatory piece about Sinclair for the December issue of *Esquire,* at that time an influential literary magazine, which appeared on the stands just before the election. Interestingly, Dreiser told *Esquire*'s publisher, Arnold Gingerich, that he had met Sinclair only a few times, "and never have I seriously discussed anything with him. If he, or you, through one of your devils, will furnish me with a little intimate character data about him I could take care of the intellectual and other phases and imports of his work in America so far."

Although not one of the more than seven hundred daily newspapers in California supported Sinclair, he still had enough of a chance at winning in mid-October to rate extensive national coverage by *The New York Times.* A major coup for the Sinclair camp was the *Time* magazine cover story for the October 22 issue, on the stands by October 17. Surprisingly objective, given Henry Luce's hostility to the New Deal and to Sinclair as one of Roosevelt's supporters, *Time* described Sinclair as "inordinately vain" but not a crackpot, an atheist, or a " 'free-love' cultist." If anything, he was an "ascetic," an old-fashioned socialist who looked "like Henry Ford gone slightly fey." Despite the opposition of the *Los Angeles Times* and the movie studios, the *Time* story concluded, Sinclair would probably carry southern California; only the sensible folk of northern California would be able to deny him the governorship.

Within days of that optimistic assessment, as the EPIC camp viewed it, Sinclair's campaign was dead. It was wounded first by an inaccurate *Literary Digest* poll that greatly underestimated Sinclair's strength, then finished off by President Franklin D. Roosevelt's calculated silence and by the active opposition of George Creel. Creel had learned that some of FDR's advisers thought Sinclair was a menace to the president and to California. One of these, said to be his most influential, was Rexford Tugwell, who had said in a review of *Oil!* in 1928 that Sinclair was a "millennial ass," a "bad novelist and a worse philosopher," the "kind of man which [*sic*] cannot learn." Another was Raymond Moley, a speechwriter for the president (and later a prominent syndicated columnist and author), who wrote an article entitled "Looking Backward with Mr. Sinclair." In it, he linked Sinclair unfavorably with Rousseau and charged that his program was a "scrambled hodge-podge of proposals, some sound and some absurd," propounded by a "man with no experience in practical administration."

Creel had joked during the primary campaign that when he visited southern California, Sinclair's base, he felt as though he were "plunging into darkest Africa without gun bearers." He had reluctantly agreed to try to win over for Sinclair the "hardheaded, hard-working native sons and daughters" of northern California. But on October 18, Creel wrote a letter to Sinclair renouncing his support. He said, "I do not question your honesty, but you have the most amazing faculty of making yourself believe the things you want to believe," such as ending poverty in California in one or two years. "This is an optimism carried to the point of delirium." Going public with his opposition, Creel announced that he was "a man without a vote," unable to support either Upton Sinclair or Frank Merriam: the choice, he joked, was between "epilepsy and catalepsy."

Anticipating the damage from Creel's defection, Dick Otto on October 21 released a letter from Jim Farley to a constituent that seemed to be the

Roosevelt administration's desired endorsement. In the letter, Farley said that every voter "owes it to himself to vote not only for [Senator Hiram] Johnson and Sinclair but for the entire Democratic ticket." In an earlier private note to Senator McAdoo, on October 3, Farley had said he and the president wanted to "see Sinclair elected."

Sinclair still thought he had the administration's support. He brushed aside suggestions by a New Deal power broker, J.F.T. O'Connor, that he resign in favor of the third major candidate, Raymond Haight, the former Republican running as a Progressive. He was still confident that FDR's long-anticipated radio "fireside chat" on October 22 would save his campaign: this was the moment when Roosevelt would come out for "production for use," fulfilling his earlier purported promise to Sinclair. But Roosevelt's address was very short, dealing with the virtues of charity; he said not a word about production for use. Events now moved swiftly. The next day, Creel hand-delivered to the White House a copy of his letter to Sinclair. On October 24, Roosevelt said in a press conference that he had no intention of intervening in any state election, and that he had made no promises of any kind to Sinclair. On October 26, an aide to Jim Farley said the letter that appeared to endorse Sinclair was the result of a complicated secretarial error: "Mr. Farley never intended to endorse Upton Sinclair and will not do so." Sinclair was doomed.

But the result was not the humiliation that he feared, or that his enemies desired. When the ballots were tallied two weeks later, Sinclair had 879,537 votes, or 37.6 percent; Merriam had 1,138,620, or 48.7 percent; Raymond Haight, whose strength was in the San Joaquin Valley, had 320,519 votes, or 13.7 percent. Sinclair drew some comfort from the evidence that between Haight and himself a majority of the voters had rejected Merriam and the Republican Party.

Robert Cantwell, in one of the better essays that has been written about Upton Sinclair, described him in the 1950s as a "pale and soft-voiced ascetic" with "a near-sighted smile," a "disarming candor," and a "strangely prim and dated prewar air of good-fellowship and enthusiasm." Always cheerful, he never indulged in self-pity. And yet he possessed qualities of character and experience developed "in knock-down and drag-out conflicts of such ferocity and ruthlessness that they might well demoralize a dozen hardened captains of industry."

Cantwell's generous assessment was only partly correct insofar as Sinclair's reaction to his loss of the governor's race was concerned. Even though at first he had not seriously believed he could win, and said repeatedly that he did not care whether he won or lost, by the end of the campaign Sinclair was bitter indeed—toward President Roosevelt, toward the corporations that had financed his defeat, including the movie studios, and most of all toward the *Los Angeles Times*. At high noon on November 5, the day before the election, he spoke for the last time to a crowd in downtown Los Angeles, within sight and earshot of the *Times* building. Returning to one of the major issues of the campaign, the purported influx of desperate bums who would bankrupt the state, he said the *Times*'s publisher, Harry Chandler, was himself a college dropout who had come to town riding the rails, in 1881. After living on the streets for a year as a penniless vagrant, Sinclair said, Chandler had landed a job at the *Times* and married the boss's daughter. Sinclair turned dramatically toward the tenth-floor window of Chandler's office, raised his arm, and shouted, "Come on, Harry! Give the other bums a chance!" The crowd roared with appreciative laughter at Sinclair's aggressive wit.

But at 10:30 the next night, when it was clear that Merriam had won, Sinclair's anger was no longer cloaked in humor. Violating political protocol, which required a graceful concession speech, he first said he thought he had been cheated of 125,000 votes by fraud at the polling places. Then he said, "My face burns when I think of the lies and forgeries circulated by men with millions to spend to defeat me. But it won't go on. Be of good cheer." He concluded by threatening Governor Merriam with a recall election, invoking once again his penchant for martial metaphor: "This is only one skirmish, and we're enlisted for the war."

CHAPTER FIFTEEN

THE NOVELIST

(December 1934–June 1943)

The physical and emotional strains of the governor's race on Sinclair had been prolonged and intense. He described himself as a man "no longer young," "not especially strong," who had daily been besieged by photographers and reporters. He had spent weeks on end talking and talking, sometimes to thousands of people in large auditoriums, many of whom hoped to trap him with loaded questions—after which, around midnight, he collapsed into a hotel room bed and tried to sleep. His first reaction on November 6 to the certainty that he had lost the election was bemused relief; he could sleep with his windows open again, take his walks, drive his own car.

Craig's reaction to the loss was more intense. She sank to her knees in tears, sobbing, "Thank God, thank God!" She had been opposed to Sinclair's candidacy from the beginning, and had stayed at home in Pasadena throughout the entire campaign. Fearful as always of violence directed toward her husband, she was appalled to learn a few days after the election that a businessman had bought a pistol and made his will; if Sinclair had won, he intended to kill him, and then himself.

Sinclair might have regarded death in battle as a fitting end for a warrior, thinking as he did that EPIC was just the first skirmish in a long war. About that, at any rate, he was correct; California would change from the most conservative state outside the old Confederacy to one of the most liberal in the next three decades. Sinclair's contribution to those changes was considerable.

But his own political war had ended. He relinquished control of EPIC as a people's movement to Dick Otto, who himself soon tired of factional disputes and left to sail his boat around the world. Sinclair then broke his ties with Sheridan Downey and Culbert Olson on the ground that they were insufficiently loyal to him, and charged that the communists who had helped to sabotage him were now infiltrating the movement.

He wrote two books almost immediately about his dream for California. The first, *I, Candidate for Governor, and How I Got Licked,* was finished before Christmas 1934. It is the definitive account of the campaign as he saw it, valuable for its delineation of his ideas and of the concerted opposition that defeated him. Although Sinclair had cause to be bitter, his querulous tone often undercuts his effectiveness, as one exchange with his old enemy at Caltech, Robert Millikan, indicates. A decade earlier, Sinclair had foolishly endorsed a physician named Abrams, who claimed he could diagnose illness by measuring electronic reactions in a drop of a patient's blood. During the campaign Millikan sarcastically remarked that EPIC was "just as desirable and effective" as was Dr. Abrams's imbecilic device: Sinclair was constantly meddling in areas he knew nothing about, ranging from medicine to government. Sinclair retorted that Millikan might be a Nobel Prize winner but "how many times" had he "invaded *my* field of economics, expressing opinions unworthy of a child in high school!" Sounding childish himself—his credentials as an economist hardly matched Millikan's as a physicist—Sinclair cited the praise of Albert Einstein, a "greater scientist" than Millikan. His young son, Einstein wrote Sinclair at the end of the campaign, had once tried to cut wood with his father's shaving razor: "You can be sure it was less bad for the wood than the razor." But whatever his campaign had cost Sinclair, Einstein hoped he would be comforted in the knowledge that he had fought the good fight.

In *We, People of America* (1935), Sinclair sketched another hopeful scenario of EPIC sweeping the nation by 1938. In 1936 Farrar & Rinehart published his first novel in four years, called *Co-Op;* it was based on the experiences of a colorful EPIC volunteer named Hjalmar Rutzebeck who had earlier directed a successful co-op in Santa Barbara. The novel's chief value in fictional terms is in its convincing portrayal of a family of poor southern sharecroppers who make their way across the country to California in a beat-up car. The Jett family survives various hardships during its journey, arriving just in time for the mother to have a child—foreshadowing John Steinbeck's more famous sound-alike Joad family in John Steinbeck's *The Grapes of Wrath* (1939).

Several other works grew out of the EPIC campaign. The first, *What God Means to Me,* also published by Farrar & Rinehart in 1936, was prompted by campaign charges that Sinclair was an atheist. Although dismissed by reviewers as a rambling repetition of his earlier musings on Emersonian Transcendentalism and on spiritualism, it usefully reveals Sinclair's state of mind at the time: close to despair but fighting to resist it. Returning to his early years as a writer, he recalled H. G. Wells's advice to adopt a "sturdy atheism" instead of a religious belief. He continued to reject that advice, linking it with the "vanity and materialism" that he said killed Jack London, that "shining soul." Too many besides London had destroyed themselves out of nihilistic angst: George Sterling, his wife, Carrie Sterling, and the poet Nora May French in the past, and Eugene O'Neill and Sinclair Lewis "and others I could name" who were still doing so in the present. The great fault of the age lay in taking literally the second law of thermodynamics—meaning that life is a mechanical winding down "like a clock, and a billion years" from now we'll all be dead. Such pessimism was inconsistent with the "brotherhood of man," which constituted the "backbone of my religion," Sinclair insisted. His "hunger and thirst after social righteousness" had provided him with a "formula [that] makes life comparatively simple, and it makes religion simple. I took God's help for granted in the work I was doing."

That work continued apace as Sinclair's energy revived. Another indirect result of EPIC was a short novel, *The Gnomobile,* later turned into a Disney film, *The Gnome-Mobile* (1967). In June 1935, Sinclair bought a new Ford sedan (for $774) and set out with Craig on a cross-country drive and speaking tour to help him recoup some of his $10,000 campaign debt. En route to their first stops in San Francisco and Seattle, they passed through several different redwood forests. Debates about cutting stands of old timber had been stimulated as a result of Roosevelt's election. So too had Sinclair's memories of camping out as a young man for months at a time in upstate New York and Canada. He wrote a story, dedicated to his three-year-old granddaughter, Diana, about a little girl who helps a race of woodland elves, or gnomes, frustrate the evil designs of greedy timber pirates. Whimsical and often charming, the tale harks back to Sinclair's early juvenile novels, though with the knowledge gained of hard experience—as reflected in his reference to Jack London's Valley of the Moon ranch being "cut up into tracts," so that the public could "buy romance at so much per front foot."

═══

In fact, Sinclair's mood during these post-election months and years was not very whimsical. He was consoled to some degree by the fact that nearly nine hundred thousand people had said they wanted him to be their governor. He had received many letters of support, some from old friends like Dell Munger, who said that he had had a wonderful chance to convert new believers, and Albert Einstein, who said he had done enough, and could leave the rest to "men with tougher hands and nerves." And scores of strangers also wrote, including a Wordsworthian businessman who offered him the free use of one of his furnished cabins at Big Bear Lake so that he could "commune with the visible forms of Nature" and restore his spirits.

But he had lost, after all—decisively. Many who did vote for him said later that they did so as a protest against the Republicans, not because they thought Sinclair would be an effective governor. Even some influential old friends had declined to endorse him, including Manchester Boddy at the *Daily News* and Rob Wagner, the editor of *Script,* who had drawn the first sketch of the EPIC campaign symbol, the bumblebee. From Kansas, Sinclair's longtime publisher and goad at *Appeal to Reason,* Emanuel Haldeman-Julius, linked him with Huey Long and Father Coughlin, the right-wing Detroit Catholic, as a patent-medicine huckster; concerning Sinclair's plan to organize industry in California, Emanuel Haldeman-Julius reportedly said that "Sinclair knew as much about factories as he himself did of the science of vulcanizing casings for hot-dogs." And, not surprisingly, that arch-skeptic H. L. Mencken ridiculed EPIC and its leader mercilessly in the pages of *The American Mercury,* to the point where Sinclair ceased to regard him as a friend.

The cause of their falling-out was contained in one of Mencken's published attacks on the New Deal, in early 1936. He made a passing reference to Sinclair that at first seemed to be consistent with his earlier fond mockery; his old friend was a "sunkist Utopian" and "an early Christian demonologist," certain that the nation was "a den swarming with devils" whose souls were "black all through." But Mencken also warned against the impulse toward absolutism implicit in much of what Sinclair had written: if Sinclair were ever to gain power, Mencken said, he would destroy his enemies "with the kind of ferocity that will make that of Hitler and Mussolini look puerile." Beware of apostles, Mencken said; they were all "carnivores with sharp teeth."

Outraged at being linked with Hitler and Mussolini, Sinclair told Mencken, "you ought to be ashamed of yourself." In the past, Mencken had "desired to be considered as a friend. But I am not basing this letter upon any claim of friendship. . . . I challenge you to justify your attack upon my character, and I expect and await your reply."

Mencken's reply was that Sinclair had devoted his life to "making reckless charges against all sorts of people . . . and yet you set up a horrible clatter every time you are put on the block yourself." He said Sinclair was "far, far better on the give than on the take. No man in history has denounced more people than you have, or in more violent terms, and yet no man that I can recall complains more bitterly when he happens to be hit. Why not stop your caterwauling for a while, and try to play the game according to the rules?" Sinclair retorted that Mencken's rules seemed to be to "have a brainstorm and without paying any attention to facts, pitch in and slam out all the phrases you can think of without regard to anything except their being picturesque and startling." Their correspondence ceased almost entirely, one of the last letters coming in 1951, after Mencken's disabling stroke, when Sinclair wrote, "Let us forgive each other . . . before we take our departure from this time and place of world wars, both political and military."

Sinclair's most significant work in the post-EPIC period was an attack on Henry Ford, a short labor novel called *The Flivver King* (1937). This book was also prompted in part by Sinclair's recent campaign experience. Among the contributing reasons for his defeat had been labor unrest in San Francisco, where a longshoremen's strike in July 1934 ended in violence and a short-lived general strike. Harry Bridges, the leader of the Longshoremen's Association, was a Communist Party member. Governor Merriam looked forceful as he called out the National Guard to restore order, and Sinclair was tarred with the image of an insurrectionist and a Red for supporting the strikers, just as he was winning the Democratic primary.

Labor problems during the Depression had accelerated nationwide, nowhere more dramatically than in Detroit, where the United Auto Workers were in virtually open warfare with the big automobile companies. In the years since Henry Ford had chatted with King Gillette in Sinclair's living room, his company had prospered even as Ford himself grew old and erratic, or worse—the *Dearborn Independent* that Sinclair had encouraged him to start was notorious as an anti-Semitic rag until threats of a boycott against the Ford company forced its discontinuation in 1927. Ford's generous salaries and benefits had kept the union at bay until the Depression forced the company to cut back on hours and benefits. When the UAW under Walter Reuther launched a concerted drive to unionize Ford Motor in 1937, the company crossed the line from determined opposition to strong-arm tactics. The result was the worst labor-management violence in decades.

For Sinclair the Ford-UAW confrontation as dramatized in his new novel was a reprise of his two earlier experiences in Chicago and in Colorado, an effort to return to his roots as a muckraker. But *The Flivver King* was a less ambitious effort than *The Jungle* or *King Coal,* a much shorter book that did not involve on-site research. It relied on techniques that Sinclair had used before, and would soon use again, to better effect, in the Lanny Budd stories: essentially, a counterpoint between real and fictional characters designed to create a documentary realism. But as the decision by the UAW to pay for the printing and distribution of two hundred thousand copies of Sinclair's book to its members suggests, *The Flivver King* was propaganda rather than history or fiction. Its flavor is best suggested by Sinclair's interesting depiction of Henry Ford as an emperor: the "Ford empire was not a metaphor but a fact, not a sneer but a sociological analysis. Henry was more than any feudal lord had been, because he had not merely the power of the purse, but that of the press and the radio; he could make himself omnipresent to his vassals, he was master not merely of their bread and butter but of their thoughts and ideals."

The Flivver King allowed Sinclair to reestablish his credentials as a crusader for social justice, but it was no work of literary art; nor were the three works that followed it, though each has its moments. The best part of the fantasy he called *Our Lady* (1938) is its delightful premise—that the mother of Jesus would appear through "some celestial wire-crossing," as John Ahouse puts it, during the Notre Dame–University of Southern California football game at the Los Angeles Coliseum. As he did in *Roman Holiday*, Sinclair contrasted past and present cultural and religious values to good effect. In a longer work also published in 1938, *Little Steel*, he combined his interest in labor-management problems and his recent EPIC experience. In this instance the elderly factory owner is a good man who wants to do the right thing, and the villains are two public relations experts hired to make him do otherwise. Sinclair had always resented those who shared his gifts for expression but who used them for what he considered ignoble ends, from Arthur Brisbane to Harry Carr: advertising copywriters and public relations flacks, as he thought of them, were near to the lowest circle of his inferno. The enterprising team of Leone Baxter and Clem Whitaker, so instrumental in his recent defeat as the public relations advisers to Governor Merriam, takes a final bow in *Little Steel* as Matt Joyce and his wife, Ernestine, "a brainy woman."

Although Sinclair's creative energy during the years following EPIC seemed undiminished, he was obviously casting about for a subject. He even wrote a satirical sketch in 1936 called "Wally for Queen," about the crisis provoked in England by his distant relative Wallis Warfield Simpson's love affair with King Edward VIII. But two more serious works about European politics from this period suggest that he was on the verge of finding a new channel for his energies. The Spanish Civil War, widely seen as the first round of a larger European conflict, prompted Sinclair to write and self-publish *No Pasaran!* in 1937. Returning to the pattern of *Jimmie Higgins*, Sinclair followed the adventures of a group of young American volunteers against Franco. A thinly developed thesis novel about the siege of Madrid, the book's main interest is in its anticipation of Sinclair's turning to contemporary world events for his inspiration. In the play *Marie Antoinette,* written in 1938 and published the following year, Sinclair returned to the subject of European politics, but with an intriguingly different style and tone. Eschewing propaganda, he objectively re-created the political and social tensions of pre-revolutionary France, largely from the perspective of the French court and its social milieu.

Sinclair turned sixty in September 1938. One month later, after nearly four years in search of a proper subject, and at an age when most men retire, he began his new career as a historical novelist. Before that career ended, in 1953, the first year of President Dwight D. Eisenhower's administration, he would write eleven novels about a charming spy named Lanny Budd— a heroic saga admirable both for its achievement and for the unique combination of qualities it required of its irrepressible creator.

═══

Sinclair's best writing had always reflected his abilities to master huge quantities of information and to convey it vividly. So strong was his documentary sense that it often compensated for his weaknesses, especially as a novelist. These weaknesses would have been less important a hundred years earlier, when certain kinds of fiction were expected to be didactic instruments for education and for social improvement, but for many of his contemporaries they were profoundly disqualifying. Even Sinclair's admirers concede that his indifference to the complexities of human psychology and his aversion to modernist innovations in narrative technique prevented him from writing works that the twentieth-century literary establishment would praise as high art. So too did his insistence that the world had always turned on the struggle between the haves and the have-nots, and that everything writers said was propaganda, on the side either of good or of evil—a core conviction of some of the postmodernists who came to prominence after Sinclair's death, but not one that has led them as yet to rediscover his work.

But now Sinclair acquired a substantially greater interest in human psychology, even as he became less doctrinaire about the notion of all literature as propaganda. Why these radical shifts in orientation should have happened so late in his life is unclear. In a general sense, given the outsized figures of the age, from Roosevelt and Churchill to Hitler and Mussolini, it was hard for anyone not to become caught up in speculating on the relationship of character, personality, and national destinies. More personally, Sinclair's exposure to so many people during the EPIC campaign and the adulation and condemnation he had experienced may have jarred him into a greater sensitivity to the complexities of human nature. He had always been a solitary and reclusive man, despite his fame and his public image, and the campaign had been a life-altering experience.

World events now presented Sinclair with the greatest challenge yet to his talents: this was nothing less than showing how and why Western civilization was on the verge of extinction, and doing what he could to save it.

Sinclair credited Craig with the title *World's End* for his first Lanny Budd novel. As they listened to a radio broadcast on Hitler's triumph at Munich in October 1938, she said, "Well, our world is at an end." They had been following the rise of Hitler for years, with more than casual apprehension— Sinclair's fear that economic conditions in the United States might encourage fascism at home had helped decide him to run for governor, just as it had led Sinclair Lewis to write his cautionary tale *It Can't Happen Here,* in 1935. He had also talked and corresponded with Thomas Mann, who warned him of the "dreadful nightmare" that was at hand. Sinclair was certain that the coming war was a direct result of the failed peace following the Great War, a notion widely accepted today but less so at the time. He intended to dramatize the ideas, personalities, and events relating to that series of failures in a novel that would end in 1919, with the peace negotiations at Versailles.

Sinclair's situation in 1939 was comparable to that in 1904, in Chicago, before he came upon the Lithuanian wedding party that showed him the path to take in *The Jungle.* He had a thesis, and he had no shortage of material, in part based on his own experiences and on those of his many contacts through the years in Germany, England, and the Soviet Union. But he did not yet have "the calling" to undertake such a massive project.

The needed inspirational spark was ignited shortly after the radio broadcast, Sinclair said later, as he walked one night in his garden. Though he does not make the connection, the moment he describes sounds much like the one when he was sixteen years old and had a vision that he would become a writer. As a consequence of that "strange and portentous experience," he had written in *American Outpost,* his juvenile sense of self gave way to his fancy and to the "people of his dreams." Now, nearly half a century later, he "was walking up and down in my garden" in Pasadena when suddenly "a spring was touched" and "a novel came rolling into the field of my mental vision; a whole series of events, with the emotions that accompanied them, a string of characters, good and bad, old and young, rich and poor." The "mass and persistence" of his vision was such that Sinclair went for thirty-six hours in a state of "absorption," lying in bed wide awake as he "saw" his theme.

This account of his inspiration, or epiphany, was written after *World's End* was finished. An earlier, more prosaic remark to Fulton Oursler omits the walk in the garden but uses another pair of metaphors to explain his new "big idea," which would be "the biggest story I have ever written," going beyond even the ambitious scope of *World's End.* "The scenes are to be laid all over Europe during the past twenty-five years. It was perfectly marvelous the way the thing just unfolded itself like one ocean wave rolling in after another. . . . This novel has been knocking at the gate of my mind for several years, but I would not let it in, because it seemed impossibly big and some of the episodes were so terrible, but apparently the story has gone on writing itself in my subconscious mind all the time."

Of the various reasons for the success of *World's End* and its sequels, Sinclair's creation of Lanny Budd is the most important. Lanny is the perfect vehicle to carry Sinclair and his readers through the first half of the twentieth century. He is also Sinclair's first fully realized fictional character, one who grows and changes with his times. Lanny, born in 1900, is just one year older than Sinclair's son, David, and he too has a difficult relationship with his father, who has caused him to be born illegitimate. Lanny, the child of Sinclair's imagination, is considerably more tractable than his flesh-and-blood son, and Sinclair seems to have given Lanny much more attention that he ever gave David. The Lanny-Sinclair relationship is further complicated by the degree to which Lanny appears to be an idealized alter ego of his creator—like many of Sinclair's characters in past books, but with important differences.

One of these differences is that Sinclair spent only fifteen months of his long life in Europe, while Lanny is born in Switzerland and doesn't even see the United States until he is sixteen, when he stays for less than two years. Sinclair needed a protagonist who was born rootless and without allegiances, a blank slate on whom experiences could be written as he matured. Prior to the events of the novel, Lanny's father, Robert Budd, called Robbie, was the scion of a Connecticut arms manufacturer on a business trip to the Continent when he fell in love with Mabel Blackless, a young American working as an artist's model. Threatened with disinheritance if he married Mabel—nicknamed "Beauty"—Robbie settled her and their infant son into a villa on the French Riviera, and returned home to marry an acceptable wife.

In the course of the novel, Beauty marries a French artist of genius whom Lanny idolizes, and who is killed during the war. Lanny is raised bilingual in

French and English, and is nearly as fluent in German. Brought back in mid-war by Robbie to Connecticut, he is guardedly accepted into the Budd family and briefly attends a prep school. (All of his education otherwise is through tutors.) On his return voyage to France after the war, in 1918, Lanny meets an envoy of President Wilson who needs the boy's language skills to assist him with the peace negotiations at Versailles—where Lanny subsequently observes the great men of the age, David Lloyd George, Woodrow Wilson, and Georges Clemenceau, at work, and meets many others, including Sinclair's old sponsor, George Herron.

Sinclair divided his long novel into six "books," reflecting his ambition to write an epic history of the period that Herron had told him in 1914 would be the most important in the past two thousand years. In past novels, even those with similarly epic scope, his titles had often been little more than labels (witness *Manassas, Oil!,* and *Boston*). "World's End" is far more evocative. Sinclair also effectively uses snatches of poetry and scripture throughout the novel and its sequels: Book One is "God's in His Heaven," a sentiment consistent with the opening scene of the summer festival at Hellerau, where Lanny and his friends meet George Bernard Shaw, as Sinclair and Craig had on their wedding journey. The last book, which describes the aftermath of the war and Wilson's failure to secure a just peace at Versailles, is ominously titled "They Shall Reap the Whirlwind." It was that failure, Sinclair argued, that had sowed the seeds for the Second World War.

Like the Victorian novels it resembles, *World's End* overflows with characters, scenes, subplots, contrivance and coincidence, debates and quarrels, and re-creations of actual events and of the real people who were involved in them. Always, though, it's Lanny's story, even if that simply means he reacts to what he learns—for this is also an education novel as well as a coming-of-age or initiation story, with sufficient problems for its hero to overcome to keep the reader involved. Lanny is a young man of many talents: a capable pianist; a natural linguist; intellectually curious enough at fifteen to read Racine and Molière on his own—and, like Sinclair, all of Shakespeare; intimately familiar with all weapons through his father; and an engaging conversationalist, able to talk about art with his stepfather and about arms with his father's business acquaintance and competitor Basil Zaharoff. But for all his gifts, Lanny is modest and likable, good company no matter who he is with, and more interested in others than in himself. Small wonder that he later becomes the perfect spy.

The reviews of *World's End* frequently praised Sinclair's vivid re-creations of actual historical figures. Of these, the most successfully realized is Basil Zaharoff, the Turkish-born lord of the arms trade. Lanny, by the end of the novel a mature young man of nineteen, is employed as an interpreter for Wilson's aide and thus privy to secrets concerning the ongoing peace talks. The wily Zaharoff, variously likened to a spider, a tiger, and an "old grey wolf," tries to buy Lanny's services as a spy. He even suggests that Lanny might be interested in marrying one of his two beautiful daughters. "It was really a fascinating thing to watch," Sinclair allows Lanny to observe, "most educational for a young man with a possible future in the diplomatic world. The perfection of a Grand Officer's technique: the velvety softness of manner, the kindness, the cordiality, even affection; the gentle, insinuating voice; the subtle flattery of an old man asking advice from a young one; the fatherly attitude, the strong offering security to the weak. Won't you walk into my parlor? It is warm, and the cushions are soft, and there is no sweeter honey provided for any fly." Sinclair returns to his favorite metaphor of the temptation on the mount as Lanny declines Zaharoff's offer. "The munitions king realized that he had wasted his afternoon. He didn't show any signs of irritation, but brought the interview politely to a close and parted from the youth on terms which would make it possible for the duqesa [Zaharoff's mistress] to invite him again."

Sinclair's most effective fictional character in *World's End* other than Lanny is Robbie Budd. Urbane, intelligent, and a loving father, Robbie also wants to enlist his son's services as his successor, just as "Dad" Ross had hoped to do with his son, Bunny. George Bernard Shaw had created the perfect model for a sympathetic villain in *Major Barbara*'s arms merchant, Sir Andrew Undershaft. Just as Shaw gave his best lines to the devil, so does Sinclair, who lets the well-read Robbie quote Undershaft's persuasive arguments that nations need arms for their defense, and that his calling was as moral as any other. Through Robbie, Sinclair offers an effective description of what would later be called the "military-industrial complex," one that transcends more than borders. German fighter pilots during the Great War flew Fokker planes that were "manufactured in neutral Switzerland from bauxite mined in enemy France." To Lanny's protest of "treason," and his demand to know who was responsible, Robbie answers, "It's business." The company is a "big concern, with a lot of stockholders; its shares are on the market, anybody can buy them who has the money." Its directors sit on the boards of "hundreds of different companies, all tied together in a big net—steel, oil, coal, chemicals, shipping, and, above all, banks. When you see those names, you might as well butt your brains out against a stone wall as try to stop them, or even to expose them—because they own the newspapers."

"But, Robbie," Lanny protests—he always addresses his father so—

"doesn't it make any difference to those men whether the Germans take France?" Robbie responds, "They're building big industry, and they'll own it and run it. Whatever government comes in will have to have money, and will make terms with them, and business will go on as it's always done. It's a steam roller; and what I'm telling my son is, be on it and not under it!"

Sinclair has resurrected his old themes of the interlocking directorates and the underlying evil of capitalism, as well as his continuing war against the press. But now he allows them to be voiced by an attractive character who is not easily refuted. David reproached his father for creating such a sympathetic merchant of death—while also noting that Robbie was a good deal more tolerant of Lanny's errors than Sinclair had been of his. Sinclair said David had misread what he was trying to do with Robbie Budd; the critic who called him a "villainous, traitorous animal" was closer to the mark. In earlier novels, no readers would have been able to misconstrue Sinclair's intentions.

=====

Living as he did so close to Hollywood, Sinclair knew the rule that a director was only as good as his last picture. His own last books had been so lackluster that Farrar & Rinehart, his publisher since *Mental Radio,* passed on the chance to publish *World's End.* Only James Henle at Vanguard Press, an underfunded radical publisher, seemed interested. Then even Henle begged off, in the early summer of 1939, saying the book would be too long and too difficult to market. When Sinclair tried Farrar & Rinehart again, a "reader" there said he missed the strong sense of social conscience that had previously marked Sinclair's work. Sinclair protested to John Farrar that he had "been scolded all my life for writing propaganda and thesis novels." Here he was, doing what his critics had so long asked him to do, "trying to tell the story and show the facts, and let them preach their own lesson," only to find his effort rejected as " 'a triumph of futility.' "

Fortunately, an old ACLU friend, Ben Huebsch at Viking Press, saw both the merit and the marketing potential of *World's End.* A few weeks after the contract was signed in February 1940, an in-house memo at Viking said Sinclair's novel had everyone "romp[ing] about like schoolboys with their first football." Sinclair had "baited his hook with so many bright and dancing lures that it will be the sluggish reader indeed who doesn't strike at one of them." On April 15, Huebsch wired Sinclair that *World's End* was a Literary Guild choice for July, with an initial printing of sixty thousand copies. Between then and 1953, Viking would sell nearly half a million copies of *World's End* and its ten sequels—not quite blockbuster numbers on the order of those for *The Jungle,* to be sure, and declining considerably toward the end of the series, but solid enough to earn Sinclair not only financial security but a degree of critical respect that he had never before received.

These books—generally called the *World's End* series or "the Lanny Budd novels"—also won for Sinclair an audience he had never before sought: middle-class readers with no vested ideology other than a generalized belief in American democracy. He called the series "contemporary history," though it became more like "current events" as it drew closer to the times of composition and publication. *World's End* went as far back as 1913. The second novel, *Between Two Worlds* (1941), describes the 1920s, ending with the stock market crash of 1929; *Dragon's Teeth* (1942) concentrates on the rise of Hitler, ending in 1934; *Wide Is the Gate* (1943) goes through the debates over appeasement and the Spanish Civil War, ending in 1938; the fifth book, *Presidential Agent* (1944), covers the 1937–1938 period, up to the eve of Munich; *Dragon Harvest* (1945) goes from 1938 through 1940, focusing on Munich, Dunkirk, and the occupation of Paris. *A World to Win* (1946), from 1940 through 1942, includes the establishment of Vichy France, the Battle of Britain, Rudolf Hess's flight and capture, and the war in China. *Presidential Mission* (1947) is about the critical events of 1942–1943—the Africa campaign, the Pacific war, and the bombing of Berlin. *One Clear Call* (1948) covers the period from 1943 through 1944, concentrating on the Allied invasion of Sicily, D-Day, and the election of FDR to his fourth term. *O Shepherd, Speak!* (1949), on the years 1944 through 1946, takes in the Battle of the Bulge, Yalta, Roosevelt's death, and the Nuremberg trials. Although Sinclair intended to end the series with this volume, he published *The Return of Lanny Budd* in 1953 as a Cold War sequel, with the Soviet Union as Lanny's new enemy.

Sinclair traveled the world from his study, weaving his stories out of his own imagination and material from a vast array of books, magazine articles, and personal correspondence. He relied on an extensive network of epistolary friends, some of whom agreed to read sections of the manuscripts. Some respondents were important men, like the diplomat Adolph Berle, who said Clemenceau's gloves were made not of suede but of silk, and that Wilson's chief adviser, Colonel House, never took notes, simply closing his eyes to concentrate when he wanted to record something in his photographic memory. Others were plainer sorts, like the steelworkers' union organizer who said Lanny needed a livelier sex life.

Two correspondents were particularly important. The first, Martin Birnbaum, was Sinclair's old Lower East Side schoolmate and violin teacher. After law school, Birnbaum had become a successful international art dealer, with a particular expertise in helping wealthy Americans like Charles M. Schwab, Joseph Widener, and the Taft family, in Cincinnati, acquire great European paintings. Birnbaum was an elegantly handsome man, widely traveled and on comfortable terms of intimacy with various social sets of artists, musicians, and millionaires. He served willingly as a partial model for Lanny Budd, and provided Sinclair with detailed and highly intelligent suggestions not only on art matters but on theme, plot, and characterization. Lanny's profession is critical to his success as a spy, allowing him to cross borders, to pose as a playboy dilettante without principles or scruples, and to gain access to Nazi art collectors and thieves like Hermann Göring and the inner Nazi circle, including Hitler. His instructor, guide, and confidant is Zoltan Kertezsi, a Hungarian art dealer whose protégé Lanny became as a boy: an inside joke for Sinclair and his former violin tutor, because "kertezsi" is the Hungarian word for the German "birnbaum," or "pear tree."

Sinclair's second most important aide was S. K. Ratcliffe, an English journalist working in Glasgow, who read every word of the manuscripts and offered both factual corrections and good-humored as well as useful stylistic suggestions—which Sinclair, once so resistant to criticism of any kind, willingly accepted. Where Sinclair had written "ardent in his belief in," Ratcliffe suggests "it is well, I think, to avoid these little repetitions. An ardent believer in . . ." Shuddering at Sinclair's "He voiced the question"—"Horrid!"—Ratcliffe substitutes "He put the question." Concerning Sinclair's phrase "A significant sign," Ratcliffe asks, "Is this not a pleonasm? A sign is of course significant. A revealing sign?" Sinclair's sentence "Two years only had passed" earns a sympathetic sigh: "As R. L. Stevenson said, we all put 'only' in the wrong place." But Ratcliffe also frequently voices his great admiration for Sinclair's achievement: "Trifles again, no more. There is almost nothing for the hack reader to mark in these chapters, which you seem to be producing with ease and enjoyment."

=====

On May 3, 1943, Sinclair received another welcome telegram from Ben Huebsch:

PULITZER PRIZE AWARDED DRAGONS TEETH. THE WORLD IS CATCHING UP WITH YOU. ALL OF US HERE SHARE PRIDE WHICH YOU MUST DESERVEDLY FEEL.

A letter arrived the next day, in which Huebsch said his first wire had been bounced back "after an hour with the stern notice that congratulatory telegrams were taboo" (a peculiar Western Union stricture during the war). He would understand if Sinclair had a "slightly cynical feeling about a verdict from a jury which is only a slow echo of the verdict of the people." Nevertheless, the prize now "makes you the most conspicuous of American writers for the time being." Inasmuch as the postmaster general had not yet forbidden the use of the word in letters, Huebsch concluded, "I congratulate you."

Although *World's End* had been a better novel, *Dragon's Teeth* won the prize because of its plausible insights into the political and social world of the Nazis. Its greatest virtue lay in Sinclair's brilliant and sustained linking of bad art and bad politics, a theme he had introduced in *World's End*. He used Lanny's slightly older German friend, the greatly gifted composer Kurt Meissner, to develop his central idea. Kurt is the paradigm of the Romantic who for idealistic reasons becomes a Nazi, and his new concerto proves to Lanny that his friend's art had "lost its vitality." His "sweeping melodies" had become formulaic: "He is trying to pump himself up and sound impressive," his genius a servant of his fanatic ideology. But Lanny realizes also that he is himself "an intriguer, a double-dealer, using art and art criticism as camouflage for *his* kind of ideology, *his* set of formulas." Although Lanny is not really on the horns of a dilemma—he never doubts that his deceptions are necessary—the revealing moral relativism of this passage is a far cry from the reductive oversimplifications of Sinclair's earlier comments on art and propaganda in *Mammonart* and *Money Writes!*

A similarly effective passage—one of dozens throughout the novels—appears earlier, in *Between Two Worlds*. Here Sinclair recounts an incident so grotesque that it had become a kind of bad joke: the death in 1927 of the vain and aging dancer Isadora Duncan, whose long scarf became entangled with a wheel of her car. Sinclair trusts that his readers in 1941 will see that Duncan's death foretold the death of art and beauty in Europe, just as Gluck's 1912 *Orpheus* at Hellerau had foreshadowed, for Sinclair in fact and for Lanny in fiction, the First World War. His use of violent details is not gratuitous but purposeful, oddly restoring Duncan's dignity as a tragic heroine destroyed by fate: "By the time the car had moved a few feet the tightening fabric had become a strong rope wound about Isadora's neck; it drew her lovely face against the side of the car and crushed it, broke her neck, and severed her jugular vein." At the funeral, "thousands stood and watched the pale gray smoke rising from the chimney of the crematory, and wondered to what heaven the soul of their adored one was bound."

Among the letters of congratulation that Sinclair received for the Pulitzer were several from old friends and acquaintances with whom his relations had been strained. Michael Williams had turned his life around after their Bermuda sojourn in 1909, and was now the devoutly religious editor of the Catholic magazine *Commonweal.* In a "Dear Mike" reply to Williams's letter, Sinclair wondered if his wife, Peggy, had joined him in his newfound religiosity. Another former admirer-turned-antagonist was Carey McWilliams, who had supported Sinclair's run for governor but later accused him of becoming a red-baiter. Sinclair had counterattacked, in a biting article, "The Strange Case of Carey McWilliams." Now McWilliams wrote to tell Sinclair that the award was "long over-due" and "richly deserved." Irving Stone, rejected as Sinclair's biographer a few years earlier by Craig because he had asked leading questions about "sin," said he and his wife, Jean, "let out a 'yip' of joy" when they heard the good news; Stone promised to send him a copy of his new book, *They Also Ran,* about worthy failed aspirants for the presidency, in which Sinclair would find himself included in a chapter on Horace Greeley.

Perhaps the most interesting letter from a former antagonist was that of the venerable Gertrude Atherton, a California writer with whom he had once sparred (in 1904 in an article for *Collier's,* "Our Bourgeois Literature: The Reason and the Remedy"). Now eighty-six years old, Atherton wrote that Sinclair's *Dragon's Teeth* was "enthralling," though it made her "bloodthirsty": "I would revel in seeing, with my own eyes, Hitler, Goering *et al* boiled in oil." Like so many readers, she incorrectly assumed that Sinclair must have found time somehow to travel widely and for extended periods in Europe, in order to "learn so much, not only about the psychology of peoples, but of art, music, literature—no man ever lived a busier life."

And from Washington came two letters from unambiguous admirers at opposite ends of the federal bureaucracy. Ernest Greene, Sinclair's former secretary and advocate for the Nobel Prize, took time out from his boring job with the War Department to say that the Pulitzer was at least a modest recognition for Sinclair's achievement. Harold Ickes, the member of FDR's brain trust most sympathetic to Sinclair's run for governor, was still the secretary of the interior. Ickes "rejoiced" at the way Sinclair had "fought [his] way through to the front rank of living authors."

===

But had Sinclair really joined that illustrious assembly, however it might be counted? The Pulitzer Prize had prompted him in the past to question the motives as well as the literary and political sensibilities of those who awarded it. Now his own selection was being questioned—but not on the old ground that he was a propagandist. A number of newspaper reviewers as well as literary critics agreed with *The New York Times,* which praised Sinclair for having, in *World's End,* "mastered his earlier tendency to put the idea and the symbol first and the character last." The artist in him had routed "the old crusader," who now saw that "human life is too complicated to fit into a formula." In his seventh decade, Sinclair had become "the successful painter of an epoch, as a first-class mingler of fiction with historic fact."

The chief objections to Sinclair's new inclusion among the great writers of his time—or even the "first-class" writers—came from two allied camps. The first was composed of historical purists who argued that mixing real figures with invented ones inevitably distorted history according to the author's vision—a version of Sinclair's own earlier argument in *Mammonart.* This objection rested on the assumption that the truth could somehow be objectively verified. It ignored the fact that from Homer and Virgil onward, through Plutarch and Livy, Shakespeare and Goethe, Carlyle and Tolstoy, the dead have always been effectively brought back to life through the devices of fiction. There are different kinds of truth, and the kind that comes through the artist's imagination has its own value. Sinclair was a member in good standing of an honored tradition, whose most noted recent practitioner had been John Dos Passos. More recently, Philip Roth, Thomas Pynchon, Norman Mailer, E. L. Doctorow, and Don DeLillo have also mixed history and fiction, as have lesser writers like Gore Vidal, James Michener, Kenneth Roberts, and Herman Wouk, whose *The Winds of War* employs Sinclair's technique of a single ubiquitous protagonist. The real question was, where on the ladder of achievement did Sinclair fit?

The answer to that question depended on how far one agreed with the second camp of objectors, who said Sinclair was merely a vulgar popularizer. The formidable and astringent literary critic Diana Trilling, for one, dismissed Lanny and his adventures in *The Nation,* in 1943, as "fatuous." (Sinclair showed gentlemanly restraint in his reply to the editor concerning the "very high standards" of his "lady-critic." Twelve years earlier, when Trilling was a beginning writer and a friend of Bettina Sinclair, she had asked Sinclair to help her sell a piece to Bernarr Macfadden's *True Story* magazine. Although Fulton Oursler, Sinclair's good friend and the editor of the magazine, had rejected the story she then submitted, Trilling wrote a warm thank-you note to Sinclair for his generosity.)

Sinclair's chief appeal, according to a remarkably supercilious later critic, Ivan Scott, was "to those readers who regularly buy trade books, people with an average education and an above average interest in contemporary events." These readers were presumably unbothered by Lanny Budd's unbelievable ability to be everywhere, to know everyone of importance, and to come through so many adventures safely. The Harvard scholar of Puritan America, Perry Miller, compared Lanny to Superman and to Casanova for his many love affairs (none of which would earn more than a PG, or even a G, rating today in Hollywood). He also found Sinclair's style "corny" and marred by excessive didacticism: "When the travelers pass through the Panama Canal, [Sinclair] must point out, 'If an enemy could knock it out, the American fleet would be cut into two halves, and neither half would be big enough for any military purpose.' "

Some critics were even less polite. Howard Mumford Jones said in *The Atlantic Monthly* that Sinclair's style was simply "vulgar" and that Lanny was a character only in the sense that Captain Nemo, Phileas Fogg, and Dick Tracy were characters. Lewis Mumford, in a letter to Van Wyck Brooks, dismissed Sinclair as a man with a "decent but commonplace mind" who somehow got geniuses like Einstein to say they liked his books: "indeed, he extracts praise in the way a broken down actor, known to everybody in his palmy days, extracts dollars from people who once knew him at least by reputation."

Sinclair did not see Lewis Mumford's comment. But he responded to Jones that "somebody has to write for the masses and not just the Harvard professors." He had, he said, always "tried to make my meaning plain, so that the humblest can understand me." For once, Sinclair was too modest in his estimation of what he gave his readers, humble and otherwise. Although examples of weak writing can be found in the two-million-plus words of the eleven Lanny Budd novels, Sinclair's prose is often subtle and sophisticated, by anybody's standards. Lewis Mumford's surprise that great minds could admire Sinclair says more about his own limitations than it does Sinclair's.

It is true that Sinclair's Lanny Budd books are "literary" in a rather old-fashioned sense. He was self-consciously trying to create an epic, drawing on the resources of language in every way he thought useful. This included its rich literary history. His pages are dense with scores, perhaps hundreds, of unidentified allusions: to Keats while Lanny, on a drive through the English countryside one fall day, enjoys "this season of mist and mellow fruitfulness"; to the lesser-known Allen Cunningham when a forceful young woman suggests to Lanny "one of those old-fashioned, full-rigged clipper ships with every sail set—a wet sheet and a flowing sea, a wind that follows fast, and fills the white and rustling sails and bends the gallant mast!"; and more than once to Swift, as Lanny wonders how one can tolerate a world ruled by knaves or fools, or both.

A proper epic hero, Lanny had been "born in the crater of a volcano." In the earlier novels "he still played about its slopes, catching pretty butterflies and making garlands out of flowers, but he heard the rumble and smelled the sulphur, and knew what was going on below." As he matures, he comes to understand "the peculiar duality of the artistic temperament, which is bowed down with grief, horror, or other tragic emotion, then finds a phrase to express it, and slaps its knee, exclaiming: 'By God, a masterstroke!' "

Blessed with a well-stocked mind, like his creator, Lanny achieves a degree of compassionate insight that his superficial critics overlooked: "The anatomists tell us that the heart has four chambers," Sinclair allows him to reflect, "but this poet says two; in one dwells joy and in the other grief. When joy wakes in one, grief sleeps in the other. The poet whispers to joy to be careful and speak softly, lest grief should awaken. *O Freude, habe Acht! Sprich leise, dass nicht der Schmerz erwacht!*" Sinclair had used this same allusion to "The Heart," by the German Romantic poet Hermann Neumann, in his second work, *King Midas.* At that time, in 1901, he was himself a solipsistic Romantic; now he could say "Surely the primary purpose of art is to communicate to others, and not alone to the artist." Some of his materials remained the same, but Sinclair's purpose had radically changed.

George Bernard Shaw and Thomas Mann, who knew from their own experience how difficult a task Sinclair had set himself, were generous in praise of his early Lanny Budd books. Shaw's encomium was especially welcome because he was known to be sparing in his praise; indeed, he had told Sinclair years earlier that *Naturewoman* was a terrible piece of writing. Now he wrote to say that, at age eighty-five, "When people ask me what happened in my long lifetime I do not refer them to the newspaper files and to authorities but to your novels." Less formally, he added a postscript: "by the way," Lanny "is just the right choice for a peg to hang your history on."

Mann, who in *The Magic Mountain* (1924) and the later *Doctor Faustus* (1948) did so much to explain the nature of the two great European wars, was equally complimentary: "Some day the whole [*World's End*] cycle will certainly be recognized as the best founded and best informed description of the political life of our epoch."

Sinclair also valued the letter from another long-ago Helicon Hall friend, Edwin Bjorkman. Now in his late eighties, Bjorkman wrote to say that "the conception of the entire series is as audacious as the execution is perfect. It seems to me that you may be said to have inaugurated a new literary category—the novel of current history." Bjorkman found the stories "full of intense human interest, dealing with a group of living and growing" characters, altogether constituting "work of genuine greatness, no matter from which angle you may regard it." Sinclair responded that he knew Bjorkman did not "praise easily," and that he could think of very few men whose good opinion "would please me as much."

One of those men was Van Wyck Brooks, whom Sinclair had known since they met at Gaylord Wilshire's house in England in 1912, and whose important early biography of Mark Twain had helped to shape Sinclair's ideas of an artist's obligation to his society. Although Brooks liked Sinclair, he had for a long time agreed with those who dismissed him as an earnest propagandist, and Sinclair had responded in kind. But by the time the *World's End* series had run its course in the mid-1950s, Brooks told Sinclair that he now regarded him as "one of the great figures of our time." Even then, of course, Brooks was hedging—is it better to be a great "figure" or a great "writer"? But he also acknowledged—correctly—that Sinclair was "a very difficult person to be right about."

CHAPTER SIXTEEN

THE RECLUSE

(July 1943–April 1961)

U pton Sinclair's life before he began the Lanny Budd books had been filled with incident; its apogee was reached with the winning of the Pulitzer Prize in 1943, when he turned sixty-five. For most of the following eighteen years, he would lead a restricted and nearly solitary existence, with only his wife for companionship. As a writer, he continued to display a remarkable ability to maintain his artistic and intellectual pace. As a father, he grew even further estranged from David until Jean Sinclair, his son's second wife, effected a reconciliation. And as a husband, he showed a touching capacity for self-sacrifice in caring for his ill and dependent wife until her death. Intricately interwoven, these three major threads of Sinclair's later years reveal the texture of a personality that continued to grow more withdrawn, more complex, and, in some respects, more appealing.

The mystery of Sinclair's rejuvenation as an accomplished novelist in his seventh decade is solved, at least in part, by noting the frequent references in the *World's End* series to his youth. He tapped not only his early personal experiences with Shaw and Herron, among many others, but the original wellspring of self-centered energy that he had described in *Love's Pilgrimage*. At that time, in his early twenties, "He went quite alone, and spoke to no man; he was self-absorbed, and walked about with his eyes fixed on vacancy; he was savage when disturbed, and guarded his time unscrupulously."

Now he was similarly absorbed. For ten years, from 1939 to 1948, when he turned seventy, he wrote on average a thousand words a day, following a regimen that few writers can adhere to for more than a few months. Moreover, he was writing with greater attention to style than he ever had before, as his meticulous corrections and revisions of the Lanny Budd manuscripts reveal. He had become at last the perfect type of the artist, as described by Lanny in *Between Two Worlds:* an "anarchist" who "lives in the freedom of his own imagination, and represents the experimental element of life. If 'authority' should intervene and tell him what to think or to feel, the experiment would not be tried, the brain-child would be born dead."

Sinclair believed that he had achieved his artistic fulfillment in part because of Craig, just as he thought Meta had earlier failed him. In a striking instance of reaching back into his past, perhaps without even realizing it, he wrote to the Pasadena public library to verify the spelling and punctuation of a poem by Sir Walter Scott he wanted Lanny to quote:

> Maiden! A nameless life I lead,
> A nameless death I'll die;
> The fiend whose lantern lights the mead
> Were better mate than I!

In 1900, Sinclair had quoted the same warning to Meta, as he recounted in *Love's Pilgrimage.* Forty-two years later, in *Between Two Worlds,* Lanny thinks of the Scott poem as he reflects that there are two kinds of women. One is "the artist-soul whose cravings would never be satisfied," clearly a Meta-type—indeed, the female counterpart to himself. The other, just as clearly Sinclair's idealized version of Craig, is "the mother-soul who thought about what she could give to a man instead of what she could get." The latter "merges her life with" the man she loves. Elsewhere, Lanny says that insofar as love and marriage were concerned, "the most indispensable thing is intellectual harmony." Nietzsche was right, says Lanny: "The most important question for a man to consider is whether he's going to be bored by what the woman says to him at breakfast every morning; for that is what marriage comes down to."

Sinclair was immensely grateful to Craig for mothering and sustaining him for so many years, and he was willing to do whatever she thought would make her happier and healthier. In 1943, at her insistence, he agreed to move to Monrovia, a small town fifteen miles east of Pasadena. By 1949, when he had finished the last of the scheduled Lanny Budd books, he was devoting most of his time to caring for her, a task that would end only with her death in 1961.

The coming move to Monrovia, Sinclair wrote to David in October 1942, was entirely Craig's idea—not that he had any objection. Their old house had been stitched together twenty-five years earlier, out of shacks that were probably fifty years old at the time. He was too busy to keep it up properly, and couldn't find good help to do the work. Black widow spiders, silverfish, termites, and rats were infesting his stacks of papers and records and books. Mesquite and creosote bushes filled the gully over which the house perched, a fire hazard waiting to explode during the hot late-summer months. Pasadena itself no longer had much attraction. Wartime industrialization had brought prosperity back to southern California, but along with it came worsening smog and growing crime. The area around their home on Sunset was becoming predominantly black, which Sinclair and Craig both connected with an increased number of incidents of vandalism on their property.

The new house was a Spanish-Moorish-style two-story stucco dwelling, built in 1926. Craig, still alert to real estate bargains, had bought it for just $11,500—about $130,000 in today's currency. Smaller than the rambling Pasadena house, with only six rooms, it was solidly built on a steel frame and came with a large garage where Sinclair's papers would be secure, with enough yard room for his additional storage sheds. It was comfortably situated on the outskirts of town, on North Myrtle Avenue, next to a hill where no houses could be built, but within walking distance for Sinclair of the post office and library, his two essentials. Not long after they moved in, Craig had a high fence built around the property, which she seldom left and which few people ever visited.

David Sinclair was not among those few visitors. Father and son had fallen out politically before the war. They had also quarreled about Sinclair's effort, or lack of effort, to help David get a job, and David also resented his father's seeming indifference to his divorce from Bettina in 1939 and his marriage to Jean Weidman in April 1944. By that time, as the world war was about to enter its final year, the Sinclair wars were entering a new phase of hostilities. As usual, the combatants were on opposite sides of the continent; David and his father did not meet at all from 1934 until 1955, and there are several gaps of more than two years in their correspondence during this time.

Their political arguments had centered on what to do about Stalin's increasingly bloody repression in the Soviet Union and on America's role in the war. David had been horrified by Stalin's purges in 1937 and 1938 and wondered how his father could credit the confessions of men when they were obviously obtained through torture. Sinclair, who had brilliantly described in *Jimmie Higgins* how the bravest could be broken, said in March 1938 that he was "wholly unable to believe that those men would have confessed unless they were guilty . . . most Russian revolutionists stood the torture of the Czarist police for their faith, and they would do it today if the charges were frame-ups." (Even three years later, in *A World to Win,* Sinclair could coolly write, "if Stalin hadn't purged his pro-Nazi elements, including his generals, there wouldn't have been any Soviet Union at this moment.") After the treacherous truce between Hitler and Stalin in October 1939 freed Hitler to attack England, Sinclair told David, "It seems to me that Stalin has gained a tremendous diplomatic victory in having got his two deadliest enemies to fighting each other . . . for twenty years the British government has been doing everything in its power to overthrow the Soviets."

"I can understand a Russian citizen falling for Soviet propaganda," David replied, "but I see no excuse for you or anyone else in this country believing it." His neatly typed letter, three full single-spaced pages long, ended with this dramatic reproach: "It may be possible for you, like the locomotive of history, to follow the C.P. line through forced collectivization, the Moscow trials, the purges, collective security with British and French democratic imperialism, the appeasement of Germany, the 'diplomatic victory' over Poland, and now the Blitzkrieg in the Baltic, but it is too much for your socialist pupil." Taking a leaf from his father's book, David published his letter, with Sinclair's responses, in the socialist newspaper that had long published Sinclair's own columns and letters, *The Call.* Sinclair complained privately to David that he was greatly offended by this violation of his privacy. Publicly, he said he regarded the Russian invasion of Finland—the "Blitzkrieg in the Baltic"—as "the most painful public event in my lifetime." But he refused to condemn Stalin, and sounded cynical and callous in citing Talleyrand's comment on a needless execution ordered by Napoleon: "It is worse than a crime, it is a blunder."

Sinclair was much shrewder about Hitler than he was about Stalin, and his son the reverse. In September 1940, David asked his father to read "every word" of a Norman Thomas article opposing American entry into the European war. Sinclair said Thomas was living in a "fairy tale" and his argument was "pathetic"; the United States had as much chance of keeping the peace "as the man who finds himself at the bottom of a well with a hungry tiger." As late as September 1941, when Germany seemed close to conquering Great Britain, David agreed with the America First arguments against involving the United States in the European war. Sinclair insisted that "we have to fight because Hitler is what he is and because his system is predatory. . . . I do not see how anybody can fail to see this, and I can only guess the reason to be that you do not know as much about the Nazis as I do. A great many people think they know but they don't *really* know . . . because their badness is so completely unbelievable and because it is so cleverly combined with plausibility." A month later Sinclair wrote to say that none of the America First Committee's arguments impressed him: "You propose to sit back and let Hitler overcome first Russia and then Britain."

Pearl Harbor ended the Sinclairs' political disputes. It did not solve the problem that David had been wrestling with for several years, and which he thought his father should help him with: finding a job. Sinclair had given David enough money to live on for a time while he was working on his doctorate at Columbia, but only part-time jobs and research appointments were available in 1936 when David went on the academic job market. He seems not to have realized that Sinclair did ask a number of friends to help his son if they could, including Einstein at Princeton, J. B. Rhine at Duke, and Hamilton Holt at Rollins College. All replied cordially but said there were simply no jobs to be had. Holt added a note recalling how, as the editor of *The Independent,* he had published "My Cause" in 1903. "I have never forgotten that opening," Holt said—"I, Upton Sinclair, penniless rat."

David continued to look for work. Didn't his father have academic and political connections in California that he could exploit? Sinclair said the only physicist he knew locally was his bête noire from the Einstein days, Robert Millikan at Caltech, and "Millikan hates me." His political contacts were useless; though his former EPIC comrade Culbert Olson was now governor of California, he had been elected, Sinclair said, with the help of gambling and oil interests, and they no longer spoke. "You must understand," he said, "that I just stay in our garden and write novels."

In 1940, as Washington was gearing up for war, David was still living on research grants. When Sinclair said he thought David's socialist affiliation and his own notoriety would make it pointless to write letters for him to "Washington liberals," David exploded in anger. He agreed, sarcastically, that of course Sinclair could not recommend him: "In the first place you don't know anything about me. . . . The more I read your letter the more enraged and indignant I become. You really are the most incredibly self righteous man. . . . How on earth can I love any one who is so intolerant and self righteous and persists in treating me like a donkey?" But Sinclair should not worry about his reputation, David continued: "I wouldn't trust you to write to anyone about me. . . . I gave up trying to understand you in the days when I used to love you and worship you much too much for my own good. It didn't help me. You could only introduce me as 'your little boy' and always be very sparing and grudging of praise for me for fear it would spoil me. So now that I am fed up, I feel that I have nothing to lose but my chains. I really am fed up, I just can't stand your irrationality any longer. You make me afraid there is insanity in the family." Sinclair responded mildly, attaching a copy of a letter of recommendation for David that he had just sent to Harold Ickes.

David's troubles with his father were exacerbated by his bitter divorce from Bettina in 1939. He went through several years of psychoanalysis, and was on the verge of recovering his mental and emotional balance in January 1944 when he called his father to say that he was in Los Angeles and wanted to see him and Craig. Sinclair said no; a visit at that time would be inconvenient. A few days later he wrote to David, saying "your sudden and unexpected arrival" had caused him and Craig a serious problem. They were unable to see him, and he resented being put in the position of having to tell him this. Craig was so ill that she had even refused to see a nephew who was shipping out to the South Pacific, and she still resented the hurtful words of David and Betty in New York ten years earlier, during the occasion of the *Thunder Over Mexico* premiere. David had ignored the efforts Craig had made "through many painful years to take care of you." (David's marginal note: "Joke!") Consequently, "I am putting off any suggestion of our meeting." ("Polite, what?") "You know that you wrote me just about a year ago that you wished to be independent of me, and since then I have been adjusting my mind to that attitude." ("This hurts me more than it does you.")

A few months later, in April, David acquired both a job, with the Johns Manville company, and a new wife, Jean Weidman. Sinclair didn't reply to the wedding announcement. In December, David sent a Christmas card, saying he was "sorry not to have seen you" during his visit to Los Angeles. He thought, given Sinclair's long love of the violin, that his research project at Johns Manville, on "the cause and cure of automobile brake squeal," might be of interest: "strange as it seems," the squeal was "caused by the same physical process as the tones of a violin."

=====

Two continuing exceptions to Craig's ban on visitors were Martin Birnbaum and Cornelius Vanderbilt, Jr., always called Neil. Birnbaum frequently came to Pasadena on business—Henry Huntington was one of his patrons—and he later recalled with pleasure an evening in 1940 with Sinclair and Charlie Chaplin at Rob Wagner's house. Chaplin had just finished making his satire of Hitler, *The Great Dictator;* he delivered the "profound speech with which the picture comes to an end," and acted out several other scenes "with amazing liveliness."

What Birnbaum did not realize until Sinclair told him many years later was that Wagner and Chaplin thought he must be an agent in the pay of the

Nazis: his worldly sophistication, his command of German and French, and his accounts of moving easily through fascist Italy and Nazi Germany in search of art for his patrons were almost too good to be true.

Birnbaum's modest autobiography offers persuasive evidence that he was a trustworthy source for Sinclair. Neil Vanderbilt's stories of his escapades as a secret agent for President Roosevelt were even more enthralling than Birnbaum's, and Sinclair made ample use of them in the later Lanny Budd novels. The validity of Vanderbilt's stories, compared to Birnbaum's, was another matter. The respected Roosevelt biographer Frank Friedel reviewed Vanderbilt's 1959 autobiography as the "wildest concoction" of fantasies since Baron Munchausen, and he marveled, in a 1970 letter to Leon Harris, at Sinclair's gullibility in taking "every word of Vanderbilt's as received truth."

Born in 1898, Neil Vanderbilt was a great-grandson of "the Commodore," brought up in a mansion on Fifth Avenue near Craig's Gardner School for Young Ladies; when she was a student there in 1900 she saw him several times from a distance, attended by nursemaids and liveried servants, and wondered what kind of "fairy-tale" existence such a child might experience. By the early 1930s, Vanderbilt had a acquired a reputation as a skier, a sailor, and a playboy—and also as a pushover for women who wanted him for his money. (By 1963 he had been married six times.) On the less frivolous side, he was, at least occasionally, a working journalist; his articles about the politics and culture of Europe between the wars appeared frequently in *Liberty* magazine, edited by Sinclair's friend Fulton Oursler.

In the late 1930s, while Vanderbilt was making one of his periodic divorce sojourns in Reno, he thought he noticed an unusual influx of German ski instructors. He contacted President Roosevelt, who had known him since he was a boy, and was asked to stay in touch. FDR also reportedly sent Vanderbilt to check up on antiwar sympathies in Hollywood. Even before the war began, Vanderbilt said, he was an unofficial agent for Roosevelt in Europe. Hitler's chief propagandist, Joseph Goebbels, bugged his hotel room and ordered him out of Germany, saying, according to Vanderbilt, "If you were not a presidential agent, you would not be alive at this moment." Whereupon the secret agent hurried off to Budapest for a social call on his aunt, Gladys Vanderbilt Széchenyi.

Vanderbilt regaled Sinclair with stories like this for several years before the war began, but did not learn until January 1943 that he was one of the models for Lanny Budd. It was then that Sinclair told him that he planned to open the fifth novel in the series, *Presidential Agent,* with Lanny meeting FDR in 1937. Lanny was to "fall under his spell, and become a secret agent getting information for him in Europe." At the same time, he would try to "convince Roosevelt that our government was making a tragic blunder in turning Europe over to Fascism" by not vigorously opposing General Francisco Franco's efforts to topple the Loyalist government of Spain. Sinclair asked Vanderbilt to tell him what he could about Roosevelt, adding that "it might entertain you to scribble me some gossip on this and allied subjects." He also encouraged Vanderbilt to read the earlier books in the series, so that he would be able to see what Sinclair needed.

The episodes drawn from Vanderbilt's tales, artfully and extensively embroidered by Sinclair, are among the most entertaining in the Lanny Budd books. They are also the ones that critics used to disparage Lanny, with some cause, as a figure of fantasy—a d'Artagnan, a Superman, a Scarlet Pimpernel. But the truer point of literary reference was none of these, and it applied not to Lanny but to his creator. It was James Thurber's appealing fantasist, Walter Mitty, that famously henpecked little man who escapes the tedium of his lonely life by conjuring up wonderful adventures in which he is the hero—soldier, sportsman, surgeon, lover of beautiful women. It is unlikely that Sinclair read "The Secret Life of Walter Mitty," which came out in 1941, or that he would have seen himself in it. But there is no question that by 1943, when Lanny's adventures became more dazzling than ever, Sinclair's own life had become increasingly constrained. While Lanny dashed through countries and between continents, Craig's ill health kept Sinclair tightly tethered in a remote town where they knew nobody; he said later, in 1953, that he had not spent a night away from her side for fifteen years. He gave up tennis and quit playing the violin. His only amusement was to walk by himself to the local movie theater once or twice a week. He turned down all invitations to speak, including the one from John Burton, a Los Angeles radio station director, who urged him to remember the devoted thousands of followers who had supported him in his campaign. Wouldn't he come to the radio station just once to talk to them? Burton apologized for trying "to say what a genius should do with his time," but was sure of the "public applause" that such a talk would generate.

Nowhere is Sinclair's Mitty-like projection of himself into the character of Lanny Budd better observed than in his re-creation of two important men whom Sinclair had in fact met: Albert Einstein and Franklin D. Roosevelt. Lanny meets Einstein because FDR wants to send him to rescue a German scientist, and Lanny has to master enough nuclear physics in a few weeks to pass as an esteemed colleague of the man he must save. The great Einstein himself takes Lanny on as his very apt pupil. For relaxation they play Mozart duets on violin and piano (just as Sinclair and Meta had once done). Sinclair

admitted candidly that in real life his skills as a violinist were not up to letting him play a duet with Einstein. But Lanny is a pianist up to the challenge.
In a passage that suggests Sinclair's emotional sensitivity to music, as well as
a longing for companionship and a sad sense of the evanescence of life,
Lanny waxes lyrical: their playing was like skipping through a flower-
bedecked meadow, with "the sunlight strewing showers of golden fire"; then
you realize "that all this is going to die, and you grow very sorrowful, and
walk mournfully for a while . . . then the sun comes out again, and it is
springtime, and you realize that life renews itself," and "you rejoice in your
powers, the fact that you are equal to all emergencies, even to *allegro assai.*"

Roosevelt's relationship with Lanny is even more remarkable than Einstein's. In 1934, Sinclair had failed entirely in his effort to resist the famous
Roosevelt charm: he had been as giddy as a schoolgirl over his two-hour
chat with the president at Hyde Park. He was probably correct in saying that
with FDR's endorsement, he would have been elected governor. Instead,
the ruthlessly pragmatic Roosevelt had cast Sinclair adrift and condemned
him to defeat. Uncharacteristically, Sinclair harbored no lasting resentment
at what his more earnest supporters condemned as Roosevelt's betrayal,
agreeing that it had seemed necessary at the time. His first picture of FDR as
seen by Lanny resembles Sinclair's own impressions during the Hyde Park
visit. Lanny is struck by Roosevelt's big shoulders and physical strength, by
the indomitable will that had let him survive and, in a sense, to conquer
polio, and by his personal warmth. To Lanny as well as to Sinclair, Roosevelt
seems to be "a man genuinely interested in human beings and in what they
had to bring him." Lanny leaves their first meeting shaking his head and saying "By heck! I have fallen for the Roosevelt charm!"

Before long FDR, who had so easily resisted Sinclair, embraces Lanny,
not merely as a valued servant but as a friend, almost a blood brother. As
Lanny explains, they both "had grown up in comfort and near-luxury, never
knowing deprivation; both were generous by nature and dreamed of a kind-
lier world; but had met with disappointments and disillusionments, but
were stubborn and did not easily give up their dreams; now both were fight-
ing-mad in their hearts, but kept a smile on their lips because that was good
form, that was 'sporting.' Also, they both liked to talk, and were tempted to
ramble into the fields of philosophy and literature and what not." Roosevelt
even tells Lanny that he thinks of him as "another self, a self that had lived
abroad and knew all the people who were in the headlines there": " 'Tell me
about Hitler,' said the President; so Lanny described that strange portent,
half-genius, half-madman, who had managed to infect with his mental sickness a whole generation of German youth."

A boyish charm infuses Lanny's encounters with FDR, which Sinclair's dense matrix of solid facts and data makes more plausible than they may sound out of context—even such risible lines as "Tell me about Hitler." But the later Lanny Budd novels suffer, as does Lanny's credibility, not only from too much reliance on Vanderbilt's tales but on Sinclair's continuing fascination with spiritualism. Because the Nazis were notoriously susceptible to superstition and fraud, Sinclair's use of spiritualism does often serve as an effective plot device, especially in several scenes with Hitler and Rudolf Hess. But by the time the last of the originally planned Budd novels, *O Shepherd, Speak!,* appeared in 1949, Sinclair was losing control of his medium, so to speak. The "shepherd" is FDR, now dead but offering Lanny advice from beyond the grave. A longtime Sinclair friend and admirer, Albert Mordell, rightly shuddered at the passage in which Roosevelt's spirit, in Mordell's words, is "cracking jokes, giving way to spasms of laughter, apologizing for his agreement with Stalin at Yalta." Mordell had complained earlier to Sinclair about Lanny's spiritualist interests; he condemned this scene in print as "undoubtedly the prize piece of inanity in all of Sinclair's novels." Shaking his head, Mordell concluded that he and Sinclair's other admirers should be thankful for what they had that was great; they should say not, "What a noble mind is here overthrown," but "Look how masterly a noble mind can function, even when it is partly overthrown."

By 1953, when he resurrected his hero as an anti-communist Cold Warrior in *The Return of Lanny Budd,* many of Sinclair's readers on the left feared he had lurched rightward, like John Dos Passos and Max Eastman. The onetime apologist for Stalin now has Lanny realizing that the Russian leader is "more dangerous to the world than Hitler" because he's not hysterical or impatient, not a "blusterer and a fool." Remarkably, the first real violence to which Lanny is subjected, after more than twenty years of dangerous undercover work, occurs late in the last of his adventures, which is set in postwar Germany just before the Berlin Airlift. Charged with plotting to kill Stalin, Lanny is abducted by Soviet agents, taken to East Berlin, and tortured for more than a week before he is rescued—a gripping sequence that merits comparison with those basic Cold War texts, Arthur Koestler's *Darkness at Noon* and George Orwell's *1984.*

As was often the case with Sinclair, he was lucky (or astute) in the timing of his novel. Stalin died on March 7, 1953, and *The Return of Lanny Budd* was published in April. On April 28, Sinclair was the subject of a Voice of America broadcast. The old rebel was now an authorized and approved voice of the government—like Lanny, its agent: his "forthright portrayal of the seamier side of life [in *The Jungle*] naturally endeared him to the Communist Party," the text read. "But, with the Party's serpentine windings, Sinclair—independent thinker that he is—inevitably fell from favor. In 1948 [the] General Secretary of the Union of Soviet Writers named him among 'the finest writers, artists and scientists of the capitalist world.' Less than 12 months later, the *Literary Gazette* in Moscow was calling him a 'money-grubbing capitalist.' " Sinclair's sin was that he said "the leaders of Communism respect only force . . . therefore the free nations of the West have to unite economically and politically to defend themselves against this menace."

The radio text did not exaggerate Sinclair's feelings. American communists had slandered him in connection with the Eisenstein film, tried their best to sabotage his candidacy for governor, and maligned him for years as a "social Fascist." Craig hated them all, and both she and Sinclair ultimately ended their long friendship with Kate Gartz because of the older woman's insistence on following the party line. Lanny's voice is indistinguishable from Sinclair's when he says that the communist cause "is not the cause I believed in or ever could believe in. I was talking about social justice, brought about by honest means, by free and open discussion, and by the democratic process which we in America know and have practiced for centuries." Sounding like the Orwell of "Politics and the English Language," Lanny says the communists have "have taken up all the good words and poisoned them. You can't say 'liberal,' you can't say 'democratic,' you can't say 'people's,' you can't say 'workers' any more." The communists, Lanny has already warned his new patron, President Harry Truman, in *O Shepherd, Speak!,* are "the world's best propagandists because they put their whole minds on it, they have no doubts or scruples, and there are no shades in their ideas—everything is either white or black."

In a passage that shocked his old friends in the ACLU, Sinclair allows Lanny to wonder now "whether civil liberties should be extended to the enemies of civil liberties; to persons who were cynically and implacably determined to destroy the civil liberties of everybody in the world." Even more shocking was Lanny's decision to turn his half-sister Bess over to the FBI as a communist spy. Floyd Dell, still active on the left, saw more clearly than some of Sinclair's old admirers did that his novel was subtler than it appeared, though he warned Sinclair that "Nobody can be as right as you and Lanny are about everything." Dell wondered if Sinclair fully realized the corruption of the soul that spying, for whatever cause, entailed, making the spy into "a psychological monster and a potential criminal." He also worried

that Sinclair's preoccupation with communism had kept him from understanding "how wide and deep these fears and terroristic activities that are
called anti-Communism are in the U.S.A." He said "the zeal of anti-
Communism tends to corrupt the mind of writers into an anti-liberal and
anti-reform and anti-democratic fanaticism." But upon consideration, Dell
said, he was certain that Sinclair's "novel [is] uncorrupted in all these respects. You remain a civilized person, a liberal, and a scholar and a gentleman."

It is much clearer today than it was in 1953 that Sinclair was both correct
and courageous, though tardy, in his anti-communism, which Senator
Joseph McCarthy had come close to making intellectually disreputable. His
fictional treatment of the issue is measured and restrained by comparison
with some of his private remarks, which suggest fury deriving from a sense
of personal betrayal: "I have broken off all connections with the Soviet
Union and its supporters and all those who let themselves be duped by its
campaign of falsehood and treachery," he wrote to an acquaintance. "To me
the cold war is a hot war against the civilized world, and I have no patience
with those who support it. I cannot be interested to talk to them."

Personal betrayal of the most striking kind is suggested in a passage from
Sinclair's "Reds I Have Known," an unpublished book-length manuscript
completed in 1953. Reaching back more than half a century, Sinclair recalled
his friendship with young Hal Ware, the son of Ella Reeve—"Mother
Bloor"—his old comrade and investigative assistant with *The Jungle.* Hal was
then a teenager, living with his mother at Arden, and an avid tennis player.
He and Sinclair had "fought it out one hot summer afternoon" on the tennis court, and when Sinclair had won the championship Hal was "gracious
and friendly as always." The next day they had gone to jail together for violating the blue law against playing games on Sunday.

Sinclair ran into Hal once some years later in New York; Ware had been
to Russia and was raising money, supposedly to buy tractors for the collective farms there. Ella by that time had become a famous CP member, still a
"cheerful, nut-brown woman," constantly being arrested and joking with
the police as they carried her off to jail. After Roosevelt's election in 1932,
Ware had joined the New Deal's Agricultural Adjustment Administration,
or AAA. Sinclair did not know until the Alger Hiss spy case broke in 1947
that Hal Ware had died in an automobile accident in 1935. He was shocked
and distressed to learn that Ware, operating through the AAA, had been the
leader of a particularly important communist underground cell in Washington. Ware's assignment from Moscow was to form a network of communist
agents whose members could rise through the ranks of the government in

many different agencies. His success may be measured by the fact that it was Hal Ware who introduced Alger Hiss to Whittaker Chambers and who thereby touched off, a decade after his own death, one of the most notorious spy scandals of the century.

"I read of 'Mother' Bloor's being quoted as expressing her pride in Hal's work and in the number of 'his boys' he had left behind him to carry it on," Sinclair writes with horror. He imagines engaging his old friends in a "mental argument," still thinking of them as they had been—Ella "lively and humorous," Hal "quiet and kind." Don't they understand that the South Koreans did not attack the North? Or that "Russia is now in the hands of power-mad and cynical men . . . afraid to let any portion of [the world] remain free, because the speaking of the truth inevitably means the death of the lie?" But he knows he can make no headway with "this pair"; they have become fanatic devotees of a new religion. He can "no longer picture this mother as being humorous, or this son as being kind." They are now the enemy, intriguing against their native land.

=====

Despite its timeliness, *The Return of Lanny Budd* did not sell well. Also timely but unsuccessful were an earlier short play, in 1948, about the threat of nuclear annihilation, *A Giant's Strength,* and a longer play in 1950 about the growing arms race, *The Enemy Had It Too.* An anomalous parody of Samuel Richardson's *Pamela* called *Another Pamela* was published by Viking in 1950, of interest only for its portrayal of Kate Gartz in the form of Pamela's philanthropist employer, Mrs. Harnest. In 1952 Sinclair had returned to a favorite subject, the idea of Jesus as social activist, in *A Personal Jesus,* and in 1954 he pursued his interest in religious themes with a parable called *What Didymus Did.* As this work, which recalls the earlier *They Call Me Carpenter,* suggests, Sinclair was finally written out. Only *The Cup of Fury* found an audience; a return to his lifelong hatred of alcohol and how it destroyed Jack London and other writers of his acquaintance, most recently Sinclair Lewis (who died in 1951), it was published in 1956 by a small religious press.

Sinclair's continued interest in religion was strongly echoed by Craig. Writing to her sister Dollie some time in her fifties, Craig said that life was "not *ever* the delightful thing we all imagine it is when we are young. I have never known a really happy person who had passed the age of fifty! By that time the hopes of youth had turned into the 'realities' of life—and hopes are thus crushed, one by one." But she had found God, and believed that "life can become sweet again, even after we have become maimed and scarred by the disappointments of the years." In succeeding years, she turned to Christian Science and wrote increasingly in her many long letters to friends about how she despised "materialism." She had fallen out with Kate Gartz, she wrote after her old friend's death in 1949 at the age of eighty-four, first because of her support of communism and then because she "clutched at wealth" and failed to hear "the voice of intuition." This "materialism was her undoing."

In another undated letter to Dollie, Craig speculated about what she called "intangibles," saying that they had to be unsatisfactorily "expressed in the vocabulary of *things* since no one has ever devised a universal vocabulary for the philosophers, theologians and psychologists. Each philosopher and each theologian invents his own makeshift language. The psychologists have been ruined by Freudian terms which are so vivid, but so utterly inadequate and misleading, that they seem to have given up in all directions and adopted as final, the theory of Freud along with his popular phrases. But there is left us still the old device of symbols, and of art-forms. I like neither, because both are primitive for primitives! But they are the last resort of those who wish to convey ideas of intangibles."

Craig's religious quest was intensified by her failing health—which, previously at least partly imagined, was real enough by the mid-1940s. She had an enlarged heart and found breathing increasingly difficult. In early 1950, impelled by the spreading smog, she and Sinclair had rented out the house in Monrovia and moved to the desert town of Corona, near Riverside. They chose Corona because Craig's brother Hunter had moved to Riverside in 1948 with his wife, Sally, and their son, Leftwich, to open an automobile insurance business. He had done so in part because his sister persuaded him that she and Sinclair were growing too old to look after themselves properly, and he spent at least a few days every month in Monrovia to make sure their bills were paid and the house maintained properly. Later that same year, however, Hunter moved to Phoenix, and Craig and Sinclair bought a tiny house in the nearby suburb of Buckeye. They returned to Monrovia to be closer to Craig's doctors in late February 1954, by which time she needed Sinclair's constant attention.

Sinclair described the emergency that had prompted their return in typical fashion—by means of a newspaper article on the benefits of a rice diet that took him back to the days of *Good Health, and How We Won It,* and his advice columns for Haldeman-Julius's *New Appeal.* He had rushed to Craig's side in the middle of the night, he wrote, when he heard her moaning, unable to breathe, her lungs full of fluid. Surviving nonetheless, she returned home with him to Monrovia, where they both took up the rice diet recommended by her doctor, "the strangest menu ever followed" but one that kept her alive. Three times daily for nine months, Sinclair put a half cup of white rice and three cups of distilled water into a double boiler, cooked it for two hours, and served it without butter or salt—nothing else but fruit juice and ripe fruit. The diet, he assured his readers, "lifted her out of the grave." No trace of fluid remained in his wife's lungs or her ankles, she slept through the night, her enlarged heart had declined in size, and the "auricular fibrillation" that the doctors said was incurable had disappeared. But Sinclair warned readers to check with their doctors before trying his diet because some people are "salt-losers" and could be endangered by it.

In order to ease Craig's mind and to keep her occupied during the mid-1950s, and even earlier, Sinclair helped her write her autobiography. It was published by Crown in 1957 with the title *Southern Belle,* which she reportedly disliked. The degree to which Sinclair helped with this work is unclear, though his earlier biographer Leon Harris believed he wrote it all himself. If he did, he left some tantalizing false trails. He not only confused the location of Helicon Hall, placing it near Princeton; he also let stand Craig's description of Thomas Mann, who had so graciously praised his books and whose son Klaus he had helped to find a job in Washington, as a "narrow and austere" man whose "chilly grey-blue eyes seemed wholly absorbed in something inside himself." In the first instance Sinclair, now nearly eighty years old, let slip an error he could not have made. In the second, he may have been resisting the chance to censor his wife's opinion when it varied from his own, in keeping with his long-avowed feminism. He would hardly have described Mann in this fashion himself.

It is true that Craig wrote to Martin Birnbaum in 1946 to say that "Upton is really putting his heart & soul" into writing her life as the "lovely, noble, brilliant lady" he believed she was. And much of the manuscript is in his handwriting. But Sinclair said he merely transcribed his wife's thoughts while she lay in bed and edited them as needed. Craig herself said at several different times over the years that she had written most of the book herself. Her draft of nearly a thousand pages at the Honnold Library in Claremont is called "My Husband, Upton Sinclair." What probably happened was that Sinclair's strong personality had been deeply absorbed by his wife many years earlier and that, like many older couples, they mirrored each other's thoughts. With Craig, this process began early in her marriage. In 1950 she came upon a letter that she had written in 1914, when Sinclair was in Colorado: "It sounds as if Upton had written it," she told a friend, "so completely had I dedicated myself, in his manner, to keep on with it until victory."

More interesting than speculations about the authorship of *Southern Belle* are the places where Sinclair edited Craig's words, particularly the following passage on his "iron will." Craig had written

> I decided that he had an iron will. But an iron will was a dangerous thing. Dictators had it. Was he a dictator? Every child is. Only a few men are. But he was not invulnerable—I could always break his will! I seldom did, however. It took a mighty effort, and I was seldom equal to it. After all, a sunny disposition might be more desirable to live with than a broken spirit. He never thought of death with sadness, as I did.

Sinclair's revision, after cross-outs and insertions, reads as follows:

> I had discovered that he had an iron will. But an iron will is a dangerous thing. Dictators had it. Was he a dictator? Some people thought he was; I knew he was not. But whatever the magic that kept his sunny disposition supreme over disaster, it was a boon to me. He never seemed to think of death, as I did.

The tense changes are trivial, but the firmer denial that he was a dictator—which echoes Mencken's charge some years earlier—is not. Nor is the deletion of Craig's doubtful assertion that she could break his will. Although her influence was great in the case of David, Sinclair had ignored her objections when he ran for governor and in taking so long to extricate them from the Sergei Eisenstein venture. Most important of all the changes is the elevation of "sunny disposition" to the most prominent concept besides "iron will" in the sentence, allowing Sinclair to avoid all thoughts of death entirely, not just those associated with sadness. In a word, he re-created himself through an act of will to *become* the image that he thought best suited him, whatever he thought his original nature—that of the resentful "penniless rat"?—might have been. He was living proof that human nature could change, or be changed, because he had done it to himself.

A touching picture of Sinclair as a "good and most lovable man" is that of Van Wyck Brooks, who visited the house in Monrovia one afternoon in 1956. "In a time of great talents with small hearts," it seemed to Brooks that Sinclair had "a particularly large one. He stood at the gate of his big Spanish house with the sun beating down—there were no trees, there was nothing to shade it—and, on this bright spring day, he received me in a darkened room with all the window-shades closely drawn. Deeply shrouded electric lamps, with bowls of pink camellias, stood in every corner of the room, while his wife, who was scarcely able to move, so frail her heart was, sat in the semi-darkness like a heroine of Poe."

In writing the account of his visit, Brooks speculated on the isolation of the modern American writer, so unlike the close fellowship of nineteenth-century New England. These days, writers were "as solitary as the rhinoceros roaming the veldt or as lone wolves drifting about a wilderness." Few were as solitary as Upton Sinclair, caring for his dying wife in a placid village near the edge of the continent, far from the great literary centers of New York and Chicago where he had first made his mark as a writer.

In early October 1960, David Sinclair was once again in Los Angeles on a business trip, and Sinclair said, once again, that it would not be convenient for him to visit. But the circumstances of the refusal were different from those in 1943. In 1949 David had written to tell his father and stepmother that he was living through a rough period with his daughter, Diana, then sixteen. History was repeating itself, he said; he understood better now what they had experienced and apologized for causing them anxiety. David was being unduly generous, but the tactic worked. Warm letters from Sinclair began to flow, including one in which he told David "how impressed" he was "by having a son whose work is found worthy of publication by the Atomic Energy Commission."

Jean Sinclair, who had instigated the reconciliation, traveled with David to meet the Sinclairs for the first time in 1955. David had not seen either his father or Craig for more than twenty years. Jean was struck by Craig's egotism: the first thing she said was "Now, David, I want you to tell me all about physics. I understand physics, you know." But she also thought that Craig must have mellowed a bit in her later years—or perhaps she just didn't want to "go down in history as a witch." At any rate, Sinclair's assurance to David that he would like to see him on his 1960 visit but could not seemed sincere this time. Craig "knows she is going," and clings to him "with the most pitiful cries," he said. Sounding rather like the self-centered John Marcher in Henry James's "The Beast in the Jungle," Sinclair added, "I can't bear to think of what will become of me—alone." But his deep commiseration for his wife was unmistakable: "Her fears dominate her whole being. I am, as you know, bound to her by unbreakable ties, and if I had not done everything possible to help her, I could not bear to know it."

On March 13, 1961, Craig dictated a long letter, which Sinclair presumably typed, to Dick Otto and his wife, Shirley. She gratefully declined the Ottos' offer to come down from Santa Barbara and stay with them. She told an amusing story of how, when her feet were cold the previous night, "Upton got up and got a hot water bottle and put it in the bed with me, and pretty soon I was lying in a bathtub full of water . . . and there I was drowning when Upton discovered my plight." He was so distressed that he made himself sick rushing around in a panic. He grabbed the offending water bottle, still half-full, and put it down on the hall floor, then stripped the blankets from Craig's bed and threw them on top of the leaking bottle in the hallway, soaking them as well as her bed. By the time he went downstairs to find some more blankets and remade Craig's bed he was so exhausted that he lay down on the bed beside her and groaned, close to tears. "Go and call Lefty," Craig said. (Leftwich Kimbrough, Hunter's son, was then a young Marine officer stationed at nearby Twentynine Palms who stayed with them when he could.) "I'm sure he'll come in and help us instead of your breaking your back." "No," Sinclair said; he wouldn't leave her. Somehow they got through the night. But she really was better now, Craig concluded. She hoped to get back soon to "normalcy. Excuse me, President Harding."

Ten weeks later Mary Craig Kimbrough Sinclair died at the age of seventy-eight. The date of death was April 26, 1961, five days after she and her husband quietly observed their forty-eighth wedding anniversary.

THE SAGE

(October 1961–November 1968)

U pton Sinclair admired for its stoic dignity Goethe's assurance that "everything on the earth can be endured," but he came to doubt its truth after Craig's death. He felt "a sense of desolation beyond my power to describe." For seven years, since her first heart attack, Craig had been telling him that he could not survive on his own—"Oh, my Uppie, what will you do? What will become of you?"—and she had been right. She had also urged him to be careful in his search for a wife to take care of him, and not to get "hooked by some floozie."

Sinclair's tone as he recounts Craig's counsel in his 1962 *Autobiography,* which updated his earlier *American Outpost,* is once again deceptively sanguine, set not by the admission of "desolation" but by his claim to have been unclear on the concept of "floozies." In actual fact, his state of dejection during the months after Craig's death suggests Coleridge's ode:

> A grief without a pang, void, dark, and drear,
> A stifled, drowsy, unimpassioned grief,
> Which finds no natural outlet, no relief,
>   In word, or sigh, or tear—

Desperately lonely, Sinclair proposed marriage, unsuccessfully, to several women; he even proposed by mail to one woman whom he had never met, and whom he asked for a picture of herself. He was rescued after a few unutterably bleak months by a poet more cheerful than Coleridge, the humorist Richard Armour, and his wife, Kathleen. Armour was an English professor at Scripps College, a respected expert on Chaucer, who had met Sinclair a few years earlier. In addition to limericks, Armour wrote punning mock-histories such as *It All Started with Columbus* ("The journey over the

Oregon trail took several months. The plains were crossed in wagon trains or caravans, and the streams were crossed in Fords"). Sinclair had tried his own hand at whimsy in a tribute to his new friend: "And if you find that I'm a charmer / You'll know that I've been reading Armour."

According to Armour, Sinclair said he was "still capable of being a husband." He placed his order specifically: "Get me someone who's literate, and get me a Democrat." Through the Armours, Sinclair met Mary Elizabeth Willis, the recently widowed sister of Frederick Hard, the president of Scripps College. Both Sinclair and Mrs. Willis were invited to a party at the Armours' house in Claremont. Sinclair was chatting with Kathleen Armour. He had not yet been introduced to May, as she was known, a jolly, plump woman with horn-rimmed spectacles and a deep southern drawl. She sat down on a sofa that was covered with a treacherously smooth fabric and slid to the floor, holding her whiskey and soda aloft like the Statue of Liberty. Unembarrassed, she burst into laughter. Mrs. Armour nudged the famous teetotaler Upton Sinclair vigorously and said, "That's the woman for you."

Before the evening had ended, Sinclair later said, he asked Mrs. Willis to marry him. She said, " 'Oh, Mr. Sinclair, you aren't serious. I hardly know you.' And I said to her, 'but you will and I want you to think it over.' " About a week later, "she told me she had thought it over and she would accept. And so we got married." Sinclair was eighty-three and May was seventy-nine when they were married on October 16, 1961, a little less than six months after Craig died.

Perhaps the keenest insight into the contrast in Upton Sinclair's life before Craig's death and after his marriage to May Willis is provided by Ronald Gottesman. In 1960, Gottesman was a graduate student at Indiana University. He had chosen Sinclair as the subject for his dissertation, to be based on the vast collection of papers and books that Sinclair had sold to Indiana's Lilly Library in 1957 for $50,000. (Sinclair had previously offered his collection to the Huntington Library in Pasadena—which turned it down, he said, because former President Herbert Hoover was on the board of trustees and vetoed the purchase of an old socialist's papers.)

In the late summer of 1960 Gottesman flew to Los Angeles from Indianapolis to meet, for the first time, the man to whom he was devoting several years of his life. Sinclair had sent Gottesman his telephone number, with the warning not to release it to anyone else because his wife was still afraid that he was marked for assassination, and told him to call when he got to the airport. Gottesman did as instructed and heard a querulous woman's voice demanding to know what he wanted. The next and last sound he heard was a dial tone. Repeated efforts to call back were fruitless. He rented a car and drove to Monrovia, where he stood outside the locked gate of the house on Myrtle Avenue. He called out but received no response, though he thought he caught a fleeting glimpse of a figure behind an upstairs window curtain. A neighbor suggested that he might wait around and catch Sinclair on one of his walks to the post office. The local Western Union clerk laughed when Gottesman tried to send a telegram to Sinclair, telling him to save his money and do what they did: tie his message around a rock and throw it over the fence.

All efforts failing, Gottesman spent a day examining the collection of Sinclair's work that his physician, Elmer Belt, had donated to Occidental College, and returned to Bloomington without ever meeting the man he had come so far to see. But on his next visit, in January 1963, the new Mrs. Sinclair was Gottesman's willing hostess. Craig's camellias were long gone, as were the heavy velvet curtains and the gloom that had led Van Wyck Brooks to see in Craig a character out of Edgar Allan Poe. The room was flooded with sunlight as the young scholar sat down to describe his project, a fully annotated description of Sinclair's publications through 1932. May asked him what he would like to drink. Knowing Sinclair's aversion to alcohol, Gottesman replied that whatever she was having would be fine with him. "None of that, young man," May admonished him. "What are you going to drink?" Then she took pity on him, and said, "I'm having a margarita!"

In the days that followed, Sinclair and May showed Gottesman around Pasadena and Los Angeles. Sinclair zipped along the freeways in his pink Nash Rambler at speeds approximating his age. He always assumed he had the right of way, blithely entering and exiting lanes without bothering to look for traffic. Passing through the San Gabriel Mountains one day on a narrow two-lane road, Gottesman held on for dear life as Sinclair careened into turns, while May serenely assured him that no matter how many times she told her impetuous husband to drive normally, it had no effect. At one point Sinclair pulled to a quick stop, ran into a roadside store, and came back with two Hershey bars—a radical departure from his customary diet of rice and fruit. One bar was for him, he said; he needed an energy boost. May and Gottesman could split the other.

Frank Harris had said once that he wanted Sinclair, "this Emersonian," to "fall desperately in love," to be "intoxicated with the heady fragrance of love." Sinclair was not seeking this kind of romantic love when he married May Willis, but he found something even more valuable, almost a literal rejuvenation. Sinclair had said that he knew not a soul in Monrovia after living there for twenty years, but May was as gregarious as Craig had been solitary. She vowed repeatedly to "put the 'social' in 'socialism,' the 'sin' in 'Sinclair,' and the 'rove' in 'Monrovia.' " She made her shabby husband buy a new suit, saying he could consider the cost a donation to the garment workers' union, and sent him to the liquor store to buy her the bourbon and tequila and scotch she required for her evening libations—thereby innocently setting off the rumor that the old teetotaler had succumbed to drink in his dotage.

Sinclair had spent eighty years coping with three neurotic women, beginning with his mother. Now he enjoyed the uninhibited laughter of what George Bernard Shaw would have called a life force, and he behaved like a little boy released from after-school detention. A former antagonist at the now friendly *Los Angeles Times,* Ed Ainsworth, described a library event in Monrovia in November 1961, when Sinclair introduced Dick Armour as the main speaker. After a gracious testimonial, Sinclair "electrified the audience by nimbly leaping down four feet from the stage" to take a seat in the front row for Armour's talk. On another occasion, Sinclair wrote to David and Jean, his "blessed children," to describe a "wondrous" Christmas party he had attended with May "at a millionaire's home in the hills." They listened to "organ and piano and I ate Mexican food [and] I sang Adeste Fideles in Latin and shook the ceiling."

The man who had so jealously guarded his time, spending almost every waking moment on his work, now told David, "I'm discovering luxury." He and May were taking vacations together, and they spent endless hours playing Scrabble. Competitive as ever (and as meticulous about keeping records), he noted by early 1963 that they had played 890 games. Of the 100,000 points accumulated so far, May was ahead by 300, but he had just made his "highest score ever, 410!"

But Sinclair had not abandoned his intellectual interests, either during Craig's illness or after his remarriage. In the mid-1950s he had exchanged several friendly letters with Carl Jung as a result of his book *A Personal Jesus,* and Albert Camus wrote to thank Sinclair for the copy of his play about Cicero, and to say that he might be able to stage it in Paris; the letter arrived shortly before the French author's untimely death in an auto accident in January 1960. Sinclair also kept up his efforts to understand his son's scientific work, which gave him great pride—particularly David's patented device for making air pollution particles visible, called the Sinclair Phoenix Smoke Photometer.

With the publication of his *Autobiography* in 1962, Sinclair found himself once again in the public eye. His old fans were happy to read that he had survived his difficult years, and a new generation of college students was just beginning to discover that they had in their midst a kindred spirit who was born only thirteen years after the end of the Civil War. Sinclair's new freedom of movement and revived popularity coincided with the wave of idealism sweeping the campuses in the early 1960s, following the election of John F. Kennedy as president. His vast range of experience and his storytelling genius made him a popular attraction on college campuses, where the presidents and deans and department heads he had once castigated so vigorously now took him to lunch before he spoke to their students. "Hard to believe!" he marveled: "I'm getting respectable."

In early October 1963, Sinclair advised David Randall, the director of the Lilly Library, that he could not provide him with an advance copy of the speech he was to give there later in the month. He had never written out a speech, he said; it took all the life out of it. He did have a title, though: "Changing America and What Will Happen to You if You Try."

The occasion for Sinclair's visit to Bloomington in mid-October was the dedication of his collection at the Lilly Library, a handsome limestone building adjacent to the auditorium at the heart of the Indiana University campus. Arranged by Randall with the active assistance of Ron Gottesman, the celebration of the old radical's career in the conservative heartland had prompted a concerned letter from the chairman of the Lilly Foundation to Randall. The chain-smoking, hard-charging librarian, who had put the Lilly Library on the educational map with his acquisitions during the past seven years, ignored the complaint, secure in the support of IU's respected president, Herman Wells.

Sinclair reveled in his three-day stay in Indiana. He shook his head in amazement as he viewed the display of his books, letters, and posters that filled some forty cases in the Lilly Library, mildly protesting that "it seems very egotistical to be looking at them." He charmed Ron Gottesman's English class by reading a humorous love poem that he had written as a boy. And he entertained a group of reporters with his opinions on the current political scene: President Kennedy was doing a fine job, the Martin Luther King speech on the mall in Washington was "the most wonderful thing I've seen in years," and Barry Goldwater was alternately horrifying and comic, a fascist but an amiable man, and "one of the most amusing spectacles" on the current scene.

At the banquet in his honor, Sinclair politely refused the roast beef that was placed before him, dining instead on cold rice in a silver bowl that he always carried with him.

Sinclair wrote the following week to Edward Allatt, an English admirer and collector of his work, that he had been pleased and moved by his reception in Bloomington—and gratified by the huge crowd that had come to hear his talk on Saturday night. The hall was "packed to the doors," he said: "They told me that only two other persons had ever filled it—Eleanor Roosevelt and some comedian whose name I have forgotten." (The "comedian" was the actor Charles Laughton.)

Sinclair made only a few more college appearances following his visit to Indiana. He took particular pleasure in the invitation to speak in early November at his alma mater, now called the City University of New York. Edgar Johnson, the eminent Dickens biographer who was then the chairman of the English Department at CUNY, wrote to Sinclair that he was delighted to have the honor of hosting such a distinguished man of letters. Johnson recalled fondly his early appreciation of Sinclair's "slashing" attacks on "Nicholas Miraculous" at Columbia and the enthusiastic reaction of his students when he assigned *Mammonart* and *Money Writes!* He also wanted Sinclair to know, Johnson said, that he remained a "devoted follower" of Lanny Budd's adventures.

═══

In the few years that remained to him, Sinclair met twice with his third president, Lyndon Johnson. The first time was as a luncheon guest with May at the White House; the second was when Johnson signed the new Wholesome Meat Act of 1967 and acknowledged Sinclair's contribution to the original Pure Food legislation six decades earlier. Among the guests was Ralph Nader, newly famous for his attack on the automobile industry, *Unsafe at Any Speed*. Acknowledging Sinclair's influence and implicitly declaring himself his heir, Nader said later that "two historic consumer ages" were meeting on that day.

On December 18, 1967, Sinclair's third wife died, and he was once again alone. Thanks largely to May, however, Sinclair did not have to end his days in despairing isolation, as Meta had long ago threatened he would because of his selfish nature. "Say all the loving things that are in your heart," May had admonished him with regard to his son, and Sinclair had done his best. David and Jean had visited the Monrovia home more than once, and in 1966 Sinclair and May moved to an apartment in suburban Washington, D.C., to be closer to both of their families. Sometimes Sinclair's old vanity shone through, as when he encouraged David to write his memoirs, reminding him that "your beginning became a famous event—the birth scene in *Love's Pilgrimage*." More seriously, in what amounted to an emotional unbuttoning for this Victorian father, formerly so remote and neglectful, he assured

David that he had been "a dear and devoted son" for his entire life, and had "done nothing wrong that I know of. Quite a record."

David and Jean brought Sinclair after May's death to a small nursing home in Bound Brook, New Jersey, just a mile from their house in Martinsville. In October 1968, David wrote to David Randall at the Lilly that his father was doing "amazingly well." Though ill with diabetes and other ailments of extreme old age, Sinclair still occasionally dictated responses to the letters that continued to come to him, and he enjoyed drives through the autumn foliage with David and Jean.

Upton Sinclair died on December 18, 1968, two months into his ninety-first year. He was buried in Rock Creek Cemetery, not far from the nation's heart in Washington. The obituaries, long since prepared, must have been easy to write, for few men have been so successful in their ambitions for fame for so long, and from such an early age. He left behind remarkably revealing accounts of himself, not just in his two autobiographies but in his various novels and nonfiction books such as *The Brass Check, Money Writes!,* and *I, Governor.* He passed through many clearly marked stages during his ninety years, as suggested by the chapter titles of this book—from "Penniless Rat" to "Man of Letters" to "Sage." His successes were a matter of record. They included the role of *The Jungle* in bringing about legislation to cure the ills he described, the forming of the Intercollegiate Socialist Society and the Southern California branch of the ACLU, the enlivening effect of his EPIC campaign for governor upon the political scene in California, and his Pulitzer Prize. Finally, he knew virtually everyone of importance in the intellectual and political circles of Europe and America for half a century—or they knew him—and many of them were still alive to offer their observations on his passing.

The consistent theme of commentary on Sinclair's death was admiration for his character, linked with wonder that one man could have done so much. As a writer, it was widely acknowledged, Sinclair was energetic, principled, and humane—and seriously flawed: he wrote too much, and often with insufficient care, for an audience that was more interested in his message than his art. Apart from sections of his most sensational novel, *The Jungle,* Sinclair by 1968 had virtually disappeared from American literary anthologies, and most of his commercially published books were out of print, even the once popular Lanny Budd novels. The settled critical judgment then and now is that Sinclair's great gifts might have resulted, after his early success with *The Jungle,* in equally strong but more artful novels: many clear echoes of classics like *The Sea-Wolf, Sister Carrie, Babbitt,* and *The Grapes of Wrath* resound through his works. Such was not the case. *Oil!* and *Boston* were good novels, but not great. Nor did Sinclair's late-in-life renunciation of propaganda in the Lanny Budd books rehabilitate him in the eyes of the literary establishment. Despite the encomiums of Shaw and Mann, among many others, Sinclair's books were dismissed by the academy as too popular, too old-fashioned, and too resistant to the tools of literary criticism to be considered as works of art.

These objections are valid, but they are overstated and they miss the point. They are overstated because they focus on the poorer examples of Sinclair's writing instead of the better ones, as this book has tried to do. And they are beside the point because they ignore Sinclair's effort to reach out to an audience of less well-educated readers without talking down to them, an effort in which he was remarkably successful.

A more pertinent critique of Sinclair's career, one seldom heard, might have questioned the wisdom of devoting most of his life to a goal that never stood a chance of being reached in the United States—socialism—because its premise, the essential iniquity of capitalism, was one that most Americans would never share.

But that objection too would miss the point. Socialism, whatever its other faults or merits might be, served Sinclair very well indeed. He knew that he was not naturally "sweet and kind." He was not introspective—unusual for a writer—but he was self-centered and rigidly intolerant of frailty in others. His genial public image is often belied by the private self revealed in his letters and in his books, right up to the end of his life. His fundamental nature remained that of the driven artist. Even after he became a socialist reformer, he was largely responsible for the failure of his first marriage and for the decades of estrangement from his son during his second. He wrote so often about reenacting Christ's temptation in the wilderness that the temptations, though resisted, must have been real for him.

What saved Sinclair—what made him, in the end, a happy and contented man—was his conversion from the religion of art to the religion of socialism, which he called the religion of humanity. The religion of art is essentially selfish, at least as it is usually conceived of today. Socialism, for Sinclair, was essentially selfless. It allowed him to make himself into a better person, and to do the work that would bring him fulfillment.

The true significance of Sinclair's often derided puritanism finally becomes apparent when viewed in the light of his socialism. He was a puritan in the sense of Bunyan's Christian, searching for the true path to salvation. Socialism gave him that path. He was also a Romantic idealist who lived as though the journey, not the destination, was what mattered.

Finally, as a man born in the last quarter of the nineteenth century, Sinclair was a proper Victorian who had absorbed two key guiding principles of that earnest period. These related to work and to duty, which were often linked, and were best expressed in one of Sinclair's favorite poems, Tennyson's "Ulysses." In his 1911 novel, *Love's Pilgrimage,* Sinclair cited "Ulysses" in defining the "heroic life" as one of striving against great difficulties for "the good of all." In 1968 Sinclair would have been justified in citing Tennyson once again, as Ulysses thinks back on his life:

> Much have I seen and known; cities of men
> And manners, climates, councils, governments,
> Myself not least, but honour'd of them all. . . .

And yet Ulysses knows

> How dull it is to pause, to make an end,
> To rust unburnish'd, not to shine in use!
> As tho' to breathe were life!

Let this, then, be the final word on Upton Sinclair: that he lived a heroic life, on his own terms, and that he shone "in use."

ACKNOWLEDGMENTS

For access to their collections, I am grateful to the following libraries:

Claremont Colleges, Honnold Library: Jerry Voorhis, Richard Armour, Mary Craig Sinclair Papers
Huntington Library: Jack London Papers
Indiana University, Lilly Library: Leon Harris, David Anton Randall, Upton Sinclair, and Meta Sinclair Stone Collections
Occidental College: Elmer Belt Collection
Southern Illinois University, Morris Library: Edith Summers Kelley Papers
University of California at Berkeley, the Bancroft Library: Fay Blake EPIC interviews
University of California at Los Angeles, Special Collections, Research Library: Reuben Borough Papers
Wayne State University, Archives of Labor and Urban Affairs: John and Phyllis Collier Collection

For their assistance in obtaining interlibrary loans and purchases of dissertations and other materials, my special thanks to Susan Curzon, Doris Helfer, Marcia Henry, and Ann Perkins at the Oviatt Library, California State University, Northridge.

My debt to the Lilly Library is great indeed. An Everett Helm Visiting Fellowship helped me do my research there in 2003. Breon Mitchell, director of the Lilly Library, and his helpful staff, especially Becky Cape, Saundra Taylor, Anthony Tedeschi, and Joel Silver, made my two summer visits to Indiana both rewarding and pleasant. Upton Sinclair chose wisely in the final resting place for his treasured archives.

I am grateful for their comments on several chapters while they were in draft form to my friends Peter Brier, Barbara Kelly, and especially John Broesamle, a historian by training and an editor by instinct who read and commented usefully on every draft of every chapter. My greatest debt is to John Ahouse, who not only shared his knowledge of Sinclair's life and works with me but entrusted me with his large personal collection of primary and secondary materials, including valuable first editions of Sinclair's works, vastly expediting my research efforts. He also read the manuscript in its various stages with a searching and critical eye, saving me from errors of fact, judgment, and even taste. Not a week passed without an e-mail about a related book, a forgotten fact, a suggested approach. Between John Ahouse, librarian and literary scholar, and John Broesamle, historian—John A and John B, as I came to think of them—I may have done justice to Sinclair; if I haven't, it's not their fault.

At Random House, Bob Loomis provided me with editorial guidance that was gentle but firm and greatly appreciated, as were the thoughtful suggestions of Dana Isaacson. Finally, my thanks to Deborah Grosvenor, my agent, for her wise counsel.

NOTES

Sources and Documentation

I am grateful for the insights and information provided by my interviews with Ronald Gottesman, Leftwich Kimbrough, the late Julian "Bud" Lesser, and Mrs. Shirley Otto.

The dissertations, monographs, articles, and books used in writing this book are acknowledged in my notes, but several deserve special mention, in particular Ronald Gottesman's dissertation, "Upton Sinclair: An Annotated Bibliographical Catalogue, 1894–1932," and John Ahouse's *Upton Sinclair: A Descriptive, Annotated Bibliography,* both models of humane scholarship. For specific topics, I was particularly grateful for Margaret Ann Brown's dissertation, "Not Your Usual Boardinghouse Types: Upton Sinclair's Helicon Home Colony, 1906–1907"; William Brevda's *Harry Kemp: The Last Bohemian;* Harry M. Geduld and Ronald Gottesman's *Sergei Eisenstein and Upton Sinclair: The Making and Unmaking of Que Viva Mexico!;* Greg Mitchell's *The Campaign of the Century;* and James Michael Riherd's dissertation, "Upton Sinclair: Creating *World's End.*" For his exhaustive notes, interviews with Sinclair's friends and family, and suggestive leads, I am indebted to Leon Harris and his 1975 biography, *Upton Sinclair: American Rebel,* the only previous full-scale life of Sinclair. Harris's generosity in leaving his voluminous research files for his Sinclair book to the Lilly Library greatly eased my way.

Unless otherwise indicated in the notes, all references to correspondence, events, and works are from the Upton Sinclair MSS, Lilly Library. References to materials from the David Anton Randall, Meta Sinclair Stone, and Leon Harris collections at the Lilly Library are keyed as Randall MSS, Stone MSS, and LH MSS.

References to material from the private collection of John Ahouse are identified as JA papers.

Abbreviations

AO: American Outpost (US)
AS: The Journal of Arthur Stirling (US)
DS: David Sinclair
GS: George Sterling
HK: Harry Kemp
HLM: H. L. Mencken
JA: John Ahouse
JL: Jack London
LAT: Los Angeles Times

LL: Lilly Library
LP: Love's Pilgrimage (US)
MCS: Mary Craig Sinclair
NYPL: New York Public Library
NYT: New York Times
SB: Southern Belle (MCS)
Stone: Meta Sinclair Stone
TR: Theodore Roosevelt
US: Upton Sinclair
WE: World's End (US)

Prologue: Indiana University

xi In 1895, when Upton Sinclair: Priscilla Sinclair scrapbook, 1911–1962, DS MSS.

xi Upton Sinclair's audience: Details on the speech, which was similar to many given by Sinclair during this period, are from the author's interviews with Ronald Gottesman, and newspaper accounts: "Upton Sinclair Is Here," *Indianapolis News,* Oct. 18, 1963; "Upton Sinclair Takes Refreshing Pause for a Poke at the World," *Indianapolis News,* Oct. 19, 1963; "Upton Sinclair Speaks to Three Groups; Views Little Mellowed," *Indiana Daily Student,* Oct. 19, 1963; and "Sinclair Tells Tales of Reform," *Bloomington Daily Herald-Telephone,* Oct. 19, 1963.

xiii "dearly beloved saint": Rudolf von Lierich to US, Jan. 1, 1933.

xiii "been marked by the Gods": Dell Munger to US, May 29, 1909.

xiii "PLEASE PLEASE, Mr. Sinclair": Regina Brand Fayne to US, Nov. 3, 1963.

xiv "radical innocent": My title is derived from my reading many years ago of Ihab Hassan's provocative study of American literature, *Radical Innocence: The Contemporary American Novel* (1961).

One: The Penniless Rat

4 he was a "natty" dresser: *The Autobiography of Upton Sinclair* (New York: Harcourt, Brace & World, 1962), 20; hereafter cited as *Autobiography.*

4 "There was an incredible": US, *Love's Pilgrimage* (New York: Mitchell Kennerley, 1911), 8; hereafter cited as *LP.*

4 "The men who shoveled": *The Journal of Arthur Stirling* (New York: D. Appleton and Company, 1903, 1906), 155; hereafter cited as *AS.*

4 "the Highway of Lost Men": *LP,* 3–4.

4 Priscilla Sinclair's stubborn strength: Details here and following are from Sinclair's two autobiographies, *American Outpost: A Book of Reminiscences* (New York: Farrar & Rinehart, 1932), hereafter cited as *AO,* and *Autobiography.*

5 "dances and parties, terrapin suppers": *Autobiography,* 12.

6 Far more satisfying: Sinclair's account of his joke-writing is from *AO,* 47–49.

7 "taught himself French and Italian": Sinclair makes this claim for his autobiographical hero in *LP,* 44. See also *Autobiography,* 61–63.

8 "haunted by the ghosts": *AO,* 71.

9 "a young shark": *AO,* 72.

9 $40 a week: Currency equivalents in this and succeeding chapters are from John J. Mc-Cusker, "Comparing the Purchasing Power of Money in the United States (or Colonies) from 1665 to Any Other Year Including the Present," Economic History Services, 2001, www.eh.net/hmit/ppowerusd.

9 He later adopted: *AO,* 71, 72.

10 "barbaric screechings": *LP,* 16.

10 Helping him in his resolve: *AO,* 42–43.

10 Moir was less successful: *AO,* 44.

10 What stood in: *AO,* 75–76.

11 "a woman's soul redeemed": US, *Springtime and Harvest* (New York: Sinclair Press, 1901), 3.

12 "Last spring, because": *Springtime and Harvest,* i.

13 Now Meta and Mrs. Fuller: *LP,* 53, 52.

13 A summer romance: *LP,* 61.

13 More alarmingly: Stone MSS; Sinclair quotes directly from his and Meta's letters throughout *LP.*

13 Asked if he did not love: *LP,* 61.

14 "all female": Jean Sinclair in Leon Harris's interview of David Sinclair, nd, ca 1970, LH MSS.

14 "an inspiration direct from God": *LP,* 130.

16 Maeterlinck's *Life of the Bee: LP,* 217; on Meta's abortion attempts, see Leon Harris, *Upton Sinclair: American Rebel* (New York: Thomas Y. Crowell, 1975), 45.

16 He also loved: *AO,* 115–16. The peewees story was a favorite of Sinclair's. See also Ronald Gottesman, Interview of Upton Beall Sinclair, January 1963, at Monrovia, California, Oral History Collection of Columbia University (New York, Oral History Research Office, 1964), 148–49, hereafter cited as Columbia Oral History.

17 The young prince: US, *Prince Hagen* (New York: L. C. Page, 1903; Chicago: Charles H. Kerr, 1910), 182, 189.

18 All of these writers: *AO,* 116–18.

18 "I *want* to give": US to Markham, Dec. 7, no year.

19 On June 9, 1902: *AS,* 73.

19 They agreed that a man: *AS,* 43, 20, 87.

20 His voice was "strained": *AS,* 128.

20 George Herron: Sinclair's account of the Herron-Wilshire visit is found in *LP,* 427, 433; Wilshire details are from Signe Nakashima, *Cardinal Mine: A Ghost of the Past* (Bishop, California: Chalfont Press, 1995), 97–106.

22 "tortured him hideously": *LP,* 427, 423, 433.

22 "petrified inspiration": *A Captain of Industry* (Girard, Kansas: *Appeal to Reason,* 1906), 8.

23 "Sir, I exist!": Crane's poem, written in 1894, reads: "A man said to the universe: / "Sir, I exist!" / "However," replied the universe, / "The Fact has not created in me / A sense of obligation."

23 "My Cause": *Independent,* May 14, 1903, 1121–26.

24 "survival as a writer": *AO,* 146.

Two: The American Homer

25 Upton Sinclair began life anew: Carrie Stout Chevalier, "Upton Sinclair Builds His Dream House," *Princeton Recollector* (1976), US MSS.

26 For weeks after: *LP,* 443–45.

28 In April 1901, Sinclair: Darwin Payne, *Owen Wister: Chronicler of the West, Gentleman of the East* (Dallas: Southern Methodist University Press, 1985), 193.

28 Wister did not respond: Payne, *Owen Wister,* 219.

28 Sinclair told Wister: cited in Payne, *Owen Wister,* 219–20. Sinclair's begging letter was written on Aug. 22, 1903.

29 Sinclair's alter ego Arthur Stirling: *AS,* 106; *LP,* 413; *AS,* 46–47.

30 In late September: In an article for the June 1904 issue of *Country Life in America,* Sinclair describes the construction of his small house, with the aid of three carpenters. As

Thoreau does in *Walden,* he specifies the cost of materials, calling attention to his economy: they totaled $156.

31 "a continuous ebullition of glee": *LP,* 537.

31 Efficiency in small matters: *LP,* 475.

32 Meta knew that her husband: *LP,* 466.

33 Sinclair not only condemned: *LP,* 452.

33 Hers was a "love-nature": *LP,* 453.

33 To be *useful: AS,* 208.

33 But theory and practice: *LP,* 470, 472.

34 "Thyrsis and Corydon," Chapter 4, Stone MSS.

34 In March, the freezing weather: *LP,* 468–69.

34 They had less and less: *LP,* 480.

34 Early one morning: *LP,* 494–97.

35 Images of combat: *LP,* 484.

36 Despite some strong reviews: US, *Manassas: A Novel of the War* (Pasadena, California: Published by the Author, 1924), 392. (This is Sinclair's reissue of the original, published in 1904 by Macmillan.)

36 "a black shadow stealing": *LP,* 437.

36 Sinclair resented: *LP,* 487.

37 Sinclair's self-study plan: "Not since he had discovered the master-key of Evolution had Thyrsis come upon any set of ideas that meant so much to him." *LP,* 535.

40 The dean of this group: Sinclair describes his relationship with Steffens at this time in *Autobiography,* 107–8, and in *The Brass Check* (Pasadena, California: Published by the Author, 1920), 22–23.

40 Robbie Collier: *The Brass Check,* 24–25.

41 The *Appeal* was indignant: *The Jungle* (New York: Doubleday, Page, 1906), 391. All references to Sinclair's novel are to this first edition.

41 "You have lost the strike!": *The Jungle,* 392.

41 As proof of his credentials: Negotiations with the *Appeal* are described in *Autobiography,* 108–9, and in Ronald Gottesman, "Upton Sinclair: An Annotated Bibliographical Catalogue, 1894–1932" (Bloomington: Indiana University dissertation, 1964), 86–89.

42 A jubilant Sinclair: Gottesman, "Upton Sinclair," 89. In 1945 Sinclair stated, in the Introduction to the Viking Press edition of *The Jungle* (p. 7), that he arrived on September 20, his twenty-sixth birthday, but Gottesman convincingly shows that this is unlikely.

Three: The Muckraker

43 Ernest Poole, writing in 1940: *The Bridge: My Own Story* (New York: Macmillan, 1940), 95–96.

43 great books "which make their way": *Manassas,* 57–58.

44 "Who can thrill": Kathleen De Grave, "Introduction," *The Jungle: The Uncensored Original Edition* (Tucson: Sharp Press, 2003), xviii.

45 Its greatest figure: Harper Leech and John Charles Carroll, "Portrait of a Beef Baron," from *Armour and His Time* (New York: D. Appleton–Century, 1938), cited in Claire Eby, ed., Upton Sinclair, *The Jungle* (New York: Norton, 2003), 362.

45 a "plain merchant": Theodore Dreiser, "Interview with P. D. Armour," from "Life Stories of Successful Men—No. 10," *Success* 1 (Oct. 1898), Eby, *The Jungle,* 357. This Norton Critical Edition contains valuable notes, background materials, selections from contemporary reviews and later criticism, as well as an excellent bibliography of primary and secondary sources.

46 Russell and Hearst: James D. Hart, *The Popular Book: A History of America's Literary Taste* (New York: Oxford University Press, 1950), 205–6; for the status of the meatpacking industry in the 1880s and 1890s, see Paul S. Boyer, ed., *The Oxford Companion to American History* (New York: Oxford University Press, 2001), 460.

46 inside the "fortress of oppression": *Autobiography,* 108–9; *The Brass Check,* 24, 27. Sinclair's self-description is in the context of the publisher of *Collier's* magazine declining to print his article on Lincoln Steffens a few weeks before he left for Chicago.

46 But Sinclair was warmly received: For Kaztauskis, see Eby, *The Jungle,* [Ernest Poole], *From Lithuania to the Chicago Stockyards—An Autobiography,* 388–95. Simons is discussed in Louise Carol Wade's "The Problem with Classroom Use of Upton Sinclair's *The Jungle,*" *American Studies* 32 (Fall 1991), 83. Wade makes a strong case against the accuracy and fairness of *The Jungle.* James R. Barrett, *Work and Community in the Jungle: Chicago's Packinghouse Workers, 1894–1922* (Urbana: University of Illinois Press, 1987). Like Wade an urban historian specializing in Chicago, Barrett argues persuasively that Sinclair was more accurate than not. The general thrust of commentary concerning *The Jungle* is that it was for the most part accurate though exaggerated in the sense of concentrating on worst-case examples.

47 Of these, Jane Addams: *AO,* 155.

48 He told Addams: *Autobiography,* 110.

49 (A correspondent later): W. B. Barrows to US, Sep. 19, 1945. The German injunction read "Blutig ist ja dein Amt, O Schlaechter, / Drum uebe es menschlich!"

49 Sinclair's own account: *Autobiography,* 110.

50 This particular violinist: *The Jungle,* 7.

50 "I will work harder": *The Jungle,* 19.

50 "In the good old summer time": *The Jungle,* 21.

50 The Norwegian scholar: Orm Øverland, *"The Jungle:* From Lithuanian Peasant to American Socialist," *American Literary Realism* 37:1 (Fall 2004), 8. Concerning Jurgis's almost complete silence in the concluding pages of *The Jungle,* Øverland usefully notes (p. 18) that "Sinclair could have made him speak in broken English but chose to silence him in the company of so many literate speakers."

52 Sinclair referred: Cited passages here and following are from *The Jungle,* 112, 28, 40–41.

53 Sinclair's descriptions of the workers' lives: *The Jungle,* 116, 95.

54 Ironically, most of the abuses: Leech and Carroll, "Portrait of a Beef Baron," Eby, *The Jungle,* 365.

54 "the basic device of modern straight line production": Leech and Carroll, "Portrait of a Beef Baron," Eby, *The Jungle,* 365.

54 "a Socialist who believes in machinery": US, *Mammonart* (Pasadena: Published by the author, 1924, 1925), 238.

55 Worst of all: *The Jungle,* 161–62.

55 This was the passage: F. P. Dunne, "Mr. Dooley on the Food We Eat," *Collier's,* June 23, 1906, 15–16.

56 Federal and city inspectors: *The Jungle,* 113.

56 Some of Sinclair's more shocking: De Grave, xv–xvi.

57 a country home "with great open fire-places": *LP,* 564.

57 "would work as a laborer": *LP,* 566.

57 George Stout, Sinclair's landlord: The purchase date of the property was December 31, 1904; the deed was recorded January 6, 1905. My thanks to George Rojas of the Mercer County Clerk's Office in Trenton for searching out these details for me.

57 "Whereupon," Sinclair says, amused: *LP,* 599–600.

58 Sinclair was satisfied: *LP,* 600–601.

Four: The Warrior

59 For the first three months: *AO,* 158.

60 Nowhere does Sinclair: Gene DeGruson, *The Lost First Edition of Upton Sinclair's "The Jungle"* (Atlanta: Peachtree, 1988), Introduction, xviii. DeGruson's edition is based on copies found in 1980 of Sinclair's novel as it appeared serially, at considerably greater length, in 1905 in *Appeal to Reason.* DeGruson's speculations about Wayland's providing Sinclair with the plot for his novel are found in Max McCoy, " 'Horrible Mess' Turns into 'Literary Treasure,' " *Morning Sun,* Pittsburg, Kansas, Apr. 17, 1989. J. A. Wayland also published his own slightly modified edition of *The Jungle* in his quarterly journal *One-Hoss Philosophy.* This text is substantially reproduced as *The Jungle: The Uncensored Original Edition,* with an introduction by Kathleen De Grave.

60 Conscious or unconscious: For his excellent discussion of Sinclair's use of *Pilgrim's Progress* I am indebted to Busnagi Rajannan's "Upton Sinclair's *The Jungle* Revisited," *IJAS [Indian Journal of American Studies]* 12 (July 1982), 49–54.

61 Later commentators: See for example Christopher Hitchens, "A Capitalist Primer: Upton Sinclair's Realism Got the Better of His Socialism," *Atlantic Monthly* (July–Aug. 2002), 176–79.

61 Brett pressed Sinclair: US to Brett, Apr. 30, 1905; US to Brett, May 3, 1905; US to Brett, May 31, 1905; US to Brett, June 10, 1905, NYPL.

61 "blood and guts": *Autobiography,* 115.

62 "will and intelligence": *LP,* 604–5.

62 describes sex as a "marriage duty": *LP,* 604.

63 One source of Sinclair's success: For Sinclair's memories of London, see *Mammonart,* 364, and *AO,* 160–61. Renamed the League for Industrial Democracy in 1921, when "socialist" was an unhealthy designation, this would be one of Sinclair's most successful and long-lasting organizational efforts. Walter Lippmann would run the Harvard chapter, and members would include William Shirer, Ralph Bunche, Walter Reuther, and Sidney Hook, as well as Norman Thomas.

64 London may also have given: Harris, *Upton Sinclair,* 80.

64 But he was too late: DeGruson, *The Lost First Edition,* xviii.

65 Warren came out to Sinclair's farm: *AO,* 161.

65 Abandoned now by both his editors: US letter, Sep. 30, 1930, cited in Gottesman, "Upton Sinclair," 94.

65 Now he revealed: *AO,* 162–63; the fullest explication of the complicated publishing history of *The Jungle,* including the probable date of book publication as February 26, 1906, is in Gottesman, "Upton Sinclair," 93–99.

66 Though he did not know it: Isaac Marcosson, *Adventures in Interviewing* (New York: Curtis, 1919), 280–84.

67 Page's obvious interest: *The Brass Check,* 33.

68 This was simply an "unproven theory": *The Brass Check,* 33.

68 Keeley vouched: *AO,* 164; *The Brass Check,* 32–33.

68 "cloak for calumny": Christine Scriabine, "Upton Sinclair and the Writing of *The Jungle,*" in *Chicago History* (Chicago Historical Society, 1981), 33.

68 Luckily, as McKee: *The Brass Check,* 33.

68 Marcosson earned his keep: Marcosson, *Adventures in Interviewing,* 284.

68 When McKee returned: Sinclair, "Campaign Against the Wholesale Poisoners of the Nation's Food," *Arena* 36 (July 1906); for DeGruson on the title, see McCoy, " 'Horrible Mess' "; for the deleted jungle references, see De Grave, *The Jungle,* xx, xxi.

69 Sinclair signed his contract: Gottesman, "Upton Sinclair," 100.

69 Marcosson worked hard: Marcosson, *Adventures in Interviewing,* 286–87. Gottesman finds

Marcosson's account "rife with error" ("Upton Sinclair," 99), and it is clear that Marcosson exaggerated his influence; Sinclair himself only mildly objected to Marcosson's account in *AO* (p. 167), for failing to note that "both of us sent copies of the book to the President, and both got letters saying that he was investigating the charges." On Marcosson, see Christopher P. Wilson, *The Labor of Words: Literary Professionalism in the Progressive Era* (Athens: University of Georgia Press, 1985), 81–82.

70 No frightened ingénue: Marcosson, *Adventures in Interviewing,* 287.

70 "Few men could have stood up": Marcosson, *Adventures in Interviewing,* 287.

71 Unlike his partner: Frank Doubleday, "The Story of *The Jungle,*" in *The Memoirs of a Publisher* (New York: Doubleday, 1972), 158–59.

71 Thanks in large part: Harris, *Upton Sinclair,* 83.

71 "the conditions of life": Hugh J. Dawson, "Winston Churchill and Upton Sinclair: An Early Review of *The Jungle,*" *ALR* [*American Literary Review*] 24:1 (Fall 1991), 74–75; the reviews appeared in *T.P.O.,* an English journal that took the initials of its publisher, T. P. O'Connor, Vol. 1, No. 1, June 15, 1906, 25–26, and Vol. 1, No. 2, June 23, 1906, 65–66.

73 ("I have had three letters"): US to JL, Mar. 19, 1906, Huntington Library; TR to US, US, *My Lifetime in Letters* (Columbia: University of Missouri Press, 1960), 11–14; the information about the number of letters to the White House was given to Sinclair by Roosevelt's secretary, *AO,* 166.

73 Sinclair met Roosevelt: *AO,* 166–69. Sinclair also described his continuing relations with Roosevelt in *The Brass Check,* 28–44; in *Autobiography,* 118–26; and in *My Lifetime in Letters,* 11–18. See James Harvey Young, *Pure Food: Securing the Federal Food and Drugs Act of 1906* (Princeton: Princeton University Press, 1989), 233, for the fullest account of the Roosevelt-Sinclair interaction. Young's summary of their communications indicates messages from Roosevelt to Sinclair on Mar. 9, 15, 21, Apr. 9, 11, 13, May 29, and June 2; and from Sinclair to Roosevelt on Apr. 10 (two letters and a telegram), Apr. 12, May 20, and June 1, in addition to a "barrage" of earlier messages he had sent.

74 (Roosevelt was on record): Henry F. Pringle, *Theodore Roosevelt: A Biography* (New York: Harcourt, Brace, 1931; Harvest Books edition, 1956), 258.

74 Sinclair pondered his response: *AO,* 168.

75 Sinclair left the White House: *AO,* 168.

75 The next morning: *AO,* 169–70.

76 When Sinclair's telegram: Ella Reeve Cohen, *We Are Many* (New York: International Publishers, 1940), 82.

77 Roosevelt wrote back: TR to US, Apr. 11, 1906, *My Lifetime in Letters,* 16–17.

77 "There is filth on the floor": Roosevelt's speech is quoted in Fred J. Cook, *The Muckrakers* (Garden City: Doubleday, 1972), 10.

77 "Tell Sinclair to go home": *AO,* 173.

77 Jurgis is handed a stiff broom: *The Jungle,* 49. Edmund Morris, in *Theodore Rex* (New York: Random House, 2001), 439, points out that Roosevelt either misread or misremembered the point of Bunyan's man with the rake—he was rooting in filth in order to find money, not to uncover evil. Even their enemies admitted that the muckrakers were too idealistic to be bought. (By the same token, Sinclair may also have misread or misremembered the purpose of the raker in Bunyan, given his use of the image in *The Jungle.*)

78 Another line of attack: *The Brass Check,* 37, 314–17.

79 Seeing all of these forces: *AO,* 170; "Is *The Jungle* True?" *Independent* 60 (May 17, 1906), 1129.

80 dealing with people who "desired publicity": *The Brass Check,* 41.

80 And thus it happened: *The Brass Check,* 42–43.

80 Sinclair's story appeared: *NYT,* May 28, 1906.

80 Personalizing the dispute: *NYT,* May 3, 1906.

81 "bound to me": Young, *Pure Food,* 241.

81 "dirt, splinters, floor filth": Young, *Pure Food,* 242, citing McNeil-Reynolds report.

82 "did not like the man": TR to William Allen White, July 31, 1906, *The Letters of Theodore Roosevelt,* Elting E. Morison, ed. (8 vols., Cambridge: Harvard University Press, 1951–1954), Vol. 5, 340; TR to US, June 1, 1915, *My Lifetime in Letters,* 18.

82 He was also, Roosevelt said: Fulton Oursler, *Behold This Dreamer!* (Boston: Little, Brown, 1964), 417.

82 "I want to let in light": TR to Ray Stannard Baker, cited in Robert M. Crunden, *Ministers of Reform: The Progressives' Achievement in American Civilization, 1889–1920* (New York: Basic Books, 1982), 190, 192.

82 "the greatest publicity man of that time": *Autobiography,* 118.

83 Sinclair never quite forgave: Crunden, *Ministers of Reform,* 192. Crunden's chapter "The Muckrakers and the Pure Food and Drug Act" includes the contributions of Samuel Hopkins Adams to the drug reforms as well as Sinclair's.

83 "Mighty nice of you": TR to US, Oct. 25, 1917.

83 "bitterly disappointed": *The Brass Check,* 47.

Five: The Czar of Helicon Hall

85 "a problem to solve": US, "A Home Colony," *Independent,* June 14, 1906.

86 "Smiling almost ecstatically": "Sinclair Explains His Home," *NYT,* July 18, 1906, cited in Margaret Ann Brown's excellent dissertation, "Not Your Usual Boardinghouse Types: Upton Sinclair's Helicon Home Colony, 1906–1907" (St. Louis: George Washington University dissertation, 1993), 57. Further details on Helicon Hall, unless otherwise indicated, are from Brown.

87 By mid-July Sinclair: Brown, "Not Your Usual," 62, citing *New York Sun,* Aug. 13, 1906, "Liberty in the Home Colony."

87 "slight, pale young man": Edith Summers Kelley, "Helicon Hall: An Experiment in Living," 1934, Edith Summers Kelley Papers, Morris Library, Southern Illinois University, Carbondale, Illinois, ed. Mary Byrd Davis, *Kentucky Review* 1 (Spring 1980), 32.

88 She impressed Sinclair: *AO,* 184.

88 gigantic rubber tree: *NYT,* Oct. 7, 1906.

89 Edie Summers, who had been living: Brown, "Not Your Usual," 85–90.

89 "vision of exotic beauty": Kelley, "Helicon Hall," 32.

89 "safe, sane, conservative": Michael Williams, *Book of the High Romance: A Spiritual Autobiography* (New York: Macmillan, 1918), 140.

91 "very incarnation of insignificance": "Love's Progress," early draft, 328, US MSS.

92 the "czar" of Helicon Hall: Brown, "Not Your Usual," 108.

92 John Dewey, then forty-seven: Brown, "Not Your Usual," 106.

92 "lean, lanky": Kelley, "Helicon Hall," 35–36.

93 "a large, dark woman": The *Kentucky Review* version of Kelley's "Helicon Hall," 37, refers to Wilkins as "Miss W." Brown; "Not Your Usual," 333–34, identifies "Miss W." as Wilkins.

93 "I am not by nature personal": *My Lifetime in Letters,* x.

93 Then there was the food: US, "A New Colony," John and Phyllis Collier Collection, Archives of Labor and Urban Affairs, Wayne State University, Detroit, Michigan; Brown, "Not Your Usual," 123–24.

94 The true sustenance: Brown, "Not Your Usual," 126–28.

94 "grumpy boardinghouse table": Kelley, "Helicon Hall," 38.

94 "culmination" of her day: Brown, "Not Your Usual," 126–27.

94 The dinner conversations: Williams, *Book of the High Romance,* 129, 143.

95 The good fellowship: Kelley, "Helicon Hall," 41–42.

95 Sinclair bitterly resented: *AO,* 182–83.

96 According to her unpublished: "Thyrsis and Corydon"; Harris, *Upton Sinclair,* 96–97.

96 Sinclair described his affair: "Love's Progress," 305.

96 "It wouldn't do to have the papers": Harris, *Upton Sinclair,* 96.

97 Leon Harris aptly says: *Upton Sinclair,* 97.

97 He gave more serious: *The Industrial Republic* (New York: Doubleday, Page, 1907), 57.

98 "the best and clearest exposition": Updegraff to Edith Summers, May 17, 1912, US MSS.

98 "dreadful bugaboo": *The Industrial Republic,* 273.

98 John Armistead Collier: Details on Collier background are from Brown, "Not Your Usual," 143–44.

98 Edie Summers thought Collier was gentle: Kelley, "Helicon Hall," 43.

98 Meta said they only "petted": Synopsis, "Thyrsis and Corydon."

98 Collier grandly claimed: Phyllis Feningston, "Biography: John Armistead Collier," Collier Papers.

99 "inevitable family accessory": US to Collier, June 10, 1919.

99 "take on a harassed look": Kelley, "Helicon Hall," 39.

99 "an honest and dedicated man": Will and Ariel Durant, *Interpretations of Life: A Survey of Contemporary Literature* (New York: Simon & Schuster, 1970), 47. Although Durant and Sinclair both later lived in Los Angeles or nearby for many years, they apparently did not meet again.

99 "a little dusty": *AO,* 179.

99 "Being freaks ourselves": Kelley, "Helicon Hall," 41.

99 Hartmann sent a card: *AO,* 185.

99 "a great German body": Kelley, "Helicon Hall," 41.

100 "seven or eight feet tall": Williams, *Book of the High Romance,* 144–45. The Hartmann visit is also described in Brown, "Not Your Usual," 135–39.

100 "Why don't you get things": Brown, "Not Your Usual," 137.

100 Edie Summers on her days off: Accounts of the Helicon Hall fire are from Kelley, "Helicon Hall," 42–44; Brown, "Not Your Usual," 153–61; and *AO,* 186–88.

Six: The Wayfarer

103 The stuffy Republican neighbors: Brown, "Not Your Usual," 156, 165.

104 Sinclair was furious: *The Brass Check,* 69–71, 68–69.

104 As he noted later: *Autobiography,* 135. One nonresident stockholder claimed that she received only $600 back from her $1,000 investment, plus a full set of Sinclair's books, but this is the only documented instance of less than full repayment cited in Brown, "Not Your Usual," 173.

105 "spoiled us": *New York Post,* Mar. 19, 1907, cited in Brown, "Not Your Usual," 151–52.

105 created a "beautiful Utopia": *Autobiography,* 135–36.

105 "the least justification": *The Living of Charlotte Perkins Gilman: An Autobiography* (Madison: University of Wisconsin Press, 1991; originally published 1935), 26.

105 Privately, Sinclair was torn: Sinclair to Meta, nd, Stone MSS. Brown thinks this was "most likely written in 1909 or 1910," Brown, "Not Your Usual," 227.

105 "a weird experiment": Marcosson, *Adventures in Interviewing,* 188.

105 Sinclair's move to the isolated beach cottage: *Autobiography,* 137; Harris, *Upton Sinclair,* 99–100.

106 *The Metropolis* grew: On Brisbane, see Ferdinand Lundberg, *Imperial Hearst* (New York: Equinox Cooperative Press, 1936; Arno Press, 1970 reprint), 89. Sinclair's association with Brisbane is described in *The Brass Check,* 36, and Columbia Oral History, 40.

107 "more a travelogue": John Ahouse, *Upton Sinclair: A Descriptive, Annotated Bibliography* (Los Angeles: Mercer & Aitchison, 1994), 18.

107 " 'rest cures' and 'water cures' ": US, *The Metropolis* (New York: Phillips Publishing Co., 1907), 276, 278.

107 "regular experiment station in health": US, *The Book of Life* (Girard, Kansas: Haldeman-Julius, 1921, 1922), 116, 117.

107 "enema machine": *The Road to Wellville* (New York: Penguin, 1993), 474.

108 Meta and Upton: *The Road to Wellville,* 354, 355.

108 By the time: "Thyrsis and Corydon"; Kuttner's translation with A. A. Brill of Freud's *Reflections on War and Death* was published in 1918.

108 "endless vista of horrors": US, "Letter to My Friends," 1915; treatment details are from *The Book of Life,* 118, 119.

109 He drafted a prospectus: Williams, *Book of the High Romance,* 187–88.

110 "It's really exactly": US, *The Millennium* (Girard, Kansas: Upton Sinclair / Haldeman-Julius, 1924), 156. "*The Millennium* began life as a play in 1907; it was rewritten as a novel in 1914 and serialized in *Appeal to Reason* without appearing in book form at that time," JA, *Upton Sinclair,* 53.

110 "The uncrowned king of America": *Mammonart,* 329–32.

111 *The Moneychangers:* Sinclair discusses the origins of *The Moneychangers* in *The Brass Check,* 80–84.

112 Only marginally more persuasive: US, *The Moneychangers* (Upper Saddle River, New Jersey: Gregg Press, 1908) 214; Harris, *Upton Sinclair,* 104.

112 "declassed" himself: *The Brass Check,* 83.

113 Kemp's image: William Brevda, *Harry Kemp: The Last Bohemian* (Lewisburg, Pennsylvania: Bucknell University Press, 1986), 44, 40.

114 In an amusing echo: Harry Kemp, *Tramping on Life: An Autobiographical Narrative* (New York: Boni & Liveright, 1922), 298 (Kemp is quoting Meta on Sinclair's skin); *AO,* 206.

115 "poetry just rolled": US to Meta, nd, Stone MSS.

115 "Hotbed of Soulful Culture": *LAT,* May 22, 1910.

116 The heavy drinking: *AO,* 211.

116 Little remembered now: *Martin Eden* (New York: Macmillan, 1908), 256, 265.

116 Another play: *Prince Hagen,* in *Plays of Protest* (New York: Mitchell Kennerley, 1912), 157; Harris, *Upton Sinclair,* 114.

117 "a nice, slouchy": *Palo Alto Times,* Feb. 1913.

117 Dell Munger's own offbeat solution: *The Fasting Cure* (New York: Mitchell Kennerley, 1911), 19.

117 Sinclair wrote constantly: US to Meta, nd, Stone MSS.

117 "dear Ole Tiger-Princess": Collier to Meta, Apr. 23, 1908, Mar. 16, 1908, Stone MSS.

118 "You might as well ask me": *San Francisco Examiner,* Jan. 30, 1909.

118 Lighter in tone: *Samuel the Seeker* (New York: B. W. Dodge, 1910), 57, 6–7.

118 "guileless fool": the phrase is from JA, *Upton Sinclair,* 24.

119 "harebrained, posturing": *The Road to Wellville,* 170.

119 As the publisher: Robert Ernst, *Weakness Is a Crime: The Life of Bernarr Macfadden* (Syracuse: Syracuse University Press, 1991), 55, 29.

119 A devout believer in the enjoyment of sex: Ernst, *Weakness Is a Crime,* 30, 39.

119 Mary Craig Kimbrough: Mary Craig Sinclair, *Southern Belle* (Phoenix: Sinclair Press 1957; 1962 Memorial Edition), 61–63; hereafter cited as *SB.*

120 her charming accent: see Upton Sinclair, *Sylvia* (Philadelphia and Chicago: John C. Winston, 1913; later Sinclair issue, Long Beach, California: Published by the Author, 1927), 45.

120 ("Take her away"): "Thyrsis and Corydon."

120 Into this interesting mix: Kemp, *Tramping on Life,* 313, 314, 316, 338.

Seven: The Pilgrim of Love

123 "the greatest discovery": *Independent,* Sep. 9, 1909, 580–83.

123 Dedicated to Macfadden: First publication was in *Cosmopolitan,* May 1910, and *Contemporary Review* (London), Apr. 1910; *The Fasting Cure,* 6.

123 "food *drunkard*": US to Meta, Feb. 15, 1908.

123 the body produces poisons: *The Fasting Cure,* 15.

123 "the key to eternal youth": *The Fasting Cure,* 25, 69.

123 "many years of filth": *The Fasting Cure,* 73–74.

124 *Love's Pilgrimage* was a much more interesting exercise: Floyd Dell, *Upton Sinclair: A Study in Social Protest* (New York: George H. Dolan, 1927), 128; Van Eeden letter to US cited in Dell, *Upton Sinclair,* 128–29.

124 "rawest, reddest meat": JL to US, Feb. 10, 1910.

124 "the bondage of love": William Bloodworth, *Upton Sinclair* (Boston: Twayne, 1977), 74.

124 Sinclair was describing: US, *Naturewoman,* in *Plays of Protest,* 12, 53.

125 "You and Alfred": US to Meta, July 2 [no year, probably 1908], Stone MSS.

125 Sinclair's letters: US to Meta, undated, Stone MSS.

127 Stephens and Price called: details on Arden are from Mark Taylor, "Utopia by Taxation: Frank Stephens and the Single Tax Community of Arden, Delaware," *Pennsylvania Magazine of History and Biography,* 126:2 (April 2002), 305–26, and from George N. Caylor, untitled, nd [ca 1960], nine-page MS included in letter to Leon Harris, Oct. 12, 1970, LH MSS.

127 community kitchen: *AO,* 234. The Monopoly story is told fully by Burton H. Wolfe, "The Monopolization of Monopoly: Lizzie J. Magie," *San Francisco Bay Guardian,* 1976. Magie wrote to Sinclair (as Mrs. Lizzie Phillips) on May 6, 1939, to tell him that she had asked Parker Brothers to send him her new and improved Landlord game.

128 "had bored me": *SB,* 73.

129 "Is that the way": *SB,* 69.

129 "becoming a radical": *SB,* 76, 75.

129 she might make "good copy": *SB,* 77–78.

129 A few days later: *SB,* 84.

130 Craig omitted: Leon Harris in his 1975 Sinclair biography dismisses *Southern Belle* (p. 125) as "jejune" and "meretricious," asserting that Craig schemed to "appropriate" Meta's husband, working with a "cool and ingratiating guile." She became Meta's best friend, with the intent of stealing her husband. Either "consciously or subconsciously," Harris says, Craig decided that "if she couldn't be an artist, she could eat one." This argument seems overwrought. See Peggy Prenshaw's Afterword to *Southern Belle* (Jackson, Mississippi: Banner Books, 1999) for a contrary impression of Craig and her story.

130 "Corydon, Thyrsis": *AO,* 243.

130 Kemp came to Arden: Kemp to US, Nov. 1909; US to Fels, Jan. 3, 1910; Fels to Kemp, Feb. 7, 1910; Kemp to US, Feb. 10, 1910; all US MSS.

130 Shaw wrote Fels: Harris, *Upton Sinclair,* 128.

130 The two friends: US to Kemp, July 21, 1910.

131 Arden in mid-July: Kemp, *Tramping on Life,* 347, 349.

131 Meta—"Hildreth": Kemp, *Tramping on Life,* 348.

131 A third woman: Kemp, *Tramping on Life,* 350.

131 Sinclair recalled Kemp's arrival: "Love's Progress," later draft, 585–86; Brevda, *Harry Kemp,* 56.

132 The two men: *AO,* 239.

132 Harry was younger: Kemp, *Tramping on Life,* 351, 352; US to Kemp, July 21, 1910.

132 Kemp reacted: Kemp, *Tramping on Life,* 352, 358.

133 According to *The New York Times:* "Arden Has a Circus," *NYT,* Aug. 5, 1911.

133 Though Sinclair did not note: *The Brass Check,* 97–99. The *NYT* ran stories on Sinclair's arrest on Aug. 2, 3, and 6, 1911; the *New York World* on Aug. 1, 2, and 3; the *New York Tribune* on Aug. 3.

134 In Sinclair's absence: Kemp, *Tramping on Life,* 363.

134 There were other tensions: Kemp, *Tramping on Life,* 359.

134 Harry Kemp had listened: Kemp, *Tramping on Life,* 402.

135 Meta wrote Sinclair: Kemp, *Tramping on Life,* 402, 404; US to Kemp, July 21, 1910. Sinclair tells his side of the story most fully in *The Brass Check,* 97–113.

135 The headlines during the ensuing weeks: *The Brass Check,* 195; Brevda, *Harry Kemp,* 59–63.

135 The stories below: *The Brass Check,* 107.

136 Yet Sinclair's own actions: Brevda, *Harry Kemp,* 61.

136 The day after the press conference: Kemp, *Tramping on Life,* 407–10; Brevda, *Harry Kemp,* 62–63; "Thyrsis and Corydon," pp. D, E, 418, and pp. 413, 414, 417.

136 Sinclair devoted the autumn: *The Brass Check,* 110–11; "Statement of Upton Sinclair," nd, Stone MSS.

136 For her part, Meta: *New York Sun,* Aug. 28, 1911; "Thyrsis and Corydon," 47–48; Kemp, *Tramping on Life,* 382.

137 On November 19: Harris, *Upton Sinclair,* 133–34.

137 "give a damn about marriage": *New York World,* Dec. 24, 1911.

137 But George Herron agreed: Herron to US, June 12, 1911.

138 "If by any chance": *LP,* 543.

138 "a disorderly blend": Brevda, *Harry Kemp,* 101.

Eight: The Survivor

140 Sinclair and David crossed: *Autobiography,* 176.

140 Sinclair's initial visit with Van Eeden: Van Eeden to US, Sep. 13, 1911.

141 put Van Eeden in touch with Harry Kemp: Brevda, *Harry Kemp,* 46–47.

142 "an endless stream": *Autobiography,* 182, 181.

142 a "hodge-podge of cant": *Autobiography,* 178.

143 "fail to be happy": *Autobiography,* 176.

143 "multiplied madonnas": *Autobiography,* 177.

143 "a lovely spot on the edge": *Autobiography,* 177.

143 Craig was pregnant: For Dollie's story of Craig's pregnancy, see Harris, *Upton Sinclair,* 126 and 374 note, on his interview with Dollie Kimbrough Kling. Further evidence that Craig and Sinclair were in close touch in New York during the fall and early winter is Sinclair's letter to Craig describing Meta's behavior and character and authorizing Craig to assume guardianship of David should anything happen to him (Dec. 15, 1911, US MSS; Harris, *Upton Sinclair,* 135). Even earlier, on September 8, 1911, Sinclair had written to Craig to assure her that nothing of his "obsession" with Meta remained, and that there was no comparison between Craig and Meta in terms of character; for Craig even to consider that they may be viewed similarly is to "do yourself an injustice."

144 Craig claimed: *SB,* 85–86.

144 Craig followed Sterling's advice: *SB,* 103, 104.

144 Much of Craig's account: Concerning the date of the divorce from Meta, Sinclair wrote to Van Eeden in May 1912 to say that his lawyer had told him "I get the divorce May 24th next," cited Harris, *Upton Sinclair,* 376; "I rejoice with my whole heart at your news," Lady Russell to US, June 3, 1912, cited in Harris, *Upton Sinclair,* 376.

145 "You came and started": US to Irving Stone, Jan. 26, 1939.

146 Craig's perceptiveness: MCS, Autobiography Notes, Sinclair Papers, Honnold Library, Claremont Colleges.

147 "Damn his hide!": MCS, Autobiography Notes.

147 Sinclair later used the memory: US, *World's End* (New York: Viking, 1940), 2–3, hereafter cited as *WE*.

147 "What part do moral forces": *WE*, 680.

147 Sinclair's greatest strength: US to Emile Jaques-Dalcroze, Dec. 31, 1938.

149 "Public opinion": *Sylvia*, 355.

150 John D. Jr. was: Ron Chernow, *Titan: The Life of John D. Rockefeller, Sr.* (New York: Random House, 1998), 584.

150 The first act: *The Brass Check* 144; *Autobiography*, 198; Harris, *Upton Sinclair*, 144. Sinclair's most extended description of these events and their sequel, his quarrel with the Associated Press regarding its coverage, is in *The Brass Check*, 142–68. See also John Graham, "Introduction," *The Coal War* (Boulder: Colorado Associated University Press, 1976), lx. Sinclair was unable to find a publisher during his lifetime for this sequel to *King Coal* (1917). Graham's 100-page introduction is the best account of Sinclair's involvement with the coal strike and its aftermath, including his two novels on the subject.

151 The next morning: *Autobiography*, 199–200; Graham, "Introduction," *The Coal War*, lix.

151 Sinclair spent two days: *Autobiography*, 200.

152 "My God Mary Craig": Mrs. Kimbrough to Craig, Apr. 29, 1914, US MSS.

152 "packed to suffocation": *New York American*, May 4, 1914.

153 Bouck White: Mary E. Kenton, "Christianity, Democracy, and Socialism: Bouck White's Kingdom of Self-Respect," in *Socialism and Christianity in Early 20th Century America*, ed. Jacob H. Dorn (Westport: Greenwood, 1998), 182–83.

153 That meeting began: Graham, "Introduction," *The Coal War*, lxvii.

154 A few days later: "My Friends in Tarrytown," nd, US MSS.

154 Sinclair had an entirely different message: *Appeal to Reason*, July 18, 1914, 3.

155 As Sinclair suspected: Graham, "Introduction," *The Coal War*, lxxv, citing *NYT*, Feb. 16, 1915.

155 "Men, only when": Graham, "Introduction," *The Coal War*, vii.

155 The Colorado coal strike: Graham, "Introduction," *The Coal War*, vii–viii; Chernow, *Titan*, 581; *Autobiography*, 202.

156 Sinclair had chosen Croton: Philip S. Foner, "Upton Sinclair's 'The Jungle': The Movie," in *Upton Sinclair: Literature and Social Reform*, ed. Dieter Herms (New York: Peter Lang, 1990), 163.

156 "most effective Socialist propaganda": *Appeal to Reason*, June 12, 1914.

156 Sinclair himself played: Foner, "Upton Sinclair's 'The Jungle,' " 159.

157 Richard Harding Davis: *Autobiography*, 204.

157 Sinclair worked hard: US to Harper's, Jan. 29, 1915.

158 Jack London: JL to US, Feb. 18, 1915.

159 Judge Kimbrough offered: *Autobiography*, 207.

159 "always be a sort": Kemp to Meta, Nov. 17, 1913, Stone MSS.

160 "a perfect little monster": US to Meta, July 19, 1915.

160 "perfect simile": *Sylvia's Marriage* (Philadelphia: John C. Winston, 1914), 75.

161 "keen competition": Columbia Oral History, 99.

Nine: The Homesteader

162 In January 1916: US to Craig, nd.

163 "a little mad": "Irving Stone Recalls Upton Sinclair," *Upton Sinclair Quarterly* (Sep. 1981), 8.

163 The Sinclair house: "Our Office," *Upton Sinclair's* 1 (Feb. 1919), 16.

163 David joined the household: Leon Harris interview of David Sinclair, nd, ca 1970, LH MSS.

163 The twenty-month period: "World's End Impending," Appendix, *O Shepherd, Speak!* (New York: Viking, 1949), 584; Leon Harris interview of David Sinclair.

165 "straight-from-the-shoulder": JL to US, Aug. 16, 1916.

165 "so death must have been swift": Sterling's claim for London's death by cyanide was made in the context of the death of Carrie Sterling, his former wife, by that means. GS to US, Aug. 21, 1918.

166 He promised Brett: US to Brett, Dec. 8, 1916, and Brett to US, Dec. 15, 1916.

167 "Bear in mind": Brett to US, May 9, 1916.

167 "tell me I'm an idiot": Craig to George Brett, May 1, 1916.

167 Later, Sinclair acknowledged: *Autobiography*, 212–13.

167 "a separate race of creatures": *King Coal*, 22.

167 "what was repulsive": *King Coal*, 23.

168 "under no circumstances": "War: A Manifesto Against It," *Wilshire's*, Sep. 1909, 7.

168 "to justify the use of force": Louis Fretz, "Upton Sinclair and World War I," *Political Science* 1973 (25), 3.

168 He wrote with alarm: US to J. G. Phelps Stokes, Feb. 8, 1916.

168 He made the same point: Fretz, "Upton Sinclair and World War I," 4.

169 The incident: deposition of Frank Bohm, State of California, County of Tulare, May 22, 1917, cited in Harris, *Upton Sinclair*, 379.

170 "strangers prowl about": *The Colonist* (Hamilton, Bermuda), Feb. 4, 1914, JA papers.

170 Sinclair now wrote lightly: US to G. B. Shaw, May 19, 1917.

170 It was a chilly: Sinclair's account of this incident is in Columbia Oral History, 140; Alma Whitaker, "Women's Work, Women's Clubs," June 10, 1916, *LAT.*

170 "an effeminate young man": "Upton Sinclair's Ravings," June 25, 1916, *LAT.*

171 On July 22, 1917, Sinclair's letter: Sinclair's resignation was also reported in *NYT,* July 17 and 18, 1917.

171 An influential Mississippi cousin: Unidentified to Lamar, Mar. 23, 1918.

171 "got in some pretty good licks": Scripps to US, Apr. 16, 1918.

172 But Brett was still wary: Gottesman, "Upton Sinclair," 165–66. Sinclair published a limited number of his own bound copies of *Jimmie Higgins* in March 1919, intended for his socialist readers, and Boni & Liveright brought out a trade edition at the same time for general readers.

173 "the Beast with the Brains": *Jimmie Higgins*, 265.

173 "If at the beginning of 1917": Dell, *Upton Sinclair*, 150.

174 A few days after he signed: Sinclair's encounters with Ford and the meeting with Gillette are told in several places: *Autobiography*, 285–88, 324–25; *The Flivver King* (Pasadena: Published by the Author, 1937), 44–47; and *SB*, 254–56. Gillette details are from Tim Dowling, *Inventor of the Disposable Culture: King Camp Gillette, 1855–1932* (London: Short Books, 2001), 14, 73–78.

177 "If you can once get a man": US, *The Profits of Religion: An Essay in Economic Interpretation* (Pasadena: Published by the Author, 1918), 219–20.

178 Picture, Sinclair says: *The Profits of Religion*, 11, 73–78.

178 Sinclair couched his argument: Harris, *Upton Sinclair*, 171; Emerson quoted in US, *What God Means to Me* (New York: Farrar & Rinehart, 1936), 129.

Ten: The Civil Libertarian

180 A sympathetic editor: The advice was given to Sinclair's autobiographical alter ego Arthur Stirling in *AS*, 207.

180 "You are listening": *The Brass Check*, 28.

180 Sinclair's paranoia: *The Brass Check*, 221, 437.

181 He once explained: Judson Grenier, "Upton Sinclair and the Press: *The Brass Check* Reconsidered," *Journalism Quarterly* 49 (Autumn 1972), 429.

181 "an animal in a cage": *The Brass Check,* 39, 332.

181 Sinclair introduces: *The Brass Check,* 221, 42, 221, 224.

182 one student assured: Everett Gould to US, Mar. 11, 1933.

182 "dawn of the twenty-first century": Robert W. McChesny and Ben Scott, Introduction, *The Brass Check* (Urbana: University of Illinois Press, 2003), xxxi; see also Grenier, "Upton Sinclair and the Press," 427–36.

182 "cumulative record of blackmail": Untermeyer cited in Gottesman, "Upton Sinclair," 175.

182 Somewhat more substantial: *The Book of Life,* viii.

183 "you are a mighty unlucky person": DS to US, Aug. 13, 1920.

183 Sinclair vetoed Stanford: US to DS, Aug. 23, 1920.

183 Sinclair, who had fought Meta: *100%: The Story of a Patriot* (Pasadena: Published by the Author, 1920), 282.

183 in a play about Cicero: typescript, 1-1-5, JA papers; *Mammonart: An Essay in Economic Interpretation* (Pasadena: Published by the Author, 1925), 333.

183 As a lonely freshman: US to DS, Sep. 27, 1920.

184 Sinclair had far fewer: US, *The Goose-Step* (Pasadena: Published by the Author, 1923), 15, 16–17.

185 "merely a physical thing": *The Goose-Step,* 18.

185 "the greatest mind in America": Columbia Oral History, 154, 196.

186 Sinclair's confidants: *The Goose-Step,* 405, 50.

186 But some of Sinclair's respondents: *The Goose-Step* 247, 400, 458, 301.

186 *The Goose-Step* sold well: Harris, *Upton Sinclair,* 206.

186 In September 1922: US, *They Call Me Carpenter* (New York: Boni & Liveright, 1922), 3, 129, 37. Langston Hughes wrote an effective sketch in 1934 called "On the Road," in which Christ steps down from a crucifix to travel with a black hobo.

188 *They Call Me Carpenter* was a success: Gottesman, "Upton Sinclair," 196.

188 "rugged, strong character": Harry Carr, *Los Angeles: City of Dreams* (New York: D. Appleton–Century, 1935), 327.

189 Most of the members: Arthur A. Almeida, "Liberty Hill Shone as San Pedro Labor Beacon," *California Historian* (Spring 1998), 20; Carey McWilliams, *Southern California Country: An Island on the Land* (New York: Duell, Sloan & Pearce, 1946), 291.

189 Sinclair had long been infatuated: Richard B. Fisher, "The Last Muckraker" (New Haven: Yale University dissertation, 1953), 351.

190 Sinclair became involved: *The Goslings: A Study of the American Schools* (Pasadena: Upton Sinclair, 1924), 9 and 2–22.

190 William Burns was: *The Goslings,* 9–10.

190 On Monday, May 7: *The Goslings,* 14, 11–12.

191 When street meetings: Martin Zanger, "The Reluctant Activist: Upton Sinclair's Reform Activities in California, 1915–1930" (Bloomington: Indiana University dissertation, 1971), 122; *LAT,* May 15, 1923.

191 On Saturday, May 12: *The Goslings,* 16.

192 Sinclair and his group: *The Goslings,* 18.

192 The farcical elements: Elmer Belt to David Randall, Apr. 22, 1957, Randall MSS; Louis Adamic, "Upton Sinclair on Liberty Hill," *Upton Sinclair Quarterly,* 6:1 and 2 (Spring-Summer 1982), 6–7.

193 "You're clear. Beat it—": Hunter Kimbrough account is from *SB,* 283.

193 Kate Gartz was yet another example: *SB,* 249–50.

194 By the early 1920s: Paul Jordan-Smith, *The Road I Came* (Caldwell, Idaho: Caxton Printers, 1960), 36; *100%,* 213.

194 For all her eccentricities: Jordan-Smith, *The Road I Came,* 365; *SB,* 288.

195 Craig's dramatic account: "Sinclair Held for Trial," *LAT,* May 17, 1923; Hunter Kimbrough statement, May 19, 1923, US MSS.

195 a "splendid" young man: Bromley Oxnam to Kate Gartz, June 5, 1925. Oxnam was the pastor of the Methodist Episcopal Church of All Nations in Los Angeles.

196 Also destroyed: *Los Angeles Express,* May 16, 1923; *Autobiography,* 231.

196 In early July: "Chief Oaks, You Are Subpoenaed," *New York Call,* July 1, 1923.

196 Sinclair's own reputation: GS to US, May 18, 1923.

197 Sinclair shrugged off criticism: *SB,* 291.

197 In the weeks: Clinton Taft, "The ACLU Comes to Los Angeles," *Upton Sinclair Quarterly,* 6:1 and 2 (Spring–Summer 1982), 9.

197 John Ahouse suggests: Author correspondence, Apr. 13, 2004.

Eleven: The Man of Letters

198 In April 1924: GS to US, Apr. 10, Apr. 25, 1924; Gottesman, "Upton Sinclair," 208.

198 Its deceptively perky title: *Singing Jailbirds,* 84.

199 George Sterling, always candid: GS to US, July 2, 1924.

199 "no critic of importance": Herbert Read, "A Man Without Art," *New English Weekly,* Nov. 1, 1934, 57–59.

199 A reviewer in distant: *Sydney Bulletin,* Sep. 16, 1926.

200 Once himself the Arthur Stirling aesthete: *Mammonart,* 225, 249, 243.

200 Sinclair's readers liked him: *Mammonart,* 207, 91.

201 "from the dawn": *Mammonart,* 5.

201 Sinclair as the modern Mr. Ogi: *Mammonart,* 138.

201 "a very dignified": Priscilla Sinclair scrapbook, 1911–1962.

201 "in a painful position": US to DS, June 1, 1925.

202 As Sinclair's terminology: *Ethan Frome* (New York: Charles Scribner's Sons, 1911; Contemporary Classics edition, 1970), 53.

202 Craig believed: Details concerning the Long Beach / Signal Hill properties and relocation are from Roberta Nichols, "Idyll at Station B: The Sinclairs in Long Beach," *Upton Sinclair Quarterly* 4:2 (June 1980), 6–14, and from *SB,* 301–4.

203 "several thousand dollars": *SB,* 304.

204 "greatest benefactors": William Manchester, *Disturber of the Peace: The Life of H. L. Mencken* (New York: Harper & Brothers, 1950), 155.

204 Sinclair tried valiantly: *SB,* 294, and HLM to US, Sep. 21, 1926.

204 "salute of 21 bombs": *Pasadena Record,* Oct. 13, 1926.

204 Harry Carr: *LAT,* Nov. 16, 1926.

204 Soon after Mencken arrived: US, *Money Writes!* (New York: Albert & Charles Boni, 1927), 130, 131, 132.

205 Mencken's epistolary challenges: HLM to US, Sep. 9, 1926.

205 "due to be diddled forever": HLM to US, Jan. 28, 1920, cited in Harris, *Upton Sinclair,* 180.

205 His actual review: "On Journalism," *Smart Set* 61 (April 1920), 138–44.

205 "Well, he sat down": cited in David A. Remley, "The Correspondence of H. L. Mencken and Upton Sinclair: 'An Illustration of How Not to Agree' " (Bloomington: Indiana University dissertation, 1963), 2.

205 "a much more solid man": US to S. Hillkowitz, Apr. 20, 1931.

206 On Wednesday, November 17: *LAT,* Nov. 17, 1926.

206 "really knocked out": Charles Malamuth to US, Dec. 2, 1926.

206 Mencken returned to Baltimore: US to HLM, Nov. 26, 1926.

207 Mencken's reply: *Money Writes!,* 165; HLM to US, Jan. 14, 1927.

207 Sinclair responded temperately: *Money Writes!*, 36; US to HLM, Jan. 24, 1927; Mary Austin, "George Sterling at Carmel," *American Mercury* 11 (May 1927), 65–72.

208 *Oil!*: A new edition of *Oil!* was published by the University of California Press (Berkeley and Los Angeles: [1926, 1927,] 1997, First California Paperback Printing, introduction by Jules Tygiel). Page references are to this edition, which follows the pagination of the original Boni & Liveright edition.

208 "most sustained": Lawrence Clark Powell, *California Classics: The Creative Literature of the Golden State* (Los Angeles: W. Ritchie Press, 1971), 326, 325.

209 "The road ran": *Oil!*, 1.

209 "there was a tower": *Oil!*, 157.

210 Dell ended his study: Dell, *Upton Sinclair*, 187.

210 "Voltairean" literary warrior: Dell cited in Harris, *Upton Sinclair*, 233–34.

211 But in early May: The *Atlantic Monthly* assertion is cited in Gottesman, "Upton Sinclair," 229; HLM to US, May 11, 1927.

211 "Remember we will not tolerate": *Oil!*, 275.

212 Personalizing the dispute: *Money Writes!*, 181–83.

212 Sinclair returned to his hotel: JA, *Upton Sinclair*, 61; *Money Writes!*, 18.

212 Conkey had prepared: *Oil!*, Tygiel introduction, xi; Gottesman, "Upton Sinclair," 229.

213 "his land and his treasures": *Oil!*, 424.

213 Sinclair had deliberately: US to HLM, Jan. 8, 1927; *Mammonart*, 67; Wilson, "Notes on Babbitt and More, "*A Literary Chronicle: 1920–1950* (New York: Doubleday Anchor, 1950, 1952), 155. Wilson's *New Republic* review of *Mammonart* (Apr. 22, 1925), reprinted in his *The Shores of Light* (New York: Noonday, 1967 [1952]), 212–16, is more generous, praising Sinclair as "well informed" with "a real taste for books" (p. 215) but muddled in his thinking.

213 "conservative in his taste": *WE*, 307.

214 "more bored": *Mammonart*, 304–5.

214 Worse than merely: *Mammonart*, 305.

214 "excuse for having lived": *Money Writes!*, 306.

214 "scientist who discovers": *Money Writes!*, 18.

214 "the wilds of the west": *Money Writes!*, 143.

215 "a woman with no trace": *Money Writes!*, 143.

215 "a code of artificialities": *Money Writes!*, 136–37, 138, 139.

215 Sinclair also took aim: *Money Writes!*, 171, 174, 172.

216 Sinclair's comments: Mark Schorer, *Sinclair Lewis: An American Life* (New York: McGraw Hill, 1961), 496; Lewis to US, Jan. 3, 1928.

217 "misquotations, misrepresentations": Felix Frankfurter, "The Case of Sacco and Vanzetti," *Atlantic Online* (March 1927).

217 "super-reporter": *Boston* folder, US MSS. *Boston* was published by Albert & Charles Boni in November 1928.

218 Sinclair spent six weeks in Boston: *Boston* folder, US MSS.

219 It was Fred Moore: US, "Reds I Have Known," ca 1953, 52.

220 His old friend Robert Minor: "Reds I Have Known," 53; Minor to US, Mar. 26, 1928.

Twelve: The Venture Capitalist

221 Thornton Wilder, not: Richard Burton to US, Apr. 22, 1929; *Minneapolis Star*, Apr. 13, 1929; Richard Burton to US, Apr. 20, 1929.

221 *Boston* did include: Moncrieff's letter to Albert and Charles Boni cited in their letter to US, Apr. 13, 1928.

221 Felix Frankfurter: Frankfurter to US, May 6, 1929.

222 Sinclair was no less: *Money Writes!*, 78.

223 "says it all": JA, *Upton Sinclair*, 67.

223 "old tradition of the West": US, *Mountain City* (New York: Albert & Charles Boni, 1930), 129.

223 as Sinclair summarized: "Fiat Justitia! A Radical Seeks Justice in Denver," *New Leader*, Aug. 3, 1929, 4. The case was heard before Denver judge J. Foster Symes, beginning on June 13, 1929.

224 "practically a member": *New Republic*, Feb. 11, 1929.

225 "Sinclair has gone": US, *Mental Radio* (New York: Albert & Charles Boni, 1930), 175.

225 In *Mental Radio* Sinclair: *Mental Radio*, 5.

226 *Mental Radio* turned out: *American Mercury* 21 (Oct. 1931), xxxvi–xxxviii. The review is unsigned, but it sounds like Mencken. A study by Walter Franklin Pierce, "Mrs. Sinclair's Mental Radio," for *Scientific American* 146 (Mar. 1932), 135–38, concluded that the experiments fully established the existence of psychic powers.

226 Albert Einstein, one of those socialists: Harris, *Upton Sinclair*, 272; US to Einstein, Nov. 13, 1930.

226 "Is This Jack London?": *Occult Review* 52 (Dec. 1930), 394–400; 53 (Jan. 1931), 10–14.

227 "The Hypnotist": US to Chaplin, Aug. 18, 1918.

228 "two mentors": US, "The Chaplin Story—Gags to Riches," review of Chaplin, *My Autobiography*, *LAT*, Oct. 11, 1964.

228 Jesse Lasky, met Eisenstein: Greg Mitchell, "The Greatest Movie Never Made," *American Film*, Jan.–Feb. 1983, 54–55.

229 "a good stiff police story!": Peter A. Soderbergh, "Upton Sinclair and Hollywood," *Midwest Quarterly* 11 (1970), 183.

229 "rather cheaper, for Ronald Colman": Mitchell, "The Greatest Movie Never Made," 55.

229 Sinclair later wondered: US, letter to editor, *Manchester Guardian*, Dec. 9, 1953, US MSS.

229 "Do drop me a note": US to Eisenstein, Oct. 25, 1930, cited in Harry M. Geduld and Ronald Gottesman, *Sergei Eisenstein and Upton Sinclair: The Making and Unmaking of Que Viva Mexico!* (Bloomington: Indiana University Press, 1970), 19.

230 an important stipulation: Geduld and Gottesman, *Eisenstein and Sinclair*, 22.

231 "the new, growing Mexico": Mitchell, "The Greatest Movie Never Made," 56.

231 EISENSTEIN LOOSE HIS COMRADES: Stalin telegram, Geduld and Gottesman, *Eisenstein and Sinclair*, 212.

232 "My Dear Comrade Stalin": US to Stalin, Nov. 22, 1931, Geduld and Gottesman, *Eisenstein and Sinclair*, 212.

233 In March 1929: US to Priscilla Sinclair, Mar. 20, 1929.

233 No correspondence of interest: Priscilla Sinclair to US, Aug. 26, 1931; US to Priscilla Sinclair, Aug. 27, 1931.

233 Sinclair wrote to David: US to DS, nd, 1931.

234 More than thirty years later: Columbia Oral History, 192.

234 "of whom you must say": Harris, *Upton Sinclair*, 271.

234 "Argument for Awarding the Nobel Prize": Greene, "Argument," nd, ca Dec. 29, 1930, JA papers.

235 "quack novelists": "Quack-Novels and Democracy," *Atlantic Monthly*, June 1915.

235 "blew up when he tried": US to Wister, Oct. 22, 1931, and Nov. 15, 1931.

235 "For Wister": Payne, *Owen Wister*, 326.

235 Quinn told Greene: Quinn to Ernest Greene, Aug. 25, 1931.

235 Sinclair was still bitter: Columbia Oral History, 115. (Quinn, born in 1875, three years before Sinclair, died in 1960.)

235 his net income for 1931: Harris, *Upton Sinclair*, 230. The 1932 Nobel Prize monetary value is from the *World Almanac*, 1930–1935.

Thirteen: The Insider

237 The most perceptive: *Saturday Review of Literature,* Mar. 3, 1928.

238 William Bloodworth usefully captures: Bloodworth, *Upton Sinclair,* 126.

239 "unquestionably revised": *LAT,* Mar. 16, 1932; an earlier *LAT* story, on March 14, discussed the movie at some length without mentioning Sinclair's name.

239 "that Bolshevik": Greg Mitchell, *The Campaign of the Century* (New York: Random House, 1992), 303; the $20,000 option amount is from Harris, *Upton Sinclair,* 268 and 395 note, citing "Assignment, July 23, 1931," US MSS.

240 *The Wet Parade* offers useful insights: US, *The Wet Parade* (New York: Farrar & Rinehart, 1931), 51, 52–53.

240 On another level: *The Wet Parade,* 344.

240 *The Wet Parade* also contains: *The Wet Parade,* 157, 276.

241 The movie version: HLM to US, Sep. 9, 1931, quoted in Remley, "Correspondence of H. L. Mencken and Sinclair," 37.

241 Irving Thalberg was sufficiently impressed: Harris, *Upton Sinclair,* 270, citing Memorandum of Agreement, Aug. 31, 1932; *SB,* 346.

241 come in "for some teasing": US to DS, Nov. 29, 1932.

242 Sinclair was candid: *Upton Sinclair Presents William Fox* (Los Angeles: Published by the Author, 1933), 2.

242 Such at least seems: *William Fox,* xiv–xv, 377.

243 A workman worthy: *William Fox,* v.

243 "Hollywood as the Cosa Nostra": Kevin Starr, *Endangered Dreams: The Great Depression in California* (New York: Oxford University Press, 1990), 148.

243 "wise enough to keep": Samuel Putnam to US, Mar. 18, 1933.

244 Imagine Sinclair's chagrin: *William Fox,* xvii; *Autobiography,* 260–61.

244 During the first three months: *Autobiography,* 255.

245 "we shouldn't be afraid": Denis Brian, *The Enchanted Voyager: The Life of J. B. Rhine* (Englewood Cliffs, New Jersey: Prentice Hall, 1982), 88.

245 "Dourly conservative": Ronald Clark, *Einstein: The Life and Times* (New York: World, 1971), 453–54.

245 Sinclair had warned: US to Einstein, Nov. 13, 1930, Leon Harris research files, LH MSS.

245 "exploited" by various people: Clark, *Einstein,* 454.

245 A few days before Einstein's: *Autobiography,* 254–56; as John Ahouse has pointed out (author correspondence), Sinclair slightly miscopied the German original, which correctly reads:

> Wen ficht der schmutzigste Topf nicht an?
> Wer klopft der Welt auf den hohlen Zahn?
> Wer verachtet das Jetzt und schwört auf das Morgen?
> Wem macht kein 'undignified' je Sorgen?
> Der Sinclair ist der tapfre Mann
> Wenn einer, dann ich es bezeugen kann.
> In Herzlichkeit   *Albert Einstein*

Sinclair's own literal translation is as follows:

> Whom does the dirtiest pot not attack?
> Who hits the world on the hollow tooth?
> Who spurns the now and swears by the morrow?
> Who takes no care about being "undignified"?

> The Sinclair is the valiant man
> If anyone, then I can attest it.
> In heartiness   *Albert Einstein*

246 In *The Way Out:* US, *The Way Out: What Lies Ahead for America* (New York: Farrar & Rinehart, 1933), 91.

247 "a business man": *The Way Out,* 11.

247 The communists, Sinclair says: *The Way Out,* 94–95, 103, 73.

247 Sinclair also addresses: For the poker analogies, see US, *Letters to Judd* (Pasadena: Published by the Author, 1926), 37, and *The Way Out,* 5–7.

248 The meeting occurred: *I, Governor of California, and How I Ended Poverty: A True Story of the Future* (Los Angeles: End Poverty League, 1933), 11–12. *I, Candidate for Governor, and How I Got Licked* (New York: Farrar & Rinehart, 1935), 16–18.

249 "lost interest in novels": US to Fulton Oursler, Sep. 6, 1933, cited in Remley, "Correspondence of H. L. Mencken and Sinclair," 409.

250 These recriminations: *New York Herald Tribune,* Sept. 22, 1933; in US to DS, June 25, 1940, Sinclair says that when Craig and he arrived in New York for the Lesser movie, David and Betty met them at the train and berated them for their political opinions. "Sol Lesser was horrified, and asked Craig if we could not get you to shut up."

251 The American Communist Party created: Geduld and Gottesman, *Eisenstein and Sinclair,* 408.

251 "oil man and movies enterpriser": Guillermo Delhora to US, Sep. 25, 1933.

251 "Upton Sinclair, you have butchered": Geduld and Gottesman, *Eisenstein and Sinclair,* 408.

251 On September 18 Kirstein: Geduld and Gottesman, *Eisenstein and Sinclair,* 408.

252 The Rialto Theatre premiere: Geduld and Gottesman, *Eisenstein and Sinclair,* 412.

252 Richard Watts caught the mood: Richard Watts, *New York Sun,* Sep. 22, 1933.

252 "pure rascality from the beginning": US to editor, *Manchester Guardian,* Dec. 9, 1953, US MSS; Seton's *Eisenstein: A Biography* was published in 1952.

253 Not everyone in the film world: Stanley Kauffman, citing Otis Ferguson in his review of Geduld and Gottesman's book *Eisenstein and Sinclair* for *The New Republic* ("Something Less Than Masterly," Nov. 24, 1979), 24.

253 But passions over the Eisenstein: Kirstein to LH, Jan. 23, 1971, LH MSS.

253 "poor, forthright, psychologically obtuse": MCS to Helen Woodward, Aug. 25, 1933, in Geduld and Gottesman, *Eisenstein and Sinclair,* 404.

253 "Upton has learned his lesson": MCS to Albert [Williams], Aug. 29, 1933, in Geduld and Gottesman, *Eisenstein and Sinclair,* 407.

Fourteen: The Politician

255 His fame: US to Reuben Borough, June 27, 1934, citing Lewis Gannett in the *New York Herald Tribune,* June 18, 1934.

255 "little band of 'insiders' ": *I, Governor,* 6.

256 One of the most interesting: George G. Rising, "An EPIC Endeavor: Upton Sinclair's 1934 California Gubernatorial Campaign," *Southern California Quarterly* (1997), 110. Details on Technocracy and other groups are from Rising's account, which is among the best of the many shorter studies consulted for this chapter. The most recent account, an excellent one but published too late for use here, is that of Douglas Cazaux Sackman, "A Jungle of Representation: The EPIC Campaign Versus Sunkist," in his *Orange Empire: California and the Fruits of Eden* (Berkeley: University of California Press, 2005), 185–224.

256 A peculiar offshoot: McWilliams, *Southern California Country,* 70.

258 "So far as I know": *I, Governor,* 8.

258 Sinclair's irrepressible egotism: *I, Governor,* 15, 41–42.

259 Chief among these: Otto's background comes from author interview with Mrs. Shirley Otto, Dec. 2003; US, "Preface" to Otto's proposed book about EPIC, nd, US MSS.

259 He and Otto: *I, Governor,* 19.

260 Sinclair managed: Fay Blake, *Fifty Years After EPIC* (sound recording), Bancroft Library, University of California, Berkeley; see also Fay M. Blake and H. Morton Newman, "Upton Sinclair's EPIC Campaign," *California History* 63 (Fall 1984), 305–12.

260 Voorhis is best remembered: Jerry Voorhis, "The EPIC Campaign in California," 2, from "Book Two: The Learning Years," Voorhis Papers, Honnold Library, Claremont Colleges.

261 Voorhis did not support: Voorhis, "The EPIC Campaign," 5, 6.

261 Sinclair was a man: Voorhis, "The EPIC Campaign," 6, 7.

262 "He was, like so many": Voorhis, "The EPIC Campaign," 7, 8.

262 "Well, you see": *End Poverty Paper,* Mar. 1934, cited in *SB,* 348.

263 "All who want to starve": *SB,* 348.

263 "the brains of a pigeon": *EPIC News,* June 11, 1934.

263 The key to Sinclair's effectiveness: Alfred J. Albrecht, "A Rhetorical Study of Upton Sinclair's 1934 Campaign for Governor of California" (Bloomington: Indiana University dissertation, 1966), 196. The Lincoln comparison is reported in *EPIC News,* Oct. 15, 1934.

264 His most principled opposition: Clarence McIntosh, "Upton Sinclair and the EPIC Movement, 1933–1936" (Stanford: Stanford University dissertation, 1955), 2.

264 Creel knew: George Creel, *Rebel at Large* (New York: G. P. Putnam's Sons, 1947), 47.

264 Creel was a dangerous opponent: Creel, *Rebel at Large,* 280, 286.

266 Sinclair's account: *I, Candidate,* 77.

266 Sinclair had vowed: *I, Candidate,* 76, 77.

267 Sinclair was in high spirits: Mitchell, *The Campaign of the Century,* 99. Mitchell's subtitle, "Upton Sinclair's Race for Governor of California and the Birth of Media Politics," conveys the theme of his effective book. A musical-in-progress based on Mitchell's book premiered in a concert version in Chicago in November 2004. Michael Rupert starred as Sinclair; other figures portrayed included William Randolph Hearst, Irving Thalberg, Franklin and Eleanor Roosevelt, Louis B. Mayer, and Father Charles Coughlin.

267 The following morning: McIntosh, "Upton Sinclair and the EPIC Movement," 18.

268 Sinclair's negotiating position: McIntosh, "Upton Sinclair and the EPIC Movement," 191.

269 Other parts of *I, Governor: I, Governor,* 59, 61.

270 Careful readers noted: *I, Governor,* 15.

271 "I've been welcomed": Mitchell, *The Campaign of the Century,* 112.

272 "what a stinker": Mitchell, *The Campaign of the Century,* 337.

272 "if I am elected": Mitchell, *The Campaign of the Century,* 246; McIntosh, "Upton Sinclair and the EPIC Movement," 252.

272 Sinclair's attempt: *LAT,* Sep. 27, 1934.

273 Harry Chandler, the publisher: *LAT,* Aug. 30, 1934.

273 Boxed quotes: Mitchell, *The Campaign of the Century,* 384–85; Ed Ainsworth, "Remembering Uppie," *Saturday Review,* Sep. 30, 1967.

273 The *Times* did not stop there: US to Harry Carr, July 14, 1934.

273 Kyle Palmer: David Halberstam, "The California Dynasty," in *Atlantic Monthly* (April 1979), cited in Mitchell, *The Campaign of the Century,* 429.

274 Another former associate: Mitchell, *The Campaign of the Century,* 304.

274 Thalberg was only thirty-seven: Mitchell, *The Campaign of the Century,* 423, 499; McIntosh, "Upton Sinclair and the EPIC Movement," 263.

275 Thalberg confirmed: Mitchell, *The Campaign of the Century,* 561.

275 "He was my friend": "From Gags to Riches," review of *My Autobiography* by Charles Chaplin, *LAT,* Oct. 11, 1964.

275 "and never have I": Mitchell, *The Campaign of the Century,* 167.

276 a "millennial ass": Tugwell, *Saturday Review of Literature,* July 2, 1927.

276 Raymond Moley: Mitchell, *The Campaign of the Century,* 278.

276 Creel had joked: Creel, *Rebel at Large,* 285–86; Creel to US, Oct. 18, 1934, Roosevelt White House papers, cited in McIntosh, "Upton Sinclair and the EPIC Movement," 285.

276 "epilepsy and catalepsy": *Los Angeles Herald,* Oct. 27, 1934.

277 "owes it to himself to vote": Mitchell, *The Campaign of the Century,* 285.

277 "Mr. Farley never intended": Mitchell, *The Campaign of the Century,* 433.

277 Cantwell's generous assessment: Robert Cantwell, "Upton Sinclair," in Malcolm Cowley, ed., *After the Genteel Tradition* (Carbondale: Southern Illinois University Press, 1964), 37.

278 "Come on, Harry!": Starr, *Endangered Dreams,* 144.

278 But at 10:30: Mitchell, *The Campaign of the Century,* 533–34.

Fifteen: The Novelist

279 The physical and emotional strains: *What God Means to Me,* 74–75.

279 Craig's reaction: *Autobiography,* 278.

280 Robert Millikan: *I, Candidate,* 215.

280 "You can be sure it was less bad": Einstein to US, Nov. 23, 1934, *My Lifetime in Letters,* 357.

280 *What God Means to Me: What God Means to Me,* 53, 54, 51.

281 That work continued apace: *The Gnomobile* (New York: Farrar & Rinehart, 1936), 56. John Ahouse suggests that Sinclair may have been influenced by the 1934 MGM film *Sequoia,* a children's movie with live animals (JA e-mail to author, Oct. 11, 2004).

281 In fact, Sinclair's mood: Einstein quoted in *I, Governor,* 215.

282 "commune with the visible forms": W. L. Rideout to US, Nov. 11, 1934.

282 But he had lost, after all: Albert Mordell, *Trailing E. Haldeman-Julius in Philadelphia and Other Places* (Girard, Kansas: Haldeman-Julius, 1949), 12.

282 The cause of their falling-out: "The New Deal Mentality," *American Mercury* 38 (May 1936), 4–5. Earlier comments were "Storm Damage in Utopia," *Baltimore Evening Sun,* Jan. 28, 1935, 15, and "Forty Acres and a Mule," *Baltimore Evening Sun,* Sep. 10, 1934, 17, cited in Remley, "Correspondence of Mencken and Sinclair," 423.

282 Outraged at being linked: US to HLM, Apr. 28, 1936, cited in Remley, "Correspondence of Mencken and Sinclair," 425.

282 Mencken's reply: HLM to US, May 2, 1936; US to HLM, May 7, 1936, Jan. 3, 1951, cited in Remley, "Correspondence of H. L. Mencken and Sinclair," 434, 476.

283 For Sinclair the Ford-UAW confrontation: *The Flivver King,* 73–74.

284 "some celestial wire-crossing": JA, *Upton Sinclair,* 92.

286 Sinclair credited Craig: James Michael Riherd, "Upton Sinclair: Creating *World's End*" (Los Angeles: University of Southern California dissertation, 1978), 7; Mann to US, Oct. 14, 1938, cited in Riherd, "Upton Sinclair," 39.

286 The needed inspirational spark: "*World's End* Impending," Appendix, *O Shepherd, Speak!* (New York: Viking, 1949), 583–84.

287 "The scenes are to be laid": US to Fulton Oursler, Dec. 7, 1938.

288 Sinclair divided his long novel: Riherd, "Upton Sinclair," 18.

289 "old grey wolf": *WE,* 554, 551.

289 Sinclair's most effective fictional character: *WE,* 355–56.

290 "villainous, traitorous animal": US to DS, June 25, 1940.

290 "been scolded all my life": US to John Farrar, Aug. 25, 1939, cited in Riherd, "Upton Sinclair," 231.

290 Fortunately, an old ACLU friend: *World's End* sold more than sixty thousand copies; sales for the series, between 1941 and 1953, came to 397,168 copies plus 69,383 in export and special sales. Riherd, "Upton Sinclair," 15.

290 A few weeks after: Ben Huebsch to US, Viking log memo, Apr. 14, 1940, US MSS.

292 Sinclair's second most important aide: Ratcliffe's corrections are found in the *Presidential Agent* "Related Material" folder, US MSS.

292 On May 3, 1943: Huebsch to US, May 3, May 4, 1943.

293 "lost its vitality": US, *Dragon's Teeth* (New York: Viking, 1942), 454.

293 A similarly effective passage: US, *Between Two Worlds* (New York: Viking, 1941), 624.

293 Among the letters: US to Michael Williams, May 12, 1943; Carey McWilliams to US, May 18, 1943; Irving Stone to US, May 5, 1943. Sinclair's "Strange Case of Carey McWilliams" appeared in *Pacific Weekly* 4 (Feb. 24, 1936), 88–89.

294 Perhaps the most interesting: Gertrude Atherton to US, May 24, 1943.

294 And from Washington: Ernest Greene to US, May 4, 1943; Harold Ickes to US, May 6, 1943.

295 "mastered his earlier tendency": L. Duffus, *NYT Book Review,* June 16, 1940, 1.

295 The answer to that question: US to *The Nation,* Feb. 5, 1943; Diana Trilling to US, Feb. 27, 1931. In her memoir, *The Beginning of the Journey* (New York: Harcourt, Brace, 1993), 202–3, Trilling says that in 1932 "my friend Bettina Sinclair returned from Russia." Bettina and David gave Diane and Lionel Trilling their "first instruction in the truth of Soviet Communism," especially concerning "the brutality of Stalin's regime, the fear which lay over the land." Unfortunately, Trilling says, at the time she and Lionel still preferred the "happy inventions" of E. E. Cummings, who had "savagely satirize[d]" Bettina and David "for their unwillingness to be co-opted into the service of Stalin" in *Eimi,* his 1933 book about his travels in the Soviet Union.

295 Sinclair's chief appeal: Ivan Scott, *Upton Sinclair: The Forgotten Socialist* (Lampeter, Wales: Edwin Mellen Press), 367.

296 Harvard scholar: Perry, "Mr. Sinclair's Superman Carries On," *NYT Book Review,* June 2, 1946, and "Lanny Budd Rides Again," *NYT,* Sep. 2, 1948 (review of *One Clear Call*).

296 Some critics were even less polite: Jones, "The Confused Case of Upton Sinclair," *Atlantic Monthly* (Aug. 1946); Mumford, *The Van Wyck Brooks–Lewis Mumford Letters* (New York: Dutton, 1970), 398.

296 "somebody has to write": Harris, *Upton Sinclair,* 341.

296 It is true: *Wide Is the Gate* (New York: Viking, 1943), 44, 154.

296 A proper epic hero: *Between Two Worlds,* 604, 152.

297 Blessed with a well-stocked mind: *Wide Is the Gate,* 566, 72. Neumann's dates are 1808–1875.

297 "When people ask me": Shaw to US, cited in *Autobiography,* 292; Shaw to US, Dec. 12, 1941.

297 "Some day": Thomas Mann to US, Jan. 18, 1943, *My Lifetime in Letters,* 380.

297 Sinclair also valued: E. Bjorkman to US, Feb. 10, 1943; US to Bjorkman, Mar. 25, 1943.

298 One of those men: Van Wyck Brooks to US, Mar. 18 and Feb. 1, 1955.

Sixteen: The Recluse

299 The mystery of Sinclair's rejuvenation: *LP,* 44.

299 Now he was similarly absorbed: *Between Two Worlds,* 305.

300 Sinclair believed: *Between Two Worlds,* 174; *Wide Is the Gate,* 335.

300 The coming move to Monrovia: US to DS, Oct. 23, 1942.

301 Their political arguments: US to DS, Mar. 15, 1938; *A World to Win* (New York: Viking, 1946), 569; US to DS, Oct. 3, 1939.

302 David replied: DS to US, Dec. 5, 1939; *The Call,* Dec. 12, 1939.

302 Sinclair was much shrewder about Hitler: US to DS, Sep. 4, 1940, Sep. 24, 1941, Nov. 1, 1941.

303 "I have never forgotten that opening": Hamilton Holt to US, Oct. 1, 1937.

303 David continued to look for work: US to DS, Feb. 14, 1939.

303 "In the first place": DS to US, Aug. 26, 1940.

304 "your sudden and unexpected arrival": US to DS, Jan. 17, 1944.

304 "sorry not to have seen you": DS to US, Dec. 18, 1944.

304 "profound speech": Martin Birnbaum, *The Last Romantic* (New York: Twayne, 1960), 20.

304 What Birnbaum did not realize: Sinclair tells this story in his introduction to Birnbaum's autobiography, *The Last Romantic,* 10.

305 "wildest concoction": Frank Friedel, *New York Herald Tribune Book Review,* Dec. 6, 1959, review of Cornelius Vanderbilt, *Man of the World: My Life on Five Continents* (New York: 1959), and Friedel to LH, Nov. 13, 1970, LH MSS.

305 "fairy-tale" existence: *SB,* 17.

305 "If you were not a presidential agent": Vanderbilt, *Man of the World,* 192.

305 "fall under his spell": US to Vanderbilt, Jan. 8, 1943.

306 come to the radio station: John Burton to US, Mar. 3, 1943.

306 Lanny meets Einstein: *A World to Win,* 366. In "Albert Einstein as I Remember Him," *Saturday Review,* Apr. 14, 1956, Sinclair wrote that Einstein "played as he lived, quietly and serenely, with the precision of his mathematical formulas." He "knew better than to accept" Einstein's offer to join him in a duet.

307 Roosevelt's relationship with Lanny: US, *Presidential Agent* (New York: Viking, 1944), 13, 23.

307 " 'Tell me about Hitler' ": *Presidential Agent,* 32.

308 A longtime Sinclair friend: Albert Mordell, *Haldeman-Julius and Upton Sinclair: The Amazing Record of a Long Collaboration* (Girard, Kansas: Haldeman-Julius, 1950), 21. Mordell notes that only fifteen of the novel's 575 pages involve mediums, but they come after many similar pages in the earlier novels.

308 "more dangerous to the world": US, *The Return of Lanny Budd* (New York: Viking, 1953), 38, 39.

308 As was often the case: Central Program Services Division / Talks and Features Branch, Apr. 28, 1953, US MSS.

309 The radio text: *The Return of Lanny Budd,* 238, 298; *O Shepherd, Speak!,* 554.

309 In a passage: *The Return of Lanny Budd,* 322; Dell to US, Dec. 14, 1953.

310 "I have broken off": US to Jerome Davis, Nov. 12, 1952.

310 "fought it out": "Reds I Have Known," 5–6.

310 "cheerful, nut-brown woman": "Reds I Have Known," 7.

310 Ware's assignment from Moscow: Ware's activities are described in detail in Sam Tanenhaus, *Whittaker Chambers: A Biography* (New York: Random House, 1997), 94: "By 1934 Ware had assembled a secret Communist network in Washington, a cluster of seven cells or more, each with a leader who also belonged to an elite nucleus." During the EPIC campaign, Sinclair had opposed AAA policies of limiting food supplies as "an economic blunder and suicide" in a letter to the *Chicago Daily Tribune,* Sep. 3, 1934.

311 "I read of 'Mother' Bloor's": "Reds I Have Known," 7–9.

311 Writing to her sister: MCS to Dollie Kling, nd, ca 1953.

312 In another undated: MCS to Dollie Kling, nd, ca 1953.

313 "the strangest menu": US, "A Resort to Rice Diet," *Buffalo Courier Express,* Apr. 8, 1955.

313 In order to ease: "My Husband, Upton Sinclair," Honnold Library, Claremont Colleges, 868.

313 It is true: Harris, *Upton Sinclair,* 349, note 409, citing MCS to Birnbaum, envelope dated Mar. 17, 1946: MCS to Helen [Woodward?], nd, ca 1950, "Craig's Notes," Honnold Library.

314 More interesting than speculations: MCS, "My Husband, Upton Sinclair," 933.

314 A touching picture: Van Wyck Brooks, *From the Shadow of the Mountain: My Post-Meridian Years* (New York: E. P. Dutton, 1961), 33, 38.

315 "how impressed" he was: US to DS, Aug. 10, 1950.

315 Jean Sinclair, who: Leon Harris interview of DS.

315 "knows she is going": US to DS, Oct. 6, 1960. Marcher's concern in the James story is that his beloved friend has to die before she can learn what it is that has troubled him, his "beast," all his life—which turns out to be his own unrecognized selfishness.

316 "Upton got up": MCS to Richard Otto, Mar. 13, 1961.

Epilogue: The Sage

317 Upton Sinclair admired: Lanny Budd quotes Goethe in *Presidential Mission,* 255.

317 "Oh, my Uppie": *Autobiography,* 318; the typescript for this passage in the Honnold Library, Claremont Colleges, includes the phrase "Oh, my Uppie," deleted in the *Autobiography.*

317 Armour was an English professor: *Autobiography,* 319.

318 According to Armour: "Richard Armour, Matchmaker: An Interview" (with John Ahouse), *Upton Sinclair Quarterly* (Spring 1982), 11–12.

318 Before the evening: Roger Baldwin to Leon Harris, nd, ca 1970, LH MSS.

318 Perhaps the keenest insight: Author interviews of Ronald Gottesman, Apr. 2003, May 2004.

319 Frank Harris had said: Nina Neal to US, Oct. 17, 1929, LH MSS.

319 to "put the 'social' in 'socialism' ": Lorna Smith to Leon Harris, July 14, 1970, LH MSS.

320 A former antagonist: Ainsworth, "Readers Given Rare Treat," *LAT,* Nov. 17, 1961.

320 Sinclair wrote to: US to DS, Dec. 23, 1964.

320 The man who had: US to DS, Mar. 15, 1963.

321 "Hard to believe!": US to DS, May 1, 1964.

321 In early October 1963: US to David Randall, Oct. 11, 1963, Randall MSS.

321 "it seems very egotistical": "Upton Sinclair Speaks to Three Groups," *Indiana Daily Student,* Oct. 19, 1963.

321 "the most wonderful thing I've seen": "Upton Sinclair Is Here," *Indianapolis News,* Oct. 18, 1963.

321 Sinclair wrote: US to Edward Allatt, Nov. 11, 1963.

322 Sinclair made only: Edgar Johnson to US, Oct. 16, Oct. 30, 1963.

322 Among the guests: Charles McCarry, *Citizen Nader* (Saturday Review Press, 1972), 320–21.

322 Thanks largely to May: US to DS, Nov. 30, 1963, and Apr. 18, 1963.

323 In October 1968: DS to Randall, Oct. 12, 1968.

WORKS CITED AND
PUBLICATION TIME LINE

1901 *Springtime and Harvest*
      King Midas

1903 *The Journal of Arthur Stirling*
      "My Cause," *Independent,* May 14
      Prince Hagen

1904 *Manassas*

1906 *The Jungle*
      "Is The Jungle True?" *Independent,* May 17
      "A Home Colony," *Independent,* June 14
      "Campaign Against the Wholesale Poisoners of the Nation's Food,"
         Arena, July
      A Captain of Industry

1907 *The Industrial Republic*

1908 *The Metropolis*
      The Moneychangers

1909 "War: A Manifesto Against It," *Wilshire's,* September
      Prince Hagen: A Drama in Four Acts

1910 *Samuel the Seeker*

1911 *Naturewoman*
Love's Pilgrimage
The Fasting Cure

1912 *Plays of Protest*

1913 *Sylvia*

1914 *Sylvia's Marriage*

1915 *The Cry for Justice*

1917 *King Coal*

1918 *The Profits of Religion*

1919 "Our Office," *Upton Sinclair's,* February
Jimmie Higgins

1920 *The Brass Check*
100%: The Story of a Patriot

1921 *The Book of Life*

1922 *They Call Me Carpenter*

1923 *The Goose-Step*

1924 *The Goslings*
The Millennium
Singing Jailbirds

1925 *Mammonart*

1926 *Letters to Judd*

1927 *Oil!*
Money Writes!

1928 *Boston*

1929 "Fiat Justitia! A Radical Seeks Justice in Denver," *New Leader,* Aug. 3

1930 *Mountain City*
      Mental Radio
      "Is This Jack London?" *Occult Review,* Dec. and Jan., 1931

1931 *The Wet Parade*

1932 *American Outpost*

1933 *Upton Sinclair Presents William Fox*
      The Way Out: What Lies Ahead for America
      I, Governor of California and How I Ended Poverty

1935 *I, Candidate for Governor, and How I Got Licked*

1936 *Co-Op*
      The Gnomobile
      What God Means to Me
      "The Strange Case of Carey McWilliams," *Pacific Weekly,* 4 (Feb. 24,
         1936)

1937 *The Flivver King*

1938 *Little Steel*

1940 *World's End*

1941 *Between Two Worlds*

1942 *Dragon's Teeth*

1943 *Wide Is the Gate*

1944 *Presidential Agent*

1945 Introduction, *The Jungle* (Viking edition)

1946 *A World to Win.* New York: Viking

1949   "World's End Impending," Appendix, *O Shepherd, Speak!*

1953   *The Return of Lanny Budd*

1955   "A Resort to Rice Diet," *Buffalo Courier Express,* Apr. 8

1956   "Albert Einstein As I Remember Him," *Saturday Review,* Apr. 14

1960   *My Lifetime in Letters.* Columbia: University of Missouri Press

1962   *The Autobiography of Upton Sinclair.* New York: Harcourt, Brace & World

1964   "The Chaplin Story—Gags to Riches," review of Chaplin, *Los Angeles Times,* Oct. 11

INDEX

PERMISSIONS
ACKNOWLEDGMENTS

Grateful acknowledgment is made to the following to reprint both published and unpublished material:

Archives of Labor and Urban Affairs, Wayne State University: Excerpt from a letter from John Armistead Collier to Upton Sinclair housed in the John and Phyllis Collier Collection. Reprinted by permission.

Enoch Pratt Free Library: Quotations from the letters of H. L. Mencken to Upton Sinclair used by permission of the Enoch Pratt Free Library, Baltimore, in accordance with the terms of Mr. Mencken's bequest to the library.

Harold Ickes: Excerpt from a letter from Harold Ickes to Upton Sinclair dated May 6, 1943. Reprinted by permission of Harold Ickes.

Lilly Library, Indiana University, and the Bancroft Library, University of California, Berkeley: Excerpts from five letters from George Sterling to Upton Sinclair dated December 8, 1916; May 18, 1923; April 10, 1924; April 17, 1924; and July 2, 1924 housed at the Lilly Library, Indiana University. Reprinted by permission of the Lilly Library, Indiana University, and the Bancroft Library, University of California, Berkeley.

McIntosh and Otis, Inc., and Lilly Library, Indiana University: Quotes from various unpublished letters written by Upton Sinclair, quotes from an unpublished manuscript by Upton Sinclair, excerpts from an unpublished manuscript by Craig Sinclair, and excerpts from letters by David Sinclair, Mary Craig Sinclair, and Priscilla Sinclair housed in the Upton Sinclair, Meta Stone, and Leon Harris Collections at the Lilly Library, Indiana University, Bloomington, Indiana, copyright © 2006 by John and Jeffrey Weidman. Reprinted by permission of McIntosh and Otis, Inc., and Lilly Library, Indiana University.

The New York Times: Excerpt from an article that appeared in *The New York Herald Tribune* September 22, 1933, copyright © 1933 by The New York Times Company. Reprinted by permission.

Rare Book and Manuscript Library, University of Pennsylvania: Excerpt from an undated letter by Theodore Dreiser to Arnold Gingerich from the Theodore Dreiser Papers, Rare Book and Manuscript Library, University of Pennsylvania. Reprinted by permission.

S. Fischer Verlag GmbH: Excerpt from a letter from Thomas Mann to Upton Sinclair dated January 18, 1943, copyright © S. Fischer Verlag GmbH, Frankfurt am Main. Reprinted by permission.

Mary Davis Carol Short: Excerpt from "Helicon Hall: An Experiment in Living," by Edith Summers Kelley, as published in *The Kentucky Review,* 1 (Spring, 1980), edited by Mary Byrd Davis and found in the Edith Summers Kelley Papers, Morris Library, Southern Illinois University, Carbondale, IL. Reprinted by permission of Mary Davis Carol Short.

Jerry Voorhis: Excerpts from "The EPIC Campaign in California" and "Book Two: The Learning Years," both by Jerry Voorhis as found in the Voorhis Papers, Honnold Library, Claremont College. Reprinted by permission of Jerry Voorhis.

A former Fulbright scholar, ANTHONY ARTHUR is the author of *Literary Feuds: A Century of Celebrated Quarrels—from Mark Twain to Tom Wolfe.* Additionally, he has written *Deliverance at Los Baños* and *The Bushmasters,* both narrative histories of World War II, and *The Tailor-King: The Rise and Fall of the Anabaptist Kingdom of Münster.* A professor emeritus, Arthur retired two years ago from the English department at California State University at Northridge, where he had taught American literature since 1970. He lives in Woodland Hills, California.

ABOUT THE TYPE

This book was set in Bembo, a typeface based on an old-style Roman face that was used for Cardinal Bembo's tract *De Aetna* in 1495. Bembo was cut by Francisco Griffo in the early sixteenth century. The Lanston Monotype Machine Company of Philadelphia brought the well-proportioned letter forms of Bembo to the United States in the 1930s.